PRAISE FOR *THE GOOD*

"Dr. Naugle has provided one of the greatest convergences of scholarship, love of students, and care for culture. This volume, a collection of voices from his beloved community, brings enduring light to his influence in all of our lives, and an invitation toward the great Banquet to come."

—MAKOTO FUJIMURA, ARTIST AND AUTHOR OF *ART+FAITH: A THEOLOGY OF MAKING*

"I call Dr. Naugle both friend and guide. He has so faithfully mined the depths of what a Christocentric worldview holds. But more than that, he's one of the good guys. Today, more than ever, this counts for nearly everything. Give me one man of character like Dr. Naugle over a thousand deep thinkers. Why? With Davey, you don't have to choose. He has depth of scholarship and an abiding love for God, his people, and his planet. That's the package right there."

—CHARLIE PEACOCK, GRAMMY-WINNING MUSIC PRODUCER AND AUTHOR OF *NEW WAY TO BE HUMAN*

"In *The Good, the True, the Beautiful*, colleagues, friends, and former students have gathered to express profound gratitude and to provide a truly fitting and worthy tribute to Professor David K. Naugle for his years of investment in so many lives. In honor of Naugle's effective and transformational teaching as well as his significant scholarly publications, this volume beautifully reflects and echoes Naugle's thoughtful articulation of the importance of Christian worldview thinking, living, and engagement. The astute and insightful chapters range from the thought of C. S. Lewis, William Wilberforce, Philip Melanchthon, Augustine, and Thomas Aquinas to literature, art, movies, philosophy, apologetics, and more. The editors are to be commended for bringing together such an outstanding group of contributors. I count it a privilege to recommend this fine book."

—DAVID S. DOCKERY, PRESIDENT, INTERNATIONAL ALLIANCE FOR CHRISTIAN EDUCATION, AND DISTINGUISHED PROFESSOR OF THEOLOGY, SOUTHWESTERN BAPTIST THEOLOGICAL SEMINARY

"A fascinating potpourri of essays that takes up everything from philosophy to pop culture, aesthetics to apologetics without ever straying too far from the classroom. A fine tribute to the worldview thinking and pedagogical commitments of David Naugle."

—LOUIS MARKOS, AUTHOR OF *RESTORING BEAUTY: THE GOOD, THE TRUE, AND THE BEAUTIFUL IN THE WRITINGS OF C. S. LEWIS*

"*The Good, the True, the Beautiful* is a moving tribute to the legacy of Dallas Baptist University Distinguished University Professor, Dr. David Naugle. Dr. Naugle has been not only a stellar professor but also a beloved mentor and friend to students and colleagues. This book, which includes essays by a gallery of lives he has touched, wonderfully captures David's enduring and scholarly commitment to upholding a Christian worldview that develops our minds, engages God's truth in the arts and sciences, and transforms our moral life to glorify our Creator and Lord."

—GARY COOK, CHANCELLOR AND FORMER PRESIDENT, DALLAS BAPTIST UNIVERSITY

"While no publication can ever do justice to the impact of the greatest communicator and educator I have ever known, this tribute to Dr. David Naugle can inspire readers to climb to spiritual higher ground. I have seen and personally experienced his eternal impact on countless lives which have been shaped by the biblical mandate to be committed stewards and caretakers of our world."

—GAIL LINAM, ACADEMIC DEAN AND FORMER PROVOST, DALLAS BAPTIST UNIVERSITY

The Good, the True, the Beautiful

The Good, the True, the Beautiful

A Multidisciplinary Tribute to David K. Naugle

Edited by
Mark J. Boone, Rose M. Cothren,
Kevin C. Neece, and Jaclyn S. Parrish

Foreword by Philip Mitchell
Afterword by Steven Garber

◆PICKWICK *Publications* • Eugene, Oregon

THE GOOD, THE TRUE, THE BEAUTIFUL
A Multidisciplinary Tribute to David K. Naugle

Copyright © 2021 Wipf and Stock Publishers. All rights reserved. Except for brief quotations in critical publications or reviews, no part of this book may be reproduced in any manner without prior written permission from the publisher. Write: Permissions, Wipf and Stock Publishers, 199 W. 8th Ave., Suite 3, Eugene, OR 97401.

Pickwick Publications
An Imprint of Wipf and Stock Publishers
199 W. 8th Ave., Suite 3
Eugene, OR 97401

www.wipfandstock.com

PAPERBACK ISBN: 978-1-7252-6888-3
HARDCOVER ISBN: 978-1-7252-6887-6
EBOOK ISBN: 978-1-7252-6889-0

Cataloguing-in-Publication data:

Names: Boone, Mark J., editor. | Cothren, Rose M., editor. | Neece, Kevin C., editor. | Parrish, Jaclyn S., editor. | Mitchell, Philip, foreword. | Garber, Steven, afterword.

Title: The good, the true, the beautiful : a multidisciplinary tribute to David K. Naugle / edited by Mark J. Boone, Rose M. Cothren, Kevin C. Neece, and Jaclyn S. Parrish; foreword by Philip Mitchell; afterword by Steven Garber

Description: Eugene, OR: Pickwick Publications, 2021. | Includes bibliographical references and index.

Identifiers: ISBN 978-1-7252-6888-3 (paperback). | ISBN 978-1-7252-6887-6 (hardcover). | ISBN 978-1-7252-6889-0 (ebook).

Subjects: LCSH: Naugle, David K. | Worldview. | Philosophy. | Theology.

Classification: B53 G69 2021 (paperback). | B53 (ebook).

02/12/21

Scripture quotations marked (ESV) are taken from the ESV® Bible (The Holy Bible, English Standard Version®), copyright © 2001 by Crossway, a publishing ministry of Good News Publishers. Used by permission. All rights reserved.
Scripture quotations marked (KJV) are taken from the King James Version, which is in the public domain.
Scripture quotations marked (NIV) are taken from the Holy Bible, NEW INTERNATIONAL VERSION®, NIV® Copyright © 1973, 1978, 1984, 2011 by Biblica, Inc.® Used by permission. All rights reserved worldwide.
Scripture quotations marked (NKJV) are taken from the New King James Version®. Copyright © 1982 by Thomas Nelson. Used by permission. All rights reserved.
Scripture quotations marked (NRSV) are taken from the New Revised Standard Version Bible, copyright © 1989 National Council of the Churches of Christ in the United States of America. Used by permission. All rights reserved worldwide.

Contents

Foreword by Philip Mitchell   xi
List of Contributors   xv

1   Introduction   1
     KEVIN C. NEECE

PART 1: THE GOOD

2   To Tao or Not to Tao   7
     Heroes and Villains in *The Magician's Nephew*
     ROSE M. COTHREN

3   An Exploration of Calling   21
     William Wilberforce, Julia Sass, and Me
     HANNAH BRISCOE

4   Translation of Phillip Melanchthon's   38
     Oration on the Praise of the Scholastic Life
     D. P. FAHRENTHOLD

5   Before Outsiders   48
     Apologetics in Every Course, across Curricula, for Life
     MARK ECKEL

6   For the Cross and the Land   64
     Radical Counter-Secularization in Russia
     ARTYOM H. TONOYAN

7   From Losers to Lovers   79
     How the *It* Films Take Us to Church
     LEIGH HICKMAN

PART 2: THE TRUE

8	Ordeal by Worldview A Naugelian Study in Lovecraftian Horror JACLYN S. PARRISH	103
9	The Problem of Evil An Alternative to Plantinga's Free Will Defense SCOTT SHIFFER	120
10	Demons, Idols, and Faith RUSSELL HEMATI	135
11	A Medievalist's Journey through Science and Faith ADAM D. JONES	148
12	The Christian Philosophical Worldview of St. Thomas Aquinas DAX R. BENNINGTON	159
13	From Evidence to Total Commitment Two Ways Faith Goes beyond Reason MARK J. BOONE	172

PART 3: THE BEAUTIFUL

14	Three Poems SARA TRIANA MITCHELL	195
15	Or Whither Shall I Flee? MARK J. BOONE	201
16	Beauty, Bad Guys, and Art in God's Good World DUSTIN MESSER	223
17	A Hot Coal in My Mouth My Personal Journey with *The Last Temptation of Christ* KEVIN C. NEECE	228
18	Worship Made Flesh How Modern Worship Songs Incarnate Meaning CHRISTINE HAND JONES	241
19	Transcendent Aesthetics Training Our Spiritual Senses with St. Augustine TAVNER THREATT	260
20	Evangelism through Beauty DAVID DALLAS MILLER	284

21	In Defense of Beauty How Gardens Manifest the Unity of Truth and Prescribe a Life-Preserving Posture of Submission MARY FLICKNER	302

Afterword: Dare to Be a Davey   317
    STEVEN GARBER

Appendix: Contact Work—A Personal Letter to Davey Naugle   323
    BRETT BRADSHAW

Index   331

Foreword

Davey's Mojo. For years, this is how I have described David K. Naugle's ability to inspire students. It is an ability of which I confess that I have been envious, but it is also a gift from which I have learned much, for David Naugle has consistently put into practice a profound marriage of the casting of a vision with a life lived in community with others. Certainly, this is the path of wisdom for a scholar. He has taught me that theory has to be embodied in interpersonal ways, that the classroom is not just information, and that we are offering ourselves and our lives to our students. Davey's lifework has been to cultivate in others a profound and biblical vision of Creation, Fall, Redemption, and Consummation. He first learned this from the likes of Abraham Kuyper, Arthur Holmes, James Sire, and others in the Dutch Reformed tradition. It is a vision that extends to work and play, to art and science, to all of life and culture. For Davey there has always been a fundamental danger in treating any area of life as if it were beneath the concerns of Christ. Thus, as an academic he continually stressed to others not only the study of philosophy, history, and theology, but also their application to matters as wide-ranging as woodworking, advertising, firefighting, rock music, and urban planning. In short, his has been a comprehensive and cosmic vision with real-world implications.

Not surprisingly, then, David Naugle has been a person of action. When I first arrived on our campus twenty years ago, I found him already in the thick of it. Davey was helping organize student conferences, retreats, and faculty reading groups. His biblically rich commentary on our university mission statement became a regular text for faculty and staff reflection, and for several summers he led institutes for faculty that explored not only the Kuyperian tradition but also a philosophy and doxology of university teaching. Beyond these, one of his most-lasting impacts has been the Friday Symposium, a weekly lecture series on faith and culture that he hosted. The Friday Symposium helped initiate our sleepy Texas university into a larger world of Christian scholarship and continues to do so today. It was (and still is) an interdisciplinary "great conversation" to which all are invited. This was the venue through which Davey helped a Christian campus in the Free Church tradition encounter thinkers from the Presbyterian, Anglican, Roman Catholic, and Eastern Orthodox worlds because he took seriously Jesus's high priestly prayer that his people would be one. For some of our students, Davey helped them encounter for the first time people of conviction outside their own denominational circles. It was the Lordship of Christ enacted on a weekly basis, a practice we strive to continue.

But, again, this was more than just a matter of theory. Davey and his wife Deemie, week in and week out it seemed, shared their home and their lives with students and friends. They both strongly believed that the Christian faith calls us to a full-bodied humanness that celebrates life together around food and conversation. Their ability to befriend students and to awaken them to the possibilities of the life of the mind was shaped as much by these informal times as by Davey's teaching in the classroom. Davey long understood that his life's teaching was also in his own life's example. He strived in his teaching career to help students have a deep sense of calling, and sought to model for them the truth that calling extends beyond one's chosen vocation or career. Surely, this volume is just one example of the fruit of a life invested in others, and the wide range of topics contained herein bears witness to these lessons.

When David K. Naugle retired, a hall full of former students attended the celebration, and their testimonies and expressions of love continued for over an hour. I remember turning to one of his former students who is now a professor. We both agreed that, if we could have even a tenth said of us that was said of Davey that day, we would have had a career well spent. When Davey helped design a general education course for our university called Developing a Christian Mind, he chose as a prayer for its students a passage from Augustine's *Confessions*:

> In the ordinary course of study, I fell upon a certain book of Cicero, whose speech almost all admire, not so his heart. This book of his contains an exhortation to philosophy, and is called "Hortensius." But this book altered my affections, and turned my prayers to Thyself, O Lord; and made me have other purposes and desires. (*Conf.* 3.4)

Sometimes a stress upon a Christian worldview has been rightly critiqued as a mental set of exercises cut off from the actual lived experiences of human beings. This has not been a failing of Davey Naugle's. He has understood very well that not only the mind but also the whole person with one's embodied affections has to be shaped if real change is to take place, and he has placed that embodied life change within a Christian hope that is communal in expectation. There awaits us a new heaven and earth in which human flourishing will finally reach its full potential. Such an eschatological expectation continues to serve as the final *telos* of his commitment to academic conversation and to a life of friendship.

And I am proud to be one of that host of friends.

Philip Mitchell
Director of the University Honors Program
Dallas Baptist University
May 2020

Contributors

Dawn Waters Baker is a full-time landscape artist living in Dallas. She graduated from Dallas Baptist University with a BA in Fine Arts. Her painting, *Release,* is on permanent display in the New York Times Building. She finished five original drawings for the book *Why, O God?* (Crossway). She is a Signature member of Artists of Texas. Dawn is affiliated with Mary Tomas Gallery in the Dallas Design District, Waterfall Mansion in New York, NewYork, and Joseph Gierek Fine Art in Tulsa, Oklahoma. She has been awarded three residencies from the National Parks Art Foundation by the National Endowment of the Arts: Big Bend National Park in 2015, Gettysburg National Military Park in 2018, and Hawaii Volcanoes National Park in 2020. Her work has been in national shows, including The National Weather Biennale, Jubilee Museum of Sacred Art Biennale, CIVA Contemporary Images of Mary, and Ex Nihilo at Roberts Wesleyan College. She is also a wife and the mother of three beautiful girls.

Dax Bennington is a PhD student at the University of Arkansas. He intends to defend his dissertation in August 2021. His research focus is in analytic epistemology and Thomistic philosophy. Prior to attending the University of Arkansas, Dax received an MA in philosophy from Texas Tech University and a BS in Philosophy from Dallas Baptist University, where he graduated from the University Honors Program.

Mark J. Boone is an Assistant Professor in the Department of Religion and Philosophy at Hong Kong Baptist University. Mark earned his BA in Biblical Studies and Philosophy from Dallas Baptist University in 2005 and his PhD in Philosophy from Baylor University in 2010. He is the author of *The Conversion and Therapy of Desire: Augustine's Theology of Desire in the Cassiciacum Dialogues* and *Reason, Authority, and the Healing of Desire in the Writings of Augustine*. Mark also manages an educational YouTube channel, TeacherOfPhilosophy.

Hannah Briscoe is a PhD student in History at the University of Birmingham. Her research, supported through the Global Challenges Scholarship, explores the lives of children of missionaries in the nineteenth and twentieth centuries, focusing on the Church Missionary Society and their work in eastern Africa. Her broader research interests include the history and geographies of children, especially in global and religious contexts, and the history of Christian renewal and revival movements. She holds an MLitt in Reformation Studies from the University of St Andrews and a BA in English from Dallas Baptist University.

Rose M. Cothren retired as a Professor of English from Dallas Baptist University in 2009, continuing to teach adjunct through 2015. She participated in the first Summer Faculty Institute in Christian Scholarship led by Davey Naugle in 2000. Rose taught Advanced Written Communication, Introduction to Linguistics, and the C. S. Lewis Seminar in addition to Perspectives in Greco-Roman Thought in the University Honors Program and other composition and literature courses. Since 2015, Rose has enjoyed traveling and various editing endeavors, especially this scholarly collection honoring her esteemed colleague, Dr. David K. Naugle.

Mark D. Eckel is President of The Comenius Institute (comeniusinstitute.org) and Associate Faculty for various institutions, including Indiana University-Purdue University Indianapolis and Capital Seminary & Graduate School, Lancaster, Pennsylvania. Mark has been teaching for over three decades: junior high through PhD. He is a contributor to books on various subjects, including science fiction, education, and apologetics. He is the author of dozens of peer-reviewed journal and encyclopedia articles, several curricula, and a number of books on subjects such as reflective thinking, faith-learning integration, and movies. Mark holds a PhD in Social Science research, a ThM in Old Testament, and a MA in English. Mark writes weekly online.

D. P. Fahrenthold is the upper-school Latin teacher at the Classical School of Wichita in Wichita, Kansas. He earned his BA in General Studies (Biblical Studies and Philosophy) from Dallas Baptist University in 2008 and an MBA (Finance Concentration) from Dallas Baptist University in 2018. He is a contributor to LOGIA Forum. He is a proponent of "Living Latin," and enjoys reading, writing, listening to, and speaking Latin as often as possible, and encouraging others to do the same.

Mary Flickner is a PhD student in the Cook School of Leadership at Dallas Baptist University. She graduated from DBU with an MA in Christian Education and from Cairn University with a BS in Biblical Studies. She is an adjunct professor at DBU, where she has taught *Developing the Christian Mind* for the past thirteen years as a colleague of Dr. Naugle's. She is also a wife, mother, and of course, a gardener.

Steven Garber is the professor of marketplace theology at Regent College in Vancouver, BC, the director of the Program in Leadership, Theology and Society, and the founder of the Washington Institute for Faith, Vocation and Culture. The author of several books, his most recent is *The Seamless Life: A Tapestry of Love and Learning, Worship and Work* (InterVarsity). He has been a consultant to colleges and corporations, facilitating institutional vocation. A husband, a father, and a grandfather, he has long lived in Washington, DC, living a life among family, friends, and flowers.

Russell D. Hemati is Associate Professor of Philosophy at Houston Baptist University. After earning his BA in Philosophy from Dallas Baptist University in 2003, Russell went on to Baylor University in Waco, where he earned his PhD in 2010, writing on Augustine and free will. He has been at HBU since 2008 and currently chairs the Philosophy department. He has primarily written on Augustine, applying the saint's insights to contemporary issues.

Leigh Hickman is an adjunct professor of English at Dallas Baptist University, where she has served for ten years. Her scholarship includes lectures and articles on Flannery O'Connor, Harry Potter, Twilight, "Jesus Movement" musicals of the 1970s, the films of Mel Gibson and Martin Scorsese, *Stranger Things*, and the horror film genre. She is an identical twin and a proud aunt to her niece Eleanor and nephews Auron and Rilian. Her heart's passion is expressed in teaching people to find and savor the Gospel story embedded in pop culture and the stories that endure throughout human history.

Adam Jones is a medievalist with an MA from Southern Methodist University. His graduate research focused on the life and writings of the Venerable Bede and the role of the church in the scientific understanding of the Middle Ages. He also publishes fiction and works as a broadcast engineer.

Christine Hand Jones is a singer-songwriter and Assistant Professor of English at Dallas Baptist University, where she teaches courses in English and songwriting. She earned her BA in music business and an MLA in literature from DBU, and a PhD in literary studies from the University of Texas at Dallas. Her academic work focuses on the apocalyptic writing of Bob Dylan and the many intersections between music and literature. Her own songwriting draws from folk and blues, the Bible and Shakespeare, and everyday life with her husband Adam and their two cats. Christine has also served as a music and worship leader in churches across Texas.

Dustin Messer is the Worldview Director at Legacy Christian Academy in Frisco, Texas and a pastor at All Saints Dallas. Additionally, Dustin serves on the board of directors at both the Evangelical Fellowship in the Anglican Communion (EFAC-USA) and the Center for Christian Civics in Washington, DC. Before starting his doctoral work at La Salle University, Dustin graduated from Boyce College, Covenant Theological Seminary, and the World Journalism Institute, and completed a fellowship at *National Review*.

David Miller has a BAS of Philosophy from Dallas Baptist University and an MDiv from Perkins School of Theology at Southern Methodist University. He is an ordained Episcopal priest currently serving as the Associate Rector for Evangelism and Family Ministries at St. Luke's Episcopal Church in Dallas, TX. He and his wife, Keeley, will soon celebrate eleven years of marriage. They have been blessed with three wonderfully rambunctious children: Pierce (six), Lawther (four), and Ellen (two).

Philip Irving Mitchell is Associate Professor of English at Dallas Baptist University, where he teaches early modern and modern humanities and directs the University Honors Program. He also serves as the Book Review Editor for the journal *Christianity and Literature*. He is a contributor to *Inklings Studies*, *Logos*, *Mythlore*, *Religion and the Arts*, *Seven*, and *Tolkien Studies*. In addition, he has chapters included in *Baptism of Fire: The Birth of Modern British Fantastic in World War I* (2015) and *Approaches to Teaching Tolkien's The Lord of the Rings and Other Works* (2015). His monograph, *The Shared Witness of C. S. Lewis and Austin Farrer: Friendship, Influence, and an Anglican Worldview*, published by Kent State University Press, is forthcoming 2021.

Sara Triana Mitchell is a poet and the author of three books. She graduated from Dallas Baptist University with a BA in Philosophy in 2009. In 2013, she earned an MEd in Curriculum and Instruction with a Children's

Literature emphasis from Penn State University. She lives with her husband Mitch and their three daughters outside of Houston, Texas.

Kevin C. Neece is an author, editor, and speaker on media, the arts, and pop culture from a Christian worldview perspective. His books include the ongoing *Gospel According to Star Trek* series (Cascade) and the forthcoming *The Gospel According to Mister Rogers' Neighborhood* (Cascade). He is the editor of *Spockology* (UCP) and co-editor of *Science Fiction and the Abolition of Man* (Pickwick) and *Rags and Bones: A Multidisciplinary Exploration of The Band* (University Press of Mississippi). He also served as a contributing editor for *Imaginatio et Ratio: A Journal of Theology and the Arts* (Wipf & Stock) and has written leader guides for Abingdon Press. His writing has appeared in a number of books and periodicals, including *Light Shining in a Dark Place: Discovering Theology Through Film*, *New Identity Magazine*, Reel World Theology, and Patheos. A former professor, Kevin holds a BAS in Communication and Philosophy and an MLA in Fine Arts. He lives with his wife and son in Fort Worth, Texas.

Jaclyn S. Parrish is the Associate Director of Digital Communications at Southwestern Baptist Theological Seminary. She graduated *summa cum laude* from Dallas Baptist University in 2012, receiving her BA in English and Christian Studies. She has worked as an online marketer and journalist in South Asia and continues to serve as an editor and content marketer in the Christian nonprofit sector. Jaclyn has published articles and reviews in *The Gospel Coalition*, *Christianity Today*, *Christianity and Literature*, *Themelios*, and *The Whedon Studies Association*.

Scott Shiffer has a PhD from the B. H. Carroll Theological Institute and is an author and speaker who studies culture and theology. He has a desire to help people think more Christianly in the way they engage in and reflect on culture, especially popular culture in America. Scott teaches religion classes at Criswell College and regularly contributes to the blog "Thinking Through Christianity." He also leads Transformation Media Ministries, which helps believers learn to think more biblically about serious issues in our world today.

Tavner Threatt teaches Modern Literature at Founders Classical Academy in Lewisville, Texas. He graduated from Dallas Baptist University with a BA in Philosophy in 2014 and is completing graduate studies in Philosophy and Classical Education at The University of Dallas. He is a Certified Sommelier with The Court of Master Sommeliers.

Artyom Tonoyan, PhD, is a Research Associate at the Center for *Holocaust & Genocide Studies* of University of Minnesota's Institute for Global Studies. Since 2015, he has been a visiting research fellow at the Institute of Archaeology and Ethnography, National Academy of Sciences of Armenia. His research interests include the Armenian Genocide, sociology of religion, religion, and politics in the Caucasus and religion and nationalism in post-Soviet Russia. His articles have appeared in *Demokratizatsiya: The Journal of Post-Soviet Democratization*, *Social Science and Society*, and *Modern Greek Studies Yearbook*, among others. He received his PhD from Baylor University.

1

Introduction

KEVIN C. NEECE

For nearly thirty years, Dr. David K. Naugle was a vital part of the faculty of Dallas Baptist University, where he holds the title of Distinguished University Professor Emeritus. Most of his time at DBU was spent as Chair of the Philosophy Department. He is a globally recognized scholar in the area of Christian worldview, having written *Worldview: The History of a Concept* (Eerdmans, 2002), which was selected by *Christianity Today* magazine as the 2003 book of the year in the theology and ethics category and is considered the premier volume on the subject of worldview.

In addition to serving as a Fellow for the Wilberforce Forum, on the advisory boards of the International Institute of Christian Studies and the Bryan Center for Critical Thought & Practice, the editorial board of the journal *Intégrité*, and the Creative Council for Art House Dallas, Dr. Naugle counts among his friends and admirers such distinguished figures as Dr. Steven Garber, Gideon Strauss, Makoto Fujimura, Nancy Pearcey, and Os Guinness.

His greatest legacy, however, lies in the robust Christian worldview he has inspired in countless students, many of whom have gone on to serve at other universities and become authors, speakers, priests, parents, musicians, and culture makers of all types. It is this inspiration and life-changing work that have animated several of his former students and colleagues to collaborate in the production of this volume.

It is on Dr. Naugle's life and profound instruction in the development of a Christian worldview that this work is based. Dr. Naugle instilled in his students that there is no area of life that is not under the rule and reign of Christ, that intellectual pursuits are necessarily spiritual pursuits, and that distinctions between the intellect and the soul, the sacred and the secular, are false dichotomies. This call to a deeply considered, nobly lived life wherein all of Creation is restored and redeemed through Christ is one that has changed the lives of his students and his colleagues alike, and which they seek to share with others in his honor—but more importantly, for the honor of Christ.

This book is a love letter to a professor, a tribute to a thinker, and most of all, evidence for the idea that the scope of the lordship and life of Christ is as vast and varied as the landscape of human ideas and endeavors. Gathered from across the spectrum of academics and popular authors, artists and musicians, Protestants and Catholics, it resonates around the theme that all goodness is God's goodness, all truth is God's truth, and all beauty is God's beauty. It is our hope that in assembling and publishing this volume, we may take a step of our own toward continuing the life's work and legacy of Dr. Naugle, not simply to honor the man, but to share with others the profound change in heart, mind, and life that Christ has wrought through his work.

Many of us whose work is collected in this volume disagree with one another and even with Dr. Naugle—philosophically, theologically, and politically. That is not a weakness, either of the book or of Dr. Naugle's instruction. Rather, this diversity represents perhaps the greatest strength of the core ideas around which this work is constructed. They are broad enough to encompass and encourage growth within a variety of viewpoints. While all of us who have contributed to this work follow Christ, we each have different convictions and different life paths. But we all seek the same goal: a discovery of the fullness of our humanity in the context of Christ. We strive to carry forward in our work and lives, as Dr. Naugle put it, "The Great Conversation in light of the Greatest Conversation." That is, the grand narrative of human ideas, philosophy, and history, understood as an expression of, and part and parcel with, the dialogue between humankind and the Divine.

The Good, the True, the Beautiful is, therefore, neither a lengthy lionization of Dr. Naugle nor an argument for his particular theology or philosophy. Rather, it is a conversation around the core of what might be termed Naugelian thought—an expression of where the essential ideas Dr. Naugle has passed on to his students and colleagues have taken each of us in all our disparate journeys and within a variety of disciplines. It is our hope that, by inviting the reader to engage with what might be seen as the papers we would write for one of Dr. Naugle's classes today or perhaps things we might discuss in his living room, the beauty of these ideas may be seen through their application.

This exploration is, therefore, presented in the context of three broad categories of human experience: The Good (community life, politics, ethics), The True (intellectual life, philosophy, theology), and The Beautiful (aesthetic and emotional life, art, literature). These are the three pillars of the pursuit of a robust and deeply engaged human experience. As such, they are also the pillars of a journey toward God and toward a deeper relationship therewith. We believe that the human experience is bound up with the quest for the Divine—that human endeavors are, at their core, spiritual in nature and that nothing good, true, or beautiful exists apart from God. In fact, everything in our human experience points to the Divine and all goodness, truth, and beauty belong to God. Therefore, all goodness is God's goodness, all truth is God's truth, and all beauty is God's beauty, no matter where they may be found. In the words Dr. Naugle instilled in us, we say along with Abraham Kuyper:[1]

> Oh, no single piece of our mental world is to be hermetically sealed off from the rest, and there is not a square inch in the whole domain of our human existence over which Christ, who is Sovereign over all, does not cry: "Mine!"[2]

This anthology not only embodies the personal and professional influence Dr. Naugle has had on a generation of believers, but it also demonstrates the viability and versatility of the biblical worldview he labored for decades to communicate. Taken together, these chapters provide a broad survey of life and culture from the vantage point of Scripture's narrative of Creation, Fall, and Redemption. It is our hope that these works will inspire readers to explore not only Dr. Naugle's work but also the profound concept that all of life is bound up with our search for our Creator and that Christ has redeemed, is redeeming, and will absolutely redeem *all*.

---

1. Abraham Kuyper, it should be noted, was the namesake of Dr. Naugle's beloved dog, Kuyper, also known as "Hyper Kuyper," who is well remembered and missed by the Naugle family and their friends.

2. Kuyper, "Speech at New Church."

BIBLIOGRAPHY

Kuyper, Abraham. "Speech at New Church, Amsterdam. October 20, 1880." In *Abraham Kuyper: A Centennial Reader*, edited by James D. Bratt, 488. Grand Rapids: Eerdmans, 1998.

Part 1

The Good

2

To Tao or Not to Tao

Heroes and Villains in "The Magician's Nephew"

Rose M. Cothren[1]

It has become somewhat of a commonplace that C. S. Lewis explored the same themes in his writing of both nonfiction and fiction. He continued to develop his ideas about moral law not only in *The Abolition of Man*, where he calls it the Tao, but also in The Chronicles of Narnia. *The Magician's Nephew*, the first in Narnian chronology but the last written by Lewis, should provide his fullest development of the Tao in the Narnian series. This paper uses the yardstick of the Tao as delineated in the appendix of *The Abolition of Man* to measure the main characters in *The Magician's Nephew* in order to determine their degree of heroism or villainy. When humans exhibit "stock responses" to the Tao, they develop virtuous characters. When we look at the fictional characters of Uncle Andrew, Diggory, Jadis, and Polly, we find that those who make stock responses to the Tao, which is present as "what

---

1. I originally presented this paper at Dallas Baptist University's Honors Banquet on April 27, 2012. As a professor in the Honors program, Dr. David K. Naugle attended the banquet, and at his request, I presented the paper again at a Friday Symposium in Fall 2014. I am delighted to contribute it to this volume in his honor.

is right" or "decency," are the heroic characters whereas those who do not are the villains.

Perhaps an overview of the Lewis course that I taught at Dallas Baptist University for nine springs, from 2005 to 2013, will serve as an appropriate introduction, after which we will briefly review *Mere Christianity* and *The Abolition of Man* before diving into the Tao in *The Magician's Nephew*.

The "Doc Rose Syllabus" for English 4314 paired nonfictional with fictional works in three units to provide an in-depth exploration of his thematic development. After the introductory reading of his spiritual autobiography, *Surprised by Joy*, the first unit paired *The Discarded Image*, Lewis's defense of the medieval worldview, with his first two planetary novels, *Out of the Silent Planet* and *Perelandra*, where we witness the protagonist Ransom overcoming his chronological snobbery and learning truths from the medieval model that are much more satisfying—life-giving, even—than are modern facts and philosophies.

(We didn't read *That Hideous Strength* for at least three reasons: (1) it's longer than the other two, the semester's only so long, and there's a lot of reading to do; (2) it's so different from the other two: it takes place on planet Earth, incorporates Arthurian mythology rather than Greco-Roman, and is much darker; and (3) as Dr. Naugle points out at the beginning of his insightful blog post on "Devils in Our World,"[2] *That Hideous Strength* develops themes from *The Abolition of Man* rather than from *The Discarded Image*.)

The third and final unit of the syllabus explored Lewis's development of ideas from *The Four Loves* in his epistolary novel *The Screwtape Letters*, his dream vision *The Great Divorce*, and his myth retold *Till We Have Faces*.

Sandwiched between these two units, we find *Mere Christianity*, *The Abolition of Man*, and *The Chronicles of Narnia*. I guess you could compare the first and third units of the syllabus to two halves of a toasted English muffin, the second unit spreading one half with the peanut butter of *Mere Christianity*, the other with peanut butter of *The Abolition of Man*, and filling the middle with the grape jelly of Narnia. My students always seemed to relish sinking their analytical teeth into this concoction and to savor discovering how the sweetness of Narnia enhances the understanding of the two apparently more nutritious works.

Now, if we stand back from the syllabus a bit and take a look at the chronology of the works in this tasty unit of study, we can see Lewis's developing focus on moral behavior. *Mere Christianity* began as broadcast talks aired over the BBC during the war years of 1941, 1942, and 1944; was published in three volumes in the nineteen-forties; and finally appeared as

---

2. Naugle, "Devils."

one volume titled *Mere Christianity* in 1952. In the meantime, *The Abolition of Man*, which began as three Riddell Memorial Lectures, was published in 1944 and *The Lion, the Witch, and the Wardrobe* in 1950, with the rest of the chronicles being written and published between 1951 and 1956.

Of course, these works were all produced after Lewis became a Christian in 1931, but his interest in moral behavior predates them. Walter Hooper in his *C. S. Lewis: A Companion and Guide*, tells us that Lewis believed in an absolute moral value long before he believed in God and became a Christian. Being "much occupied with Philosophy" while studying at Oxford, Lewis wrote in his diary on July 6, 1922, the idea of "writing a dissertation on 'the hegemony of moral value.'"[3] From lectures and papers delivered in 1924, Hooper says,

> We know that he accepted the primacy of a spiritual reality, which was essentially one of divine immanence rather than transcendence—the spirit within man and all reality, rather than a personal Father above him. "I distinguished," said Lewis, . . . "this philosophical 'God' very sharply . . . from 'the God of popular religion.'"[4]

However, with his conversion (or return, as some see it) to theism in 1929 and then to Christianity in 1931, Lewis began to see moral absolutes and God and the relationship between them in quite a different light.

In *Mere Christianity*, Lewis builds his defense of mere or basic Christianity on what he calls the "Law or Rule about Right and Wrong [that] used to be called the Law of Nature," which really means "the Law of Human Nature,"[5] which he also calls the "Moral Law, or Rule of Decent Behavior."[6] He claims that this Moral Law transcends time and culture, being held in common by "ancient Egyptians, Babylonians, Hindus, Chinese, Greeks and Romans."[7]

He concludes the first chapter, "The Law of Human Nature," with these two points: "First, . . . human beings, all over the earth, have this curious idea that they ought to behave in a certain way, and cannot really get rid of it. Secondly, . . . they do not in fact behave in that way. They know the Law of Nature; they break it."[8]

3. Hooper, *C. S. Lewis*, 329.
4. Hooper, *C. S. Lewis*, 329.
5. Lewis, *Mere Christianity*, 4.
6. Lewis, *Mere Christianity*, 9.
7. Lewis, *Mere Christianity*, 6.
8. Lewis, *Mere Christianity*, 8.

In the third part of *Mere Christianity*, *Christian Behavior*, Lewis adds that, although "the word Morality raises in a good many people's minds [the idea of] something that interferes, something that stops you having a good time. In reality, moral rules are directions for running the human machine,"[9] in other words, a user's manual. And sounding rather Aristotelian, he continues: "A man who perseveres in doing just actions gets in the end a certain quality of character. Now it is that quality rather than particular actions which we mean when we talk of 'virtue.'"[10] Lewis recognizes that choice involves feelings and emotions (the heart) as well as reason or logic (the head) and instinct (the belly)—appropriating Plato's tripartite human soul in both *Mere Christianity* and *The Abolition of Man*. As Peter Kreeft says, "We are head, hands and heart. We respond to truth, goodness and beauty."[11] Kreeft goes on to specify both the ontological and psychological order of these three "transcendentals," as he calls them: Ontologically, "Goodness is defined by truth, not by will. [But psychologically] we are attracted to goodness first by its beauty, we are attracted to truth by its goodness."[12] Metaphysically, Lewis recognizes the objective reality of truth, goodness, and beauty, fearing the results of moral subjectivism. In "The Poison of Subjectivism," Lewis says that moral subjectivism is a "disease that will certainly end our species (and, in my view, damn our souls)."[13] And so, although "we know all three transcendentals immediately and intuitively," our wills must be educated to choose objective moral goodness.[14]

In *The Abolition of Man*, alternatively titled *Reflections on Education with Special Reference to the Teaching of English in the Upper Forms of Schools*, Lewis develops the theme of a universal moral law—or the lack thereof—in connection with modern education. He laments the elimination of the user's manual, the Law of Human Nature, charging educators with trying to develop men of virtue (men with chests—the heart, the seat of feelings and emotions) without the source of virtue: "The doctrine of objective value, the belief that certain attitudes are really true, and others really false."[15] Lewis regrets that educators have fallen prey to Modernist reductionism, which reduces any emotional judgment or any statement of evaluation to an unimportant,

---

9. Lewis, *Mere Christianity*, 69.
10. Lewis, *Mere Christianity*, 80.
11. Kreeft, *Between Heaven and Hell*, 25.
12. Kreeft, *Between Heaven and Hell*, 25.
13. Lewis, "Poison of Subjectivism," 73.
14. Kreeft, *Between Heaven and Hell*, 29.
15. Lewis, *Abolition*, xx.

merely subjective observation or reaction.[16] Instead of "discriminat[ing] the good from the bad [which] would have been a lesson worth teaching," Lewis says, educators discriminate between statements of fact and statements of value, judging statements of value unimportant because they are "about the emotional state of the speaker."[17] (Of course, he exposes the illogicality of that reasoning, but we'll not dwell on that.)

Into the appendix of *The Abolition of Man*, Lewis gathers examples of the universal moral law, which is "the sole source of all value judgements,"[18] and he calls this universal moral law the Tao or the Way. Peter Kreeft observes that every culture seeks the three transcendentals of truth, goodness, and beauty, but "some cultures . . . specialize in one [of the three]." For example, "China has specialized in the love of the good, the practical human good, whether Confucian or Taoist or even Communist."[19] Even though we may associate the Tao with Taoism, not only do Confucianism and Buddhism and even Communism, according to Kreeft, concern themselves with the Way or the Path of moral uprightness, but also Jesus calls Himself "the Way, the Truth, and the Life" in John's Gospel. Not only does the Tao indicate universality but it also reflects Lewis's belief that myths are partial truths fulfilled in the True Myth of Christianity. Jesus is not only the Way, but He is also the Truth and the Life—the incarnation of the Way, the manifestation of the True Myth, and the source of abundant Life.

In his appendix to *The Abolition of Man*, Lewis gathers illustrations of the Tao from Old Norse and Old English writings, Jewish and Christian codes, and Native American and Aboriginal Australian teachings, as well as from more modern Western philosophers. And he organizes them under these headings: The Law of General Beneficence; The Law of Special Beneficence; Duties to Parents, Elders, Ancestors; Duties to Children and Posterity; The Law of Justice (subdivided into Sexual Justice, Honesty, and Justice in Court); The Law of Good Faith and Veracity; The Law of Mercy; and The Law of Magnanimity.

In *The Abolition of Man*, Lewis bemoans not only the loss of the moral law but also the loss of imagination and myth from the modern educational system, and he develops both of these themes of loss throughout *The Chronicles of Narnia*. *The Chronicles* are nuanced with moral concepts. In fact, Gabriele Greggerson says, "the key for the comprehension of Narnia's World

---

16. Lewis, *Abolition*, 4.
17. Lewis, *Abolition*, 7, 4.
18. Lewis, *Abolition*, 43.
19. Kreeft, *Between Heaven and Hell*, 23.

is precisely Lewis's theological conception of *Tao* or *Natural Law*, which he had the gift to convey into imaginative language."[20]

Since my Lewis syllabus paired nonfictional and fictional works thematically, the paper assignment for the second unit asked students to select a topic or theme from either *Mere Christianity* or *The Abolition of Man* and to show how Lewis develops that topic or theme in two of the Narnian chronicles. Three students who submitted excellent explorations of aspects of the Tao in Narnia in their Spring 2012 papers (and who have all graduated since then) gave me permission to incorporate some of their insights into this paper. I know you will appreciate, as I do, the academic excellence and generosity of Elizabeth Goring, Vincent Peña, and Zachary Simmons. (And I will be sure to give them credit for their contributions as I go along.)

While Lewis's purpose in introducing the universal Moral Law in *Mere Christianity* is to defend the basic beliefs of Christianity, in *The Abolition of Man*, he champions a Tao-based education in order to develop men of virtue, "men with chests." As Lewis says in *The Abolition of Man*: "[The Tao] is the sole source of all value judgements. If it is rejected, all value is rejected. If any value is retained, it is retained. The effort to refute it and raise a new system of value in its place is self-contradictory."[21] And he continues to express in *The Chronicles* "concern . . . with the effects on children's values of positivist conditioning."[22]

Paul Ford notes in his *Pocket Companion to Narnia*:

> Lewis felt very strongly, as did Plato, that "the little human animal will not at first have the right responses. It must be trained to feel pleasure, liking, disgust, and hatred at those things which really are pleasant, likable, disgusting, and hateful." In the *Chronicles*, he wants to foster these stock responses in his readers.[23]

Peter Kreeft adds that he "think[s] the most fundamental and universal of all moral principles is what [he calls] the 'Three R's Principle: Right Response to Reality.'"[24] As Vince Peña says, "A human is most human [when choosing to live] within the Tao because it provides a true reality on which to model life."[25] When humans exhibit stock responses, make right responses to reality, they develop virtuous characters: they become "men with chests."

---

20. Greggerson, "C. S. Lewis and the Rejection," 120.
21. Lewis, *Abolition*, 43.
22. Adey, *C. S. Lewis*, 169.
23. Ford, *Companion*, 393.
24. Kreeft, *Between Heaven and Hell*, 27.
25. Peña, Untitled Manuscript, 1.

Of course, heroes—whether male or female—must have "chests," and as we follow the decidings and the doings of a few of the characters in Narnia, we find that those who make "stock responses" to the Tao are the heroic characters whereas those who do not are the villains. Of course, the Tao is not named as such in the Chronicles, but it is present as "what is right" or "decency."

We enter Narnia with *The Magician's Nephew*, which, although first in Narnian chronology, was last in Lewis's writing. As such, it should give us the fullest development of the Tao in *The Chronicles*, and that is the reason I have chosen it for this particular thematic exploration. Beginning at the beginning then, we meet two pairs of characters who contrast starkly in their responses to the Tao. Here Lewis sets the villainous Uncle Andrew and Queen Jadis against the heroic Digory and Polly, revealing Andrew's and Jadis's lack of morals in contrast to Digory's and Polly's stock responses, showing how Digory, in particular, becomes more heroic, grows more of a chest, as he makes more stock responses.

It is not that Andrew and Jadis do not recognize a moral law but that they think themselves above it. It is not that Digory and Polly are perfect in their moral choices and behaviors, but they do try to follow the Tao and are aware when they and others do not.

From the time of Digory and Polly's unwitting entrance into his study, Uncle Andrew violates the Law of General Beneficence, which obligates every individual to seek the well-being of every other human being, stated positively in the Gospel of Matthew: "'Do to men what you wish men to do to you.' (Christian. Matt 7:12)."[26] Uncle Andrew immediately tricks Polly into doing something that he does not want to do himself: using his magic ring to travel to "Another World." As soon as Polly touches a yellow ring, "immediately, without a flash or a noise or a warning of any sort, there was no Polly."[27] At Polly's disappearance, Digory screams, an indication that he knows that Uncle Andrew has acted contrary to the Law of General Beneficence.

In so tricking Polly, Uncle Andrew reveals not only that he does not seek the well-being of others but also that he is afraid of risking his own life, thus violating The Law of Magnanimity, which Zac Simmons notes "involves valiance, courage, and love for the fellow man that is greater than love for oneself."[28] One of Lewis's illustrations of The Law of Magnanimity is drawn from Beowulf: "Death is better for every man than life with shame.

---

26. Lewis, *Abolition*, 87.
27. Lewis, *Magician's Nephew*, 16.
28. Simmons, Untitled Manuscript, 5.

(Anglo-Saxon. Beowulf, 2890),"[29] and, as Simmons notes, cowardly, fearful Uncle Andrew is "bound to a life with shame outside of the Tao."[30]

When Uncle Andrew explains that he has sent Polly via magic to "Another World," excusing himself with "'A man at my time of life, and in my state of health, to risk the shock and the dangers of being flung suddenly into a different universe,'" Digory reacts with the stock response of disgust and disapproval: "'You've behaved like a coward, sending a girl to a place you're afraid to go yourself.'"[31] Digory makes it explicit that, when someone behaves in an un-Tao-like manner, one manifests oneself as unheroic.

When Digory screams at Polly's disappearance, Uncle Andrew shows that he knows the Tao by invoking its Duties to Parents, Elders, Ancestors in order to silence Digory and to protect himself, appealing to Digory's concern for his ailing mother: "'None of that!' he hissed in Digory's ear. 'If you start making a noise your Mother'll hear it. And you know what a fright might do to her.'"[32] Uncle Andrew does know the Tao, but he uses it the way he uses people—only for his own dastardly purposes. Paul Ford comments that Andrew Ketterley is "completely without conscience, he is only out for himself. . . . [He] shows himself to be the very antithesis of stock responses to human values."[33]

Uncle Andrew violates while Digory gives the stock responses not only to The Law of General Beneficence, to Duties to Parents, and to The Law of Magnanimity, but also to The Law of Good Faith and Veracity.

Digory responds with disapproval to his uncle's despicable breaking of his promise to his godmother: "'Well, then, it was jolly rotten of you,' said Digory" when Uncle Andrew relates that he did not keep his promise to burn the box, unopened, as soon as she was dead.[34] Lewis cites Confucius's *Analects*: "[The gentleman] must learn to be faithful to his superiors and to keep promises."[35]

Andrew defends himself by saying that he is above such rules:

> "Rotten?" said Uncle Andrew with a puzzled look. "Oh, I see. You mean that little boys ought to keep their promises. Very true: most right and proper, I'm sure, and I'm very glad you have been taught to do it. But of course you must understand that rules of

---

29. Lewis, *Abolition*, 99.
30. Simmons, Untitled Manuscript, 6.
31. Lewis, *Magician's Nephew*, 25.
32. Lewis, *Magician's Nephew*, 17.
33. Ford, *Companion*, 6.
34. Lewis, *Magician's Nephew*, 20.
35. Lewis, *Abolition*, 96.

that sort, however excellent they may be for little boys—and servants—and women—and even people in general, can't possibly be expected to apply to profound students and great thinkers and sages. No, Digory. Men like me, who possess hidden wisdom, are freed from common rules just as we are cut off from common pleasures. Ours, my boy, is a high and lonely destiny."[36]

Uncle Andrew makes it clear that he knows the Tao but considers himself above it, and his declaration brings to mind Aristotle's observation that a man who thinks he is self-sufficient and has no need of community must be either a god or a beast. Yet there are consequences to removing oneself from the moral community, to seeing oneself as a god. Both Uncle Andrew and Jadis, Queen of Charn, see themselves as godlike, as above moral laws that others are subject to.

Like Uncle Andrew, Jadis ignores the Law of General Beneficence and, as Zac notes, she suffers its consequences.[37] Lewis gives the consequences of not caring for others from an ancient Babylonian hymn: "Who meditates oppression, his dwelling is overturned."[38] Uncaring, Jadis sends "a whole world [her world, her dwelling] to its own demise" with one word, and at the same time she also brings upon herself the form of a statue.

Elizabeth Goring connects Jadis's immoral behavior to The Law of Special Beneficence, especially to Lewis's citation of the Greek philosopher Epictetus: "I ought not to be unfeeling like a statue but should fulfill both my natural and artificial relations."[39] Goring also notes how literally appropriate the connection to Epictetus is, seeing that, in both *The Magician's Nephew* and *The Lion, the Witch, and the Wardrobe* (where she is known as The White Witch), Jadis's being unfeeling like a statue is pictured first in her being a statue and then in her reducing both human beings and animals to statues.[40]

Rather than obeying the Tao, Jadis has set herself up as the law in Charn, a now-dying world whose demise, Goring says, she revels in when revealing that the violent war and its fatal results came after she uttered the Deplorable Word.[41] When Digory and Polly protest, Jadis pronounces, "They were all my people. What else were they there for except to do my

---

36. Lewis, *Magician's Nephew*, 20–21.
37. Simmons, Untitled Manuscript, 1.
38. Lewis, *Abolition*, 85.
39. Lewis, *Abolition*, 88.
40. Goring, Untitled Manuscript, 4.
41. Goring, Untitled Manuscript, 7.

will?"[42] The hallmark of the Tao-less Narnian villains, then, seems to be the abrogation of The Law of General Beneficence, treating other humans as things to be used for utilitarian purposes. However, aspects of the Tao seem to be closely related, even overlapping, so we could likely cite violations of all eight categories for Andrew and Jadis, but let's move on to some consequences.

While Jadis does not receive her full come-uppance until Aslan slays her in *The Lion, the Witch, and the Wardrobe,* Andrew suffers laughable consequences during the creation of Narnia. Just as he rejects the Tao, so Andrew rejects Aslan's song. Partly because he has no appreciation for myth or imagination, Andrew discounts a lion's being able to sing and convinces himself that it is "only roaring as any lion might in a zoo in our own world."[43] The narrator spells out how Andrew's continuing rejection results in his loss of ability to hear:

> And the longer and more beautiful the Lion sang, the harder Uncle Andrew tried to make himself believe that he could hear nothing but roaring. Now the trouble about trying to make yourself stupider than you really are is that you very often succeed. Uncle Andrew did. He soon did hear nothing but roaring in Aslan's song. Soon he couldn't have heard anything else even if he had wanted to.[44]

This may not seem like much of a loss to Andrew, but it has the further consequence of his being able to hear only growling when the Bulldog inquires, "Now, sir . . . are you animal, vegetable, or mineral?"[45] Neither do the animals think Andrew can talk, so the Warthog determines that he's only a tree, and the Andrew Tree narrowly escapes being fatally planted upside-down because "several animals said his legs must be his branches and therefore the gray, fluffy thing (they meant his head) must be his root. But then others said that the forked end of him was the muddier and that it spread out more, as roots ought to do. So finally he was planted the right way up."[46] Right way up or not, Andrew—outside the moral community—is no longer regarded as human; he is now neither godlike nor even beastlike, but plantlike.

Digory, however, acts within the Tao, being, as Goring notes, compelled by a strong sense of right and attempting to abide by it. After Polly's disappearance, Uncle Andrew pricks Digory's sense of honor and chivalry

42. Lewis, *Magician's Nephew*, 61.
43. Lewis, *Magician's Nephew*, 149.
44. Lewis, *Magician's Nephew*, 149–50.
45. Lewis, *Magician's Nephew*, 152.
46. Lewis, *Magician's Nephew*, 157–58.

to go after her—not to save her, exactly, but to be able to bring back experimental information for himself. Digory knows it's a trap, but he's compelled to go: "If you had any honor and all that, you'd be going yourself. But I know you won't. All right. I see I've got to go. But you *are* a beast."[47]

After alluding to The Law of Justice—"And you're simply a wicked, cruel magician like the ones in the stories. Well, I've never read a story in which people of that sort weren't paid out in the end, and I bet you will be"[48]—Digory—not quite bravely—"rings off" into the unknown. The narrator then tells us, "And he thought then, as he always thought afterward too, that he could not *decently* have done anything else."[49] In doing right by Polly in their artificial relationship of friendship, Digory obeys The Law of Special Beneficence as Lewis illustrates from Cicero: "Part of us is claimed by our country, part by our parents, part by our friends."[50]

Neither Polly nor Digory is perfect, but they do have consciences that prick them when they go against the Tao. Zac Simmons notes that Digory violates The Tao's Law of Justice, which "involves following the rules that have been placed on that society or community" and which is illustrated by The Ten Commandments.[51] Digory breaks The Law of Justice when he ignores the warning on the bell he finds in Charn:

> Make your choice, adventurous Stranger;
> Strike the bell and bide the danger,
> Or wonder, till it drives you mad,
> What would have followed if you had.[52]

Although Polly advises against ringing the bell, Digory now sets aside his obligation to listen to his friend's warnings. Digory strikes the bell and the rest is . . . well, the tale of *The Magician's Nephew*. He and others bide the danger, but Digory, after being convicted of acting outside the Tao, learns his lesson well.

In the garden in the Western Wild where an apple tree grows, Digory not only follows the rules of entering the garden (obeying The Law of Justice), but he also resists Jadis's temptations to carry out one part of the Tao by breaking two others. The choice of means is evidently as important as the ends in determining virtue and character.

---

47. Lewis, *Magician's Nephew*, 27.
48. Lewis, *Magician's Nephew*, 27.
49. Lewis, *Magician's Nephew*, 30 (emphasis added).
50. Lewis, *Abolition*, 89.
51. Simmons, Untitled Manuscript, 3.
52. Lewis, *Magician's Nephew*, 56.

When Digory arrives at the garden, he reads and abides by the instructions on the gate:

> Come in by the gold gates or not at all,
> Take of my fruit for others or forbear,
> For those who steal or those who climb my wall
> Shall find their heart's desire and find despair.[53]

Jadis disregards these instructions, having entered the garden by leaping over the wall and having taken and eaten an apple for herself, so her days do end in despair: As Aslan says, "'She has won her heart's desire; she has unwearying strength and endless days *like a goddess* . . . [but] length of days with an evil heart is only length of misery and already she begins to know it.'"[54]

Digory very nearly succumbs to Jadis's taunt of the Tao's Duties to Parents regarding his mother, but Jadis makes her fatal mistake when she asks him to ignore Special Beneficence in regard to his friend Polly. He has learned to abide by The Law of Special Beneficence. Digory is also convicted to right-deciding and right-doing when Jadis tells him that he doesn't have to keep his promise to Aslan. As Simmons notes, this would be a transgression against The Law of Good Faith and Veracity: Not only has Digory reproached Uncle Andrew for the breaking of a promise,[55] but also Digory protests that his mother:

> "Wouldn't like it—[she's] awfully strict about keeping promises—and not stealing—and all that sort of thing" . . .
> "But she need never know," said the Witch. . . . "No one in your world need know anything about this whole story. You needn't take the little girl back with you, you know." . . .
> And the meanness of the suggestion that he should leave Polly behind suddenly made all the other things the Witch had been saying to him sound false and hollow.[56]

As Lewis says in *Mere Christianity*, decent behavior "means things like . . . keeping promises you would rather not keep."[57] Digory abides by both The Law of Good Faith and Veracity and The Law of Justice when he takes the apple to Aslan instead of stealing it for his mother, for which Tao-based

---

53. Lewis, *Magician's Nephew*, 187.
54. Lewis, *Magician's Nephew*, 208 (emphasis added).
55. Simmons, Untitled Manuscript, 5.
56. Lewis, *Magician's Nephew*, 194.
57. Lewis, *Mere Christianity*, 19.

behavior he receives both Aslan's commendation, "Well done,"[58] and an apple to restore his mother's health. Digory is a hero.

Gregory Jordan says, "Lewis saw the possession of a particular set of values as an authentic and indispensable criterion for humanness."[59] And David Neff says that if we "disconnect human beings from their moral capacity you will never have another hero . . . when we prize things rightly, we become ready to sacrifice for them."[60] As Zac Simmons says, "The basic premise behind all these laws of the Tao is to live a selfless life."[61] According to Simmons, in Narnia, those who follow the Tao, who are self-sacrificing, who look out for their fellow beings, are the heroes who reap the rewards of following the Tao. Characters who live outside the Tao, who live only for themselves, are villains who experience pain, loneliness, despair, and even death.[62]

Vince Peña comments, "Lewis reveals in [*The Chronicles of Narnia*] that, while evil men attempt to subdue the objectivity of the Tao to their own volitions, they, in essence, make a useless effort to manipulate reality, which results in a path of destruction; and prudent men, in submitting themselves to its reality, reap the ultimate benefit of the appropriate unity of the Tao."[63] In *The Magician's Nephew*, Lewis shows us the rewards of following the Tao through the heroic characters of both Digory and Polly, and the consequences of living outside the Tao in the villainous characters of Uncle Andrew and Jadis.

Although her stock responses are only hinted at herein, Polly, too, is a hero because she abides by the Tao. In fact, Polly is instrumental in Digory's becoming one of the few heroic adults in *The Chronicles of Narnia*. By abiding by the Tao, by retaining the moral law, and by retaining his imagination and his belief in myth, Digory matures into the heroic Professor Kirk in *The Lion, the Witch, and the Wardrobe*. As Professor Kirk, Digory has become the kind of man Lewis says that God wants: "He wants a child's heart, but a grown-up's head."[64] You, too, can be a heroic adult and the kind of adult that God wants: Abide by the Tao as fulfilled in the true myth of Christianity, preserve your child-like imaginative heart, and develop your grown-up intellectual head.

58. Lewis, *Magician's Nephew*, 197.
59. Jordan, "Invention of Man," 4.
60. Neff, "American Babel," 19.
61. Simmons, Untitled Manuscript, 6.
62. Simmons, Untitled Manuscript, 6.
63. Peña, Untitled Manuscript, 1.
64. Lewis, *Mere Christianity*, 77.

BIBLIOGRAPHY

Adey, Lionel. *C. S. Lewis: Writer, Dreamer, and Mentor.* Grand Rapids: Eerdmans, 1998.
Ford, Paul F. *Companion to Narnia.* San Francisco: Harper & Row, 1983.
Goring, Elizabeth. Untitled Manuscript. 2012. Unpublished.
Greggerson, Gabriele. "C. S. Lewis and the Rejection of the Tao." *Dialog: A Journal of Theology* 42.2 (2003) 120–25.
Hooper, Walter. *C. S. Lewis: A Companion and Guide.* London: HarperCollins, 1996.
Jordan, Gregory E. "The Invention of Man: A Response to C. S. Lewis's *The Abolition of Man*." *Journal of Evolution & Technology* 19.1 (2008) 1–7.
Kreeft, Peter. *Between Heaven and Hell: A Dialog Somewhere Beyond Death with John F. Kennedy, C. S. Lewis, and Aldous Huxley.* Downers Grove, IL: InterVarsity, 1982.
Lewis, C. S. *The Abolition of Man.* 1944. Reprint, San Francisco: HarperCollins, 2001.
———. *The Lion, the Witch, and the Wardrobe.* 1950. Reprint, San Francisco: HarperCollins, 1994.
———. *The Magician's Nephew.* 1955. Reprint, San Francisco: HarperCollins, 1994.
———. *Mere Christianity.* 1952. Reprint, San Francisco: HarperCollins, 2000.
———. "The Poison of Subjectivism." In *Christian Reflections*, edited by Walter Hooper, 72–81. Grand Rapids: Eerdmans, 1967.
Naugle, David K. "The Devils in Our World." *Official Website of C. S. Lewis*, July 16, 2016. https://www.cslewis.com/the-devils-in-our-world.
Neff, David. "American Babel." *Christianity Today*, August 17, 1992, 18–19.
Peña, Vincent. Untitled Manuscript. 2012. Unpublished.
Simmons, Zachary. Untitled Manuscript. 2012. Unpublished.

3

An Exploration of Calling

William Wilberforce, Julia Sass, and Me

HANNAH BRISCOE

INTRODUCTION

Inspired by Dr. David Naugle's Developing the Christian Mind (DCM) course, this chapter explores the theme of calling through the interconnected links of diverse lives. It begins with a personal reflection from my own time as a student under Dr. Naugle and my winding path back to academia. It then moves forward with two historical case studies. It looks first at the high-profile figure of William Wilberforce (1759–1833) who played a significant role in the spread of the modern missionary movement (in addition to his more famous exploits for the abolition of the slave trade and other significant causes). It then follows these ripples to the mid-nineteenth century to explore a more hidden voice in history, that of the solitary female missionary, through the life of Julia Sass (a missionary from 1848 to 1869 who died in 1891)—a young woman in Victorian England who felt the call to Africa so strongly that she went despite her mother's definite and continued opposition. These historical case studies offer windows through which this chapter explores complex issues of calling, first through a comparative look at the callings of both Wilberforce and Sass and then by a focused examination of the correspondence of Julia Sass during her time as a missionary. Finally, this chapter concludes with reflections on the practice of historical scholarship and faith.

Wilberforce showed unrelenting and courageous commitment to his calling through opposition, illness, and disappointments. Sass's courage and personality, continual struggles with poor health and exhaustion, and entanglements with colonial and "civilizing" preoccupations offer a different and less familiar perspective on calling. For Sass and other female missionaries, their vocation came with both cost and reward while helping them to step beyond their own cultural constraints. This chapter does not aim to set up heroes and saints and ignore the complex historical issues surrounding Victorian morality and colonial mission. Rather, it asks how these examples might provoke us to reflect on our own spiritual journey.

A PERSONAL JOURNEY

In Dr. Naugle's DCM course at Dallas Baptist University, I was first introduced to the historical figure of William Wilberforce. This was the same year as the release of the popular film adaptation of Wilberforce's life, *Amazing Grace* (2006). I was challenged by the story of this man's life and his crisis of calling. Should he abandon his political career and become a religious minister or continue in the "secular" sphere of politics? This crisis of calling was more than a turning point in a promising young man's personal development. Wilberforce remained a member of Parliament, and his well-famed struggle for the abolition of the slave trade rallied the conscience of a generation. This theme of vocation, or calling, and the courage that it both produces and requires was one of the main lessons I took with me from the DCM course.

This has been an important theme in my own journey. I have struggled with the meaning of my wide variety of interests that have led me to such disparate hobbies and pursuits as sports, drama, music, writing, international travel, voluntary work, Christian ministry, and academic research. I have always been inspired by men and women who accomplished great things, but I was so busy doing everything that I worried I was missing my one great thing. I have come to realize, however, that this is the beauty of calling. It has the power to move one beyond dualism and compartmentalized living onto a path that (though it may twist and turn) is lit by purpose. In *The Call* (read in the same DCM course), Os Guinness gives this definition: "*calling is the truth that God calls us to himself so decisively that everything* we are, everything we do, and everything we have is invested with a special devotion and dynamism lived out as response to his summons and service."[1]

In my own life, calling has led me on a winding road. It has been a journey of discovery and delight, around bends of confusion and clarity. The decision to return to academia and postgraduate studies was born out of two realizations. First, I found myself daydreaming often about returning to university and began to realize that this was not the case with many of my peers. Though I loved what I was doing at the time, I felt that I was ignoring something deep inside me and started to pay attention to it as perhaps important. Second, as I travelled and experienced other places and cultures, history felt alive and I longed to understand the context of the world I was witnessing around me. Now, in the latter part of my PhD, I am making plans and working toward the next steps. For my research now and for my future career moves, I am wrestling with the very questions posed back in that DCM course as Dr. Naugle challenged our thinking, disturbed our comfortable perspectives, encouraged our potential, and provoked us to fully engage our minds and our hearts.

THE NATURE OF CALLING: WILLIAM WILBERFORCE AND JULIA SASS

William Wilberforce is famous for his two "great objects," the abolition of the slave trade and the reformation of manners (or morals).[2] His fight to end the trade of enslaved persons was accomplished through years of struggle and partnership with individuals and networks. In his letter to Freeholders and other inhabitants of Yorkshire, he explained his reasons for focusing so much attention on the cause of abolition. He described the slave trade as "the foulest blot that ever stained our National character," suggesting that his constituents would therefore not deem their "Representative to have been unworthily employed, in having been among the foremost in wiping it away."[3] After the trade was abolished in 1807, Wilberforce continued to campaign for the end of slavery across the Empire. He described the systemic injustice of the institution of slavery, calling it "a system of the grossest injustice, of the most heathenish irreligion and immorality, of the most

---

1. Guinness, *Call*, 5.

2. Wilberforce's famous statement, "God Almighty has set before me two great objects, the suppression of the slave trade and the reformation of manners," is from October 28, 1787 (Wilberforce, *Life of William Wilberforce*, 149).

3. Wilberforce, *Letter on the Abolition of the Slave Trade*, 1–2.

unprecedented degradation, and unrelenting cruelty."[4] The blight of slavery was a disfigurement that could only indicate a wider sickness affecting the whole of society—his calling was not complete when one battle was won, but it was ground gained for the next battle.

However lonely at times, his struggle was not in isolation. In addition to collaborating with other great abolitionists and reformers, Wilberforce had the support of networks and communities, each member playing a different role and carrying a unique burden. These included the families living around Clapham Common in London (e.g., the Thorntons, Venns, Grants, Stephens, and the Macaulays)[5] and devoted friends further afield such as Hannah More. The men and women of this "Clapham Sect" were not isolated, but they became an extensive network of philanthropies that operated as voluntary societies that promoted various evangelical objectives.[6] Many of these families were also associated with the Eclectic Society, a discussion group founded in 1783 by John Newton and other English clergymen and laymen. It had a strong anti-slavery and missions focus, and it was in these discussions that the Church Missionary Society (CMS), originally called The Society for Missions to Africa and the East, was born in 1799.[7] Wilberforce was active in these networks and supportive of the CMS and other missionary societies.

Though less commonly known than his two great objects, Wilberforce was also influential in the spread of the missionary movement. As early as 1793 he engaged in parliamentary debate to promote Christianity in India through the provision of ministers, schoolmasters, and others at the East India Company's expense.[8] Though unsuccessful at the time, when the company renewed its charter in 1813, Wilberforce and his allies succeeded in gaining the "pious" clause, which maintained that it was the duty of Britain to promote the "Interests and Happiness" of the native inhabitants within its domains in India. This included adopting measures for the introduction of "useful knowledge and of religious and moral improvement" and to afford "sufficient facilities . . . to persons desirous of going to and remaining in India, for the purpose of accomplishing those benevolent designs."[9] Andrew Porter ascribes the successful inclusion of this clause to the "astute parliamentary manoeuvring by Wilberforce and his friends and an extensive

---

4. Wilberforce, *Appeal to the Religion, Justice, and Humanity*, 3.
5. Stott, *Wilberforce*, 3.
6. Cox, *British Missionary Enterprise*, 90.
7. Stock, *History of the Church Missionary Society*, 60–71.
8. Porter, *Religion versus Empire?*, 68.
9. Porter, *Religion versus Empire?*, 73–74.

petitioning campaign pushed ahead in the country."[10] This outcome did not mean an entirely open door for missionary interests; nevertheless, for Anglicans at least the way was paved for an influx of schoolmasters, chaplains, clergy, and for the building of churches.[11] Brian Cox describes the aim of the clause "not to command the Christianization of India, but to permit voluntarist missionary societies to operate freely there."[12]

The 1807 abolition of the British slave trade helped open new mission fields. Sierra Leone was already a colony and Freetown was chosen as the landing place for the Royal Naval squadron to "liberate those slaves (Liberated Africans or 'recaptives') freed from the slavers along the West Africa coast."[13] The quick overcrowding led to the establishment of villages around the peninsula for the resettlement of these people to a new life.[14] It was into this setting that our next historical case study, Miss Julia Sass, was sent to her missionary post as the superintendent of the Female Institution, later renamed the Annie Walsh Memorial School, which survives today as an elite high school for girls.

The nineteenth century witnessed a surge of volunteerism at home and abroad, and missionary recruits grew to the thousands. Societies were formed and multiplied that recruited from and for a vast array of social strata. Many men and women, married and single, responded to "the call." There was varied and changing opinion among the different societies as to the place of women in the mission field in the early days of pioneering and experimentation; nevertheless, it is clear that "women were of fundamental importance in defining, developing, and shaping the course of the modern missionary movement."[15] The CMS had a policy from the beginning to encourage married missionaries to go abroad with their families.[16] The presence of missionary women (though not labelled as missionaries in their own right) was considered necessary to preserve the morals and reputations of missionary men, to model the Christian home, and for the essential "domestic support and comfort of husbands, fathers, and brothers engaged in the work."[17] The first female missionaries, then, were predominantly wives,

---

10. Porter, *Religion versus Empire?*, 74.
11. Porter, *Religion versus Empire?*, 73–75.
12. Cox, *British Missionary Enterprise*, 92.
13. Porter, *Religion versus Empire?*, 66.
14. Porter, *Religion versus Empire?*, 66.
15. Murray, "Role of Women," 66.
16. Murray, "Role of Women," 71–72.
17. Seton, *Western Daughters in Eastern Lands*, 22–23.

daughters, and spinster sisters who went out officially to support the men, though often with their own sense of calling.

It was not until near the end of the nineteenth century that unmarried women began to be sent in large numbers to the mission field by all of the societies, which led to women's outnumbering men in the mission field through the whole of the twentieth century.[18] Before this great movement of professional female missionaries, there were scattered exceptions in the earlier decades of the nineteenth century. It was through this slightly open door that Julia Sass stepped forward with a clear conviction of her calling to Africa. Like other forerunners, by blazing a trail she was often alone.

William Wilberforce and Julia Sass are connected across generations by their roles in different stages of the development from abolition to resettlement, and personally through their relationships to the Venn family. Wilberforce was friend and correspondent to John Venn, member of the Eclectic Society and one of the founders of the CMS. John's son Henry Venn was the Honorary Secretary of CMS whose correspondence with Julia Sass is examined below. This is but one example of how their stories are inextricably tied to each other and to multiple histories. Ripples such as these can be traced from further afield and further back in history. The story of the British Protestant missionary movement is connected to Count Zinzendorf and the Moravian missionaries and their roots to German Pietism, the Reformation, Jan Huss, and further and further back. This story is one of various confessions and societies connected through networks of friendship, kin, trade, and politics. It is a global story, a political story, an economic and social story, and the list goes on. Throughout this historical tapestry, there are many moments occasioned by singular courage, cowardice, apathy, love, hatred, and tragic and happy mistakes. Without these moments, the picture would change; yet these moments never truly stand alone. When one recognizes this, it prevents the individual, specific calling from being either despised as insignificant or worshiped as all-important.

When thinking about calling, it is easy to get caught up in the mechanics, the five- and ten-year plan, the mission statement. These can be fruitful exercises; however, these strategies can never satisfy that essence of meaning and purpose we long for in this life. When asked for the greatest commandment in the Law, Jesus responded, "You shall love the LORD your God with all your heart, with all your soul, and with all your mind" (Matt 22:37 NKJV). This first commandment goes to the very heart of purpose, of longing, of meaning—God is love (1 John 4:7–8). If God created us in

---

18. Seton, *Western Daughters in Eastern Lands*, 22–23. See also Table 1 in Cox, *British Missionary Enterprise*, 270. In this table, "Estimated Number of British Missionaries Overseas, 1889–2001," women missionaries outnumber men already in 1889.

his image, then surely he created us to be loved and to love. It is when we finally hear him calling us beloved that we begin to believe it and our world is transformed.

In the life of Wilberforce, this primary relational call is evident through his conversion experience. In Easter 1786, he wrote to his sister Sally and described how he offered his devotions "amidst the general chorus, with which all nature seems on such a morning to be swelling the Song of Praise & Thanksgiving."[19] Our understanding of Wilberforce's experience should be situated within the frameworks of the time, in which there was a strong evangelical stress on conversion narratives.[20] Yet regardless of how his experience was lived or constructed, there is evidence of its potency in his life through the testimony of others and in his future actions. The Rev. John Newton, the repented former slave trader who penned the well-known hymn "Amazing Grace," confided in a letter to Wilberforce why he held a special place in his affections: "but especially because you were pleased to make me the first acquainted with the Lord's goodness to you. The joy that I felt and the hopes I conceived when you called on me in the vestry at St. Mary's, I shall never forget. From that hour you have been particularly dear to me."[21] There was clearly a level of emotion and fervency in the exchange that caused Newton to mark the significance of the occasion. Further evidence of Wilberforce's spiritual or moral transformation can be seen by the fact that it was only about a year after his letter to his sister that Wilberforce recorded his life's mission, his two great objects.[22] His vocation was born out of his newfound relationship to his Caller.

Julia Sass did not leave behind the same record of a dramatic conversion experience like Wilberforce, but her devotional life can be seen in her letters through her deep familiarity with Scripture, her continual desire to discern and do the Lord's will, and her efforts to trust in his faithfulness despite the circumstances. As examined below, her letters acknowledge her despair, anguish, and frustration while grasping for hope and clinging to the faithfulness and promises of God. Much personality is displayed in these letters and one could easily imagine a no-nonsense, headstrong woman who was desperate for help while critical of anyone who might try to help. But it is important to step back and consider the nature of the sources. It is apparent that Sass developed a level of closeness and trust with Henry Venn, to whom she wrote freely and, in the latter years at least, he solicited her views

19. Bodleian quoted in Stott, *Wilberforce*, 25.
20. Stott, *Wilberforce*, 25–26.
21. Wilberforce, *Correspondence*, 56–57.
22. Stott, *Wilberforce*, 25–26.

of people and situations. Even so, her pleas for assistance went unanswered time and time again. As mentioned above, this was a pioneering time for professional female missionaries (as opposed to wives, daughters, and sisters). One can imagine that gaining suitable recruits to fill vacancies left by death or grave illness was a difficult task. Her letters, therefore, needed to be persistent and emphatic to accomplish their purpose. She did not need to prove her devotion, but she absolutely had to be her own spokesperson and advocate.

Her relationship with her students, the orphan girls she raised, and other members of the mission community were complex and varied, but they certainly contained deep affection and concern. She could not, however, rely on the support of a strong community of faith such as those surrounding Wilberforce (or perhaps could not see through cultural and racial differences to fully value the companionship of local African Christian women). Whereas Wilberforce could continually dine with friends and collaborators, enjoyed a full public life in the city and private life in countryside retreats, and benefited from the constant stimulation of intellectual and spiritual communities and the warmth of a family life; Sass struggled to find friendship and companionship in her position as the sometimes only or one of a few female missionaries. Wilberforce and Sass both struggled through cycles of illness and overwork, but without the same support networks, no one can know to what depths Julia was sustained and renewed through her faith.[23]

Like Wilberforce, Sass had struggled to discern the path of her calling. A fascinating series of letters has been preserved between Julia Sass, her mother Mary Sass, and Henry Venn from before she left for missionary service in Sierra Leone. Venn visited Mrs. Mary Sass about Julia's desire to go to Africa as a missionary. Mrs. Sass was impressed with him and willing to trust his decision; nevertheless, she was determined not to aid in any way and to make her disapproval clear. Julia knew her mother's intentions and wrote to Mr. Venn to prepare him for her mother's letter or return visit the next day. This letter reveals Julia's turmoil over her mother's position on the matter and her duty as a daughter. It is worth quoting a portion of her letter because it speaks to the challenge many face today with competing callings, especially when called to a task or vocation that doesn't match easily with the call to honor parents or an authority.

> She [her mother] would not prevent my taking any situation in a family abroad, and so I do consider, my dear Sir, that the real objection is on account of my engaging in Mission Work. If she needed my support, if she were in bad health I should from the

23. CMS/B/OMS/C A1 O187, 1849–1869.

first, have felt differently, knowing that duty called me to stay with her, but neither of these is the case. Indeed if such had been the case, I cannot think that the Lord would have opened the way, and hitherto smoothed every difficulty.[24]

For Julia Sass, determining when it was right to disobey a parent came down to a distinction in a hierarchy of callings (or commandments) in Scripture. She saw in general the call to honor one's parents as higher than pursuing one's own special calling or vocation; however, when it became clear that her mother's wishes were rooted in her opposition to Julia's Evangelicalism, then the calling not to deny her faith was seen as higher than the call to honor her mother's wishes.

> I certainly should have liked my mother's consent, but feeling that she never has opposed me in what I considered my path of duty for my advancement in temporal things, I cannot but think that it is Popery alone that influences her now. However, my dear Sir, much as I wish to go to Africa, I would only be what and where the Lord appoints, whether here or there I desire to be His, to do his work, and that He should be sensibly about my path leading and guiding.[25]

Several times, Julia refers to her mother's "Popery." This was a common pejorative at this time that could refer to Catholicism or to the ritualism of High Church and Anglo-Catholic parties within the Church of England.[26] Even so, she did her best to honor her mother through defending her character and motivations. It is clear that the situation weighed very heavy on Julia, as she sought to convey to Henry Venn: "My dear Sir, I will never leave her, but to engage in Missionary Work, and really when I see her fret and looking ill with anxiety about me it is a greater trial to me than any trials of sickness, privation or difficulty I may meet with in Africa, could possibly be."[27]

In this triangle as well as in Wilberforce's journey, there are examples of the competing expectations (internal and external) which so often make discerning one's call a challenge. Issues of finances, responsibilities, well-being, relationships, hopes and desires, and legal and civic duty are often cloudy when one begins to discover a calling to a specific task or journey. Both Wilberforce and Sass wrestled with these questions in prayer and

24. CMS/G/AC16/29c.

25. CMS/G/AC16/29c.

26. Maughan, *Mighty England*, 88. For a discussion on the debates and party conflicts within the Church of England and their relationship to the development of Victorian Anglican missions, see esp. chapters 1–2.

27. CMS/G/AC16/29e.

sought counsel from trusted leadership, and after discerning the path, both drew from their own well of faith and trust in the Lord to find the courage to step forward on this road. Is this always the pattern, and does every true calling begin with such faith and obedience? The truest obedience is a joyful act of worship from a place of love, but the Lord knows our broken state. How often do we obey reluctantly and begrudgingly and find ourselves met with his grace and faithfulness along the road? Our pitiable acts of service are transformed by grace. Love him and you will delight to obey. Obey him and he will teach you to love.

THE COMPLEXITIES AND SIMPLICITY OF CALLING: THE CORRESPONDENCE OF JULIA SASS

As Guinness emphasizes throughout *The Call*, there is no calling without a Caller—no vocation without a Voice. Without this external Caller a calling can only be understood as perhaps a good idea or maybe a determination to achieve a goal or to live by a principle. We should never disdain a sense of calling in someone non-religious or of another faith, for these impulses are, after all, echoes of God's grace that permeate his creation. If we become haughty in our calling from God and belittle the efforts of others or fail to recognize their contributions and achievements, we fail to obey that essential calling to love our neighbor as ourselves and, thereby, deprive ourselves of a blessing or benefit. This form of pride seeps deeper as Christians begin to compare and judge each other according to their own standards. We close our hearts and will not receive from someone whom we have decided is prideful, sinful, or uneducated. And this pride mutates into self-pity or self-hatred when we become our own judge rather than bowing at the foot of the Cross. We may do and even accomplish much while really believing that we can't possibly be used by God and that our efforts will never please him. Either we become static or we run in circles.

In the life of Julia Sass, we see these critical tendencies most clearly in her attitudes towards the local population, in her blindness to what might now be interpreted as racism and classism cloaked in compassion and respectability. This does not mean that she did not have compassion. We will see elsewhere her honest and sacrificial efforts to much good as well as her own journey of growth through her experience. A striking example of this criticism comes right away in her first letter to headquarters from her new mission station. She gave an account of the opening of her school and explained her criteria for accepting students. First of all, the parents must be able to pay for their children. This is understandable for practical purposes, but it reveals the class base from which the society desired to raise up leaders within the colony. The students accepted must also be the products of Christian marriage. She described the benefits of these selection criteria: "Had there been no restrictions as to the Class of children to be received, the School would have been already too large for one person to undertake. I am very glad a difference is to be made, and I think it will very likely be very beneficial in inducing Parents to marry for the sake of having their children properly educated."[28] Though she desired to raise the prospects of these girls, her perception of their potential as unique individuals was limited by her design to use the Institution as a civilizing agency in the culture at large. In another letter she explicitly describes her school as "my *Select* Establishment." She explained that some people feel that students of parents who later married ought to be admitted, but she pleaded for her stricter standards to be maintained to prevent those children born out of Christian wedlock from corrupting her present pupils.[29] It is clear that Miss Sass was not simply a product of her time, but acted from her own convictions and principles. She had a strong sense of her calling to raise up the wives and mothers to lead their society to be a shining example of civilized Christianity.

Through over two decades of severe trials, which will be discussed below, Miss Sass fought for this dream. The success of her efforts in the estimation of her society is evident through a sermon preached on February 18, 1900, at Lambeth Palace by the Rev. J. B. Whiting in which her name is included among the likes of Wilberforce, Clarkson, Prince Albert, and Bishop Crowther as part of the "long array of devoted men and women, both European and African" who were raised up as God's "instruments" in overcoming wickedness and righting the "cruel wrongs" that had been inflicted upon West Africa. Clearly, this woman who has been passed over by generations of historians, about whom no biography has been written that I have identified, was recognized in her day as a person of influence.

Regardless of the uncomfortable sentiments expressed in Sass's letters, she gave her all for the development of female education in Africa. She believed that these girls deserved an education and, just as important, that they were capable of learning. In a report recorded in the Church Missionary Record, she wrote, "So far as I am able to form an opinion, I do not find that the African children are at all wanting in natural ability to learn the same as English children, but should imagine that the deficiency

---

28. Sass, CMS/B/OMS/C A1 O187, February 21, 1849.
29. Sass, CMS/B/OMS/C A1 O187, July 5, 1849.

lies in their early training and subsequent mismanagement."[30] As in much missionary writing, the layers of prejudice and paternalism as they relate to skin color, culture, and civilization are not consistent or easily untangled. Even after nineteen years, when much of her early severity seems to have softened, Sass's belief in the superiority of British civilization remains. Upon her return to the Colony after an absence, she wrote with horror to Mr. Venn about the state of affairs: "You can form no idea of [the] retrograding influence of the homes of these people; it is really quite discouraging." She continues to describe this "evil" influence, and one expects that she has just discovered shocking sinful behavior, only to find her explain,

> one single instance out of a hundred I will give you of a native Pastor's family whose two girls we have been trying to bring up for these three last years & who learn while with us to sit at a table properly & eat their rice & sauce with fork & spoon, amongst many other things they go for the vacation to their father's house to eat with their fingers![31]

Sass valued and cared for these girls and believed they were meant to play a vital role in their society: "Much has been done for the boys & young men, for years past, & more would be done for these, if we could raise the conditions of the girls & young women who, in a few years, will be called upon to bring up the children given to them, to love truth and holiness."[32] Though she fully embraced the strategy of using education to raise the marriage prospects of her pupils, she did also see its "value for higher reasons." She felt that their mothers didn't recognize their daughters' potential for learning but was satisfied that they at least sent them to the school so that they could get a husband.[33] One wonders how Miss Sass felt through these years, remaining single herself as she poured out her life to educate girls whose prospects depended on their finding husbands. Despite the colonial entanglements and gendered curriculum of the Female Institution, it is striking that it was founded only four years after the boys' CMS Grammar school, "and only one year after the foundation of the first academic secondary school for women in England (Queen's College in London)."[34] In a time when some were only beginning to recognize the importance of female education, Miss Sass gave her life to it.

30. *Church Missionary Record*, 4–5.
31. Sass, CMS/B/OMS/C A1 O187, March 16, 1868.
32. Sass, CMS/B/OMS/C A1 O187, November 13, 1864.
33. Sass, CMS/B/OMS/C A1 O187, February 21, 1849.
34. Leach, "African Girls," 339.

Though Sass survived to retire after over two decades of service in Africa, she endured an astonishing amount of illness, exhaustion, anxiety, and depression. Such suffering is a main feature of her letters, and her openness about her mental health challenges is especially poignant. From her first years on the field, she was already reporting cycles of fever and doctors' recommendations for a change to England. Most of the time, she ignored the doctor's suggestion because she "could not possibly leave [her] institution."[35] She wrote to Mr. Venn that she loved her work and in it found pleasure and comfort, though she was facing troubles that only those who bear them could know. She was committed to the prosperity of the Institution "amid sickness, depression, and anxiety" which she said was their frequent experience.[36] She saw her school as a "nursery for the garden of the Lord" and clung to his promise that he would be with her wherever she went and would strengthen and guide her and make the rough places smooth.[37] She quoted similar scriptures throughout her letters and often stressed her unworthiness.

Her letters were sometimes direct appeals for help and sometimes a therapeutic sharing of her burdens: "I am constrained to write you again not indeed to give you much information, but to release a burden and weary heart, for I know how much interest you always take in everything that concerns either Miss Wilkinson or myself and that on my losing her, you will truly sympathize."[38] She did not lose Miss Wilkinson because of death but because of Wilkinson's return to England due to severe illness. It was a protracted loss as for several years there was the hope that she would become strong enough to return. Miss Sass didn't seem to find until very late as companionable a partner in the work, and she suffered much anxiety over recruiting replacements—often finding new workers more stressful and difficult to deal with than to go without. She moved from pleading for a replacement as soon as possible to getting more specific and urgent with her appeals. She asked that help be sent by November or October, and entreated, "dear Mr. Venn, leave no one Lady here alone again!"[39] Later in the same letter, she raised her request for two ladies to be sent and in a later letter doubled her request to four. A deep sadness and despair seeps through another letter, mingled with vision and hope: "I have been exceedingly cast down when hearing constantly of your unsuccessful endeavours to procure

35. Sass, CMS/B/OMS/C A1 O187, December 13, 1851.
36. Sass, CMS/B/OMS/C A1 O187, January 12, 1852.
37. Sass, CMS/B/OMS/C A1 O187, June 7, 1852.
38. Sass, CMS/B/OMS/C A1 O187, March 10, 1857.
39. Sass, CMS/B/OMS/C A1 O187, July 17, 1857.

a suitable Lady for this Establishment. Is it possible that not one is found willing to come over and help us in this most important work?" She held onto hope for efficient help so that before her eyes were "closed in death" or before she became a "Disabled Missionary," she would "see this Institution flowering, and waxing great, with many branches, shooting out on all sides, and a place also to which many Christian Mothers & Daughters may point & say 'I was born there!'"[40] From time to time, she did receive more help, but the school and its burdens continued to grow.

Sass was not the only one who suffered, and she discussed the mental stress and physical pressures of several individuals at length in her letters. Whether it was the mental instability and strangeness of one or the weakness and severe illness of another, Sass's burdens were increased. In a letter she wrote from bed, not being able to sit up for more than five or ten minutes, she wrote to Mr. Venn, saying, "I have much very much to tell you but may only be able to give you an outline of the whole of my troubles, yes, troubles."[41] She was writing about Miss Adcock, who had been ordered home immediately by the doctor. Sass recounted Adcock's tendency to "make a martyr of herself" and her frenzies of jealousy. She wrote with a bit of humor that "The anxiety on her account has been so great & the strain on my nerves so distressing that she has well done for me what the climate has hitherto failed to accomplish, and I only hope we shall not have her ill again before the mail arrives, for it would kill me."

Several years earlier Sass had lost a mentor and maternal figure, and her expression of loneliness and disappointment at this loss is one of the most poignant moments in her letters. Julia spent four days and nights with Mrs. Bowen and attended to the last duties at her death. Mrs. Bowen had suffered with great pain, yet Sass recounted her sweet smile and calm and pleasant tone as she spoke that all was well. Sass felt her loss profoundly, stating, "With the exception of the Rhodes, no one has ever taken the interest she had in this Institution, & no one has been such a comfort to me personally, or ever made me more welcome at all times."[42] Mrs. Bowen had told her that Mr. Venn had particularly commended Julia to her care and affections. Sass recalled that, since their first acquaintance, Mrs. Bowen had taken the greatest interest in all that concerned her and that their affection had been mutual. Knowing that Julia's own mother was far away and unsupportive of her life's work, one can only imagine the pain she felt at this loss.

40. Sass, CMS/B/OMS/C A1 O187, October 19, 1857.
41. Sass, CMS/B/OMS/C A1 O187, August 12, 1866.
42. Sass, CMS/B/OMS/C A1 O187, August 14, 1858.

Through the examples of hardship and struggle demonstrated throughout these letters, many issues around calling come to the fore. How often does someone take a giant step of faith only to find herself seemingly alone? What does it mean when the Lord calls one to something that requires a team or community, but no one else seems to hear or heed the call? One might ask if this was truly God's calling. Or to personalize it, how do we discern if we were hasty and lacking wisdom, or if we have been called to be forerunners and challengers to complacency and cold Christianity? It is when considering the complexities involved in walking out a calling in real life in a broken world that the light of our primary calling dawns once more in our hearts. Calling cannot be judged according to societal hierarchies or measured by the efficiency, focus, or adventure of our life's path. It must be seen through the reflection in the eyes of the God who is calling, who calls himself "the way." Ultimately, as Os Guinness reminds us, God is our source, our motivation, and our destination. When we examine our own lives, may we also be able to say, "I live for the Audience of One. Before others I have nothing to prove, nothing to gain, nothing to lose."[43]

CONCLUSION: FAITH AND HISTORICAL SCHOLARSHIP

In this chapter, the lives of two historical figures, separate yet woven into the same tapestry, have served as windows through which to observe, question, and consider the implications of the theme of calling. It should be noted that, in the space of this chapter, Julia Sass underwent deeper scrutiny and analysis than the prominent figure of William Wilberforce. Wilberforce has been written about at length in biographies and critical works. Much of his personal correspondence, writing, and speeches have been transcribed and widely published and digitized. There are many who would see his involvement in the spread of missionary activity throughout the British Empire as negative or at least problematic; however, in bringing him into this discussion, the aim was to provide a starting place and introduction to a figure who is easily accessible for further study. Sass, on the other hand, represents the marginalized voices of women (and many others such as children and the disabled) in the past who actively shared in the making of history while simultaneously being written out of it. When her letters were examined, the aim was not to air her weaknesses or immortalize her strengths. No. It was examining her letters and exploring the different facets of her life and character that stirred the very questions and reflections considered in this chapter.

43. Guinness, *Call*, 112.

When looking at history we can simultaneously be inspired and discouraged by the disappointments we see according to our current standards. As Christians we must have the humility to grapple with the uncomfortable truths in our past. Our faith should give us the confidence to search out and inquire more deeply. This does not mean that historical persons are excused because of the days in which they lived. When looking at history with open eyes, we should ask, since they could not see the plank in their own eyes which seems so obvious to us now, what might be blocking our vision today? It should challenge us to honest reflection and a cry for mercy. Conversely, when we realize that it is imperfect people who embody our heroes, we should be inspired not to count ourselves out or diminish our own potential as ripple makers in this life. William Wilberforce and Julia Sass are also important because they remind us that many people doing or attempting great things may also be bearing burdens that need lifting. For the church to grow and thrive today and to live out its purpose as a light to the world, it must walk in its identity as a *family* that is interdependent and *alive*.

Whether it is in government, Christian education, academia, leading a revolution, or showing kindness to a neglected street cat, the call of the Christian is the same. Christians are called to walk daily into the loving embrace of our Father; to follow our Shepherd through valleys and meadows; to allow the Holy Spirit to be our constant helper; and when everything seems to be out of order and awry, to, like Peter in the waves, grab on to Jesus. When we truly journey with him, our ears are tuned to his voice, our hearts safely trust him, and we have the courage to respond to his call. And when our loves are in order, it won't matter how glorious or ordinary the path; we are on it with him, for him, and to him.[44] For William Wilberforce, this meant staying in a position marked by power and prestige as well as by scorn and trials. For Julia Sass, it meant leaving her family and enduring hardships far away for a purpose she believed in but others ignored. For many, it means steadfastly treading a familiar and perhaps expected path while spreading salt and light in a million little ways. No matter how this path looks, following it takes courage: courage to face the unknown, courage to dare the unthinkable, courage to be faithful in small things, trusting God to make them matter.

---

44. See Naugle, *Reordered Love, Reordered Lives*.

BIBLIOGRAPHY

Church Missionary Record 30.1 (1850) 4–5. Church Mission Society, Crowther Library, Oxford.

CMS/B/OMS/C A1 O187 (1849–1869). Church Missionary Society Archive, Cadbury Research Library, University of Birmingham.

CMS/G/AC16/29. Church Missionary Society Archive, Cadbury Research Library, University of Birmingham.

Cox, Jeffrey. *The British Missionary Enterprise since 1700*. New York: Routledge, 2008.

Guinness, Os. *The Call: Finding and Fulfilling God's Purpose of Your Life*. Twentieth Anniversary ed. Nashville: Nelson, 2018.

Leach, Fiona, "African Girls, Nineteenth-Century Mission Education, and the Patriarchal Imperative." *Gender and Education: Gender Balance/Gender Bias* 20 (2008) 335–47.

Maughan, Steven S. *Mighty England Do Good: Culture, Faith, Empire, and World in the Foreign Missions of the Church of England, 1850–1915*. Studies in the History of Christian Missions. Grand Rapids: Eerdmans, 2014.

Murray, Jocelyn. "The Role of Women in the Church Missionary Society, 1799–1917." In *The Church Mission Society and World Christianity, 1799–1999*, edited by Kevin Ward and Brian Stanley, 66–90. Grand Rapids: Eerdmans, 2000.

Naugle, David. *Reordered Love, Reordered Lives: Learning the Deep Meaning of Happiness*. Grand Rapids: Eerdmans, 2008.

Porter, Andrew. *Religion versus Empire? British Protestant Missionaries and Overseas Expansion, 1700–1914*. Manchester, NY: Manchester University Press, 2004.

Seton, Rosemary E. *Western Daughters in Eastern Lands: British Missionary Women in Asia*. Santa Barbara, CA: Praeger, 2013.

Stock, Eugene. *The History of the Church Missionary Society: Its Environment, Its Men and Its Work*. Vol. 1. London: Church Missionary Society, 1899.

Stott, Ann. *Wilberforce: Family and Friends*. New York: Oxford University Press, 2012. DOI:10.1093/acprof:oso/9780199699391.001.0001.

Wilberforce, William. *An Appeal to the Religion, Justice, and Humanity of the Inhabitants of the British Empire*. New York: Cosimo, 2007.

———. *The Correspondence of William Wilberforce*. Vol. 1. Edited by R. Wilberforce and S. Wilberforce. Cambridge: Cambridge University Press, 2011. https://doi.org/10.1017/CBO9780511792052.002.

———. *A Letter on the Abolition of the Slave Trade: Addressed to the Freeholders and Other Inhabitants of Yorkshire*. Cambridge: Cambridge University Press, 2012. https://doi.org/10.1017/CBO9780511791949.

———. *The Life of William Wilberforce*. Vol. 1. Cambridge: Cambridge University Press, 2011. https://doi.org/10.1017/CBO9780511792007.

4

Translation of Phillip Melanchthon's

Oration on the Praise of the Scholastic Life

D. P. FAHRENTHOLD

TRANSLATOR'S INTRODUCTION

Philip Melanchthon (1497–1560), known as *Praeceptor Germaniae*, or the Teacher of Germany, was very influential not only in the Lutheran Reformation, but also in the establishment of schools. Melanchthon was both a Renaissance humanist and a theologian, and so, like Dr. Naugle, he was intimately interested in both *res humanae* and *res divinae*, the things of man and the things of God—the cultivation of a theological humanism.

Melanchthon himself composed this speech, but Melchior Fendt delivered it at the graduation of teachers in 1536. Fendt was a physician, so you will notice several references that Melanchthon makes to the vocation of doctor. The three main themes of the speech are: (1) the necessity of the scholastic life; (2) the sacredness; and (3) the pleasantness. These are three themes that I learned originally from Dr. Naugle, and so I have no doubt that he would agree with Melanchthon's argument. Melanchthon's Latin is extremely straightforward, and it is, in Milena Minkova's words, "simple, pure, elegant."[1]

I must give thanks to Ian Mosley, who introduced this speech to me, to Matthew Colvin for help in tracking down the Euripides quote and other references, and to Dr. David Noe of Calvin University, a university important to Dr. Naugle, for encouraging me in this task and offering suggestions for my translation. Thanks also to the editors for their help and encouragement. Any remaining errors or infelicitous locutions lie with me. Finally, thanks are due to Dr. Naugle for being such a large influence on my formation, both intellectual and moral. I dedicate the translation of this speech, which, as far as I have been able to gather, has not been rendered in English before, to him.[2]

Magistro atque Professori optimo, David Naugle, Melanchthonis orationem hanc, nunc primum sermonem in Anglicum convertam, quod sciam, ego gratissimus discipulorum dedico.

ORATION ON THE PRAISE OF THE SCHOLASTIC LIFE

Delivered by Melchior Fendt in the Graduation of Teachers

When I think that those who come here to speak delight the audience either with the novelty of their argument or their eloquence, I know that I have great need of your kindness and fairness. For I have found no new argument suitable for this place and I can add no elegance to well-known arguments in my speech. Moreover, because the concern for public service places on me the need to speak, it will be characteristic of your politeness to preserve public decorum with your reserve, to hear me not unwillingly, and to think well of my speech.

I have decided to speak about the inherent value of the scholastic life and about the comparison of your station in life with the other stations and kinds of life. I know how great the argument I have undertaken is. Although I cannot cover it exhaustively now, nevertheless it will be useful to touch on the main topics. Just as, in the rules for good health, doctors advise that we should diligently observe the quality of the air in which we move, it is

---

1. Minkova, *Florilegium Recentioris Latinitatis*, 133. "Sermo autem Melanchthonis fuit simplex, purus, elegans." This text has a contemporary printing of Melanchthon's speech and an excellent introduction in Latin from which I quote regarding Melanchthon's life and work.

2. For the original text, see Melanchthon, "Laus Vitae Scholasticae," 298–306.

also extremely beneficial to perceive the kind of life in which we have been employed either by our own choice or that of another. It is a particular part of philosophy to consider and discern correctly the degrees of human duties and rank. Then something happens to others—at least it does to me in this thin fortune and in these difficulties with which I am contending, namely that the scholastic life brings comfort—because I think this kind of life is the most sacred, the most suitable to human nature, and the most useful. When I consider these good things, I endure the difficulties of life quite cheerfully. There are very many troubles that accompany this kind of life. For poverty is added to the difficulties of studies, and the endurance of poverty is not typically considered greatness of soul. In addition, we are most pridefully considered unimportant not only by the ignorant, by merchants, by Centaurs,[3] but also by the demigods who rule in palaces because they think they have learning or wisdom. Finally, not only are we considered unimportant, but we are also hated. The discussion shows how non-trivial these troubles are. They prevent a great many from literature. Nevertheless, I do not hesitate to recall those things here so that you may know that there is a certain courage in not abandoning the study of literature. Then I shall advise that you set the true and genuine goods of the scholastic life against these troubles.

In the beginning I want to say that I do not disparage the value of any station. The Cynic philosophical viewpoint that finds fault with all arts, all kinds of life is not acceptable to me. It is better, says Aristotle, and more refined that a state be composed not of a doctor and a doctor, but a doctor and a farmer, i.e., many stations.[4] Therefore, I honor each individually, but there are stages of reflecting that very often fools confuse. In this way, therefore, you will think in the first place that the scholastic life is necessary for the body politic[5] and that it brings the greatest benefits to our common life, then that it is the most sacred and pleasing to God, and finally the most delightful. In addition, we receive so many benefits from the scholastic life, and there is so much true value in this life, that although kings and bishops are distinguished because of their title, nevertheless in reality the scholastic station is equal to both. Because you have determined in your mind and will have to make the effort to build up this life with all zeal in order to endure steadfastly the toils and all the difficulties which accompany this kind of life.

---

3. Centaurs, in classical mythology, were half-man, half-horse hybrids. On Centaurs, see Griffiths, "Centaurs," 297. Melanchthon, however, is here following in his fellow Renaissance humanist Desiderius Erasmus's footsteps and portraying the Centaurs as being "mindless." See Erasmus, *Adages* 2.10.8.

4. See Aristotle, *Nichomachean Ethics* V.5 (1132B33–1133A20).

5. The Latin *res publica* has been translated here and throughout as "the body politic."

Why do we praise the scholastic life? The crowd judges that it is a leisurely life, and therefore they call it scholastic.[6] The Latins called these gatherings of learners "games."[7] What value can there be in the leisurely life or in games? I will speak about these words subsequently, but first I will show that there is very little inactivity in this profession of ours. These studies of literature are not games, but a serious investigation of the greatest matters.

Anyone can see that human nature has nothing better or more divine than the two possessions of truth and justice, the investigation and explanation of which has been handed over to the schools. It is not unknown that the knowledge of truth and justice is especially necessary for living well, and it brings the greatest benefits to life. For without instruction religion cannot be practiced, and laws cannot be established or retained. If no one were teaching or learning medicine, how great a protection would have abandoned life? If no one were learning mathematics, if no differences of historical periods were understood, if ancient events and the histories entrusted to literature were unknown, how many literary enhancements would we, by necessity, have been without? The extent of these advantages is known to you who are engaged in these studies. Therefore, you will easily judge that schools are a necessary part of the body politic, and that from them particular benefits come to our common life. For who does not see that there is a greater need in life of religion, laws, and literature than of laborers and craftsmen?

But there are some who contend that the churches, the court, and the marketplace are the abode of truth and justice rather than the schools. They call the scholastic life "esoteric," because they say intellectual abilities are employed there in idleness. They say that truth and justice are engaged in a contest there. To think respectfully of the churches, the courts, and marketplace is characteristic of a moderate and well instructed soul. And so truth and justice ought to reign in those places. But there is wide agreement that these enhancements are brought from the schools into the former places. What sort of instruction would there be in the churches if the schools had not deliberated upon and explained truth and justice? What sort of barbarity would exist in law courts and the marketplace if there were not some learned instruction on the law? It is important that the schools be consulted on all important matters, not the bishops, or courtiers, or lawyers. Finally, the purpose of inquiring into and revealing topics is the schools' sole focus.

---

6. The root of the word "scholastic" is the Greek word σχολή (scholē), meaning leisure and from which we derive "school."

7. *Ludos.* Melanchthon here is punning on the Latin word *ludus* which can mean either school, or as here, a game. The Latin word translated throughout as "school" is *schola*, which comes from the Greek word mentioned in note 6.

In the churches, many people say things in the worship services improperly; many things also are left unmentioned because the people cannot understand them. Now—terrible to say—there is so much sophistry in the palaces and the marketplace. Therefore, I often recall the ancient tale of Astrea[8] who they say was driven out from cities and thereafter typically addressed farmers in the countryside for a long while. Thus it seems to me that Astrea, i.e., instruction in truth and justice, almost driven out from the courts, from the marketplace, from churches, and the other places where people gather together, still remains in schools. Therefore, because there is less sophistry in schools than elsewhere and because the good have only the desire to search out the truth, the scholastic life must receive the highest praise. The scholastic life is a certain image of the very happy condition in which people lived in that well-known golden age, if it ever existed, or certainly in which they were about to live if the golden age had existed, if human nature had been free from the blemish of sin and from death. What then would the life of human beings have been except a certain most pleasant school in which the older and more distinguished would have taught everyone else about divine matters, about the nature of the universe, about the immortality of human souls, about the heavenly motions, about all the duties of life? The older and the younger would have spent all their time in this philosophy and discussions of this sort. I conclude that Adam's life and that of the other first people was no different. The scholastic life is a likeness of this most blessed way of life.

I spoke briefly about the necessity and the usefulness of this life. I will also add a discussion about the sacredness of this life. No duty is more pleasing to God than the concern for and the transmission of truth and justice. For these are the chief gifts of God in which we can especially discern the presence of God. God above all demands that these gifts be preserved, and He created human beings chiefly so that some teach others about God and other important matters. For this benefit, God joined fellowship through conversation to the human race. Therefore, there is no doubt that this kind of life, which is engaged in teaching and learning, is the most pleasing to God. The schools surpass the churches and courts in reputation, because the pursuit of truth is greater in schools. Therefore if anyone seeks a sacred purpose in life, let him not go away into solitude, nor think that there is a more sacred kind of life, but let him remain in these gatherings of learners, try to serve the human race well, teach others, and know that this service is useful to conserve and transmit the best things. Let him instruct wavering

---

8. Astrea is the name Roman poets assign to the Greek goddess Δίκη (*dikē*). She left the earth when the Bronze Age began. See Richardson, "Dike," 451–52.

consciences, give responses concerning the law and about all the duties of life; let him investigate the nature of the universe, the cures of diseases, reasons for changes in nature, heavenly motions and effects; let him prepare youth for the greater arts, interpret past events, commit deeds to literature, explain the arts. Everyone who does these things is responsible for a culture most pleasing to God and serves the human race very well; he preserves learning most useful for life, shapes morals, the opinions of human beings, maintains peace, and makes many public disasters less serious. Such a life not only surpasses the monastic life, but truly is divine.

Cicero criticizes Plato for his assertion that the philosophers, because of their investigation of great subjects, are just even though they abstain from the management of the body politic.[9] Plato, however, thought most correctly about the topic. For it is justice for each person to do his own duty and to give the benefit of this duty to the general well-being of the human race. The philosopher who explains religion, the nature of the universe, and the proper concern of all lawful vocations and laws especially does this. The philosopher also communicates these divine matters to others; he explains the arts or teaches them. Finally, the philosopher is the one who is eager to give instruction in truth and justice for the benefit of others. We should not think either any lawyers who give accounts of disputes in the marketplace or settle them or aediles[10] who build bridges or merchants who import useful goods at a just price serve the human race better. Plato, therefore, spoke rightly when he said that the philosophers who teach learning useful for life are just.[11] Isocrates did not hold civil offices, but guided the very praiseworthy general, Timotheus, by his advice, and shaped the talents of many who thereafter were the leading men in the body politic.[12] Aeschines the advocate did not serve the body politic more than Aristotle who, although he held no civil offices and pled no cases, nevertheless formed Alexander and many other leading men in respect to justice and beneficence.[13] Even today Aristotle serves the body politic well because he has left behind written works useful for interpreting theology and the laws; he produces doctors, and shapes the judgements of many who busy themselves in the

---

9. See Cicero, *De Officiis* 1.9.28.

10. The office of Aedile was one of the steps of the Roman *cursus honorum* (the order of political offices in the Roman Republic), and one of the functions of the aediles was to supervise public building projects, including bridges.

11. Melanchthon is perhaps referring to book 6 of Plato's *Republic* (489b), where Plato compares philosophers with the captain of a ship.

12. Isocrates (436–338 BC) was an Athenian orator. Timotheus (fourth century BC) was an Athenian General and associate of Isocrates.

13. Aeschines (fourth century BC) was one of the ten "Attic Orators."

marketplace and with commercial interests. Azo the lawyer guided a large part of Italy.[14] Nevertheless, Bartolus, who only lived in scholarly study, did not serve the body politic less.[15] Philip the doctor followed the army of Alexander and freed the king himself from great danger.[16] And yet Galen, who followed no army, but stationed himself in a school, and wrote the literary records of his teaching, does not serve the body politic less.[17]

Because there is no other kind of life more useful to the human race, more necessary, or more sacred, than the scholastic life, one can sufficiently understand that this is the most outstanding station of life. It is proper for those of good character to be inspired by genuine praise so that they delight in the scholastic life more and apply their zeal and diligence worthy of so great a profession and provide for this life with lives beyond reproach. For what is more shameful than that many live in schools in such a way that, first, they do not understand their own duty; then that they employ the time for literary study to engage in the most shameful pleasures, and that they take the license of all wicked deeds as if the schools were a laboratory not of truth and justice but of licentiousness? You ought to have the same purpose when entering the schools as the devout do when entering the churches to worship God. For we are treating theological matters. We must take great care that we celebrate our religious ceremonies rightly, lest we corrupt the arts by our ignorance or some other fault. It is no less a sin to corrupt the arts than to cause harm to church services with abuse. The schools assumed their name from leisure, because by that name the body politic attests that it frees us from base occupations so that we can devote ourselves to divine matters. It also has added rewards, just as to soldiers. Moreover, although the usefulness is scant, although the unlearned not only condemn but also fiercely hate literature as if they were the shackles of their own lusts, nevertheless God does not entirely permit those teaching and learning literature to be without rewards. The better a particular body politic was established, the more generous it is with respect to those engaged in studies. Meanwhile, it is right for us to endure the unfairness of fortune with philosophic resolve and understand the reasons why all the greatest things especially have been scorned openly. Then, let us also set the advantages against the

---

14. Azo de Bologna (c. 1150–1230) was a well-respected glossator, or commentator, on Roman law.

15. Bartolus de Saxoferrato (1314–1357) was an important lawyer in fourteenth-century Italy.

16. Philip of Acarnania (fourth century BC) was Alexander the Great's physician. On his saving Alexander's life, see Arrian, *Anabasis* II.4.

17. Galen (129–c. 199/c. 216 AD) was a Roman physician who made contributions to medicine and philosophy.

disadvantages, namely the grandeur and the sacredness of the profession, and finally also the pleasantness. And so I will also add a few things about the aforementioned topic, namely that there is no other more pleasant life than the scholastic life.

All sound minds derive an extraordinary pleasure from the knowledge of truth. Human beings were created especially for examining the truth. There are many reasons this pleasure is increased in schools. First, there is a great variety of skills there. There typically exist teachers of all disciplines, whom students can consult on any subject. There is also a large number of students who have great differences in natural abilities and opinions. Therefore, we are able to compare our ideas with many other ideas, hear what others conclude, and imitate better examples. Hence, there is the praise of strife in the works of Hesiod, concerning which he says that a neighbor is challenged by a neighbor hastening to riches.[18] And on that account, Euripides, in his works, says correctly that we find the arts by sharing opinions in large gatherings.[19] Cicero says that the eagerness to discuss things together, which he calls συζήτησις (*suzētēsis*),[20] has great power in learning. Solomon says, "Iron sharpens iron in the same way as one man builds up another" (Prov 27:17). He means that now the combining of discussions and opinions form intellects, now examples excite them. Due to these great benefits, it is proper for those devoted to learning to involve themselves gladly in this multitude. Finally, it happens naturally that we delight in the fellowship of those like us, and especially those who share our intellectual interests. Even gathering together for its own sake delights us. It is pleasant to see a multitude of learners and teachers well ordered. There is no more pleasant enjoyment than to hear what those who are more learned think about the greatest subjects, every diversity of nature, the body politic, and religion. The saying is old: "Outside the university, there is no life."[21] This signifies that the most pleasant life is in schools. I imagine that this saying came from the learned and wise who understood how much power this companionship and conversation has and how much pleasure it creates.

---

18. See Hesiod, *Works and Days* 11–25.
19. See Euripides, *Andromache* 683–84.
20. "Joint investigation." See Cicero, *Ad Familiares* 16.21.
21. *Extra universitatem non est vita*. This expression goes back at least to Peter of Blois (c. 1130–c. 1211), and was adopted by the Renaissance humanist Jacob Wimpheling (1450–1528). It is possible that it is referring to and modifying the ancient Christian dictum that there is no salvation outside the church (*extra ecclesiam nulla salus*), expressed in its most well-known and earliest guise by the third-century St. Cyprian of Carthage (*salus extra ecclesiam non est*). See Cyprian, *Epistula* 73.21 (sometimes numbered as 72).

The excellence of those who teach others generously, and sincerely try to look after future generations, also delights people of good morals. Moreover, although there is disorder in the great weakness of the human race, there is no station, no kind of life entirely without fault; nevertheless, in the schools there is a little less deceit, hateful behavior, and other examples of bad character than in other kinds of life. First, liberal learning moves moderate abilities to virtue. There is almost no one who has such a hard-hearted character that does not soften with literature and a moderate amount of instruction. Moreover, friendship is much more pleasant with the educated who understand the proper concern of all lawful vocations than it is with the uneducated whose opinions differ from ours in many matters. Then, I would dare to affirm that he who is used to finding pleasure in and seeking after the truth in studies also likes sincerity and honesty in character and life. But deceitful instruction[22] distorts the desires, for the tendency to misrepresent ideas carries over to morals. Moreover, the more devoted to study one is, the more he is inspired by the love of truth and detests deceitful instruction most vehemently. Most pleasant is the fellowship with the learned and upright, who look to do what is right and set limits to their behavior and their impulses by a certain sure method, as if they guide them with a bit. And so there are no friendships more sweet or more enduring than those devoted to philosophy, i.e., friendships of the learned produced by the fellowship of studies.[23] Compare, in contrast to these scholastic assemblies, conversations with the uneducated; although some of them are good men, nevertheless gatherings with them have less pleasantness because we are not able to discuss things we have learned with them. Not even Laelius and Scipio would have had so much enjoyment from their friendship if they had been ἄμουσοι (*amousoi*).[24] The narrowness of time does not permit us to think about and describe all the advantages of the scholastic life. I have set forth these things first in order that youth may understand and delight in the kind of life in which they are engaged. Then that they may know, in turn, how much attentiveness they need to have, and how much restraint in doing every duty in order to build up this kind of life. The learned have

---

22. *Doctrina sophistica.*

23. Bearing in mind that philosophy, classically conceived, is the love of wisdom and not one among many rarefied academic disciplines—which is how we are more likely to think of "philosophy" these days.

24. Referring to the Muses; in other words, if their souls had been less refined and cultivated by learning, they would not have been such good friends. Melanchthon is referring to Publius Cornelius Scipio Aemilianus (185–129 BC) and Gaius Laelius (190–ca. 128 BC), two second-century BC Roman statesmen. Cicero's *De Amicitia* is a dialogue featuring Laelius after the death of Aemilianus.

been placed in the greatest situation in human life. Therefore, we must train our minds very eagerly, so that we may fulfill the most difficult task of all. To preserve and pass on learning useful for life is both the most sacred kind of life and the most pleasing to God. Let us understand, therefore, that God will punish those who dishonor schools with their way of life, and do not make an effort to preserve learning. Finally, the scholastic life is the most pleasant. Therefore, they are worthy of contempt who, like the Centaurs or the Lapiths, cause unrest in the schools and confuse the calm of the entire body.[25] They subvert discipline, and after they do this, it is necessary to dissolve the association. We ought to exhort the morally upright also to hold these advantages before their eyes, and to set them against the disadvantages which keep many from studying literature. Let the value of literature and the people's benefit be more influential among the good than the unjust opinions of the mob, than the hatred of tyrants, than poverty.

I conclude that these youths,[26] who have sought a degree, were influenced in such a way that they bind themselves publicly to the defense of literature. Rightly, therefore, do we congratulate them for this purpose and we thought that we ought to have furnished them with the customary honors. I have spoken.

BIBLIOGRAPHY

Griffiths, Alan. H. "Centaurs." In *Oxford Classical Dictionary*, edited by Simon Hornblower et al., 297. 4th ed. Oxford: Oxford University Press, 2012.
Melanchthon. "Laus Vitae Scholasticae." In vol. 11 of *Corpus Reformatorum*, edited by Karl Gottlieb Bretschneider, 298-306. Halle: Schwetschke, 1834.
Minkova, Milena, ed. *Florilegium Recentioris Latinitatis*. Leuvein: Leuven University Press, 2018.
Richardson, Nicholas J. "Dike." In *Oxford Classical Dictionary*, edited by Simon Hornblower et al., 451-52. 4th ed. Oxford: Oxford University Press, 2012.
Rose, Herbert Jennings, et al. "Pirithous." In *Oxford Classical Dictionary*, edited by Simon Hornblower et al., 1150-51. 4th ed. Oxford: Oxford University Press, 2012.

---

25. For the battle between the Centaurs and the Lapiths, see Griffith, "Centaurs," 297; Rose et al., "Pirithous," 1150–1151.

26. I.e., the graduates at the ceremony for which Melanchthon prepared his speech.

5

Before Outsiders

Apologetics in Every Course, across Curricula, for Life

Mark Eckel

INTRODUCTION

Seniors from my high school class were assigned to visit a local college campus. They had been given four questions to ask:

1. Who is Jesus?
2. What is truth?
3. What is my purpose in life?
4. What is the basis for right and wrong?

College students then and now are fairly open. They generally don't mind mugging for a video.

"After you get a number of responses to these questions," I began, "Huddle up and pick out the one response which you want to share with the class. Your assignment is to give an oral report of your findings with the video clip."

My students could not wait. For most, any day outside the classroom is a good day. Upon their return, the class and I heard many interesting responses. One report stood out to everyone. The team showed their video clip without preamble. Then the team leader spoke.

"I was shocked," she began. "I kept thinking of M. C. Escher staircases while each person responded to our questions." One of the other members of the group held up an Escher painting.

"Do you see that each flight of stairs leads to nowhere?" she continued. She pointed to the picture her teammate held.

"Steps leading nowhere is exactly what we heard from our respondents."

She paused. "Their views of Jesus, truth, purpose, and ethics go nowhere." The student pointed again to the Escher painting. "It's one thing to hear about these ideas in class," she smiled at me. "It is something else altogether to hear these ideas expressed by real people who believe these ideas work. I will never again separate the importance of ideas from people or the world."

Now I was smiling.

"What I learned today will stay with me the rest of my life," she concluded.

I noticed heads around the room bobbing up and down.

"That's exactly what we found!" someone else blurted out excitedly.[1]

And we were off. The class's discussion was no longer an assignment. The discussion was now a theological-sociological commentary about life. Without a standard outside ourselves, our views of Jesus, ethics, purposes, and truths go nowhere. A transcendent paradigm informs apologetics across curricula, through each classroom, with all people, in every assumption, permeated by Christian theology, informing each methodological approach.

THE CLASSROOM

Students in my Christian high school "Bible" classes were shown how a biblical view of other subjects could be commended or defended. Since the 1980s we had been reading *The Humanist Manifestos I* and *II* and watching videos from The American Humanist Association. We held panel discussions with local disc jockeys from local radio stations about sexuality in music. Physicians joined with our classes to discuss medical ethics. Professors from public universities were invited to discuss philosophy, sociology,

---

1. Conversations recorded throughout the essay are true stories occurring at various times throughout my teaching years. The quotations include the exact ideas expressed with verbiage allowing for smooth flow of thought.

public policy, atheism, mythology, and a myriad of other topics. We read the latest editorial pages to teach young minds how to write letters to the editor with gentleness, respect, and resolve. Classroom projects invested attention in Christian responses to creation: How does one produce from and protect the "environment" (see Gen 2:15)? Listening to and reading the lyrics from the latest popular music engendered an opportunity to think critically about the content being mentally ingested.

We wrote letters to cultural celebrities asking about their views of life. A missive was sent to George Lucas after watching *Star Wars* film clips requesting that he respond to our question, "Does your view of reality in the science fiction story originate from a Buddhist perspective?" Poetry from Shakespeare, W. H. Auden, Edgar Allen Poe, E. E. Cummings, and others was read and evaluated Christianly. The literature teacher and I would team-teach an American literature writing project that included a rubric with authors' backgrounds and how their writing could have influenced their views of life. Instructional units would include the viewing of a full-length Hollywood film that directly coincided with the subject so as to teach how to write movie reviews. Discussions about the consequences of actions in historical settings engendered a constant review of the past and history's instructions for the present. Theological grounding for mathematics out of Genesis was established, showing dozens of universal principles that apply to daily life. Scientific models, laws, and theories were investigated from a Christian perspective, showing creational design. Writing in classes was encouraged not only to create a product but also to instruct a process, encouraging the practice of reflection. These and a myriad of other discipline-directed, life-infused student learning processes were initiated by an apologetic mindset: We commended and defended biblical authority.

Curricular components in Bible colleges and theological seminaries often orphan the study of apologetics by setting it aside, mainly teaching the course from the vantage point of answering questions posed to the Christian worldview. Apologetic philosophies, methods, and beliefs tend toward a review of problems posed and solutions offered to arguments brought to bear by nonbelievers. Only in recent days through the fine work of Nancy Pearcey, among others, has university apologetics begun to see its importance in the realms of science, aesthetics, and sexuality—in brief, in all of human culture.

It turns out that what we need is a thorough reinvestment of apologetics throughout the Christian university setting. Academic deans and department heads have an opportunity to reconsider all subject areas as opportunities for apologetic learning. Each discipline has its own set of beliefs whereby its professors exercise their studies. Economics programs may have dogmatic commitments to Keynesian or Austrian economic theories. Social sciences may commit to quantitative, qualitative, or mixed method research. Literature courses could defend either authorial-intention or reader-response theories. Biologists may subscribe to evolutionary, theistic evolutionary, intelligent-design, or creation models. Law professors could rely on natural law theory or legal positivism as the starting point for jurisprudential practices. Each one of these ideas within any given discipline proposes a launching point from which to explore any study. Every philosophy, then, prescribes a purpose for learning in a given university, and, hence, in any given course. Every professor in every syllabus subsequently lays out her desired outcomes for the semester premised upon a defense of her field, school mission, and department through weekly coursework. Every lecture, assignment, lab, discussion, or practicum is a reinforcement of her belief in what she teaches, a defense of her faith, her commitment to a line of reasoning. In short, no one teaches because she thinks she is wrong. Every professor professes because she believes her curriculum communicates needed, meaningful information about her teaching. She is also an interpreter of her subject, dependent upon assent to certain interpretive ideals acceded to in her discipline. She is, in essence, an apologist for her work in the classroom.

So, I would submit, "apologetics" should not be simply a stand-alone undergraduate- or graduate-level course. Defense of Hebraic-Christian belief should be present in every Bible and theology course. Old and New Testament courses, for instance, should require engagement with the reliability of the canon of Scripture. Further, theology courses ought to critique present reincarnations of ancient heresies. But the Faith must be defended in every sphere, influencing the arts, business, conservation, data-acquisition, engineering—and all the way through to zoology. Moreover, the Christian message is not only to be intellectually defended but practically productive. The church is on the offensive: The gates of hell cannot withstand the onslaught of Truth (Matt 16:18). How Christians live, speak, and respond to outsiders—nonbelievers—depends on instruction that weaves biblical thinking through every domain of life (1 Thess 4:11–12). Beginning in Christian undergraduate studies, then, students should learn the what, the why, and the *how* of belief (Titus 2:1–10). Teaching future generations in the church includes the responsibility to give in every course of study examples of methods and means that prove the beneficence of the Christian message (Matt 5:16). The gospel has offensive firepower when believers show "outsiders" *how* Christian studies impact all lives ("do good," Titus 3:1, 8, 14). Apologetic tools across curricula woven with biblical texts will demonstrate common truth for the common good for the common person (Pss 64:9; 65:8; 66:4–5; 67:1–7).

THE COMMONALITY

"Commonality" suggests the need for life connection to everyone, everywhere. Common folk are interested in what is personal, emotional, cultural, usable, and real. Christian theologians refer to this as "common grace": The goodness of all creation profits all people. The scriptural emphasis is on God's beneficence and kindness in weather, language, discovery, or agriculture being bestowed on "insiders" and "outsiders" alike (Gen 39:5; Pss 107:8, 15, 21, 31, 43; 145:9, 15–16; Matt 5:44–45; Luke 6:35–36; John 1:9; Acts 14:16–17; 1 Cor 7:12–14). Apologetic evangelism begins for Christians with what we have in common with other humans. It is our approach, our method of engagement—wedded with our doctrine—to which we must commit ourselves. The content of our belief is nothing without its proper communication. And how we communicate with one person in one venue may totally change in the next encounter. The commonality all people share includes the following:

1. Common Longing. Call it a wish, desire, hunger, or yearning. Everyone *wants* something they know will fulfill and satisfy. But no one finds it on their own.

2. Common Questions. Eight basic questions summarize human entreaties. What is real? Who is God? Who are humans? What is human purpose? What is the basis for knowledge? What is our view of history? What is right and wrong? What happens when we die? Everyone everywhere asks these questions.

3. Common Law. Cultural standards—no matter the culture—are inbred within the group. The standards, however, have an ultimate source. Every culture, every human person, intuits standards that cannot be fully explained if the origin is only the human heart.

4. Common Sense. The physical world works in a certain way. Order, arrangement, organization, stability, and completion sustain the cosmos. Our sense of life is derived from the sensible universe.

5. Common Ground. Cooperation, collaboration, and community operate best when we are able to speak the common truth, for the common good, for common folk.

Our desire for inclusivity, however, is derived from exclusivity: Jesus is creator, sustainer, and Lord of all things. The reason that the apostle Paul references the Christian's responsibility to "outsiders" is the very basis for everyday apologetics (1 Cor 5:12; 11:11; Col 4:5; 1 Thess 4:12; 1 Tim 3:7; see also Mark 4:11). The figurative idea of people being "outside," not being a member of a certain group, extends to the Christian's interaction in life's every sphere. Prescriptive processes of declaring the good news are absent. Paul's descriptive evangelism is for the daily witness of a person's lived life (2 Cor 3:2). For the believer, sharing the good news is up-to-the-minute, 24/7, 365 news rather than the once-a-day news broadcast (1 Thess 1:8). Living as a Christian is the Twitter feed that identifies trending hashtags. It is the Facebook wall describing the latest events and people. It is the news ticker, the news crawl on the bottom of any television station scrolling the latest headlines: Nothing is missed; everyone is informed.

Where is daily life observed? Where do believers live "before outsiders?" In the vocational pursuits of homemakers, office workers, builders, students, doctors, lawyers, police officers, political appointees, even educators. For what is the Christian academy preparing students? To practice their vocations through the whole of their lives (Gen 2:15; 2 Thess 3:12). To do good benefitting all people (Gen 1:28-29; 1 Pet 2:13-17; 3:13-17). To make the gospel attractive, gaining a good report from all around (Deut 4:5-8; 1 Tim 3:7; Titus 2:10). To buy up opportunities in this life to declare truth (Exod 19:5-6; Eph 5:16; Col 4:5). To preserve the cultural welfares that create blessings for everyone (Jer 29:5-7; Col 1:5-7, 10). To practice giving the gift of grace (Prov 10:32, 22:11; Eccl 10:12; Eph 4:29). When can Christians be practicing apologetics? All day, every day, in every way. Preparation of students to interact apologetically with outsiders necessitates that we teach lifelong, enduring, permanent apologetic tools.

One of the assignments I gave students in discussions of apologetic ethics was to create a story (without chapter and verse) which would demonstrate Christian thinking through living. I will never forget the story Karen told of a young person in politics who made an intentional move away from people who were maligning others. The result in her story pointed toward a generous relationship and hints of "serving before kings" (Gen 41; Prov 22:29). Reading and discussing in my class Hemingway's "Hills Like White Elephants"—an abortion story without the word—was the basis for one student to tell her story of her mom who considered aborting her. She wrote a similar paper the next year in her public university setting to unbelieving professors and classmates. To this day I have students like Taylor, whose haunting tunes now impact the music and movie industry, winsomely drawing listeners to consider eternal questions. I could recount vocation upon vocation, story upon story, student upon student, whose testimony to those outside the Faith reverberates through the harmonic chords of meeting people where they are, commending and defending Christianly with their words and ways. Christian educational institutions need to equip students apologetically in all their courses, for life.

THE ASSUMPTIONS

We were discussing an engineering problem over lunch: his latest experiment application in the tech world.

"Do you know anything about this field of math research?" he wondered.

I smiled. "I know about research. And research is the same, no matter the subject."

He cast a questioning look in my direction.

"After listening to your explanation about some troubles you were having with your experiment, I wonder if you have considered these assumptions."

I offered four or five questions to ponder for his task.

The next week we continued our discussion. "I had not considered these starting points before. Even my prof talked about the importance of these inquiries as we worked through the experiment. Your questions helped me think in different directions I would not have considered."

I smiled. "I'm glad they were helpful. God made his world to work in a certain way. The order of the cosmos is implanted in every creational process. The subjects we study may vary, but the creational laws never do. God's order is imprinted everywhere."

My interest was to help my young, believing university friend understand that Christian belief originates from a biblical source and that it is applied in every cultural context, giving opportunity for Christian impact. If people think, they do so based on their belief, informing their point of view which creates cultural benefits. Colossians 2:3 declares, "In Christ are hidden all the treasures of wisdom and knowledge," which means neutrality is a myth. Note the very next verse where Paul's desire is apologetic: "I say this so that no one will delude you with plausible arguments" (Col 2:4). The Christian life is governed by a belief system through relationship with the Personal Eternal Triune Creator.

How I view reality depends on my doctrinal "glasses." Scripture demands doctrinal regularity, accountability. Doctrine forms the basis for our assumptions leading to application (Rom 6:17; 1 Tim 1:10–11, 15, 18; 2 Tim

1:13–14; 2 Thess 3:6). Our beliefs begin because of Jesus's saving work in our lives. Thereafter, our sources of knowledge as Christian thinkers shape our knowing. There is a Spirit-driven, unconscious impact on our conscious study. Biblical sensitivities then permeate everything. Our theology informs our sociology. We intentionally apply our lifeview to life. Assumptions by which Christians live include a commitment to (1) beginning and end (what God started He will finish); (2) order in creation which posits a cosmos, not a chaos; (3) supernatural and natural realities which exist; (4) a uniformity and consistency producing dependability; and (5) induction and deduction through logic producing a pro-science viewpoint. Assumptions give us the following launching pads for any course of study.

1. The Source of Authority. Where do we get the information that we need? Is it reliable, authentic, and authoritative? How is the information interpreted? If God has revealed himself in his world, then he can be known (Ps 19:1–11; Col 2:3). The laws of science—motion or properties—come from the authority and law of God (Gen 2:16, 17; 8:22; Deut 4:5–8; Ps 147:15–20; Matt 6:25–34; Col 1:15–20).

2. God, not Matter, Is Eternal. If we know from whence everything originated, then we know to whom we're responsible. God is both transcendent and immanent—apart from and close to—caring for—his creation at the same time. God created. Matter was brought into being (Neh 9:6; Job 12:10; Acts 17:25, 28; Col 1:17; Heb 1:3).

3. Predictable Patterns in God's Creation. Mathematicians and scientists rely on God's stable universe. His world is stable and consistent because of his word (Lev 26:4; Ps 148:6; Prov 8:29; Eccl 3:11; Jer 8:7; 31:35–37). Order establishes logic, logic constitutes pattern, pattern produces models, models make possible determinations of probability, determinations of probability allow for prediction, prediction predicates hypothesis, and hypothesis identifies proof. A proof demonstrates "true Truth."

4. Discovery and Invention in God's Creation. People all over the world and throughout time uncover truth by collecting data, applying information, exploring, and observing. What is true in one place is true in another (Pss 64:9; 65:8; 66:5). Diligent probes can reveal new information. However, we uncover only "the tip of the iceberg" of God's works (Job 28:3, 11; 26:14).

5. Unity and Diversity in God's Creation. Like puzzle pieces put together to make a picture, so the world fits together showing similarities and differences. The orderly arrangement of the parts makes the whole

(Gen 1:3-2:3). God's wisdom is the basis for how the world works, thus helping Christians apologetically inquire in any course, for life (Prov 3:19-20; 8:22-31; 25:2).

THE THEOLOGY

"We were discussing how judgmental attitudes hurt people's feelings," they reminisced about the class. "The prof specifically called out absolutes coming from the Bible as a source of hatred."

"If there aren't any absolutes, then why would anyone's feelings be hurt?" I offered.

My young Christian friends looked perplexed.

"It's like this," I began the explanation. "Why would people be 'hurt' if there were no standards to judge that they had been hurt?" Their eyes brightened as I continued: "People like to say 'don't judge,' but the fact that folks think someone has been hurt shows that a standard of conduct has been breached. 'Hurt feelings' is the same as saying 'the way you have treated me is wrong.' But if there are no absolutes, no standards by which we can evaluate wrongdoing, then how can feelings be hurt?"

"Oh, I get it," one student responded. "You can't hurt someone if there is no right or wrong to judge whether or not they were hurt! And the only way we can judge hurting someone's feelings is if absolutes exist in the Bible!"

"Exactly," I confirmed. "Hurting people does not violate any moral law unless there really are moral laws, and moral laws require a moral lawgiver."

Exactly.

There are two theological baselines that crisscross through every subject of study: absolute truth and the inherent corruption of humanity. The second demands the first. If, as literature substantiates, there is a problem with "the human condition," then there must be a standard by which corruption is recognized as such and by which it is also overcome or, at least, held at bay. "Racism" is not the direct result of history, nationality, ethnicity, or privilege. Racism is the direct result of the sin in every human heart. "Greed" is not a result of big business, banking institutions, capitalism, or economic class. Greed begins in every human heart. "Hate" does not originate in ethnicity, nationality, political persuasion, or economic class. Hate originates in every human heart.

The only true change against privilege, negative home situations, or psychological dispositions is the saving grace of Jesus. The gospel changes our "hearts," then motivates us to "do good." Titus 2:11–14 leads right into Titus 3:1, 8, 14. If we begin by believing that "doing good" is our first response to sin, then our view of salvation begins with us rather than with the redemption we need, which is found only in Christ. If "doing good" has solely a human origin, then humans get to define "the good." The motivation of "doing" belongs to the individual. What is "good" for me may not be "good" for you. But if "doing good" is a focus on others because of Another, then the origin of and motivation for "good" is prompted by Someone who is Good. "Good" now has a standard. Only the exclusivity of the gospel allows for the inclusivity of help. If we don't have the first, then the second is up to the whim of the individual or institution. If we do not have a biblical foundation for government, law, policy, or jurisprudence, then biblical truths will not permeate the culture. My students have heard me say this for decades: "My environment, or biology, or psychology may accentuate my behavior but it is not the root cause of it" (Mark 7:21–23). The theological foundations of absolute truth providing a transcendent standard of conduct will mitigate the problems caused by our human condition. When Christian students are taught the theological underpinnings of sociological concerns, they then provide the possibility of apologetically commending the restorative power of order in God's world.

I had to ask her if she would type out "cytotechnology" to me on my cell phone. I had not heard of it before even though I had seen its effects in medical research.

"Does your professor ever talk about origins, where things come from, in your study?" I began.

"No," she shook her head. "We don't discuss ideas such as creation or evolution. Evolution is a given."

"Let me ask a different question. Does your professor ever use the words 'awe,' 'beauty,' 'wonder,' or 'amazement' when talking about human cell structure?"

"Oh, yes! All the time! He will say things like, 'If the molecular structure changed a fraction or the cell structure shifted ever so slightly in this direction the immune system would not work.'"

She paused. Then she said, "You know, now that I think about it, my professor assumes design all the time! He will use the word and I will think to myself, 'How can you use that word if you believe in evolution?'"

"And there it is!" I declared, looking around the table. "No one—Christian or non-Christian—can operate in their respective fields of study without depending on concepts that come from outside themselves."

I looked at the young mathematician sitting across from me. "I bet your math courses suggest that one of the ways a math proof is identified as true is if the equation is beautiful."

He agreed, nodding. "Mathematical computation depends on beauty."

The student who had fallen in love with forensic linguistics concurred: "We depend on the framework of logic as we investigate law. We assume logic as the basis for our study."

"Do you see?!" I exclaimed. "The Christian worldview provides the presuppositions for everything! Humans describe the results of any investigation as beautiful, logical, or wonderful without giving a thought about where those ideas originate."

Our discussions around the lunch table continued over a myriad of topics.

But we were all reminded again that our scholastic lives are governed by The One who has designed, sustains, and enjoys all things in his creation.

Teachers and students all assume:

- an origin for our study, which makes us ask, "Where did that come from?";
- boundaries for our schoolwork, which causes us to question, "Why are limitations built into the world?";
- exploration in our field of research, which suggests, "What else is there to learn?";
- delight as we pursue creative alternatives thinking: "How can I make this better?";
- a lack of fulfillment in our discoveries unless we can answer, "When will I feel satisfied?"

One student in our group told of a conversation she had overheard in her department. "You can hear everything from where I sit," she explained. "Two accomplished PhD professors were musing aloud, saying things like, 'After all our accomplishments, publications, and credits, is *this* all there is?'"

"I wish I could have had the liberty to engage that conversation. Maybe they should talk with us over lunch."

The theology of divine standards and human sin can be apologetically witnessed throughout Scripture, throughout life. "Wisdom" confirms an order, what the Egyptians called *ma'at*. Proverbs 8 sets the stage for wisdom—order to saturate every area of study, every discipline in the university, every curricula in K–12 schools. In contrast, "foolishness" is diametrically opposed to the wisdom-order embedded in God's world (Ps 147:15–20; Isa

28:23–29). Set regulations—what some scientists may refer to as "laws of nature"—have their conception and continuation in God's transcendent moment of creational beginnings. Creation brings cosmic order. Law brings societal order. Etiquette brings relational order. Government brings political order. Justice brings preservation of order. Institutions bring the conduit for order. Paradigms bring models of order.

For years I have used a compare-and-contrast approach to help students understand how a Christian view of an orderly life creates the possibility for flourishing. The Christian must be able to articulate other worldviews accurately, to argue their truth and error cogently, while identifying the problems and solutions possible for living together in our world. One such paper outline invited students to consider the following evaluation of where any idea begins and ends:

- Worldview: The underlying assumption(s) is . . .
- Proponent: A major contributor believed . . .
- Policies: Governments or societies responded by . . .
- Consequences: The end result was . . .

In another class I began a discussion with the question, "What is necessary to begin a world religion?" The answers flew around the room. "Priests!" "A book of rules!" "A path to follow!" "An authority figure!" "Hope!"

After students had exhausted their proposals, we discussed two more questions:

1. How is this religion different from other religions?
2. Why is this religion necessary?

We maintain three theological differences between Christianity and other religions: Christianity depends on (1) history, documentation from eyewitness accounts; (2) Jesus, a real person in time-space history who died a physical death, rising from the dead; and (3) grace, salvation which is undeserved, unrivaled in the offer, without one iota of effort from the recipient. Why is this discussion important in one's classroom? We give our students apologetic tools that will commend and defend a Christian view of life, for life.

THE APPROACH

Spiders can fly. In fact, spiders have been found one thousand miles from any land and two and a half miles up in the sky. Scientists are just now discovering that spiders in flight use something they call "ballooning." The same silk used by spiders to build webs is the silk that creates make-shift canopies catching the wind for air travel. It seems human understanding of arachnids is just now catching up to age-old spider practices. Charles Darwin, on his famous *HMS Beagle* voyage off the coast of South America, wrote about hundreds of spiders all over the ship, sixty miles off the coast of Argentina. As *The Atlantic* tells it in its July 2018 issue, "Darwin himself found the rapidity of the spiders' flight to be 'quite unaccountable' and its cause to be 'inexplicable.'"

I love science for the same reason Darwin could not account for it. Science, simply defined, is an observation of the world around us. But the question of a spider's flight plan, or any other unanswered questions about weather, earth movements, or animal behavior, leads us to the ultimate question. What or who established the orderly system of creation where we still make daily discoveries? The reason I love the science found in creation is because I love The Creator of the science.

Over three thousand years ago, Job best described human discoveries about science. In fact, he and Darwin would agree about creation being inexplicable. In Job 26:14, Job declared about human discoveries: "And these are but the outer fringe of His works" (NIV). Translation? We may be gaining in knowledge through scientific discovery but if our understanding of how spiders fly is fairly recent, how much do we really know about our world?

The creational designs of spiders are the Creator's sermons. The whole world is one big pulpit. All we have to do is find a creational pew, and listen to a scientific apologetic found in daily life. The question "How?" signals the approach curricular apologetics could take in any Christian university classroom.

Our apologetic approach should be winsome. Our presentations should focus on points of agreement with anyone. Any potential audience should see how much we have in common with shared creational architecture. Apologetic claims can be in evidence at the end of our dialogue. Training conversant tactics with those holding widely divergent viewpoints could be part of any course advancing a Christian lifeview. Respecting the discipline within which we dialogue is essential. Our use of language should invite, not alienate. Speaking publicly or privately about potential disagreement should be tempered with kindness. Supporting another's right to speak even if we disagree is an others-centered statement. Listening to those whose voice, culture, or background is different from our own is an imperative.

In sociology, for instance, some want us to accept their self-identity based on their individual definitions of sexuality or gender. My agreement or disagreement with self-identity in the culture means little if I do not accept people as fellow human beings. Worth, value, and dignity are based on our being made in God's image according to God's creational law (Gen 1:26–27). If I approach individuals as people rather than as categories, reception may be reciprocal. Hospitality of ideas should be just as much a practice as hospitality of guests in our homes. Showing care does not concede consent but offers a winsome extension of love. Since we know that love is the greatest apologetic (John 13:34–35), the life practices of others matter little in relation to the lives of others.

In politics, there are those who vilify anyone with whom they disagree. Responses to the president, congress, judges, or law enforcement cross the line of visceral hatred for some. I may be willing to listen to reasoned responses to people or policy, but I will not abide disrespect of anyone. The biblical vantage point begins with the admonition to honor those in authority (1 Pet 2:13–17). If I approach authorities with a spirit of generosity—no matter their belief or behavior—my approach may bring with it an opportunity for collaboration and conciliation. Listening to another person's political views does not mean that I give them assent (Prov 15:1–7). It means that my approach cares for them as people before wrestling over views about government.

In journalism, if we are only given to one media perspective on any given issue, we will never be able to live with each other in cooperation. Those on the so-called "left" tend to read *Slate*, Salon, Huffington Post, *The New York Times*, NPR, or *The Washington Post*. Those on the so-called "right" tend to read The Drudge Report, *The Washington Examiner*, *National Review*, *The Washington Times*, *City Journal*, or *First Things*. Scripture clearly teaches that one should consider the second point of view after the first (Prov 18:17). If I approach other perspectives with an attitude of respect—without giving up my perspective—it could lead to everyone's being heard. Every side of an issue should be fairly represented; objectivity and accuracy are paramount (Deut 19:15–18). Thus, teaching a style of apologetics that cares for everyone even sets precedent for reception of daily news coverage.

All academic disciplines must consider how to prepare their students vocationally. Why any calling exists could be presented in an apologetic fashion. A reflective report could be a way of preparing students to address the public practice of their respective fields. Additions to such an account could continue from the freshman to the senior year, addressing the following questions:

- Need—Why is your vocation necessary?
- Outcome—What do you expect to accomplish in your vocation to benefit others?
- Content—What is necessary to know in your vocation?
- Community—Who will be impacted by your vocation?
- Setting—When and where will your vocation have impact?
- Methods—How will you communicate your Christian vocational ideals? Finding ways to commend and defend biblical principles can begin with apologetic questions in any university setting, preparing students for life.

CONCLUSION

The story is told of a young boy and his dad who were practice-casting in anticipation of bass season opening the next day. The lure flashed in the full moonlight as the child learned under his father's tutelage. Without warning, the next cast hooked a fish. Reeling it in, two generations gazed on a beautiful bass, the largest either had ever seen. "Can we keep it, Dad?" came the plaintive cry. The father lit a match and noted the time on his wrist watch. It was 10 p.m., two hours before bass season opened. "No, son. The season begins tomorrow." The boy glanced around the lake. They were alone. "But, Dad! No one will know! The season begins in two hours! Please, can we keep it?!" The father's insistence was resolute. Lowering the big bass into the lake, the two watched as the animal swam away. Neither saw a fish that size ever again. But the boy sees that same fish every time he is asked to cut corners, fudge numbers, or submit half-truths in his job.

Persuasion through apologetics may be best taught through story. Stories pry their way into our attitude. Stories loosen prejudices. Stories open new vistas of thought. Stories broaden our perspectives on life. Stories help create character. Character—a person's internal ethical code—is best developed by a story. Stories can tell the biographical detail of any subject of study. Stories can carry the authority of assumptions in winsome ways. Stories are attractive to everyone, including outsiders. Robert Coles in his book *The Call of Stories* explains that powerful stories can affect us, excite us, and cause us to see more clearly.[2] C. S. Lewis in his essay "On Stories" says simply, "The story is the image of the truth."[3] Stories dot the landscape of this essay to show that lifelong commitment to apologetic thinking can be applied within any Christian university department, curriculum, coursework, or lesson. The best apologetics may be best taught in the classes students take in preparation for a life lived before outsiders. And the truth of any academic field may best be communicated with a story.

BIBLIOGRAPHY

Coles, Robert. *The Call of Stories: Teaching and the Moral Imagination*. Boston: Houghton Mifflin, 1990.
Lewis, C. S. *On Stories and Other Essays on Literature*. 1966. Reprint, Boston: Houghton Mifflin, 2002.

2. Coles, *Call of Stories*, 197.
3. Lewis, *On Stories*, 20.

6

For the Cross and the Land

Radical Counter-Secularization in Russia

Artyom H. Tonoyan

Much has been written on the forced secularization in Russia during the Soviet reign of terror, and two recent works by Paul Froese and Christopher Marsh have extensively documented both its intended and unintended consequences.[1] However, literature on the de-secularizing and counter-secularizing trends in Russia since the collapse of the Soviet Union still seems to be lacking even though a number of books and studies that have come out recently seek to reverse the trend and give us a more fine-tuned insight into the forces that led the charge to de-secularize Russia since the collapse of the Soviet Union.

I take as a point of departure Peter Berger's argument that, contrary to the prognostications of the secularization theory, religion—especially in its furiously orthodox forms—has made a comeback through what he calls its rejection of the "*aggiornamento* with modernity."[2] This paper will try to identify some of the more influential religious groups, individuals, and organizations leading the charge to desecularize the Russian public discourse

---

1. See, respectively, Froese, *Plot to Kill God*; Marsh, *Religion and the State*.
2. Berger, "Desecularization of the World," 6.

and to steer contemporary Russian statecraft away from the "false promises" of modernity. Whether this counter-secularizing process (at least in their Russian context) is meant to rearticulate the pre-modern taken-for-granted certainties in a contemporary idiom or whether it is an incipient "project of eliminating doubt"[3] is a topic for another discussion. What is obvious, however, is that this process has re-written the contemporary Russian socio-cultural and religious script and has given rise to "a new paradigm" in the religio-political dialogical continuum, "redefin[ing] the role of Orthodoxy in the Russian state and Russian society"[4] with political implications far beyond that country's physical borders. The present essay pursues two principal aims—to (briefly) discuss the complex and misunderstood dynamics present in contemporary Russian Orthodoxy, and to shed light on the unsettling and often disturbing ideological crosscurrents animating the more radically minded wing of the Russian Orthodox Church.

For the purposes of the present paper I have adopted Slava Karpov's definition of desecularization: "a process of counter-secularisation, through which religion reasserts its societal influence in reaction to previous and/or co-occurring secularising processes."[5] This process, inorganic and uneven as it may be, nevertheless is propelled forward by a varied group of actors "with specific visions of desecularisation" and more or less coherent programs of action. It is precisely these actors, along with their thematic preoccupations, who interest us here.

It is not surprising that much of the western commentary about the recent history of the Russian Orthodox Church (ROC) and its relationship with the Russian government has focused on the aspects of the relationship that has arguably challenged Russia's official constitutional secularism. The two institutions have, over the years, *seemingly* (to outside observers at least) worked on many significant issues of concern in tandem, or at least seem to have not gotten in each other's way, with the state support of the Church growing with every passing year.[6] Yet despite the abundance of titles dealing with church-state relations in Russia, what is striking is the portrayal of the ROC as a singularly powerful institution capable of inducing political changes throughout Russia almost by a whim. Although the ROC remains a cultural and political force to be reckoned with, it is far from being a unitary actor, its many decisions being alternately challenged

---

3. Berger, *Many Altars of Modernity*, 32.
4. Schroeder and Karpov, "Crimes and Punishments," 285.
5. Karpov, "Social Dynamics of Russia's Desecularisation," 256. For a fuller treatment of the concept, see Karpov, "Desecularization," 232–70.
6. Anderson, "Putin and the Russian Orthodox Church," 185–201.

or ignored, depending on the political climate within the Church leadership as well as in the broader socio-political climate in the county. Nevertheless, far from inducing paralysis, however, these challenges reveal a complex set of determinants at work in intra-church processes and the Church's engagement with its wider socio-political context.

As Irina Papkova has shown in her work,[7] within the Orthodox church there are three broadly defined groups—traditionalists, liberals, and fundamentalists—engaged in what can only be described as Heidegerrian *gigantomachia* (battle of giants) for ideological hegemony within both the more formal structures of the Orthodox church and its informal networks. Although we are speaking of three groups with various, if fluid, political agendas, it is not the same as to say that the boundaries between these groups do not at some point—or, rather, over some questions—overlap. These thematic overlaps are especially noticeable between the traditionalist and fundamentalist camps, differing only in the degree of intensity these themes have been espoused by the competing camps, ranging from constructive and gradual integration of the Russian Orthodoxy into the political life of the country (traditionalists) to a more radical reversal of the current status quo (fundamentalists). A shared traditionalist and fundamentalist concern that consequently undergirds and directs most of their political activities is the belief that the best way to ensure a strong Russia is to match Russia's economic wealth with its rich spiritual and cultural heritage. For both traditionalists and fundamentalists of primary importance in this process is Russia's spiritual renaissance whereby the Orthodox Church, which was all but incapacitated during the Soviet era, reclaims its institutional relevance/dominion in the political life of the country. Meanwhile, a secularism with its underlying emphasis on individual human rights and radical separation of church and state, ideas one usually associates with the Enlightenment and western liberalism, is seen as the principle and the most powerful enemy that stifles Russia's quest to restore its sacred and political *raison d'etat*.

The traditionalists, who vastly outnumber the fundamentalists, have been able to occupy the most important leadership positions in the Moscow Patriarchate, the formal administrative structure of the Russian Orthodox Church (ROC), thereby steering the Church's formal discourse on social and political matters. While it is expected that they will be able to continue to do so in the foreseeable future, it is not guaranteed that their reign will continue indefinitely, given the powerful challenge they face from the more conservative and reactionary groups in the ROC.[8] A growing sign of the po-

---

7. See Papkova, *Orthodox Church and Russian Politics*.
8. Verkhovsky, "Politicheskoe Pravoslavie."

tency of the fundamentalist camp is best illustrated by the fact that Patriarch Kirill, the current head of the ROC, in order to secure his election to the office, sought to assuage the reservations of fundamentalists and conservatives by holding consultations with a number of leading conservative voices such as archimandrite Tikhon (Shevkunov, the now rumored *dukhovnik* or the confessor of Vladimir Putin), Kirill (Pavlov) and Ilia (Nozdrin), spiritual elders at the Holy Trinity Lavra of St. Sergius and the Optina Hermitage respectively.

The liberals, meanwhile, have been outnumbered and outmaneuvered into the margins of the intra-church discourse, failing to halt the ascendancy of either the traditionalists or the fundamentalists. Although they favor broad-based reforms within the Church, seeking a meaningful institutional separation of church and state (not discursive, faith still has a say in public matters), they are yet to turn their political platform into something more palpable than abstract appeals to their traditional allies among the liberal intelligentsia.[9] For liberals the separationist paradigm is the true form of the *symphonia* because it grants the Church true independence, weaning it off the grotesque caesaro-papist and politically subordinationist[10] *modus vivendi* since the days of Peter the Great. They also have come to see the role of the Church as a prophetic witness rather than a quasi-state institution or an arm of the state in any other form.[11]

The liberal group had a brief period of visible success immediately after the fall of the Soviet Union when it was informally headed by the likes of Fr. Alexander Men, the late reformist priest who was assassinated for what seems to be his reformist convictions, and Gleb Yakunin, the dissident priest who was all but defrocked by the Church for his opposition to both state and church—by the former for its antireligious totalitarianism and by the latter for collaborationism during the Soviet era.[12] Although the liberal camp is still actively maintaining close relationships with other human rights activists and liberal Russian intellectuals, since they lack resources and broader public support, they have been operating in relative unimportance compared with either the traditionalists or the fundamentalists. Moreover, a large part of the lay intellectuals who had sympathized with the

---

9. Basil, "Problems of State and Church," 212.

10. Here the term is not to be confused with the theological subordinationism, which describes the relationship within the Holy Trinity, and is rejected as theological heresy.

11. See Payne, "Spiritual Security," 712–27.

12. See Marsh, *Religion and the State in Russia and China*, 85–89.

liberal wing of the Church have simply left the ranks of the faithful, leaving it with an ever-decreasing intellectual gravitas.[13]

It is the fundamentalists, however, who interest us, if for no other reason than the fact that it is fundamentalists who are at the forefront of the efforts to redefine the entire sweep of the Russian religious ecosystem. They do so by advocating two principal notions—(a) the articulation and implementation of broad-based changes in the legislative field that aim to elevate the Orthodox Church as the chief arbiter of public morality in Russian social life, and (b) closing the gap between institutions of power and religious institutions. The closure of the gap does not mean a total overlap between the two realms, but a near total collaboration. It must be pointed out that religion in this context denotes exclusively Russian Orthodoxy, other religious confessions being accorded only secondary or even tertiary importance, depending on these confessions' ideological distance from the religio-political prerogatives of the fundamentalists. This position rests firmly on the widely accepted claim that Russia is not just a country that has Orthodox believers among its citizenry, but that it is chiefly an Orthodox country.

Below are some of the themes and ideas that animate the fundamentalists in the ROC. The fundamentalist movement is, first of all, animated by a yearning to relive *L'Âge d'Or* (the golden age) exemplified in the pre-revolutionary Holy Russia with its "superior" spiritual culture and value system and by the quest to reawaken Russia's "national-religious self consciousness" and its "national historic memory."[14] Meanwhile modernity in its Western liberal-pluralistic incarnation emerges as the principal force inhibiting the political and moral revival of the Russian national spirit and faith.[15] As Konstantin Kostiuk has observed, according to the fundamentalists, "all contemporary forms of political expression—democracy, constitutional state, market economy, civil society—are actively destroying the idea of Orthodox state and in essence are nothing less than the invention of the 'evil one,' intended to destroy Russia."[16]

Another favorite object of derision for the fundamentalists is the Moscow Patriarchate, towards which they express uninhibited distrust and which, in their estimation, has continued in its old ways by striking a rather cozy relationship with the state, the same state (of course in its earlier permutation) that essentially oversaw the near-destruction of the Church during Soviet years. To add insult to injury, the Patriarchate is also actively engaged

13. Sergeichik, "Sovremennoe Pravoslavie i intelligentsia," 343–53.
14. Ioann, *Bitva Za Rossiiu*, 5 (translation by author).
15. Ioann, *Bitva Za Rossiiu*, 5.
16. Kostiuk, "Pravoslavnyi Fundamentalism," 142.

in dialogue with other religious traditions, practicing the heresy or the "sin of ecumenism."[17] Led by Orthodox laymen and a loose network of like-minded priests and bishops under an umbrella organization known as the Union of Orthodox Brotherhoods (UOB), the fundamentalists moreover believe that the formal administrative structure of the ROC is corrupt, full of conceit, and unwilling to listen to the concerns of the faithful; therefore, they rely on the informal networks of *dukhovnye startsy* (spiritual elders) or monks who, having no contamination from worldly powers, continue to receive charismatic gifts and wisdom from God.[18] The 2011 movie by the Russian film director Pavel Lungin called *The Island*, about a monk who practices the gifts of clairvoyance and healing, is highly illustrative of this way of thinking; indeed, it is a remarkable demonstration of how these themes have been revived and have seeped into the popular cultural discourse.[19]

Although some of their ideas are resoundingly outlandish even for Russia (e.g., Canonization of Stalin and Ivan the Terrible), fundamentalist groups and organizations have nevertheless managed to gain considerable following through outreach efforts and clever uses of media and popular culture. Moreover, no major gathering of the leadership of the ROC has taken place without many priests and even monks from the fundamentalist camp pushing their agenda in these meetings. In addition to using conferences, print, and audiovisual media to spread fundamentalist propaganda, mass letter-writing campaigns have become another of the favorite method of the fundamentalists to push for changes in Synodal proceedings. The fundamentalists' use of mass media and the Internet has been particularly impressive, dominating the market and, as a result, shaping the popular discourse on religion and politics. In many cases, their ideological postulates have become in the popular mind the true paradigm of Orthodox belief and praxis.[20] Although fundamentalists do not yet enjoy the amount of popular support that would allow them to be politically more effective than they already are, they nevertheless have been able to bring several issues they feel strongly about into intra-church discussions. They have been especially successful in steering the debate about the ROC's involvement in ecumenical contacts of various kinds, pressuring the Moscow Patriarchate to abandon interchurch and interconfessional initiatives.[21] Despite the general tendency toward distrust of the Patriarchate, these groups still see it as an important

17. See Mitrokhin, *Russkaya Pravoslavnaia Tserkov'*, 186.
18. Mitrokhin, *Russkaya Pravoslavnaia Tserkov'*, 185–87.
19. For a critical discussion of Pavel Lungin's film, see Bodin, "Holy Fool," 1–9.
20. Kostiuk, "Pravoslavnyi fundamentalizm," 135.
21. Kostiuk, "Pravoslavnyi fundamentalizm," 135.

institution, with enormous—albeit misused and often underutilized—political potential.[22]

Other issues that the fundamentalists have taken up are sex education programs at schools and government implementation of the taxpayer identification numbers (*Individual'nyi Nomer Nallogoplatel'shchika* or INN), both of which they have opposed with varying degrees of success.[23]

Meanwhile, the main outlet of their ideological concerns has become the journal *Rus' Pravoslavnaia* (*Russia the Orthodox*) and its corresponding website, founded in 1993 under the aegis of the Metropolitan Ioann of St. Petersburg, whom many Russian observers consider the chief ideological guru of the movement.[24] In 2013 the journal launched a successful YouTube channel, which at the time of this writing has over three hundred thousand active subscribers and nearly two hundred million views.[25]

Ironically, however, it was through Ioann's publications in the communist *cum* nationalist newspaper *Sovetskaia Rossiia* that some of Ioann's early political positions, and by extension the network of fundamentalists, were becoming systematized and articulated, providing the nascent fundamentalist movement with ideological foundations. Many of Ioann's chief ideological concerns and preoccupations, coupled with the writings of conservative writers V. Rasputin and I. Shafarevich and the works of S. Nilus (the editor of *The Protoclos of the Elders of Zion*), in time became the movement's unofficial discursive leitmotifs.

After Ioann's death in 1995, the *Rus' Pravoslavnaia* came under the editorship of Konstantin Dushenov, who is thought to have been the real author behind Metropolitan Ioann's earlier essays. With Dushenov, the movement's center of gravity almost completely shifted from theological and moralistic concerns to political ones, recruiting in the process even more followers. Some choice examples of the thinking that goes on in the fundamentalist circles and that provide us with examples of clearly counter-secularizing efforts of the movement are to be found in the pages of the periodical, *Rus' Pravoslavnaia*.

In a May 2004 issue of the journal, Dushenov, who by now had assumed the role of the chief proponent of fundamentalist dogma, interviewed the composer and poet Gennadi Ponomarev, whose musical compositions as well as verse are said to be inspired by Orthodox themes and the idea of Russian *derzhavnost'*. In the interview Ponomarev was asked about his

22. Verkhovskii, "Politicheskoe Pravoslavie," 11, 30.
23. Kostiuk, "Pravoslavnyi fundamentalizm," 135.
24. Verkhovskii, "Politicheskoe Pravoslavie."
25. https://www.youtube.com/user/ruspravoslav/about.

views on Russia's political future, to which he replied in what can be only assessed as one of the central themes of the fundamentalists in their quest to transform the Russian state from its current form, i.e., managed democracy, to its true *raison d'etat*:

> An orthodox autocratic monarchy is the only possible God-pleasing option for our religious-political organization. . . . [At the same time] the figure of the coming Russian Orthodox Tsar—God's Anointed One—becomes the mystical center of our aspirations and hope for the freeing of the Russian people and the Russian state from the current yoke of non-Orthodox and non-Russians, who seized power in 1917 and are still holding our people enslaved. . . . From this point of view, the redemptive sacrifice of the holy Tsar-martyr Nicholas II becomes central.[26]

Ponomarev's interview is illustrative of the inner logic of the fundamentalist movement, revealing its primary socio-political preoccupations and pursuits. Notably we learn of the movement's ardent monarchism, the wish to integrate the church and nation-state and the subsequent religious homogenization of the country, whereby identity markers "Russian" and "Orthodox Christian" become coterminous.[27] With the insistence of the 1917 October Revolution as a Jewish plot to dismantle Russian Orthodoxy we also learn of the movement's unflinching anti-Semitism. Moreover, using widespread anti-Semitic tropes, the movement's advocates argue that the current levers of power remain in the hands of the Jews who are determined upon exploiting Orthodox Christians. Yet another preoccupation that is revealed is the devotional, almost cultish, reverence towards the Christ-like figure of Tsar Nicholas II, who is endowed with robustly redemptive features.[28] In a prayer composed to the Tsar known as the *akafist* and widely circulated among the faithful, Nicholas II is portrayed in divine terms resembling the suffering Christ: for example, "like a sheep led to the slaughter" and "like an innocent lamb you are foreordained for redemption of our sins, let all praise you unceasingly: Rejoice, sacrifice beloved by God."[29]

According to fundamentalists, then, the post-Soviet situation in Russia is seen as the last chance that has been sent to Russia from above, as it were, to achieve spiritual transformation and renewal through repentance for the murder of the Romanovs, one of the greatest crimes committed not

---

26. Ponomarev quoted in Papkova, *Orthodox Church and Russian Politics*, 62.

27. Echoing Vladimir Solovyov's position that the Russian state "forges a nation from the church." See Solovyov, *Chtenia o bogochlovechestve*, 244.

28. Verkhovsky, "Politicheskoe Pravoslavie."

29. Chistiakov, "In Search of the 'Russian Idea,'" 55–56.

only against the Russian state but also against God himself. Repentance, thus, will allow Russia to achieve its previous glory, assume the role of a world leader, and stand up against forces of darkness currently represented by NATO, globalization, and Judeo-Masonic conspiracy against the divine order of things, the final battle being against the forces of anti-Christ himself.[30] In line with the argument about the Judeo-Masonic conspiracy, some fundamentalists have even argued that they hindered Stalin (according to them a devout Orthodox believer), to turn the Soviet Union into an Orthodox monarchy.[31] The notion that Stalin was a devout Orthodox has, in turn, been picked up by Russian communists, with whom the fundamentalists have become strange bedfellows indeed. In a booklet published on the eve of the 2011 Russian *Duma* elections titled *Kommunisty i Russkoe Pravoslavie* (*Communists and the Russian Orthodoxy*), the author Yuri Belov argued that "Stalin as a person well versed in the fundamentals of Orthodoxy was never a godless militant, i.e., a person aggressively intolerant to belief in God."[32]

Meanwhile Fr. Dmitri Dudko, a dissident anti-communist priest who spent years in prison camps under Stalin and Leonid Brezhnev for his struggle for religious freedom, in a complete *volta-face* would embrace the unseemly symbiosis between communism and Orthodoxy in what can only be called a case of Stockholm syndrome taking place in Moscow. In a controversial interview in 2012, Fr. Dmitri went on to declare that "as an Orthodox Christian and as a Russian patriot I bow to Stalin."[33] Elsewhere he declares that "Stalin was an atheist on the surface, but in reality was a believer. Facts could demonstrate this."[34] During a 2001 Victory Day march, a group of fundamentalists were seen intermingling with Communists and carrying a banner for "Freedom for Colonel Budanov," the Russian military officer accused and subsequently convicted of raping and murdering a young Chechen girl.[35] Years later, Budanov himself would be violently killed by unknown assailants, later to be identified as Chechen vigilantes.[36]

An Orthodox priest Fr. Mikhail, a long-time spiritual advisor to the slain Colonel, having visited the latter in prison on many occasions, would declare at Budanov's funeral that "We have gained a new saint. In heaven, he will be saying prayers on behalf of all of us alongside Aleksandr Nevskii,

30. Papkova, *Orthodox Church and Russian Politics*, 63.
31. Kostiuk, "Pravoslavnyi fundamentalizm," 136.
32. Belov, *Kommunisty i Russkoe Pravoslavie*, 17.
33. See "Svyashchennik Dmitry Dudko."
34. Chistiakov, "In Search of the 'Russian Idea,'" 60.
35. Rock, "Fraternal Strife," 331.
36. Gutterman, "Chechen Convicted of Killing Russian Colonel."

Dmitri Donskoi and Evgenii Rodionov."[37] The religious valorization of Budanov was in line with the tradition of heroizing Russian military personnel in the wake of the Chechen wars that went back at least to the publication of Aleksandr Shargunov's biography of Evgeny Rodionov, the Russian soldier who was killed by his Chechen captors for reportedly refusing to renounce Christianity and save himself by converting to Islam.

These and similar apocalyptic, conspiratorial, xenophobic ideologies in combination with a siege mentality have continued unabated in the fundamentalist circles and in the pages of *Rus' Pravoslavnaia*. For instance, in 2004 *Rus' Pravoslavnaia* published the resolution of a Moscow gathering of a group of fundamentalist priests and theologians in which the participants warned the leadership of the Church and Russian believers that "the main ideologues of globalism have declared Orthodoxy their Enemy Number One. There is a merciless undeclared war being fought against Russia. . . . [In order to stop this onslaught, we demand that the government] must . . . recognize Orthodoxy as the state religion."[38] The underlying assumption behind the declaration is that, only through the redemptive power of Orthodoxy and the God-given mission the Church has been bestowed from on high, will Russia survive, thrive, and maximize its political power, meanwhile offering the world true faith and salvation: Either Orthodoxy is recognized as the foundation of the Russian nation and culture and the substance of its public life, or moral chaos coupled with Russian political decline will be the only logical outcome. As Metropolitan Ioann put it, Russia is the Third Rome; therefore, "the last bastion of the true Orthodox faith" is by divine design predestined to "to keep the purity of the Orthodox faith and doctrine, which teach the ultimate triumph of divine truth and love."[39]

Similar themes have been voiced at other fundamentalist gatherings throughout Russia in various regional cities and capitals, again and again calling for the restoration of the monarchy with an underlying ideal of an Orthodox social collectivism, introduction of church teachings in schools as well as in law enforcement structures in contravention of the constitution,[40] and robust action (legal or extralegal) against foreign missionaries who represent a threat to the ROC and the Russian national identity. The fundamentalists do not shy away in their pronouncements from virulent xenophobia, a disturbing fact given the polyethnic makeup of the Russian

---

37. Kashin and Muradov, "Yuriya Budanova pokhoronili pod vystrely."
38. Papkova, *Orthodox Church and Russian Politics*, 64.
39. Ioann, *Bitva Za Rossiiu*, 8.
40. See Mitrokhin, *Russkaia Pravoslavnaia Tserkov'*, 328–37.

Federation.[41] On the question concerning the missionaries, their position is not much different from the position of the Patriarch Kirill, who voiced the same concern at a World Council of Churches gathering in 1996 while still a Metropolitan of Smolensk and Kaliningrad:

> We expected that our fellow Christians would support and help us in our own missionary service. In reality, however, they started fighting with our church, like boxers in a ring with pumped-up muscles delivering blows.... For many of Russia today, "non-Orthodox" means those who have come to destroy the spiritual unity of the people and the Orthodox faith—spiritual colonizers who by fair means and foul try to tear the people from their church.[42]

Another organization loosely affiliated with the fundamentalist camp and engaged in a full blown *kulturkampf* against the perceived decay of Russian society, the forces of globalization and the "dictatorship of consumerism"[43] is the *Obschestvennyi Komitet* founded and led by Fr. Aleksandr Shargunov, the charismatic rector of a downtown Moscow parish.

Although Shargunov himself is a cleric, the organization is considered by and large as a lay organization with broad-based support among leading conservative intellectuals and other cultural figures with powerful connections. Moreover, the *Komitet* was able to lobby and receive the blessing of the late Patriarch Aleksii II, but since then it has maintained no formal or structural ties to the Patriarchate and is thought to operate largely independently.

The stated mission of the *Komitet* as articulated in its founding documents is "to combat the spread [in Russia] of moral degeneracy and Satanism."[44] However, some of the activities of the organization have raised more than a few eyebrows since its founding in 1994. Soon thereafter the militant activities of the church were directed at newspapers and fashion journals, the perceived purveyors of both degeneracy (which the *Komitet* meant exclusively as sexual deviancy and homosexuality) and Satanism, broadly defined. The *Komitet* first gained notoriety in the mid-nineties when it organized and successfully carried out the boycott against Martin Scorsese's scandalous adaptation of Greek writer Nikos Kazantzakis's novel *The Last Temptation of Christ* on the Russian national television. In 2003 *Komitet* went even further by wreaking havoc during an art exhibit at Moscow's Sakharov Center, known for taking up various human rights

---

41. Verkhovskii, "Politicheskoe Pravoslavie."
42. Kirill of Smolensk, "Gospel and Culture," 73–74.
43. Golovushkin, "On the Issue of Religious Tolerance in Modern Russia," 103.
44. Papkova, *Orthodox Church and Russian Politics*, 137.

initiatives. The exhibit, provocatively titled *Ostorozhno, Religiia!* (*Caution, Religion!*),[45] featured installations by a group of Russian artists' works mocking religion, not unlike the scandalous installations and photographs titled *Piss Christ* by Andres Serrano. When Sakharov Center tried to have the militants prosecuted, the case was not accepted by the prosecutor because he did not find the necessary *corpus delicti* upon which to build his case. Moreover, in a strange turn of events, the museum itself and the curator of the art exhibit were countersued and were brought up on charges and subsequently found guilty of violating the Article 282 (2b) of the Russian Penal Code for "performing public actions which led to incitement to hatred and humiliating the dignity of a group of people because of their relation to an ethnicity or religion."[46] Two of the three defendants were found guilty and were ordered by the court to pay punitive damages in lieu of imprisonment. Meanwhile, one of the artists fled Russia after receiving death threats by unknown individuals, presumably members of the *Komitet*. Perhaps more than any other initiative, *Komitet*'s vandalism of the exhibit along with the prosecution and conviction of the curators of the exhibit solidified the perception that radical and militant wings within the ROC and its informal networks were increasingly becoming influential in the race to gain the upper hand *vis-à-vis* the more moderate groups.

More troubling still has been the recent *détente* between Orthodox fundamentalists and Eurasianists, followers of Aleksandr Dugin, the erstwhile professor of sociology at the prestigious Moscow State University. Known for his charismatic if brusque style and recognized easily by his unruly beard, Dugin is one of the most influential thinkers/writers to emerge in Russia since the collapse of the Soviet Union. He is also one of the very few thinkers in post-Soviet Russia whose writings and pronouncements have (or seem to have) purchase on the political thinking in the Kremlin. Eurasianism, a political ideology grounded in the idea that Russia—which occupies a vast landmass stretching from Europe to Asia and is the only country to have borders with the European Union, China, and the United States—is neither an exclusively European country nor an exclusively Asian country. It is rather, lest we in our quest for a golden middle think it to be a mix of both, a civilization unto its own, superior to anything either the West or the East is and offers. Moreover, it is a civilization that finds its footing, and more important, its meaning only if it pays heed to Orthodoxy and its religious, historical, cultural, and political claims. These are ideas that have

---

45. For more information on the reaction and the court proceedings following the Komitet's activists' actions, see Sakharov Museum, "'Осторожно, Религия!' Выставка."

46. See Rypkin, *Svastika, Krest, Zvezda*. See also Agadjanian, "Search for Privacy," 169–70.

consequences. They do not appear in a vacuum, and they have an indefinite expiration date. The recent conflict in East Ukraine is, apart from Russia's geo-political calculations, also a result of this kind of cynical essentialization and instrumentalization of Orthodoxy, since many of the leaders of the insurgency in the East are one way or another socialized into the Eurasianist ideals and are known to be closely associated with them.

Whether Patriarch Kirill has blessed these groups is open to both debate and interpretation. At least the Patriarch has refrained from openly endorsing them, given the precarious situation of the Moscow Patriarchate in Ukraine, and appears thus far to be a neutral bystander who is calling for peace and cessation of hostilities. But that the radical wing of the Church is leading the charge is beyond doubt. Whether the trend will continue remains to be seen, however, as these actors are getting disturbingly ever closer to the levers of political power. Which is not to say that in the near future Russia will turn into a full-blown theocratic state, an Orthodox *mullahcracy* of sorts, but that, without a significant countering from within Russia itself, radical elements in the ROC may bring about another period of *smuta*, from which Russia will find it difficult to recover.

In conclusion, I would like to conclude with the words of the late Fr. Georgii Chistiakov, one of the most influential Russian priests in recent memory and a close friend of Fr. Alexander Men, the reformist Russian priest:

> We must keep in mind that there are many spiritually healthy people in the church today as well. . . . Faith is not an ideology and not a call to battle with ubiquitous enemies. Orthodoxy cannot accept racist, anti-Semitic, or xenophobic attitudes, because it is based on the Gospels, which Christ gave to all peoples without exception. . . . Aggressive nationalism is not the ideology of the majority. . . .
>
> Russians must be fed not on propagandistic myths, but on concrete facts. Myths lose their attractiveness once people possess information about what a phenomenon actually represents. It is vital to build an open society in Russia. Once that occurs, the situation in the church will normalize as well.[47]

BIBLIOGRAPHY

Agadjanian, Alexander. "The Search for Privacy and the Return of a Grand Narrative: Religion in Post-Communist Society." *Social Compass* 53.2 (2006) 169–84.

47. Chistiakov, "In Search of the 'Russian Idea,'" 63.

Anderson, John. "Putin and the Russian Orthodox Church: Asymetric Symphonia?" *Journal of International Affairs* 61.1 (2007) 185–201.

Basil, John D. "Problems of State and Church in the Russian Federation: Three Points of View." *Journal of Church and State* 51.2 (2009) 211–35.

Belov, Yuri. *Kommunisty i Russkoe Pravoslavie [Communists and the Russian Orthodoxy]*. Moscow: KPRF, 2011.

Berger, Peter L. "The Desecularization of the World: A Global Overview." In *The Desecularization of the World: Resurgent Religion and World Politics*, edited by Peter L. Berger, 1–18. Grand Rapids: Eerdmans, 1999.

———. *The Many Altars of Modernity: Towards a Paradigm for Religion in a Pluralist Age*. Boston: de Gruyter, 2014.

Bodin, Per-Arne. "The Holy Fool as a TV Hero: About Pavel Lungin's film The Island and the Problem of Authenticity." *Journal of Aesthetics & Culture* 3 (2011) 1–9.

Chistiakov, Georgii. "In Search of the 'Russian Idea': A View from Inside the Russian Orthodox Church." In *Religion and Identity in Modern Russia: The Revival of Orthodoxy and Islam*, edited by Juliet Johnson et al., 53–64. Burlington, VT: Ashgate, 2005.

Froese, Paul. *The Plot to Kill God: Findings from the Soviet Experiment in Secularization*. Berkeley: University of California Press, 2008.

Golovushkin, Dmitry. "On the Issue of Religious Tolerance in Modern Russia: National Identity and Religion." *Journal for the Study of Religions and Ideologies* 7 (2004) 101–10.

Gutterman, Steve. "Chechen Convicted of Killing Russian Colonel." *Reuters*, April 30, 2013. https://www.reuters.com/article/us-russia-chechnya-killing/chechen-convicted-of-killing-russian-colonel-idUSBRE93T0EM20130430.

Ioann. *Bitva Za Rossiiu: Pravoslavie i Sovremennost' [The Battle for Russia: Orthodoxy and Modern Times]*. Saratov: Soyuz Pravoslavnykh Bratstv Sankt-Peterburga, 1993.

Karpov, Vyacheslav. "Desecularization: A Conceptual Framework." *Journal of Church & State* 52 (2010) 232–70.

———. "The Social Dynamics of Russia's Desecularization: A Comparative and Theoretical Perspective." *Religion, State & Society* 41 (2013) 254–83.

Kashin, Oleg, and Musa Muradov. "Yuriya Budanova pokhoronili pod vystrely." *Kommersant*, June 14, 2011. https://www.kommersant.ru/doc/1659554.

Kirill of Smolensk. "Gospel and Culture." In *Proselytism and Orthodoxy in Russia: The New War for Souls*, edited by John Witte Jr. and Michael Bordeaux, 66–76. Maryknoll, NY: Orbis, 1999.

Kostiuk, Konstantin. "Pravoslavnyi Fundamentalizm [Orthodox Fundamentalism]." *Polis* 5 (2000) 133–54.

Marsh, Christopher. *Religion and the State in Russia and China: Suppression, Survival, and Revival*. New York: Continuum, 2011.

Mitrokhin, Nikolai. *Russkaya Pravoslavnaia Tserkov': Sovremennoe sostoianie i aktual'nye problem [The Russian Orthodox Church: Its Contemporary State and Actual Problems]*. Moscow: Novoe Literaturnoe Obozrenie, 2006.

Papkova, Irina. *The Orthodox Church and Russian Politics*. New York: Oxford University Press, 2011.

Payne, Daniel. "Spiritual Security, the Russian Orthodox Church, and the Russian Foreign Ministry: Collaboration or Cooptation?" *Journal of Church and State* 52 (2010) 712–27.

Rock, Stella. "Fraternal Strife: Nationalist Fundamentalists in the Contemporary Russian Orthodox Brotherhood Movement." In *Orthodox Christianity and Contemporary Europe: Selected Papers of the International Conference Held at the University of Leeds, England, June 2001*, edited by Jonathan Sutton and William Peter van den Bercken, 319–42. Eastern Christian Studies 3. Leuven: Peeters, 2003.

Rypkin, M. *Svastika, Krest, Zvezda: Proizvidenia iskusstva v epokhu upravliaemoi demokratii* [Swastika, Cross, Star: Works of Art in the Age of Managed Democracy]. Moscow: Logos, 2006.

Sakharov Museum. "'Осторожно, Религия!' Выставка." 2012. Online. https://web.archive.org/web/20120504090959/www.sakharov-center.ru/museum/exhibitionhall/religion_notabene.

Schroeder, Rachel L., and Vyacheslav Karpov. "The Crimes and Punishments of the 'Enemies of the Church' and the Nature of Russia's Desecularizing Regime." *Religion, State & Society* 41.3 (2013) 284–311.

Sergeichik, Yelena. "Sovremennoe Pravoslavie i intelligentsia [Contemporary Orthodoxy and the Intelligentsia]." In *Orthodox Christianity and Contemporary Europe: Selected Papers of the International Conference Held at the University of Leeds, England, June 2001*, edited by Jonathan Sutton and William Peter van den Bercken, 343–53. Eastern Christian Studies 3. Leuven: Peeters, 2003.

Solovyov, Vladimir. *Chtenia o bogochlovechestve* [Readings About God-Manhood]. Vol. 2. Moscow: Pravda, 1989.

"Svyashchennik Dmitry Dudko: Ya nizko klanyayus' pered Stalinom [Priest Dmitry Dudko: I Bow Before Stalin]." *Svobodnaia Pressa*, April 16, 2012. http://svpressa.ru/society/article/54473.

Verkhovsky, Aleksandr. "Politicheskoe Pravoslavie v Rossiiskoi publichnoi politike: Pod'iom antisekuliarnogo natsionalisma [Political Orthodoxy in the Russian Public Politics: The Rise of Antisecularist Nationalism]." *SOVA Center*, May 21, 2005. http://www.sova-center.ru/religion/publications/2005/05/d4678.

7

From Losers to Lovers

How the "It" Films Take Us to Church[1]

LEIGH HICKMAN

In 1990, Tim Curry scared audiences in a TV miniseries adaptation of Stephen King's 1986 horror opus, *It*.[2] While Curry's performance as Pennywise, the Dancing Clown, has cultural staying power, the adaptation as a whole hasn't aged well with its poor special effects and a dismal second act. So, in 2017, audiences finally saw a full-length theatrical release of *It*. This version, directed by Andy Muschietti, updates the original nineteen-fifties setting of the book to the nineteen-eighties, cashing in on the current craze for eighties nostalgia stirred up by the success of *Stranger Things*. With literally gallons of blood, New Kids on the Block references, and an incredibly talented cast of child actors, *It* became the highest grossing horror film in history. When one looks at the nostalgic appeal and sheer talent in front of and behind the camera, it's easy to conclude that the film's success stems from arriving at the perfect end-moment in the cultural zeitgeist. But is there more to *It* than meets the eye? *It* is the story of seven friends battling a demon who transforms into

---

1. Originally published in two parts by *Mockingbird* (2019). My thanks to the editors of *Mockingbird* for allowing this reprint.
2. King, *It*.

and feeds on their worst fears. It is a coming-of-age story about what people do with their vulnerability and shame. More than a summer popcorn flick, *It*'s cultural resonance remains because the film shows the power of a community whose bond is cruciform. *It: Chapter 1* takes its audience to church, and this church is a place where children lead.[3] *It: Chapter 2* gives us a fuller picture of the church graciously triumphant over evil.[4]

FROM LOSERS TO LOVERS: HOW *IT: CHAPTER 1* TAKES US TO CHURCH

The first sign that the child heroes of *It* model Christ's church is the title they give themselves in relationship to one another: the Losers Club. Sadistically bullied by a gang of boys led by Henry Bowers (Nicholas Hamilton), the children transform the denigrating label "loser" into the moniker of their distinctive community. Instead of denying or running from this abusive title, they embrace this identity as their own, and thus the term "loser" loses its harmful power over them. In fact, this choice to embrace curses and to transmute them into blessings is at the heart of how the kids eventually overpower Pennywise (Bill Skarsgård). The Losers win through being willing to lose their own lives in order to rescue others. The Losers Club follows in the footsteps of the early Christians who chose the cross as the symbol for their faith. Crucifixion was among the most shameful ways to lose one's life. It was a manner of death reserved for the worst criminals. In other words, the early Christians formed the first Losers Club. They wore the cross in honor of their Savior, whom they believed won over sin and death by willingly losing his life on the cross. The first sign that the protagonists of *It* will win over the darkness is the fact that they embrace the group identity of Losers.

"They all float down here. You'll float, too." This declarative statement is the tagline for the film. The line self-consciously breaks the fourth wall. Not only is Pennywise threatening children in Derry, Maine, but he's also threatening the film's audience and implicating them in the horror. Almost every time he speaks in the film, Pennywise threatens the children with floating rather than dying. His aim is not merely to kill people. Pennywise wants to keep them as floating trophies of his potency. When considering the themes of friendship and community in the story, it becomes clear why Pennywise is bent on making his victims float in his underground kingdom of death. In order to float, someone must be deprived of a firm foundation.

3. Muschietti, *It*.
4. Muschietti, *It: Chapter 2*.

He must be buoyed up, unanchored to anything stable. Lack of stability and of rooted foundation are the optimal environmental factors to grow evil in *It*. Almost every time a character is attacked in *It*, he is first drawn away from his friends. Beverly Marsh (Sophia Lillis) is right when she warns the boys, "This is what it wants. It wants to divide us. We were all together when we hurt it. That's why we're still alive." Pennywise is only as powerful as his victims are isolated and autonomous. In every advertisement for the film, the viewers are warned that, without a firm foundation, they are subject to becoming Pennywise's floating victims, too. Countering the popular veneration of the rugged individual in American culture, *It* warns that individuals actually lose what makes them distinctively strong outside of community. Without a united community, it's "time to float."

In *It*, friendships aren't merely pleasantries of childhood. Intimate community and friendships are essential to survival. This theme is incarnated in the actions of the characters throughout the film. For example, when Eddie Kaspbrack (Jack Dylan Grazer) is separated from his friends in an abandoned, condemned house, Eddie falls through the decaying floor and breaks his arm. He is unconscious for a while on the floor and helpless while Pennywise plays a cat-and-mouse game with him, tauntingly snapping and snarling at his arm to provoke greater fear in the child. Right before he is consumed, his friends find and rescue Eddie. As Pennywise approaches, Richie Tozier (Finn Wolfhard) grabs Eddie's face and directs his eyes away from the clown to his own face. Pennywise's power is determined by how much his victim fears him. The more fear provoked, the more tasty the victim is to the victimizer, so Richie's strategy to help Eddie in this moment of fear is significant. In redirecting Eddie's focus, Richie destroys the power of Eddie's enemy. By privileging relationship and community over the fear of being consumed, Eddie is rescued by his new focus. It is precisely the expulsive power of something stronger than Eddie's worst fear that saves him: the fact that, even in his darkest, broken moment, Eddie's friend is there to protect and love him.

When Pennywise slinks away, against Eddie's loud protestations, Richie resets Eddie's broken bone and helps his friend out of the house. This painful and comedic moment indicates a major theme about the salvation achieved in *It*. Richie doesn't obey Eddie's command not to touch him or reset his arm. Richie resets it anyway, against the will of Eddie. In *It*, the victim's will to be saved or healed prior to salvation is not consulted. In *It*, people are saved in spite of their lack of willingness or ability to choose to be saved. Modeling the church, the Losers pursue people who don't ask to be rescued.

Among a few iconic images from *It*, few are as memorable as Eddie's arm cast. After surviving his attack, Eddie goes to the pharmacy to pick up more of his prescriptions, his arm in an unsigned cast. Noticing him, the pharmacist's bully daughter feigns sympathy and offers to sign his cast. The next time the cast is shown, the viewer sees what she wrote over his brokenness: "Loser." Yet, this label is changed by Eddie who writes over the black "S" a vivid red "V." His broken arm now bears the title "Lover." This word change from "Loser" to "Lover" is the visual thesis for *It*. The story is about what people do with their brokenness and shame. The "It" of the film's title is ambiguous on purpose because *It* focuses on the labels people are given by others or give themselves and what they do with those given identities and their brokenness. More than a play on words, *It* is about broken losers who become broken, healing lovers equipped to face their own and others' monsters. Becoming a lover of others is the only way to survive in the context of the story.

In order to savor this identity transformation, the antagonist working against the heroes needs to be identified. The antagonist is as hard to name concretely as the pronoun "it" is. The first villain in the story isn't the demonic clown. The villain is Derry, Maine, itself. In the book and film, the environment around characters in *It* is absolutely necessary for the horrors of the story to happen. All seven children who comprise the Losers Club have no protection or covering from any parent or authority figure. They are all very much orphans even if they have parents. More disturbing than getting eaten alive by Pennywise, when Georgie (Jackson Robert Scott) is pulled into the sewer at the beginning of the film, an elderly lady and her cat are watching the murder happen. The woman looks away while Georgie cries for help, and the camera focuses on the house cat, who is the only one looking at the child. In another scene, Beverly's abusive father cannot see the blood covering his daughter's entire bathroom. Only the children can see the mess and clean the carnage up. Derry is a town where adults are blind to the evil happening around them. It is either the passivity toward evil or the aggressive participation in evil that serves as the welcome mat to usher in a demon like Pennywise. Apathy and active violence are likewise damned in *It*. Ironically, each child's unique experience with a perverse or absent parent determines what each child fears most. The absence of loving parents is part of the horror in *It*. Each manifestation of Pennywise is a reflection of each child's unique fear and how the child tries to cope with his or her personal shame.

Bill Denbrough's worst fear manifests in visions of his murdered brother Georgie. Anytime he seeks to torment Bill (Jaeden Martell), Pennywise shows him his brother and mimics his voice pleading to come home, mourning the fact that Bill didn't protect him. Bill's fear takes the form of the event of which he is most ashamed. Tellingly, these ghostly visitations actually work to destroy Pennywise. The clown's name significantly denotes his lack of wisdom. He has only a penny's worth of insight. Like C. S. Lewis's White Witch, Pennywise's knowledge of his victim's weakness is ultimately his downfall because he does not count on Bill or the others using the manifestations of their fear and shame as galvanizing weapons against him, again taking curses and changing them into blessings. Inspiring the rest of the Losers to confront Pennywise in his haunted house, Bill says, "I go home, and all I see is that Georgie isn't there. His clothes, his toys, his stupid stuffed animals, but he isn't. So walking into this house, for me, is easier than walking into my own." Pennywise doesn't understand the potency of love that makes a loved one's absence more tormenting than their faux presence. Every time he shows Bill his brother, Pennywise fails to understand that Bill's love for Georgie prompts him to confront evil rather than run from it.

Mike Hanlon (Chosen Jacobs) shares a similar fear and shame. Mike's parents burned to death in a house fire, screaming for their son to help them. Like Clarice Starling in *Silence of the Lambs*, he is haunted by his failure to save victims he should have saved. Ironically, Mike works in a slaughterhouse where he resists killing sheep. Like Clarice, he's still haunted by "that awful screaming of the lambs." So Pennywise manifests to Mike in the screams of his burning parents, his greatest shame and also the fount of his empathy for other people. Again, Pennywise doesn't know that showing Mike his fear inadvertently motivates him to save others.

To torment Ben Hanscom (Jeremy Ray Taylor), Pennywise becomes a headless mummy that attacks him in Derry's public library. Ben is the "new kid on the block" in Derry. Overweight and a lover of knowledge and books, Ben is labeled a nerd. The librarian warns Ben that boys his age should be more athletically outgoing instead of poring over books. Ben's intellectual curiosity makes him less of a boy in the eyes of adults. He instantly forms affection for Beverly when she is the only person who signs his yearbook. Beverly and Ben share interest in the same boy band—and something more personal. They know what it's like to be sexually objectified. Because of his weight, Ben is nicknamed "Tits" by Henry Bowers's gang. In one of the most horrific scenes in the film, Henry carves an H in Ben's exposed stomach and threatens to mutilate his chest. Then, a couple of adults drive by the boys who are circling Ben. They look right at the attack and do nothing. It is as if Ben and his attackers are invisible to adults. Hence, it makes sense that Ben's fear and shame would manifest as a headless mummy. He already feels invisible to adults. The headless mummy also suggests that Ben fears losing his intellectual capacity. His intellect and size are used as weapons to shame him, but they are also some of his greatest strengths. His sexual objectification stirs his empathy for Beverly. His intellectual curiosity helps him understand Derry's long history of apathy toward evil.

Stanley Uris's fear and shame are manifested as a distorted woman with huge teeth coming out of a portrait in his father's office. His father is the local rabbi. During their first conversation in the film, the boys of the Losers Club discuss Stanley's upcoming bar mitzvah. Stanley (Wyatt Oleff) says that, after this ceremony, he will "become a man." The theme of what constitutes real maturity and masculinity is a major focus of the story. The audience then sees Stanley in his synagogue, struggling to read from the Torah as he practices for his coming-of-age moment. Standing over him in the shot, his father reprimands him, "You're not studying, Stanley. How's it going to look? The rabbi's son can't finish his own Torah reading." It is right after his father dismisses him with disgust that Stanley has his first visit from Pennywise as a distorted woman who jumps out at him from a portrait. Stanley's fear and shame revolve around appearance. He sees the bar mitzvah as his masculine initiation, and his father is concerned about how his son will "look" to others. So it is fitting that Stanley's fear would manifest as a woman who transgresses the limit of her frame. Stanley fears not looking like a man to others, and he's ashamed that he doesn't stay inside the expectations of his father. Tellingly, when Stanley is later attacked by Pennywise, the distorted woman jumps out at him and starts to eat his face. His identity is literally under attack. The Losers rescue both their friend's life and his identity. Still, the attack on Stanley reveals the real demonic motive: to efface and subsume identity.

Stanley's initial response toward evil is comically immature. When Bill and Richie find a missing girl's shoe in the sewer, Eddie and Stanley refuse to try to find her. Stanley complains, "It's summer. We're supposed to be having fun. This isn't fun. This is scary and disgusting." Throughout *It*, the children use their lack of physical maturity as their primary excuse for not facing the evil in Derry. As the story progresses, this excuse becomes a call to action. Adults in Derry can't see and don't act to protect what only their children can see and protect. Part of the appeal of the story is the fact that children are able to confront and conquer darkness not in spite of their weaker status as children but because of their weakness. In *It*, being a child is an advantage. Being an adult is dangerous.

Eddie's fear and shame are ironic since he is, apparently, the most protected child of the Losers. Pennywise manifests to Eddie as a decaying leper who pursues him. Eddie's mother is one of Stephen King's monster-parents, perversions of what loving parents are to their children. She is constantly reminding Eddie of how frail and sickly he is. Eddie's fears and shame are very much bequeathed to him by his mother, who teaches him to fear both germs and relationships with others. Her overprotectiveness is tantamount to psychological child abuse that stunts Eddie's maturation. Eddie is aware of this abuse because his shame looks like a leper, a person who loses pieces of themselves without the ability to feel. Like the leper, Eddie begins the story unable to feel appropriately the reality around him. Eddie rejects looking for missing children, saying, "What if I don't want to find them? I don't want to go missing either." He begins the story concerned only with self-preservation because that is what he's been trained to value by his mother. The story says that children need to be protected, but over-protecting children is potentially just as abusive as neglecting them.

Beverly Marsh, the only girl in the group of heroes, is sexually abused by her father. Her father is particularly attracted to his daughter's long red hair. Blaming herself for her abuse, Beverly cuts her hair off and tries to look more like a boy to protect herself against her father's attention. Secretly expressing his affection for Beverly, Ben writes Beverly a haiku: "Your hair is winter fire / January embers / My heart burns there, too." Tellingly, while her father fetishizes his daughter's hair, Ben's poem is an example of pure and age-appropriate love. It is right before she is first attacked by Pennywise that Beverly reads and visibly enjoys Ben's love poem. She holds the postcard close and smiles before Pennywise attacks her with her own hair as the form of entrapment. Her hair forms bonds on her hands and face as it shoots out of the sink. She is then sprayed with a huge fountain of blood that floods over her and her bathroom. Beverly's shame and fear center around female sexual menstruation and development. She fears sexual maturity because she only becomes more alluring to her father as she gets older. Still, her enslaving hair and maturity are not merely curses. Ben's pure attraction for Beverly and his childlike attraction to her hair shows that she can experience what it's like to be appropriately cherished instead of objectified.

Richie Tozier's fear and shame is the icon of *It*. Richie's number one fear is clowns, the form Pennywise takes most often. Ironically, Richie is the last child to see a manifestation of Pennywise. Richie has poor eyesight and wears thick glasses throughout the story. His lack of physical eyesight reflects his lack of spiritual sight. In key moments in the film, as in the scene where the boys help clean Beverly's blood-soaked bathroom, the rest of the Losers leave Richie outside. They don't trust his vision or his ability to control his mouth. "Can only virgins see this stuff?" Richie asks when the rest of the children are discussing Pennywise. Richie, like the other kids in Derry, has no positive adult role model. How he articulates his manhood is almost exclusively through sexual innuendo and boasting about his supposed sexual experience. While Stanley says his bar mitzvah will make him a man,

Richie quips, "I can think of funner ways to become a man." The statement is grammatically and spiritually wrong. Like boys who haven't seen examples of mature older men, Richie's view on masculinity is extremely shallow and cynical. On some level, Richie must be aware of his lack of maturity and vulnerability because he talks incessantly in an effort to mask his weakness. He even calls his ability to over-talk anyone "a gift." Of all the kids, Richie drops the most F-bombs in *It*. His "strong language" shows his weakness as he hides his insecurities behind profanity. Richie fears clowns because clownishness is how he tries to mask his shame.

The first time he attacks Richie, Pennywise exploits his poor vision. Entering the haunted house, Richie sees a "missing" poster with his image on it. Looking at himself in horror, Richie starts listing concrete details in his panic: "It . . . It says I'm missing. Police Department, City of Derry. That's my shirt. That's my hair. That's my face." Richie immediately believes the deception. His emphasis on the specific details in the image is his evidence justifying his perception. Bill counters Richie's proof, telling him, "You're not missing, Richie. It's playing tricks on you." In light of all the proofs he's cited, Richie chooses to believe his friend over the paper in his hands.

The next time he is confronted by Pennywise, Richie is alone, drawn away from his friends and isolated behind a locked door. He sees a coffin surrounded by clown mannequins. When he sees himself now, Richie sees himself as another mannequin, another clown, in the coffin. Over his body is the same missing poster with the word "Found" written over it. This play on words is explicitly demonic in nature, a perversion of the biblical idea of a lost soul's being found. Richie slams the coffin lid shut in response to his vision. Pennywise springs out of the box in clown form and runs straight at Richie. In response, Richie opens the once-locked door and shuts it in Pennywise's face. More than just the proverbial jump scare, Richie's salvation scene shows his budding maturity. Still believing Bill's voice, Richie rejects the lie that he's already a victim. He closes the door twice on Pennywise. For the first time, Richie sees rightly by rejecting what he sees and choosing to believe what he can't see: that he's alive, that he's able to resist the lie of the Enemy.

The full arc of Richie's maturation comes in the final confrontation when he is the first of the Losers to attack Pennywise. Ironically, right before Richie attacks, he uses his language to lull Pennywise into a state of false confidence in his cowardice: "I told you, Bill. I don't want to die. It's your fault. You punched me in the face. You made me walk through s****y water. You brought me to a f*****g crackhead house. And now . . . I'm gonna have to kill this f*****g clown." Richie is not a threat to Pennywise as long as he's cynical and focused on self-preservation. The clown doesn't move to attack Richie because this litany of profanity-laced complaints is exactly what one can expect from Richie, the clown. Yet, in the moment that Richie pummels Pennywise, his verb tense changes from the past to the present tense. Richie may have been a selfish clown, but he isn't one now when he acts to save his friend. With new vision, Richie Tozier is now a man.

In the second act of the film, two fathers die. Henry Bowers murders his father and Beverly accidently kills her father in self-defense when he tries to rape her. This patricide is the ugly end of the bad parenting on display. However, these deaths mark different identity embarkations in Henry and Beverly. Henry becomes Pennywise incarnate while Beverly becomes a fairytale heroine. Even as Beverly overcomes her paternal monster, Pennywise instantly attacks and kidnaps her. Angered that Beverly refuses to fear and empower him, Pennywise entrances Beverly and causes her to lose all control of her body as she begins to float with the rest of the victims. Bill finds her and tries to pull her back to earth, but he cannot reach her by himself. Only when the Losers form a human ladder are they able to reach Beverly and anchor her to the ground. In *It*, community literally saves the lost. Trying to save a floating victim autonomously never works. Beverly, like Eddie, cannot ask to be rescued or even use her will to save herself. Her friends become a literal cord of lovingkindness to bind and drag Beverly away from death. Ben, in classic fairytale fashion, brings Beverly out of her sleep of death by giving her a kiss of pure love. Perhaps one of the most appealing things about this horror film is that, for all the perversions of love Pennywise and the adults of Derry manifest, the story is profoundly uncynical about the power of childlike empathy and unselfish love. Horrors happen in fairy tales, and, in the end, *It* is a fairytale. It's a reimagining of the story of the church.

The film opens with music. A child sings a nursery rhyme about "the bells of Saint Clarence." The first invocation of children coincides with the first reference to a church. The next time a church is literally referenced in *It* is right before Eddie is first attacked by Pennywise. Eddie walks slowly by the All Saints Anglican Church as the congregants sing, "Nobody knows the troubles I've seen. Nobody knows my sorrow." The juxtaposition of the spiritual blindness of Derry with the lyrics of the Negro spiritual highlights two different perceptions. Unlike Derry, the church is a place of real seeing, a place where the horrors of the world are acknowledged. The church of Losers pushes back darkness that they correctly see and know.

Interestingly, the Losers Club comes into being in the film through baptism. In a rare moment of innocent joy, all seven children agree to meet at the quarry to swim. To enter the water, they must jump off of a literal cliff. The boys look down nervously, unsure if they will jump. They are all stripped down to their underwear. Running up behind them in her bra and shorts, Beverly fearlessly jumps off the cliff, and the boys, inspired by her bravery, take the plunge after her. After this communal leap of faith, the cinematography revels in childhood nostalgia. The kids simply play, splashing and lifting one another onto their shoulders in the water. The fact that all characters in this scene are in their underwear sharply contrasts the innocence of the children with the sexual perversion perpetrated by adults. The kids have the almost edenic experience of being naked and knowing no shame. The scene is made especially tender by considering Beverly's sexual abuse by her father. With these boys, Beverly experiences simple love that doesn't objectify her. Theirs is a community forged in their willingness to be courageous together, and their bond is sealed in a summer water baptism. The Losers Club is a picture of the church united.

The midway point between the first and second acts of the film is denoted by another explicit reference to the church. Almost destroyed by Pennywise the first time they go into his lair, the Losers are too frightened to continue their search for the lost kids of Derry. Beverly tries to galvanize the boys, saying, "We all know no one else is going to do anything. We can't pretend it's gonna go away. I wanna run toward something. Not away." In one line, Beverly indicates the telos or ultimate direction for the Losers. Life isn't just dark, scary, and covered by shame. There's something to run toward because there's a real purpose for human life. There's something people are meant to be and do in community with one another. Outside of this community, there is only nihilism, denial, and despair. This certain nihilism is voiced by Richie in his rejection of Beverly's appeal: "I'm just saying let's face facts. Real world. Georgie is dead. Stop trying to get us killed, too." One of the signs of Richie's lack of knowledge is ironically his stress on facts and what appears real. Before his worldview changes, Richie believes the real world is only the world he sees, the world where children are taken and killed. There's no reason for courage in this "real world," where missing posters are always correct. The lost can't be found, so there's no point in seeking them. Right after this statement, Bill punches Richie in the face, and the church of Losers breaks apart.

The scene that follows this communal disunity is a musical montage showing each of the Losers by themselves. The lyrics sung over the scene are a prayer. The song "Dear God" by XTC is about the existential crisis of faith.[5] Facing the fact of human suffering and evil, if people are created in God's image, God must be cruel or non-existent. This song plays over the dissolution of the Losers, the loss of their church because they no longer believe there's a purpose for their community. It is while the Losers are divided

---

5. XTC, "Dear God."

that Pennywise is empowered to kill people and kidnap Beverly. Their love for Beverly ignites the fuel that unifies the Losers again. Significantly, when the Losers come back together, they pedal their bikes past All Saints Anglican Church as they enter their final confrontation with Pennywise. They are the church again, united in purpose and empowered to push back darkness.

Pennywise's final threat to the Losers reveals the source of his power and their power over him. Pennywise says, "I'll feast on your flesh as I feed on your fear." In a single sentence Pennywise says that "flesh" and "fear" are inextricably tied. Pennywise is paraphrasing the Apostle Paul's warning in Romans 8:6: "To set the mind on the flesh is death, but to set the mind on the Spirit is life and peace." Peace is the ultimate antithesis to Pennywise, who lusts after fear and flesh. Those people who live according to their flesh are prime prey for Pennywise. Yet, when the Losers refuse the fleshly desire to survive autonomously, they are the only people able not only to survive but also to literally beat Derry's demon. The victimizer becomes the Losers' victim as they become real lovers, people united by a communal love greater than the love of self. In the end, it is Pennywise who cowers in fear and falls back into darkness. He has no power without fear, and he can't inspire fear in people who don't live in the flesh.

The last scene of the film again ties the Losers to the Church. They make an oath to come together and confront Pennywise if he ever returns. To make this oath, each of the children cuts his or her hands with the same knife. Forming a circle and holding bleeding hands, their community is bound together by blood. This blood, the sign of their individual lives bleeding into one another, is their unity. The scene images the Eucharist with the Losers' circle as the table. The Losers' table, like the Eucharist, is a place to remember, a place of intimate, communal commitment. Christians, the other Losers Club, are likewise sealed together by blood, but, unlike the kids in King's story, it isn't their own blood which unites them. The church is a bunch of losers who aren't afraid to lose, and in that grace-empowered fearlessness they overcome. They are losers who become lovers, and that's *It* . . . or at least it was until September 6, 2019, when the final chapter of *It* hit theaters.

A NOT SO "GOD-FORSAKEN TOWN": *IT: CHAPTER 2*

The first line of voiceover in *It: Chapter 2* starts with the word "Memory." Like an invocation of the muse in a Homeric epic, the film announces its theme at the beginning. In their underground clubhouse, the Losers Club have the movie poster for *The Lost Boys*, the 1987 teen horror classic about forever-young vampires. Yet, the child heroes of *It* (2017) aren't the lost boys who never grow up, and Derry, Maine, isn't Neverland. While childhood is usually associated with innocence, play, and a lack of responsibility, *It: Chapter 2* is about adults forced to reckon with the violation of their innocence as children and the horrific responsibility they swore to bear. The film is set twenty-seven years after the Losers almost fatally wounded Pennywise. Each of the Losers, for the most part affluent adults, is called back to Derry by Mike Hanlon (Isaiah Mustafa), the only character who chose to remain in his cursed hometown. As they are summoned home, each of the characters experiences the reappearance and pain of their shared scars. The Losers had cut their hands and made a blood oath to return to Derry if Pennywise ever came back. Scars are wounds that haven't completely healed. The shared scar of the Losers is the visual thesis for *It: Chapter 2*. How do people heal from the memories that cut them most deeply? Can people truly mature if they try to avoid the memories of which they are most ashamed? It's empowering to recall times of personal heroism, victory over destructive behaviors, and intimacy with friends. But *It* won't let its characters or its audience off without confronting their old scars. Since, as I have shown above, the Losers Club is a story of the church reimagined in a horror film, scars aren't just unhealed wounds. Scars are sacred for Christians and Losers alike. They are the sacramental doorways through which people experience grace and give grace to others.

As in *It: Chapter 1*, the physical and social environment around the characters is an essential component of the horror. Derry and Pennywise are equally villainous. Mike refers to Derry as a "God-forsaken town." It's a statement that hangs like a question mark over the entire story as the Losers literally reach the heart of what's wrong in Derry. The first scene of the film sets the adult tone for what follows: It's a violent hate crime. In the midst of a carnival, a young gay couple is brutally attacked by bullies. One of the victims, Adrian Mellon (Xavier Dolan), is thrown off a bridge into the river. As he tries to swim and cries for help, he vaguely sees Pennywise on the embankment in the posture of a potential rescuer. His boyfriend watches in terror as Adrian is swept up by Pennywise, who takes a huge, gory bite out of his side. The fact that Pennywise at first appears to be saving Adrian only to murder him begins a pattern in the film of expectation reversal.

What makes Pennywise seem more mature in his methods than in the first film is the way in which he uses his victims' empathy and expectations against them as a trap. Before he is attacked, Adrian kindly gives a stuffed animal he wins in a carnival game to a small girl named Victoria (Ryan Kiera Armstrong), who has a birthmark on her face. This stuffed animal connects Pennywise's first victim to his second. The girl, like Adrian, is bullied for being different in Derry. Bullying is a major motif in the film, and Pennywise is the monstrous amalgamation of the culture of bullying in Derry. Victoria is bored watching a local baseball game with her mother. Pennywise entices her to come to him in the darkness by manifesting as a lightning bug. Entranced by its beauty, she follows the light into the darkness, where she meets Pennywise. When the clown speaks to her, she rightly rejects his overtures of friendship, saying that her real friends don't talk to her in the dark. Pennywise then begins to cry and explains to Victoria that he's sad because no one wants to play with him because of his scary face. The girl, bullied for the same reason, empathizes with Pennywise. In this scene, Pennywise's means of baiting his victim is reminiscent of the tactic used by Ted Bundy, who often lured his victims by wearing an arm cast and faking an injury. In *It: Chapter 1*, empathy was a weapon the Losers used against Pennywise. It was their desire to protect other kids that inspired their battle with him. In *It: Chapter 2*, Pennywise successfully weaponizes his victims' empathy against them. Even more insidious, Pennywise entices Victoria by offering to remove her birthmark. He says he can remove the mark causing her shame in a single "poof." Victoria, like the Losers, wants to get rid of a scar causing shame. Pennywise removes Victoria's mark by eating her whole face. The cost of removing her scar is the removal of her identity. In one cruel scene, the film says that the alluring promise of a quick fix to human scars is fool's gold. People become whole through their marks of suffering, not through attempting to live like they've never been marked by suffering. The lightning bug's light that attracts Victoria to her death is a false light. The demonic Pennywise, like Lucifer, masquerades as an angel of light. This intentional juxtaposition of false and real light, of true empathy against its perversion, is at the narrative heart of the film. *It: Chapter 2* is about the discerning of spirits, and its protagonists and audience are warned that they must learn to discern light from darkness.

The film's narrative structure reflects this intentional emphasis on discernment and the significance of scars. After the Losers return to Derry, they struggle to remember the summer twenty-seven years earlier that defined them as a group. They eventually recall wounding Pennywise and making the oath to return and defeat him, but their memory is selective. People have a tendency to edit out moments of special shame or vulnerability. As Mike says, "We are what we wish we could forget." In order to defeat Pennywise, the Losers must remember the sources of their deepest personal wounds. Tellingly, each wound was opened during the brief span of time the Losers disbanded in *It: Chapter 1*, when they chose self-preservation and autonomy over friendship and empathy. The audience coming to see the film is, in its own way, just as shocked as the Losers that they don't have the full story they assume *Chapter 1* gave them. With this narrative strategy, the filmmakers again break the fourth wall and implicate the audience in the characters' assumptions that they understand what happened in the previous film. Mike tells the Losers they must do what, stereotypically, no characters should do in a horror film: Split up. Each character must leave the group and revisit the places they were when they were alone and separated from the group in *Chapter 1*. Each individual must collect a token from that time of loneliness and exposure. Admittedly, *It: Chapter 2* is almost three hours in runtime because of this focus on how one brief moment of separation affected seven characters. Yet the sometimes tedious pacing serves a point: Facing shame and scars is often frustrating, and healing takes time.

The collected tokens are emblematic of each character's scar, and they are to be used in a ritual to conquer Pennywise, their very personal demon. While each of these remembered events is painful, the token that each character retrieves is a physical talisman of their irrevocable membership in the Losers Club. Ultimately, each Loser learns that their personal struggles and shame have no power to excommunicate them from their church of losers. Their group and individual identity is established and safeguarded in grace. The Losers in *It: Chapter 2* incarnate the identity-security guaranteed by Jesus in John 10:27–29: "My sheep hear my voice, and I know them, and they follow me. I give them eternal life, and they will never perish, and no one will snatch them out of my hand. My Father, who has given them to me, is greater than all, and no one is able to snatch them out of the Father's hand" (ESV). The fact that each character remembers what happened to them when they tried to leave the Losers Club makes this parallel more explicit. Even when they try to break apart and experience disunity, they don't have the power to remove themselves from the group because they are each bound together by some force stronger than their will to stay. The blood that binds the Losers, a shadow of the blood that binds the church, keeps those whom it covers. If *Chapter 1* pictured the church as a community of losers who become lovers able to see and push back spiritual darkness, then *It: Chapter 2* pictures the security of those inside that grace-empowered community. No matter what they've feared, suffered, or believed wrongly about their identity, the Losers Club is ultimately safe because the Losers Club is a picture of the church, and the church, protected by Christ, is eternally safe.

Stanley Uris's token is a shower cap. The Losers wore shower caps as they built their underground clubhouse. While the other kids are playing, Stanley (Wyatt Oleff) is pensive and asks aloud if they will all still be friends once they grow up. Stanley, who was excited about his upcoming bar mitzvah and "becoming a man," is also the child and adult who is most afraid of dying in the story. He looks forward to maturing and dreads it as well because maturing eventually means facing human mortality. Significantly, when the Losers are called back to Derry, adult Stanley (Andy Bean) is too frightened to face the demon of the past and kills himself in his bathtub. By far one of the weakest narrative choices in *Chapter 2* is to make Stanley's suicide an act of heroism and self-sacrifice. One of the strengths of King's novel is its honesty about the consequences of losing faith and letting despair win. Unfortunately, the film doesn't have the guts to be as dark as the novel when it comes to Stanley.

The shower cap token that the rest of the Losers collect for him foreshadows where Stanley will die. But the shower cap also represents where Stanley lived and to which church he actually belonged. During his bar mitzvah, which occurs while the Losers are disbanded in *Chapter 1*, Stanley discusses the idea of change and transformation. He then formally rejects his Jewish faith in front of his rabbi father and the rest of the congregation. He identifies himself as a Loser over a Jew because that is his legitimate community of faith. The shower cap token is a sign of Stanley's exchange of the Jewish yamaka for a new head covering. Stanley doesn't reject faith; he converts to a new faith. In this conversion, he distances himself from his biological family and chooses to be part of a new family.

Beverly Marsh (Jessica Chastain) returns to her childhood apartment to collect her token, the love poem Ben Hanscom (Jeremy Ray Taylor) wrote for her. She returns to the apartment where she grew up. Beverly digs behind one of the baseboards to retrieve Ben's hidden poem. The poem is significant to Beverly because it connects her to one of her only memories of pure romantic attention from her childhood. While she looks for the poem, Beverly remembers a conversation she had with her father (Stephen Bogaert) when he sprayed her with her mother's perfume after blaming young Beverly (Sophia Lillis) for her mother's death. The audience sees Beverly blaming herself for her own sexual abuse in *Chapter 1*. *Chapter 2* implies that her father tried to make Beverly a sexual replacement for his dead wife and that the sexual abuse was punishment for his wife's absence, for which he blames his daughter. Tellingly, Beverly remembers her father's trying to make her smell like her mom. In the same room where she finds the love letter, Beverly sees a manikin wearing a dress; this image further suggests that this apartment has been a place where Beverly was made to dress up and pretend to be her father's property. He tried to make her someone she was not. Juxtaposed with this memory, the love poem is important to Beverly because it reminds her that she is loved precisely for being herself and no one else. The love poem is Beverly's link to the Losers Club and who she actually is.

Ben Hanscom's token ironically links him to Beverly's security in her identity. Ben's token is the yearbook page that Beverly alone signed for him. Beverly was the first person in Derry who claimed Ben as a friend, and that claim helps define him in relationship to her and the rest of the Losers. When he returns to Derry in *Chapter 2*, Ben (Jay Ryan) has transformed from an overweight, highly intelligent boy into a fit, successful architect. Nevertheless, Ben's fear remains the same: that he will ultimately be alone because of his weight or intellect. Ben fears Pennywise as a mummy, a symbol of paralyzed intellect and physical decay. Countering this fear, Beverly warmly recognizes and values Ben's mind and friendship. During his time separated from the Losers, Ben remembers playing by himself in school until Pennywise, disguised as Beverly, came to join him. Confiding their mutual loneliness to one another, Ben tries to kiss Beverly but is cruelly rebuffed by her. She calls him fat and disgusting, saying that there's no way someone like her would romantically like someone like him. Beverly's head then bursts into flames as she pursues him into a locker, chanting his love poem after him. The image intentionally perverts Ben's poem and, like the headless mummy in *It: Chapter 1*, again suggests that this attack is explicitly against Ben's mind. Finding the yearbook page, Ben looks at Beverly's signature and reminds himself, "Beverly would never say something like that." He defeats Pennywise's lie by remembering who Beverly is and who he is to her. Pennywise's accusation is smoke without substance because Ben knows who he is in remembering who loves him. A major theme in both the book and film versions of *It* is that identity is formed and safeguarded not merely by individual choice. Identity is perhaps more powerfully given than it is made. It is about who people choose to be in community and the community that chooses people.

In the final confrontation, Ben and Beverly undergo two different baptisms, from which they both raise one another. Their salvation stories are entwined and dependent upon the other. In *Chapter 1*, Pennywise could draw the Losers away from one another by curiosity. That strategy doesn't work in *Chapter 2*, so Pennywise has to physically drive characters away from one another by force. Rather than suggesting Pennywise's strength, this physical coercion suggests his growing impotence. He drives Beverly away from Ben into a locked bathroom stall covered with graffitied accusations and cruel labels. She is then bullied by the same girl who bullied her in *Chapter 1*, by Henry Bowers (Nicholas Hamilton), and by her father. All of these people accused Beverly of being a slut and continue the accusation in this scene. As the three accusers torment her, the stall begins to fill with blood. Beverly is covered in gore. Beverly becomes a reflection of Stephen King's first bullied protagonist, Carrie White—the protagonist of his first book, *Carrie*. Carrie destroyed her entire school when she was doused in the public judgment of others. Carrie is what Beverly Marsh could be if she didn't belong to the Losers.

Ben is forcefully separated from Beverly by Pennywise. The clown tries to bury Ben like a mummy under the earth. As he is being buried alive, Pennywise accuses Ben again and says that he will die alone despite all his weight loss and intelligence. Although he can't see Beverly, he can hear her scream for help as they are both being buried. Right before the earth closes over his head, Ben cries out that he loves Beverly. More than a romantic confession, the words are exactly what Beverly needs to hear and believe to overpower the accusations around her. She isn't a slut. Beverly is purely seen and loved. Hearing Ben and believing him, Beverly kicks open the bathroom stall and is freed from condemnation. The blood that covers her is now no longer a sign of her shame. The blood is now a sign of something else: grace and new identity. Coming out of her blood baptism, Beverly reaches down to Ben, takes him by the hand, and pulls him out of the grave. Grace received is grace to give, and Beverly incarnates that truth when she raises Ben from death to life with her bloody, grace-drenched arm.

Bill's token is the paper boat he made for Georgie (Jackson Robert Scott), the one that went down the sewer before he was murdered. Adult Bill (James McAvoy) still struggles with blaming himself for Georgie's death. Significantly, Bill's memory from his time away from the Losers is the only one actually seen in *It: Chapter 1*. There, young Bill (Jaeden Martell) goes down into his family's basement and sees Pennywise as a manifestation of Georgie who blames Bill for his death. Bill collects the paper boat from the sewer where he thinks he hears Georgie crying for help. When he reaches into the drain to grab Georgie, several small hands of dead children grab his arm. Pennywise isn't just accusing Bill of his brother's death. He's accusing him of all the child deaths in Derry. Pennywise, like Satan, is the accuser. That Georgie's paper boat is Bill's token to help defeat Pennywise again shows the pattern of expectation reversal in the film. For twenty-seven years the memory of making the boat was used by Pennywise as a weapon to shame Bill. In *Chapter 2*, Bill uses the boat to arm his weapon against Pennywise. In one of four symbolic baptism scenes, Bill goes under water in his confrontation with Pennywise and has a vision almost exactly the same as the one he had in *Chapter 1* where Pennywise accused Bill for Georgie's death. In this vision, adult Bill is in the water between Georgie and himself as a child. Georgie again accuses Bill of his murder and young Bill agrees with the accusation, saying that he wasn't really sick the day Georgie died and just didn't want to spend time with him that day. In the midst of this scene, young Bill points a gun at adult Bill's head while the adult assures his younger self that he loved Georgie well and wasn't responsible for his death. At that moment, Pennywise as young Bill shoots adult Bill in the head, but the gun is unloaded. The bullet of accusation is no longer in the gun, so the accuser is powerless to kill Bill. The accusation doesn't define his character anymore. In the end it is adult Bill who shoots Pennywise in the head with the truth. The lie goes down into the water as adult Bill pushes the false Georgie, still accusing him, under the water. Bill drowns out the lie, and at the same moment comes out of the water a new, blameless man. The paper boat is now what it always was meant to be: a symbol of Bill's love for Georgie. This memory is both scar and sword for Bill, who disarms Pennywise and shoots condemnation in the face through grace.

Eddie Kaspbrak's token is his asthma inhaler. Eddie's mother (Molly Atkinson) instilled in her son an almost absolute belief in his own frailty and helplessness. When young Eddie (Jack Dylan Grazer) is separated from the Losers, he again encounters Pennywise, who manifests to him as the leper. Yet, this time, the leper captures Eddie's mother, ties her up, and tries to infect her with its disease. The scene is particularly affecting because, without the Losers, Eddie's mother is the only person he has in his life. If he loses her, he loses his only family relationship. Adult Eddie (James Ransone) remembers the awful powerlessness he felt as he was unable to free his mom and abandoned her in order to save himself. The vision, as is every accusation Pennywise makes against the Losers, is a lie. It prophesies that Eddie will choose self-preservation over the lives of the people he loves. After remembering this vision, adult Eddie is again attacked by the leper, who puts his hands on him. In *Chapter 1*, the leper only threatened to touch Eddie, but, this time, Pennywise opts for an actual physical fight with Eddie. Reversing the leper's expectation, Eddie fights back and seizes the leper by the throat. The fact that Eddie touches the leper means that he no longer fears what the leper represents to him: sickness, frailty, and death. The attack on Eddie transforms from another scene of victimization into a scene where the victimizer becomes his target's victim. As Eddie easily strangles the leper, he becomes comically gleeful in his discovered physical strength. All Pennywise can do is dissolve in Eddie's hands into goo that washes over his face. As Pennywise dissolves, the Juice Newton love song "Angel of the Morning" plays over the scene. The music choice denotes what's just happened: If Pennywise is a demon, then Eddie is a representative from the other supernatural team. Angelic power overpowers demonic power. Eddie's inhaler becomes his token because he discovers that his weakness is actually his strength. All Eddie did was resist the Devil, and the Devil always flees resistance.

Richie Tozier's token is actually a game token for his favorite video game, *Street Fighter*. In *Chapter 2*, adult Richie (Bill Hader) is a successful standup comedian, still using his trash-mouth wit. Richie remains the clown in the scary film about another clown. His humor still masks some of his intimate insecurities. In *Chapter 1*, young Richie (Finn Wolfhard) was scared of clowns, an externalization of his inner self-loathing. Richie's chief fear is not being perceived as "man enough" by people around him. In *Chapter 1*, the audience saw Richie aggressively playing *Street Fighter* while he dealt with his anger toward Bill for punching him in the face. The violent disagreement between Bill and Richie in *Chapter 1* instigated the group's disunity. Without the Losers, Richie is desperately lonely, and his personal insecurities about his masculinity are cruelly exploited by Henry Bowers's gang. Richie's memory of his time apart from the Losers centers around a moment he played *Street Fighter* with Henry's cousin. When the game is over, Richie doesn't want to be alone and asks the boy if he wants to play with him again. Henry and the other bullies enter and immediately accuse Richie of having sexual intentions toward his friend. Henry's cousin asks Richie, "Why are you being weird?" In that moment, Richie's loneliness and vulnerability are labeled perverse. Running out of the arcade and crying by himself on a park bench, Richie is suddenly attacked by Pennywise, who manifests as Derry's huge Paul Bunyan statue come-to-life. The fact that Bunyan is trying to chop Richie in half with his huge axe suggests that Richie is scared of idealized masculinity because he feels he isn't masculine enough. This idea of falling short of the manly norms is constantly referenced in *Chapter 1* when Richie tells the other Losers, "It's a good thing we're not measuring dicks." The joke veils the suffering that Richie feels inferior to other boys. Pennywise threatens adult Richie that he will expose Richie's "dirty little secret." The whole attack is an accusation to make Richie feel "dirty" and "little." Almost allowing Pennywise to win, adult Richie tries to leave Derry in order to save himself, again doing exactly what he did in *Chapter 1*. It is seeing Stanley's synagogue and remembering Stanley's public identification of himself as a Loser that helps Richie turn around and recommit himself to the Losers. In *It*, one character's faith doesn't affect only that one person. Individual faith ripples implications beyond itself and draws others to faith even in the midst of their doubts. Richie may be the "doubting Thomas" in the Losers Club, but his acceptance in that community is not threatened by his doubts. Richie's token symbolizes his true identity that disarms the curse. For all of his insecurity and doubts, Richie is a street fighter. Returning from Stanley's synagogue, Richie kills adult Henry Bowers (Teach Grant), who is trying to kill Mike. In *Chapter 1*, Richie is the first person to injure Pennywise in the final confrontation. In *Chapter 2*, Richie is the character who disarms the clown. He literally rips the enemy's arm off. The curse and accusation inadvertently help Richie believe the truth: he does measure up because he's not being measured. He's a Loser, and, in embracing that grace-fused identity, Richie and the other Losers "have nothing to lose." With no weapon that can stand against him, Richie simply takes weapons away from Pennywise.

Mike Hanlon's token is a bloody rock from the rock fight the Losers won against Henry Bowers's gang. Henry's attack on young Mike (Chosen Jacobs) instigated the rock war. The rock is Mike's identity tie to the Losers because they entered the fight to save him before they even knew him, before he was their friend. Mike was helpless and viciously attacked, and the Losers chose to fight his attackers away. Of all the tokens, the bloody rock is most emblematic of the Christian story. Biblically, rocks are signs of judgment and accusation. In the ultimate reversal of expectation, Jesus walks out of his tomb, sealed by Roman authority, the highest human authority of that time, after rolling the stone away from his grave. In his resurrection, Jesus breaks the human authority to condemn and to keep buried. When the Losers rescued Mike in the rock war, they, like Jesus, entered a fight they didn't have to enter. They were all bloodied in the fight to deliver someone they didn't have to save. One of the hallmarks of bullying is that bullies are empowered by the thought that no one will actually call their bluff. The bully will inflict the pain and terror, not the other way around. During the rock war, another reversal of expectation takes place. Stones of condemnation become weapons against the one who condemns. The rock war in *Chapter 1* prefigures the final ultimate defeat of Pennywise in *Chapter 2* when the Losers conquer Pennywise by making "him small." Individually, Pennywise is larger than life to each one of the Losers in *It: Chapter 2*. However, when they are all together they are able to call Pennywise's bully bluff. When they are the church united, the Losers can accurately say, "You're just a clown. You're just a mummy. You're just a leper." They use their enemy's attack against their enemy and make him small by calling out his lies for what they are. Without believing the lies and accusations that make Pennywise so terrifying to each of them, the accusations lose power and so does the accuser, who goes from being huge in the scene to being a cowering infant in form. If Pennywise accused each one of the Losers individually, he'd have power over them as he does throughout *Chapter 2*. Yet, when they are together as a corporate body, their perspective of him changes. In the final confrontation, the Losers reach into Pennywise and pull out his beating heart. They crush his heart in their hands and finally conquer him. In one moment, they've literally given Derry a heart transplant. They metaphorically remove the heart of stone from their community; thus, they can heal and remember rightly again. The rock war is over because the rocks of judgment and the stone heart of Derry are finally rolled away.

After they defeat Pennywise, the adult Losers once again jump off the cliff into the same water they played in as kids. The baptism that inaugurated the Losers Club again washes over them at the end. Richie loses his thick glasses in the lake, and the others dive under the water to find them for him. Huddled together in the water, holding onto one another, and mourning the loss of two of their own, the Losers are a beautiful, resilient picture of Christian community. They mourn with those who mourn. They find lost lenses when someone can't see. They push back darkness and disarm the power of accusing lies. The last line of *It: Chapter 2* is true of Losers and Christians alike on this side of eternity: "Remember, we're Losers, and we always will be."

BIBLIOGRAPHY

King, Stephen. *It: A Novel*. New York: Scribner, 1986.
Muschietti, Andy, dir. *It*. 2017. DVD. Burbank, CA: Warner Bros., 2018.
———. *It: Chapter Two*. 2019. DVD. Burbank, CA: Warner Bros., 2019.
XTC. "Dear God." *Dear God*. CD. Los Angeles: Geffen, 1986.

Part 2

The True

8

Ordeal by Worldview

A Naugelian Study in Lovecraftian Horror

JACLYN S. PARRISH

INTRODUCTION

Though confined to the margins of culture during his lifetime,[1] Howard Phillips Lovecraft today enjoys a position of considerable renown. A pioneer in twentieth-century science fiction, his influence is felt even where his name has yet to be heard. Direct homages to his work can be found in toys, T-shirts, and tabletop role-playing games,[2] and echoes of his ideas can be heard from the screenplays of Joss Whedon to the furthest reaches of the Marvel universe. Yet, despite his ubiquity in the wider world, H. P. Lovecraft remains a veritable nonentity within the Christian subculture. This, however, is due less to his theological bent (atheism) or his sociological convictions (white supremacism), and more to his generic affinity: horror.

Christendom is, after all, not entirely hospitable to the horror genre. Thrillers are acceptable. Science fiction is allowed. Fantasy is on probation in certain spheres, but still widely tolerated. Even romance novels are

---

1. Luckhurst, "Introduction," viii.
2. "Arkham Horror."

permissible, provided consummation occurs after matrimony and well out of the reader's sight. Seemingly, if authors are able to respect a few moral boundaries, Christians are willing to partake of almost any genre. Horror, however, is rejected not merely on the evidence of individual narrative transgressions, but on the basis of its essential nature. A bodice-buster might be redeemed with some chaste redaction, but a chest-burster is irredeemable. Joshua Infantado's tone is as merciless as his typography in "Top Seven Reasons Christians Should Not Watch Horror Movies," but neither his argument nor his aggressive use of italics is original. He might be histrionic, but he is not alone in contending that "*Satan inspired the minds of these movie producers and directors.*"[3] And considering some of the juicier scenes in *The Exorcist*, his position is not wholly without grounds.

But this wholesale condemnation of horror is ultimately unjustified. After all, much of the content to which Infantado himself objects can be found within the very pages of Scripture, for "carnage, mayhem, scream, and bloodshed" along with "violence, death, and suffering"[4] could just as easily describe the Book of Lamentations as it could *Carrie*. And although Infantado is right to insist that we obey Philippians 4:8 by thinking of that which is true,[5] the truth is not exclusively pleasant. Often, it is downright horrific. Of course, believers ought not be indiscriminate in our consumption of horror (just as we ought not be indiscriminate in our consumption of anything), but we ought to take the time to understand and appreciate the horror genre on its own terms. For horror—be it written, filmed, painted, photographed, or sung—holds a unique power over the human soul, and the effects of that power can be and often are profoundly salutary. And who better to exemplify the best horror has to offer than that dark prince of cosmic dread himself, H. P. Lovecraft? This chapter will outline a definition of horror as an artform whose core purpose is to place the worldview of the audience in crisis and force them to confront the possibility that their conception of reality is wrong or inadequate. This experience of worldview-in-crisis, moreover, will be shown to be a psychologically healthy one, and perhaps even essential to the human experience. We will then conclude with a brief overview of the fictional works of H. P. Lovecraft and an examination of how his work both illustrates and exemplifies the experience of worldview-in-crisis.

---

3. Infantado, "Top Seven Reasons."
4. Infantado, "Top Seven Reasons."
5. Infantado, "Top Seven Reasons."

THE NATURE OF HORROR

Quality is a function of quiddity: so, before horror can be morally or aesthetically evaluated, it must first be defined. But the horror genre is not easily bound in any particular generic straitjacket. Contrary to Infantado's pious hand-wringing, a work of horror may or may not depict scenes of graphic violence or sexuality—Henry James's *The Turn of the Screw*, for example, is neither bloody nor unchaste. It might involve the supernatural (Stephen King's *The Shining*), or it might not (Edgar Allan Poe's "The Cask of Amontillado"). Whatever villains it features might be vanquished by the story's end (Bram Stoker's *Dracula*) or they might not, as in the multitudinous films featuring Freddy Krueger, Michael Myers, and Jason Voorhees. More irksome still, many horror films and books bleed across generic boundaries, such as Thomas Harris's *Silence of the Lambs* (a horror/thriller) or the *Alien* films, with their rock-star status among horror and sci-fi fans alike. The only expectation the audience can hold with any certainty is that they are in for a fright, but in some way qualitatively distinct from that of mystery, fantasy, science fiction, or adventure. For horror's defining characteristic is not the setting it appropriates, the style it adopts, or the narrative structure it utilizes, but rather the emotion it arouses. Just as "the genres of suspense, mystery, and horror derive their very names from the affects they are intended to promote.... The cross-art, cross-media genre of horror takes its title from the emotion it characteristically or rather ideally promotes."[6]

That emotion (horror) is distinct from plain fear in that the threat in question—be it tangible or fictional—is not practical, but existential. The prospect is not the mere breaking of bones, but the "breakdown of intelligibility."[7] Horrific monsters, both natural and supernatural, "breach the norms of ontological propriety presumed by the positive human characters in the story."[8] These monsters horrify, not because they are deadly or revolting or morally transgressive, but because they *are*. The creatures and characters of fantasy and sci-fi, on the other hand, fit without question into their fictional ontologies, and the audience reacts to them in keeping with the temporary suspension of disbelief accorded all fiction. As Sigmund Freud points out in his own examination of "The Uncanny," when reading a fantastical work, "we order our judgement to the imaginary reality imposed on us by the writer, and regard souls, spirits and spectres as though their existence had the same validity in their world as our own has in the external

---

6. Carroll, *Philosophy of Horror*, 14.
7. Asma, *On Monsters*, 10.
8. Carroll, *Philosophy of Horror*, 16.

world."[9] But within the world of "the uncanny," the weird, and the horrific, the rules are altered. Here, the characters must confront evidence that debunks their own cognitive structure for reality.

Hermione Granger and the Blair Witch, for instance, might share a job title, but their narrative functions are entirely distinct. Hermione's magic is a normal and explicable part of life for the characters of J. K. Rowling's universe, whereas the Blair Witch's powers and effects represent a transgression of the understood order of things within the world of the film. This witch's very existence shatters the conceptual schemas of the other characters, and it is that confrontation with the inexplicable and incomprehensible that affords *The Blair Witch Project* its status as a work of horror. As weird author and critic China Miéville so aptly puts it, "The Weird is the assertion of that we did not know, never knew, could not know, that has always been and will always be unknowable."[10] Horror, it seems, is closely bound to the concept of worldview.

According to David K. Naugle, a worldview is a *"semiotic phenomenon,"* one which "consists primarily of a network of *narrative signs* that offers an interpretation of reality and establishes an overarching framework for life," providing a "foundation or governing platform upon or by which people think, interpret, and know."[11] Stephen T. Asma might use the language of "intelligibility"; Noël Carroll, the term "ontological propriety"; and Miéville, the notion of "knowability"; but the theme remains constant: horror is nothing less than the theater of *Weltanschauung* in crisis, the spectacle of worldview on the rack. Carroll even makes explicit use of the term in his *Philosophy of Horror*, suggesting that "the confrontation and defeat of the monster in horror fictions might be systematically read as a restoration and defense of the established *world view* found in existing cultural schemas."[12] Horror's distinguishing ability as an artistic enterprise is to create a space where both artist and audience can confront the possibility that the interpretive structure that allows them to interact sanely with reality could, in fact, break beyond repair.

Because of this, horror artifacts retain a visceral connection with the cultures that birth them and the prevailing worldviews of their *Sitz im Leben*. Seung Min Hong, for instance, notes the proliferation and success of the "vengeful spirit" motif in Japanese and Korean horror films, and observes that "in these cultures where ancestor veneration and appeasing the souls

---

9. Freud, "Uncanny," 17.
10. Miéville, "On Monsters," 380.
11. Naugle, *Worldview*, 291.
12. Carroll, *Philosophy of Horror*, 200 (emphasis added).

... are still being practiced, movies such as *Ju-on* or *Ringu* have the ability to scare people in a unique way."[13] After all, within a cultural framework whose regular rhythms are attuned to keep the spirit world in equilibrium, the presence of an unappeased spirit represents a serious fracture in the established order. Sometimes, moreover, this conflict between horror and worldview is practically explicit, as in the case of Mary Shelley's *Frankenstein*, a cautionary tale of scientific overreach if there ever was one. Philip Tallon reminds the reader that this Enlightenment-era novel "was a work both of its time and against its time."[14] In an age "which represented huge leaps forward in terms of human understanding of the world,"[15] Shelley's work "cast doubt . . . on the human assumption that progress in knowledge is always good,"[16] presenting the nineteenth-century audience with a universe where the very principle their era trusted so implicitly (scientific progress) was proven untrustworthy.

On other occasions, the conversation between horror and worldview is more subtle and complex. Within the conceptual relativism of the postmodern age, for example, the horror genre has become a haven of moral objectivity. Audiences who increasingly profess skepticism in universal truths nevertheless choose to pay good money for narratives in which good and evil are clearly identified and starkly contrasted. Scott Derrickson, director of *The Exorcism of Emily Rose* and devout Christian, has gravitated toward horror for that very reason, arguing that it is "the perfect genre for a person of faith to work in. You can think about good and evil pretty openly."[17] The fact that a postmodern audience can still leave the latest *Paranormal Activity* sequel feeling queasy belies the relativistic worldview they proclaim, for "there is no such thing as horror—true horror—in a morally relative universe."[18] *Saw*, it seems, is as much an assault on relativism as it is an assault on the senses. In the words of the reigning Master of Horror, Stephen King, "We love and need the concept of monstrosity because it is a reaffirmation of the order we all crave as human beings. . . . It is not the physical or mental aberration itself which horrifies us, but rather the lack of order which these aberrations imply."[19]

---

13. Hong, "Redemptive Fear."
14. Tallon, "Through a Mirror," 36.
15. Tallon, "Through a Mirror," 37.
16. Tallon, "Through a Mirror," 38.
17. Greydanus, "Interview."
18. LeSweatman, "What Horror Movies Can Teach Us."
19. King, *Danse Macabre*, 50.

Audiences are not afraid of Cthulhu, Frankenstein's monster, or It; rather, they are afraid of the conceptual frameworks that would allow such beings to exist. Demons, murderers, and tentacled freaks are simply the narrative means by which artists reach the emotional end of *Weltanschauung*-in-crisis. We scream because our worldview is being dismembered before our eyes. However, while the nature of horror is established easily enough, the fascination of horror remains more difficult to explain.

THE APPEAL OF HORROR

One of horror's most deeply puzzling facets is its appeal. The genre would seem, after all, to be by its very nature intentionally unappealing. Examined from every angle, the very existence of horror as a cultural phenomenon is counterintuitive: its subject matter is invariably disturbing (death, torture, insanity, mutant freaks, giant spiders), and its audiences traditionally respond with all the visible signs of discomfort and even distress (screaming, cringing, crying, flinching, fleeing). A censorious critic might suggest that these audiences are driven by some form of sadism or masochism and derive a twisted pleasure from viewing physical or psychological pain. This, however, would be both uncharitable and unsatisfying since similar questions could also be asked of the tragedy genre, yet even the most puritanical critic is unlikely to condemn the reading of *Hamlet* (despite the fact that the play contains more deaths than the average Wes Craven film). By all appearances, horror ought to be the least successful genre on the market. Yet, audiences continue to flock to the endless *Final Destination* sequels, Stephen King's books continue to top bestseller lists, and high schools across America continue to make Edgar Allan Poe required reading. Why? Whence comes this "simultaneous lure and repulsion of the abnormal or extraordinary?"[20] Prevailing answers to that question fall habitually into one of two categories: one rooted in the mind; one, in the soul.

One explanation currently in vogue in critical circles is the psychoanalytical perspective, founded primarily on the study and work of Sigmund Freud. According to Freud, "every emotional affect, whatever its quality, is transformed by repression into morbid anxiety,"[21] and "the uncanny is nothing else than a hidden, familiar thing that has undergone repression and then emerged from it."[22] Ernest Jones skillfully applies this theory to the phenomenon of unpleasant dreams in his *On the Nightmare*, arguing that

20. Asma, *On Monsters*, 6.
21. Freud, "Uncanny," 13.
22. Freud, "Uncanny," 15.

"the reason why the object seen in a Nightmare is frightful or hideous is simply that the representation of the underlying wish is not permitted in its naked form so that the dream is a compromise of the wish on the one hand and on the other of the intense fear belonging to the inhibition."[23] From this point of view, artistic horror, like the sleeping nightmare, is a kind of emotional and psychological release valve on the psyche, allowing audiences to experience the *frisson* of a forbidden wish while still outwardly maintaining the taboo. Horror's "lure and repulsion" are nothing less than the products of repressed desire and artificial societal standards, respectively.

Yet, while certainly adaptable to some works of horror, the psychoanalytic approach is not ultimately or universally conclusive. First, Freud's ideas were and remain solidly in the category of respectable conjecture, founded largely on informed speculation and rendering conclusions drawn therefrom suspect. As anecdotal evidence is wont to do, Freud's model certainly provides grist for innumerable interesting interpretations, but Miéville is nevertheless justified in observing that "even if those readings are 'interesting,' surely the truthiness or not of any paradigm has some impact on the usefulness of readings based on it."[24] Admittedly, some of the more obvious and popular figures of Western horror literature mold easily into a pattern of repressed desire—the deadly and seductive vampire, for instance, could arguably be a stand-in for a titillating array of psychosexual urges, from incest to necrophilia to your run-of-the-mill oral fixation. But as the litany of horrific icons progresses from vampires and werewolves to giant squids and lizards to amorphous slimes and swarms of carnivorous slugs, the argument for horror as repressed desire becomes painfully strained. In the end, "the psychoanalytic reduction of horrific creatures to the objects of repression is not comprehensive for the genre; not all horrific creatures portend psychic conflict or desire,"[25] and so alternatives (or at least additions) must be sought.

Another popular explanation for horror's perennial fascination customarily goes by the name of the "quasi-religious," an emotional, psychological, and possibly even spiritual draw that Lovecraft himself argues is "coeval with the religious feeling and closely related to many aspects of it."[26] Much of the language associated with this perspective is drawn from Rudolph Otto's *The Idea of the Holy*. In this work, Otto argues: "To keep a thing holy in the heart means to mark it off by a feeling of peculiar dread . . . to appraise it

23. Jones, *On the Nightmare*, 78.
24. Miéville, "On Monsters," 381.
25. Carroll, *Philosophy of Horror*, 173.
26. Lovecraft, "Introduction," 444.

by the category of the *numinous*,"[27] and he goes on to describe an encounter with this "*numinous*" as being stamped by an emotional experience he calls the "*mysterium tremendum*."[28] This experience, he contends, is highly complex, and contains elements of "awefulness,"[29] "overpoweringness,"[30] "urgency or energy,"[31] and a keen awareness of being in the presence of a being "wholly other"[32] than oneself.

And, lest any critic dismiss this transcendent experience as incongruous with the average penny dreadful, Otto himself observes a direct connection between the *mysterium tremendum* and the common horror story. He argues that the "first crude, primitive forms" of the *mysterium* not only characterize "the so-called Religion of Primitive Man" but also remain a potent force within the human soul even when developed into more sophisticated forms of religion: "That this is so is shown by the potent attraction again and again exercised by the element of horror and 'shudder' in ghost stories, even among persons of high all-round education."[33] The horror genre, from Otto's perspective, is simply an echo of eternity down a dark alley, the instinctive human longing for the holy born twisted and deformed—we look to Dracula because we long to see God.

Despite the incompatibility of their own respective worldviews, Otto's approach to the horror genre has much in common with Freud's. For both, the unpleasantness of the horror genre is simply the psychological price rendered by the audience in order to experience a desired emotion, either a release of a repressed emotion or a shiver of the *numinous*. In fact, Freud's own words could easily be used in the service of Otto's theories, for primitive religion is one of the primary sources of repressed desire in Freudian thought, which argues that "as soon as something actually happens in our lives which seems to support the old, discarded beliefs, we get a feeling of the uncanny."[34] Any adept apologist, moreover, could just as easily argue that what Freud calls the resurgence of "old, discarded beliefs" is, in fact, the reassertion of a theistic Ultimate Reality on the irreligious mind.

However, the quasi-religious theory is also akin to the psychoanalytical in that it, too, while providing useful insights into the appeal of certain

---

27. Otto, *Idea of the Holy*, 13–14.
28. Otto, *Idea of the Holy*, 12.
29. Otto, *Idea of the Holy*, 13.
30. Otto, *Idea of the Holy*, 20.
31. Otto, *Idea of the Holy*, 23.
32. Otto, *Idea of the Holy*, 25.
33. Otto, *Idea of the Holy*, 16.
34. Freud, "Uncanny," 17.

horror artifacts, does not provide a comprehensive explanation of the appeal of the full panoply of the horror genre. Carroll is right in observing that "surely there are many horror stories that fall short of raising cosmic fear," citing such unprepossessing works as Guy N. Smith's *Crabs on the Rampage*.[35] The pulp fiction of slime monsters and gelatinous blobs certainly falls miserably short of the *mysterium tremendum*, but the fact that such literature remains both plentiful and profitable leaves the question of its appeal unanswered. It might be terrible, but it remains attractive, and neither the psychoanalytic perspective nor the quasi-religious explanation can fully resolve the tension of horror's paradoxical appeal because neither takes into full account the unique relationship between horror and worldview.

Ultimately, the horror genre continues to appeal to audiences not in spite of its nature as *Weltanschauung*-in-crisis but precisely because of that nature. In his acute and insightful examination of the genre's mysterious fascination, Noël Carroll concludes that "art-horror is the price we are willing to pay for the revelation of that which is impossible and unknown, of that which violates our conceptual schema."[36] So much of human culture and experience, from textbooks to worship services, is designed to affirm worldview; but audiences come to horror, again and again, for the express purpose of having their worldview strained to the breaking point. Moreover, from a biblical perspective, this is not a macabre exercise in psychological masochism, but an essential function of *Weltanschauung* within the human experience.

According to Naugle, the Christian use of the term "'worldview' entails God's gracious redemption that delivers the hearts of men and women from idolatry and false views of life . . . and enables them through faith in Jesus Christ to come to a knowledge of God and truth about his creation and all aspects of reality."[37] In short, the human person exists within the broad ontological narrative of created good (Gen 1), comprehensive brokenness (Gen 3; Rom 3:23), and cosmic redemption (Rom 8:19–23; Rev 21:5). This, from the Christian perspective, is the essential flow and movement of all reality within time. The regenerate experience reality within time as the sanctifying process of conformity to the image of Christ (Rom 8:29) whereas the unregenerate experience it as the incessant call of both the church and creation to repentance and belief (2 Cor 5:20; Rom 1:18–20). On both sides of the cross, the call is the same: "Do not be conformed to this world, but be transformed by the renewal of your mind, that by testing you may discern

---

35. Carroll, *Philosophy of Horror*, 163–64.
36. Carroll, *Philosophy of Horror*, 186.
37. Naugle, *Worldview*, 260.

what is the will of God, what is good and acceptable and perfect" (Rom 12:2 ESV). Thus, the Christian worldview itself calls for humans to live in a constant state of worldview crisis, holding tight to one's body of knowledge and understanding while relentlessly stretching it "until we all attain to the unity of the faith and of the knowledge of the Son of God, to mature manhood, to the measure of the stature of the fullness of Christ" (Eph 4:13 ESV). An aesthetic activity that "violates our conceptual schema," therefore, is not a deviation from healthy psychological practice, but a microcosm of the whole human experience.

Within this framework, both the psychoanalytical and quasi-religious approaches to horror gain fresh meaning and power. After all, if one's worldview is intended to stretch to infinity, then it surely must eventually contain both the depths of the psyche and the heights of eternity. The human mind does, indeed, contain much discomfiting content, which both the individual and society have chosen, consciously or unconsciously, to bury under the weight of memory. "Uncanny" art is not the only means of drawing out repressed truths, thoughts, and emotions, but it certainly is one means of doing so. Indeed, many of the darkest and most execrated works of horror deal head-on with the disquieting facts of human sin and depravity, such as insanity, abuse, murder, demons, and disease. As Derrickson argues, "It's not about putting something evil in the world. It's about reckoning with evil. We don't need any more evil in the world. We need a lot more reckoning with it."[38] Horror affords audiences the opportunity to lay aside the masks of confidence and self-assurance and scream, both figuratively and literally, "All is not well!"

Likewise, horror (supernatural horror, in particular) exists not only to frighten but also to remind the viewer that there are more things in heaven and earth than are dreamt of in our philosophy. It forces the eyes up and beyond the banal rhythms of everyday life to consider the possibility of a world (and for Christians, a God) that does not play by our rules. As Bryan Stone so aptly states, "When horror is at its best, it satisfies our curiosity about both the metaphysical and the psychological unknown while, at the same time, casting an unsettling light on the shadow elements both of the human condition and of the cosmos."[39] Horror trains us to make room in our thoughts for the unthinkable. True, most horror books provide only dull twinges of worldview crisis, just as most action movies offer only scraps of the cosmic battle between good and evil. The horror genre as a whole is here described, not any individual horror artifact, and there is room for "good"

---

38. Greydanus, "Interview."
39. Stone, "Sanctification of Fear," 4.

and "bad" aesthetic quality within a morally positive generic category. H. P. Lovecraft, however, wrote some of the best expressions and examinations of worldview crisis that the horror genre has to offer.

WELTANSCHAUUNG ON THE RACK: A LOVECRAFTIAN STUDY

H. P. Lovecraft has eluded the public eye for many years, and even with his recent explosion of popularity and the tireless work of critics such as S. T. Joshi, many more years will pass before the full breadth of his work receives a fraction of the scholarly attention it deserves. History remembers him (or rather, has rediscovered him) as a prolific and accomplished writer of weird fiction, but Lovecraft also churned out an impressive array of writing on literary criticism, science, philosophy, travel, and journalism, as well as an extensive collection of poetry and a mountain of personal correspondence. A comprehensive analysis of his full body of work would lie far beyond the scope of this essay, but the presence of worldview conflict is so poignant and so prevalent within his fiction that few authors can be better said to typify the phenomenon. Even a glancing survey of his short stories and novellas is sufficient to demonstrate the ubiquitous presence and compelling power of *Weltanschauung*-in-crisis, both as a theme within his stories and a dynamic between his stories and their corresponding *Sitz im Leben*.

Some artists of horror drape the existential dread of worldview crisis in the fleece of physical danger. The destruction of moral order might arrive dressed as a serial killer, or the imbalance of the natural world might present as a carnivorous fog. Within Lovecraft, however, the fears are explicitly existential. Characters do, from time to time, tussle physically with nightmarish creatures, but these moments of outright violence are almost a relief compared to the agony of reckoning with the fact of these monsters' presence in the waking world. Lovecraftian protagonists spend the better part of their fictional lives in an acute state of *Weltanschauung*-in-crisis, and most do not survive the ordeal with their sanity intact. Again and again, Lovecraft lays the worldviews of his characters on the rack and stretches them mercilessly, often to the point of snapping beyond repair, for within Lovecraft, it is far better to die than to know.

Such is the choice of the nameless narrator of "Dagon," for example. Marooned on the open sea, he learns a terrible secret that has lain buried on the ocean's floor for millennia. A ship eventually finds and carries him to safety, but the man's mind is shattered and he turns to morphine in an attempt to drown out the memory of what he has seen. Eventually, the money and drugs run out and he resolves to end it all, raving as he throws himself from his upper-story window, "I cannot think of the deep sea without shuddering at the nameless things that may at this very moment be crawling and floundering on its slimy bed."[40] In the end, he dies simply because he is unable to make space in his worldview for what he knows. Likewise, the "hero" of *The Shadow over Innsmouth* is so completely shattered by the monsters he encounters that his only means of incorporating their existence into his ontology is to embrace his identity as one of them. The novella, which recounts many a rousing chase and escape scene from the amphibious Deep Ones, degenerates in the end into a cacophony of wild dreams and incomprehensible language, the narrator declaring, "*Iä-R'lyeh! Cthulhu fhtagn!* . . . We shall swim out to that brooding reef in the sea and dive down through black abysses . . . and in that lair of the Deep Ones we shall dwell amidst wonder and glory for ever."[41]

Other Lovecraftian protagonists are hardier folk. In fact, the scientists of "At the Mountains of Madness" manage to traverse most of their ordeal by worldview with considerable cognitive agility and flexibility, allowing the evidence of their own senses to steadily (if painfully) expand their own conceptual schema. As they comb through the ruins of the ancient race that first populated the earth, they are driven by a sensation not at all unlike Otto's *mysterium tremendum*, for "half-paralyzed with terror . . . there was nevertheless . . . a blazing flame of awe and curiosity."[42] Even their level-headed trek through oblivion, though, ends in insanity. Their delvings into the primordial city eventually bring them face to face with a Shoggoth, one of the amorphous slave races bred by the Old Ones. Lovecraft's language stumbles and gasps even as his characters run screaming from the thing: "a terrible, indescribable thing . . . a shapeless congeries of protoplasmic bubbles, faintly self-luminous, and with myriads of temporary eyes forming and unforming."[43]

Yet even this abomination is not the ultimate threat, for as the two survivors scramble into their aeroplane and fly away, one glances back and sees . . . something, a being the Old Ones and even Lovecraft himself only hint at, the sight of which unhinges young Danforth entirely: "He has on rare occasions whispered disjointed and irresponsible things about 'the black pit,' 'the carven rim,' 'the proto-Shoggoths,' 'the windowless solids with

---

40. Lovecraft, "Dagon."
41. Lovecraft, "Shadow Over Innsmouth," 381.
42. Lovecraft, "Mountains of Madness," 261.
43. Lovecraft, "Mountains of Madness," 279.

five dimensions,' 'the nameless cylinder,' 'the elder pharos,'"[44] and another half-paragraph of incomprehensible gibbering. In the end, the narrator resolves to recount his tale only in order to prevent other men of science from exploring the Antarctic regions where his discoveries took place.[45] He has survived the racking of his worldview, but at so high a cost to his comfort and sanity that he would have no other follow his example.

Though their experiences are of course fantastical, the emotions undergone by these and other Lovecraftian characters are profoundly human. Their struggle to process the unthinkable cognitively is the same suffered by every human being, including believers. The fact that nearly all these stories end in disaster does not detract from their moral or aesthetic quality any more than the triumph of Mephistopheles renders *Doctor Faustus* unreadable for Christians. As finite and fallen beings, we see only "through a glass, darkly" (1 Cor 13:12 KJV) even when we see our clearest, and until we are made new, there will always be a measure of pain in our attempts to comprehend the Incomprehensible. An evening with H. P. Lovecraft (alone, perhaps by candlelight) is as clear an echo of our desperation to know and understand as an afternoon with Jane Austen is an echo of our desire to love and belong. But if worldview conflict appears as a recurring theme within Lovecraft's fiction, it also occurs as a fascinating dynamic between his fiction and his own worldview.

H. P. Lovecraft was a man firmly situated in the prevailing philosophy of the early twentieth century, and his work accordingly reflects Western culture's shift from theism to materialism. In the previous century's atmosphere of behavioral rectitude, Gothic horror had focused on the breakdown of the moral and societal order, featuring such tropes as "tyrannical priests, virgins menaced in convents, or men tempted to Faustian pacts by the Devil."[46] But "the religious dread of the supernatural is snapped off in Lovecraft's materialist tales,"[47] for his is horror written for the age of science, and it focuses instead on the breakdown of the natural order.

One of the means by which Lovecraft achieves this effect is by repositioning the source of the fear in question. In Gothic literature, the monster comes from without: a bloodsucking menace, a sentient and cadaverous golem, a demon luring the hero to his doom. In Lovecraft, however, the monster is frequently found within. Arthur Jermyn, for example, discovers he is the descendant of an unholy line founded by a bestial union between

---

44. Lovecraft, "Mountains of Madness," 283
45. Lovecraft, "Mountains of Madness," 182.
46. Luckhurst, "Introduction," xiv.
47. Luckhurst, "Introduction," xiv.

his ancestor and a white ape and, like the nameless sailor in "Dagon," kills himself rather than incorporate this information into his worldview. Lovecraft even enlarges the horror by intimating that the Jermyn clan is not so freakish as our stuffed-shirt science would prefer to believe, arguing, "If we knew what we are, we should do as Sir Arthur Jermyn did; and Arthur Jermyn soaked himself in oil and set fire to his clothing one night."[48] "The Outsider" suffers a similar fate in his tale, in which the prisoner of a mouldering crypt manages to make his escape into the moonlit world. He stumbles eventually into a beautiful castle, but the moment he steps hopefully into the light, the revelers all take flight in terror. The narrator likewise catches sight of the monster that has frightened them and throws an arm out to protect himself, only to have his hand brush the smooth surface of a mirror. His eyes rest on "a compound of all that is unclean, uncanny, unwelcome, abnormal, and detestable," and he realizes that this "ghoulish shade of decay, antiquity, and desolation," this "putrid, dripping eidolon of unwholesome revelation," is none other than himself.[49]

Again and again, Lovecraft forces his materialist readers to consider that the natural laws upon which their worldview depends might be overthrown, if not precisely within their own bodies, then certainly within their environment. In "The Colour out of Space," the denizens of a country community must contend with a meteorite that buries itself in a local farm, slowly dissolving into globules whose color lies nowhere on the known spectrum. The thing itself dissipates, but it leaves behind a blight that infects the crops, livestock, minds, and eventually bodies of the farmer and his family, slowly turning all to brittle ash. The community is powerless against the thing and eventually is simply forced to flee, the narrator concluding in uncomprehending terror, "It was just a colour out of space—a frightful messenger from unformed realms of infinity beyond all Nature as we know it; from realms whose mere existence stuns the brain."[50] The foes of "The Dunwich Horror" are more successful in their battle (exceptionally so, for Lovecraft), but even they admit that the creature they've vanquished was beyond their understanding, "a kind of force that doesn't belong in our part of space; a kind of force that acts and grows and shapes itself by other laws than those of our sort of Nature."[51]

This breach of natural law is, by Lovecraft's own testimony, the thematic centerpiece of his horror literature. "The true weird tale," he insisted,

---

48. Lovecraft, "Facts Concerning."
49. Lovecraft, "Outsider."
50. Lovecraft, "Color Out of Space," 79.
51. Lovecraft, "Dunwich Horror," 120.

must intimate "that most terrible conception of the human brain—a malign and particular suspension or defeat of those fixed laws of Nature which are our only safeguard against the assaults of chaos and the daemons of unplumbed space."[52] Whether or not he achieved such a sensation of cognitive crisis could certainly be argued from an aesthetic standpoint, but worldview crisis was certainly his goal, and the specific worldview he had in mind was materialism. In fact, in his "Notes on Writing Weird Fiction," he confesses:

> I choose weird stories because they suit my inclination best—one of my strongest and most persistent wishes being to achieve, momentarily, the illusion of some strange suspension or violation of the galling limitations of time, space, and natural law which for ever imprison us and frustrate our curiosity about the infinite cosmic spaces beyond the radius of our sight and analysis.[53]

One might, in examining his fiction and such comments as the above, begin to wonder if Lovecraft was, in fact, an enemy of materialism, utilizing the horror genre as a means of re-injecting supernaturalism into his empiricist culture. Yet such an assumption would bespeak an essential misunderstanding not only of the personality of H. P. Lovecraft but also of the nature of *Weltanschauung*-in-crisis.

Elsewhere in his letters, Lovecraft clarifies his goals in writing horror, insisting that "the normal revolt against time, space, and matter . . . must be gratified by images forming supplements rather than contradictions of the visible and mensurable universe."[54] Lovecraft's goal was to strain his ontological schematics not in order to break them, but in order to expand them. For such, after all, is the natural function of worldview crisis: to reach incessantly beyond what is known in order that knowledge might be complete. H. P. Lovecraft's horror is, from this perspective, not only a *depiction of* worldview crisis but an *exercise in* worldview crisis, for he not only portrayed the phenomenon in his characters, but he also embodied it within the very act of writing. He was able, by the peculiar power of horror to fascinate and repel, to hold unflinchingly to his particular *Weltanschauung* while stretching it, staring deeply into the inconceivable in order that he might manage to conceive it. He possessed enough faith in his worldview that the thing would not break entirely; nevertheless, he longed, as do all humans, to know and understand completely, fully, and perfectly the reality we inhabit.

52. Lovecraft, "Introduction," 446.
53. Lovecraft, "Notes on Writing Weird Fiction," 7–9.
54. Lovecraft, *Selected Letters*, 295–96.

BIBLIOGRAPHY

"Arkham Horror." *Fantasy Flight Games*, August 3, 2018. https://www.fantasyflightgames.com/en/news/2018/8/1/arkham-horror-third-edition.

Asma, Stephen T. *On Monsters: An Unnatural History of Our Worst Fears*. Oxford: Oxford University Press, 2009.

Carroll, Noël. *The Philosophy of Horror: Or, Paradoxes of the Heart*. New York: Routledge, 1990.

Freud, Sigmund. "The 'Uncanny.'" 1919. Translated by Alix Strachey. http://web.mit.edu/allanmc/www/freud1.pdf.

Greydanus, Steven D. "Interview: Filmmaker Scott Derrickson on Horror, Faith, Chesterton and His New Movie." *National Catholic Register*, July 1, 2014. http://www.ncregister.com/daily-news/interview-scott-derrickson.

Hong, Seung Min. "Redemptive Fear: A Review of Sacred Terror and Further Analyses of Religious Horror Films." *Journal of Religion and Popular Culture* 22.2 (2010). http://www.questiaschool.com/read/1G1-238178979/redemptive-fear-a-review-of-sacred-terror-and-further.

Infantado, Joshua. "Top Seven Reasons Christians Should not Watch Horror Movies." *Becoming Christians*. October 20, 2017. https://becomingchristians.com/2017/10/20/top-7-reasons-christians-should-not-watch-horror-movies.

Jones, Ernest. *On the Nightmare*. London: Liveright, 1971.

Joshi, S. T. *A Subtler Magick: The Writings and Philosophy of H. P. Lovecraft*. 2nd ed. Gillette: Wildside, 1996.

King, Stephen. *Danse Macabre*. New York: Everest, 1981.

LeSweatman, Victoria. "What Horror Movies Can Teach Us about Christianity." *Relevant Magazine*, October 13, 2017. https://relevantmagazine.com/culture/film/what-horror-movies-teach-us-about-christianity-2017.

Lovecraft, H. P. "At the Mountains of Madness." In *H. P. Lovecraft: The Classic Horror Stories*, edited by Roger Luckhurst, 182–284. Oxford: Oxford University Press, 2013.

———. "The Colour Out of Space." In *H. P. Lovecraft: The Classic Horror Stories*, edited by Roger Luckhurst, 53–79. Oxford: Oxford University Press, 2013.

———. "Dagon." *The Vagrant* 11 (1919) 23–29. http://www.hplovecraft.com/writings/texts/fiction/d.aspx.

———. "The Dunwich Horror." In *H. P. Lovecraft: The Classic Horror Stories*, edited by Roger Luckhurst, 80–120. Oxford: Oxford University Press, 2013.

———. "Facts Concerning the Late Arthur Jermyn and His Family." *The Wolverine* 9 (1921) 3–11. http://www.hplovecraft.com/writings/texts/fiction/faj.aspx.

———. "Introduction to 'Supernatural Horror in Literature.'" In *H. P. Lovecraft: The Classic Horror Stories*, edited by Roger Luckhurst, 444–47. Oxford: Oxford University Press, 2013.

———. "Notes on Writing Weird Fiction." *Amateur Correspondent* 2.1 (1937) 7–9. http://www.hplovecraft.com/writings/texts/essays/nwwf.aspx.

———. "The Outsider." *Weird Tales* 7.4 (1926) 449–53. http://www.hplovecraft.com/writings/texts/fiction/o.aspx.

———. *Selected Letters*. Vol. 3. Sauk City: Arkham, 1965.

———. "The Shadow Over Innsmouth." In *H. P. Lovecraft: The Classic Horror Stories*, edited by Roger Luckhurst, 320–81. Oxford: Oxford University Press, 2013.

Luckhurst, Roger. "Introduction." In *H. P. Lovecraft: The Classic Horror Stories*, edited by Roger Luckhurst, vii–xxviii. Oxford: Oxford University Press, 2013.

Miéville, China. "On Monsters: Or, Nine or More (Monstrous) Not Cannies." *Journal of the Fantastic in the Arts* 23 (2012) 377–92.

Naugle, David K. *Worldview: The History of a Concept*. Grand Rapids: Eerdmans, 2002. https://www.questiaschool.com/library/120083042/worldview-the-history-of-a-concept.

Otto, Rudolph. *The Idea of the Holy: An Inquiry into the Non-Rational Factor in the Idea of the Divine and Its Relation to the Rational*. Translated by John W. Harvey. 1923. Reprint, Oxford: Oxford University Press, 1936. https://archive.org/stream/theideaoftheholy00-ottouoft/theideaoftheholy000ttouoft_djvu.txt.

Stone, Bryan. "The Sanctification of Fear: Images of the Religious in Horror Films." *Journal of Religion & Film* 5.2 (2001). https://digitalcommons.unomaha.edu/jrf/vol5/iss2/7.

Tallon, Philip. "Through a Mirror, Darkly: Art-Horror as a Medium for Moral Reflection." In *The Philosophy of Horror*, edited by Thomas Fahy, 33–41. Lexington: University Press of Kentucky, 2010.

9

The Problem of Evil

An Alternative to Plantinga's Free Will Defense

SCOTT SHIFFER

INTRODUCTION

In 1974, Alvin Plantinga published a work titled *The Nature of Necessity*; in this work he dedicates a section to the problem of evil and his Free Will Defense. This view was expounded upon and written about in a way that is more easily understood by the non-professional philosopher in *God, Freedom, and Evil*, released that same year. In the latter work, Plantinga spends the first half of the book dealing with the logical problem of evil. This argument is in response to the works of John Mackie, who argued that the existence of God and evil were an implicitly contradictory set of beliefs.[1] Plantinga showed that Mackie had not proven his claim and, in fact, was recognized by Mackie (as well as others) as having done so.[2]

However, disproving the atheist's claim that God and evil cannot coexist takes more than merely showing that the atheist has not proven his claim.

---

1. Mackie's argument was that these ideas are implicitly contradictory as opposed to their being explicitly or formally contradictory. For further explanation, see Plantinga, *God, Freedom, and Evil*, 13–14.

2. Rowe, "Problem of Evil," 10n1.

THE PROBLEM OF EVIL   121

To defeat the atheist's argument, the theist must also prove that God and evil *can co-exist*. The theist must prove logical consistency. Proving logical consistency entails providing an account of how things could be, or a model (S) that contains a set of claims where all the members of the set could be true in some possible state of affairs. The set does not have to be actual, but it must be consistent. Plantinga chose to argue for a model that is not true in actuality but that would be consistent if it were true. Plantinga attempted to do this using the Free Will Defense.

This defense included something known as Middle Knowledge and is argued on the basis of the counterfactuals of creaturely freedom (CCFs)—the free choices creatures could have made but didn't. In the following essay, I will briefly review Plantinga's argument showing that Mackie had not proven his claim and briefly discuss both the Free Will Defense and the idea of Middle Knowledge that it is founded on. In explaining these two concepts, I will also give a critique of them. Following this, I will give a more biblical theodicy of what I believe to be a model proving logical consistency based on traditional theistic beliefs as an alternative to Plantinga's Free Will Defense.

MACKIE'S CLAIM THAT THEISM IS INCONSISTENT

Consider the following set of statements that Mackie uses to argue that theistic beliefs are inconsistent or incoherent:

1. God is omnipotent,
2. God is wholly good, and
3. Evil exists.[3]

Plantinga contends that Mackie's argument requires additional premises in order to demonstrate the alleged inconsistency. Mackie uses statements (2) and (3) to draw out the following rules:

   a. There are no limits to what an omnipotent being can do, and
   b. A good thing always eliminates evil as far as it can.[4]

Plantinga refers to these as Mackie's Quasi-Logical rules because they are too specific to be logical rules and are not specific enough to be necessary truths. Plantinga points out that these rules do not, in fact, make (1) and (2) inconsistent with (3)—namely, because these rules are false. There are,

3. Plantinga, *God, Freedom, and Evil*, 13.
4. Plantinga, *God, Freedom, and Evil*, 17.

in fact, logical limits to what an omnipotent being can do. For example, an omnipotent being cannot make something true and not true at the same time (and in the same way). Moreover, an omnipotent being cannot create a law so that [a + b = c] *and* [a + b = not c]. As a necessary truth, 2 + 3 = 5 always equals 5; it cannot ever not equal 5.

Plantinga states that God could not create a square circle or a married bachelor, illustrating that God does, in fact, have logical limits as to what he can do. Thus, Plantinga changes Mackie's claim to read that "there are no non-logical limits to what an omnipotent being can do."[5] He then takes Mackie's first claim, (A), and points out that it assumes omniscience: There are some good beings who do not eliminate evils simply because they do not know about them, and that in no way makes them less good. This claim also assumes that eliminating one evil will not bring about a greater evil. Therefore, what Plantinga does in order to strengthen Mackie's argument is transform (A) and (B) into the following:

c. There are no non-logical limits on what an omnipotent and omniscient being can do, and

d. An omnipotent and omniscient good being eliminates every evil that it can properly eliminate.

However, Plantinga adds, "An omnipotent and omniscient being cannot properly eliminate every evil state of affairs." This argument prevents the atheologian from coherently arguing that the set (1), (2), (3), (C), and (D) is inconsistent or contradictory.[6]

Before he may say that he has won the argument, Plantinga must still show that his beliefs are consistent. Thus far, he has shown only that Mackie has not proven inconsistency, thereby giving all theists a good starting point to resolve the logical problem of evil. To prove consistency, Plantinga implements his Free Will Defense. If free will is a thing of great value and if God cannot logically prevent all possible evil without preventing free will, then God's omniscience and omnibenevolence are consistent with the existence of evil. By allowing evil to exist, God preserves free will. God refrains from placing any non-logical limits on himself, he still eliminates what evil he can properly eliminate, but he remains good while evil exists.

---

5. Plantinga, *God, Freedom, and Evil*, 17.
6. Plantinga, *God, Freedom, and Evil*, 18–22.

THE FREE WILL DEFENSE AND MIDDLE KNOWLEDGE

To further unpack the ways in which the existence of evil, God's existence, and free will can logically exist together, one must understand how Plantinga explains his Free Will Defense by examining the extent of divine knowledge. His defense builds its foundation on the concept of Middle Knowledge. Middle Knowledge is the view that God possesses counterfactual knowledge. Counterfactual knowledge holds that God's omniscience allows him to know what *might* have been or *would* have been, given any circumstances.[7] Middle Knowledge is different from Natural Knowledge, which claims that God knows all necessary truths, including facts about the worlds he might possibly create. It is also different from Free Knowledge, which states that God knows all contingent truth about the real world; in other words, he knows the past, present, and future.[8]

The problem with the Free Will Defense is that it bases Middle Knowledge on the idea of counterfactuals of creaturely freedom (CCFs). These CCFs restrict God by taking control away from him in reference to his ability to cause someone to choose (X) in any given circumstance. According to Plantinga, if someone would freely do (X) in circumstance (P), then there is nothing God can do to change this. As a result, Middle Knowledge appears incompatible with God's sovereignty and free will as described in the Bible, but this is not necessarily the case. God can still bring about circumstances, as some have argued, so that a person will make a certain decision. However, it does limit God in that he cannot make someone choose not to do (X) in circumstance (P) if she would freely choose (X) in circumstance (P).[9] When this is argued, Molinists (proponents of Middle Knowledge) are also claiming that they can be compatibilists (with respect to divine foreknowledge and human freedom).[10]

In addition to God's not having control over CCFs, Plantinga argues that every creature could logically suffer from what he calls *transworld depravity*. Because of this depravity, Plantinga claims that God could not have brought about a world with more moral good and less moral evil. Transworld

---

7. Craig, "'Middle-Knowledge' View," 120–21.
8. Craig, "'Middle-Knowledge' View," 121.
9. The result of CCFs is that an additional logical limit is placed on omnipotence. Some may not worry about merely logical limits on omnipotence, but others do on the grounds that the whole point of a theodicy is to justify God by some means other than simply placing limits on his power.
10. Perszyk, "Molinism and Compatibilism," 11–33. Compatibilists believe that free will is compatible with determinism. Determinism is the belief that the world is governed by necessity so that everything that happens is inevitable. This idea is closely tied to cause and effect.

depravity is the state of a free person who will do at least one bad thing in his life. It has been argued that this leads to futility because, if someone rejects Christ in the actual world, he would reject Christ in any world.[11] Nonetheless, there are no grounds to claim that CCFs or transworld depravity is true. While it is possible, Plantinga's free will defense is not likely because in his view God's ability to create whatever free creatures he wants to is limited.[12] This is probably one of the strongest objections to Plantinga's version of Free Will Defense.[13]

Others still see that it is hard to understand how God's sovereignty and man's free will are compatible without Middle Knowledge.[14] Regardless, scripture is not completely clear on how God's sovereignty and free will are compatible, and no one on this side of Heaven has that completely figured out.

So far, what we have seen is that, if Middle Knowledge is possible, then God knows about what anyone would do in a situation (P) or what decision (X) she would make if she were in any given situation. This knowledge is possible because of counterfactuals of creaturely freedom that prohibit God from changing our wills or what decisions we would make in any given circumstance. Furthermore, God could not create a sinless world or a world containing less evil than the actual world because all creatures suffer from transworld depravity. Transworld depravity has made circumstances such that, whatever world God determines to actualize, that world will have evil because every creature in that world will do at least one wrong act. The strength here is that the concept of free will involves moral good, and this good outweighs the amount of evil we find in our world. God, knowing this, has decided to actualize a world containing moral good.[15]

---

11. Hunt, "Middle Knowledge," 13.

12. Mark Boone has observed that Mackie makes an additional mistake that Plantinga seems not to even notice: Mackie thinks that a good and omnipotent God would, given a choice between creating a creature who *would* and a creature who would *not* sin, necessarily create the one who would *not* sin. That means that, if even *one* of the trillions of possible creatures lacks TWD, then there is a zero-percent possibility of God's creating Adam and Adam's sinning. If there is no possibility of Adam sinning, then the standard view of libertarian freedom does not hold. The result is that the Principle of Alternate Possibilities is not true; in other words, there is *not* a genuine possibility of any free creature sinning. Boone's observation continues to support the idea that this is the best possible world and shows that it is not very helpful to think of God's creation of this world in terms of a choice between multiple possible worlds.

13. Cowan, "Grounding Objection," 93.

14. Davison, "Foreknowledge," 29–44.

15. To read Plantinga's argument for this, refer to Plantinga, *God, Freedom, and Evil*, 29–59.

Because Plantinga's use of CCFs to show logical consistency appears to put non-logical limits on God's power, some have concluded that there is no truth to the idea of CCFs. This problem (among others) causes some theists to claim that Plantinga has not sufficiently provided a model of logical consistency. Mackie argues that there are no limits on God's power, and Plantinga responds by saying that there are no non-logical limits. Thus Plantinga has proven his point with Mackie, based on logic, but he has not done so by showing consistency based on actual doctrinal beliefs.

A better and stronger case can be made by showing the atheist that theistic belief is warranted despite the existence of evil not by using some possible world but by using the actual world. This would not only show the atheists that theistic belief is, in fact, logically consistent, but it would also show them what Christians actually believe. Presenting what we actually profess to be true gives Christians an opportunity to share the gospel as well as to argue for the consistency of the faith. It is still necessary that the theist proceed with caution, however, because no one will be argued into Heaven. Salvation comes when the Holy Spirit moves in someone's heart to convict him of sin and righteousness and to remove the blinders from his eyes so that he can see the truth of God (2 Cor 4:4).

LOGICAL CONSISTENCY WITHOUT MIDDLE KNOWLEDGE

Let's briefly review the claims that we've already considered. It is true that

1. God is omnipotent and omniscient,[16]
2. God is perfectly good, and
3. Evil exists in the world.

It is also true that

4. There are no non-logical limits on what an omnipotent being can do, and
5. An omnipotent and omniscient good being eliminates every evil that it can properly eliminate.

To this we now add several additional truths about the Christian faith.

6. God creates a world containing evil and has a good reason for doing so.
7. God created a world containing moral good.

---

16. Additional items for this list have been taken from Plantinga, *God Freedom, and Evil*, 54; Stump, "Problem of Evil," 392–93, 398.

8. Adam fell.

9. Natural evil entered the world as a result of Adam's sin.

10. After death, either human beings go to Heaven or they go to Hell, depending on their state of belief in Christ at the time of their death.[17]

Taking these into account, what we will see is that God—through his plan of creation, fall, and redemption—was able to bring about a world containing moral good as well as evil and that he had a good reason for doing so. After creating that world, he had a plan to redeem it from its fall and then to recreate it perfectly. This perfect recreation will cause the final state to be better than the original state in which God created the world.

To show logical consistency between the existence of God and evil, I will describe God's attributes, as we understand them to be, and then argue that he created the world with free creatures and had a good reason for doing so.

GOD'S ATTRIBUTES

God's attributes are such that he is spirit and omniscient (John 4:24; 21:17). Therefore, God's knowledge never changes. God is also omnipotent. He can do anything and everything he wills to do—and this is always in harmony with his perfection (Heb 6:18; Job 42:2). This also means that God, being omnipotent, cannot do certain things. These things include anything that goes against his nature, such as lie (Heb 6:18), or that causes him to deny himself (2 Tim 2:13). It also means that he cannot break the laws of nature; because he has authority over nature, even the weather obeys his commands (Luke 8:22–25).[18]

God is holy; this holiness makes him separate from moral evil and from sin. God is righteous and just, and as a result, God treats his creatures righteously and justly. God possesses the attribute of goodness. He is the final standard of good, and all that he does is worthy of approval (Luke 18:19). Our knowledge of his goodness encourages us to give thanks to him in all circumstances (1 Thess 5:18), including even the times when bad things are happening. God's mercy is his goodness toward those in distress, his grace is his goodness toward those who deserve only punishment, and

---

17. There are numerous other truths about the Christian faith—such as beliefs about bodily resurrection, a day of judgment, and a refashioning of the heavens and earth—but the points listed above are most pertinent to the current argument.

18. This idea should still leave room for miracles, which generally overrule natural law.

his patience is his goodness toward those who continue in sin over a period of time (Rom 2:4). God also possesses the attribute of truth. He is true God and his words are the true and final standard of truth (1 John 5:20). He will always do what he says he will do, and he will always fulfill what he promises. God is wise, and his wisdom always chooses the best goals and the best means to those goals (Rom 16:27). God is perfect in his wrath, and, because he is holy, he cannot look favorably upon sin. God, being eternal, must have his wrath satisfied eternally. This necessity limits him from doing away with punishment after death, not because he is evil but because his holiness is so great that it cannot warrant anything less than eternal satisfaction.

God, being omniscient, knows what is best; being omnipotent, can actualize what is best; and being perfectly good, does what is best for his creatures. Therefore, this is the best world for those creatures. We, as his creatures, were created for eternal life in the presence of God; thus, the way this world works now is the best means to that goal. God, being separate from moral sin, did not create moral sin; neither does scripture tell us that He did. Regardless, moral sin does exist, and it exists because God's creatures have the free capacity to choose to sin. This capacity to choose now raises the question, "Why is this the best world that God could have created for his creatures, knowing that they were created for eternal fellowship with him?"[19]

THE CREATION AND THE FALL

In a nutshell, God, being who he is, created a world that was perfectly good, and this world included free creatures to take care of it, to subdue it and rule over it, and to multiply and fill it (Gen 1:1, 28, 31). These creatures were sinless when they were created, so they were, in a sense, perfect. These creatures did not remain perfect, however, because they were perfect only in the sense that they had not sinned and not in the sense that they could not sin. These free creatures were tempted by the devil (Gen 3) and sinned in the garden by eating the forbidden fruit. As a result of Adam's sin, evil was brought into the world and this included death.

Now, because of Adam's sin, all of us have an inclination to sin once we are capable of making moral choices (Rom 5:18–21). We live in a depraved world where disasters destroy homes and crops, and kill millions every year; where people do not treat each other with love or respect; and where robberies, rapes, and murders occur among people of all ages and cultures.

19. For further information on the character of God, see Grudem, *Systematic Theology*, 156–225.

Some argue that God could have created a world with moral evil but no natural evil, but as we see here, natural evil is a result of the choice that Adam made and, therefore, all evil in a sense is a form of moral evil (Gen 3:17–19). There were no natural disasters before the fall that we are aware of. The question now remains, why did God create this world in such a way that Adam would fall? Could God not have created him with free choice but without the possibility of ever falling? Could God not have also created the world in such a way that there would never be any sin? Or maybe just that no other human born after Adam would sin? Possibly God could have, but he must have had a good reason for creating this world that contains evil. In God's infinite knowledge he chose to create Adam and Eve knowing they would choose sin, and he had a reason for specifically creating these two creatures knowing what would ensue. Perhaps God's reason is that free choice may have been better than no choice or no free choice, but we are in no position to know that one way or the other. Another option, which seems more likely, is that God created a world which would contain a fall for the sake of redemption.

What we do know is that God is good and that his ways are not our ways: We do not understand his ways fully, but we do know that we can trust him in whatever he has done. Regardless, God knew we would fall, so he predestined his Son to be a sacrifice on the cross, as a substitute for us, even before the foundation of the world (Eph 1:4–5).

GOD'S ACT OF REDEMPTION

God sent his Son into the world to live a sinless life and to die as a substitute on our behalf (2 Cor 5:21). In doing this, he created a way to reconcile us to God. Because we now have a way to have communion with God, we must decide to follow him. Even this decision, however, comes from the conviction of God's Spirit, who convicts of sin and righteousness (John 16:8–11). Because the Spirit convicts us of both, both must be present; without sin, we would not be convicted of our need for God or for a Savior. We must choose to obey God in spite of the fact that he calls us.

Eleonore Stump states that, since free will "is a necessary condition for union with God, the significant exercise of free will employed by human beings in the process which is essential for their being saved from their own evil is of such great value that it outweighs all the evil of the world."[20] While free choice may not actually outweigh all the evil in the world, it may be seen as a necessary condition for union with God. Rather than argue for

---

20. Stump, "Problem of Evil," 415–16.

logical consistency based on free will, which may not be as free as what we would sometimes like to think, one should argue that consistency comes from the results of the final state of being—namely, union with God. Those who share fellowship with God in the eternal state will know what they have been saved from.

After death, every human will spend eternity with God in glory or apart from him in eternal punishment. Where a person spends eternity depends on each person's state of being in this world at the time she dies.[21] When someone accepts Christ, he washes that person of her sin and she stands before God as perfect. Those who do not accept Christ stand before God as sinful, and because God cannot look favorably upon sin, he must punish them in accordance with his nature.

What is now seen is that God, although he allowed both sin and redemption to come into the world, applies redemption to his creatures on an individual basis. One thing is certain: All suffer from a sinful nature and are in need of redemption. God could have chosen to save no one and would still be perfectly just because we are the ones who have sinned. Instead, he, in fact, has decided to save at least some and he is no less just for not saving all. This is partially due to the fact that we have free will. God knows whether we will accept him or not, and if we do not, we are punished for our sins. If we do accept him, we are rewarded for being made righteous in Christ. Free will gives us the ability to see one reason for allowing evil into the world, and that reason is redemption. Whether or not free will is a good enough thing to outweigh the existence of evil, redemption leading to the eternal state is because it allows us to see what we have been saved from.

Some may still think that, if we did not have free will, we would be better off on the whole, but once again, we are in no position to say that there would be no evil if there were no free will. Nor may we say that having no free will would be a better condition for us as creatures. If we did not have free will, we might want to do evil but would be incapable of it; thus, we would live in a state of unactualized degenerateness. Neither would we ever see our need for God, nor could we choose to love and worship him. We would not even be capable of *deciding* to give him thanks for creating us.

GOD'S WAYS ARE PERFECT

What may now be said is that God is wholly righteous, omniscient, omnipotent, holy, and perfectly good. He does not act in any way that is contrary to his character, but he always acts in whatever way is best for his creation.

---

21. Stump, "Problem of Evil," 398. This statement was also listed above as (10).

Therefore, it was best for his creation that he give them free will. It was also best for his creation that Adam sinned, but only so that the creation could be redeemed. Free will is necessary for the acceptance of Christ, and entrance into the final state, which Christ is bringing about, will outweigh evil because we will know what we have been saved from. Moreover, unlike Adam, who was created perfect with the ability to sin, we will be made perfect in this final state and we will not sin ever again. Thus, God has a good reason for creating a world that contains evil. He also eliminates every evil he can properly eliminate through redemption.

In the end, all evil will be properly eliminated because he is redeeming all of creation. The last evil to die will be the nemesis of life—death. The elimination of evil will be seen in the eternal state for all those who will live with God eternally there. So we see that, because God is perfect in all his ways and because evil will be outweighed by the condition of the eternal state for believers (knowing what we were saved from and being made perfect in such a way that we will never again sin or suffer from sin), it is logically consistent that God and evil co-exist, and, therefore, the theist is warranted in his beliefs about God.

OBJECTIONS TO THESE CLAIMS

There are several objections that may be made at this point. Why would God not bring about a scenario that results in all humans going to Heaven? How can a good God allow eternal torment in Hell? Why doesn't he give second chances? How could he allow infinite torment for someone who lived a finite life? Why did God not destroy the human race immediately after the fall of Adam? Why did God not keep humans from the inclination to do evil with respect to moral choices after Adam fell?[22]

These are all very good questions, and while the theist may easily answer some, he does not easily answer all of them. As has already been stated, God cannot look favorably on sin, and all have sinned, so not all can live with God forever because not all believe in God. Only those who give their lives to Christ are made guiltless in the sight of God. He could have made it so that all would come to know him, but that would eliminate free will, and scripture teaches that humans have free will. One single sin is enough to condemn a person to Hell for eternity, not only for a short time, because God is holy and perfect and anything less than perfect does not have the right to be in the presence of God. Because God is an eternal or infinite

---

22. Stump, "Problem of Evil," 399, 404.

being, his wrath must be eternal, so those who reject him must suffer his wrath for eternity.

This suffering for eternity leads to the question concerning second chances. There are no second chances because God has deemed it to be that way. Theists cannot give a concrete answer to this question as we can the others because we do not know exactly why God decreed for it to be this way. However, who are we to say that God, already knowing whether we would accept him or not, also knows whether we would accept him after death if given the opportunity. It very well may be that if one would not accept God in this life, she would never accept him after this life ends. Furthermore, the Bible does teach that we are immediately in God's presence after we die. This being the case, if we are not covered in Christ's blood at that point, God's wrath must immediately receive satisfaction, not because God is evil but because he is perfectly holy.

The question about infinite torture for a finite life seems to be little more than a rewording of the previous question about Hell. Still, it could be that God created us as beings who would never cease to exist completely. Because God was rejected, the creature has no other choice but to suffer for eternity because (a) there are no second chances and (b) God's wrath is eternal, being consistent with his character. Two things are certain: Humans were not ultimately created for death, and God is so great that his wrath must be eternally satisfied.

God did not destroy the human race after Adam because his plan was a plan of redemption. Furthermore, if we as humans did not inherit the inclination to sin as a result of Adam, we would either (a) not all be in need of redemption or (b) not have all been able to be reconciled to God through his Son, and God has deemed that to be of greater importance than not falling because he brought it about in actuality. Furthermore, we see that Adam had to fall because, without the fall, there would be no reconciliation and without reconciliation there would be no ability to have union with God the way that we do today and the way we will in the eternal state.

Adam and God had union and community before the fall, but that is no reason to think that the union Adam had with God before the fall is better than the union with God that we have through Christ. Christ, in the end, will redeem the elect in such a way that they will be free in the eternal state and no longer sin at all. Adam could and obviously did sin; therefore, it is argued here that the final state after sin has been properly eliminated may actually be better than the state that God originally brought about, which was all good (Gen 1:31).

If it is, in fact, the case that the eternal state will be better than the original state, then it could also be that it is better for us to have free will and to live in a fallen world than it would have been for us not to have fallen at all. It can certainly give us a deeper understanding of the way God cares for his creatures (enough to allow his Son to die on their behalf). Free will also lets us have the assurance of knowing both that we chose God and that he chose us. We are his covenant people and his love is made manifest by his choosing to redeem us. We know we are his because we have chosen to love and obey him.

Furthermore, by obeying God, we can show his love to others in a way that allows him to use us to aid in his reconciliation of other souls to himself. This being the case, we can, by obeying him, bring about good and be a living example of how he properly eliminates evil over time. He is currently eliminating it in the elect. While bad things still happen, he will eventually eliminate all evil.[23] When bad things do happen, Christians may also give him glory because those bad things ultimately work out for the Christian's good in the end. We cannot know the reason for all evils on this side of eternity; we may still not know what they are once we reach the eternal state, but God is trustworthy. Even when we do not see the reason or when someone performs an evil act that appears to us as being utterly pointless, God can still use it for good because his plans cannot be thwarted (Gen 50:20–21).

FINAL THOUGHTS

In conclusion, what has been shown is that Alvin Plantinga formulated an argument that worked exceptionally well to show that the atheist had not shown logical inconsistency between the belief that God is omnipotent and good, and the fact that evil exists. However, Plantinga did not decisively show logical consistency between the claims that God is omnipotent and omniscient and that good and evil exist. His argument rests on Middle Knowledge, requiring CCFs and trans-world depravity, which many orthodox Christians find to be at odds with traditional Christian thought as well as with doctrinal beliefs about God's character. Philosophical speculations are helpful in this argument, but they often do not reflect the reality of beliefs when it comes to practitioners of religion. For Christians to be satisfied with their arguments for God's existence, they must look to scripture to show that actual beliefs contain the same logical consistency as arguments based on speculation. For this reason, an alternative model of consistency was proposed—a theodicy. This model follows the work of Eleonore Stump, but it intends to show consistency through God's plan of creation, fall, and

---

23. All evil minus hell, but hell here is viewed as God's punishment of evil rather than in itself a state of evil.

redemption. The atheist may not believe all of the claims laid forth in this last section, but to prove consistency the model need not actually be obtained. Therefore, even if the atheist does not think the theist is correct in his beliefs, if the beliefs espoused would be true if actual, and if they do not contradict one another, then the theist has proven logical consistency. To bring this essay to a close, I will lay out the model of consistency as simply as possible to show how it fits together, using as few claims as necessary to show the set consistent. Remember, what we need is a set of claims, a subset of which entails the other claims and proves the set consistent.

1. God is wholly/perfectly omniscient, omnipotent, wise, holy, and good.
2. God has no non-logical limits and acts according to his attributes, which actions include properly eliminating all evil that can properly be eliminated.
3. God created humans as moral agents with free choice.
4. Adam, the first human, fell because he chose to sin.
5. Sin now exists in the world as a result of Adam's choice.
6. God chose to redeem the world through Christ's death on the cross.
7. At the time that humans die, they go to Heaven or Hell for eternity based on their free will and whether they have chosen to believe in God.
8. Because the final state is more perfect than the first, God created a world containing moral evil and had a perfectly good reason for doing so.

What can be deduced from this is that (1) and (2) describe God's character; together they entail (3). (4) results in (5); and therefore, God has brought about (6). (7) is a result of (1) through (6); thus, (8) shows how they all fit together in a way that is consistent because (8) retains God's holiness and man's freedom and shows that the fall of Adam and the redemption through Christ bring about the most perfect state of being in the end. This perfect state is one where humans are free and made perfect in such a way that there will never again be any sin.

We have now shown logical consistency with respect to a set of claims that entails the existence of God, evil, and free will without employing Plantinga's version of a Free Will Defense. Instead, we have shown what many orthodox Christians believe about God and salvation. In doing this, we may see not only that it is logically possible that God exists, but also that it is actually both possible and logical that these things are the case.

BIBLIOGRAPHY

Cowan, Steven B. "The Grounding Objection to Middle Knowledge Revisited." *Religious Studies* 39 (2003) 93–102.

Craig, William Lane. "The 'Middle-Knowledge' View." In *Divine Foreknowledge: Four Views*, edited by James K. Beilby and Paul R. Eddy, 119–43. Downers Grove, IL: InterVarsity, 2001.

Davison, Scott. "Foreknowledge, Middle Knowledge, and 'Nearby' Worlds." *International Journal for Philosophy of Religion* 30 (1991) 29–44.

Grudem, Wayne. *Systematic Theology: An Introduction to Biblical Doctrine*. Grand Rapids: Zondervan, 1994.

Hunt, David P. "Middle Knowledge and the Soteriological Problem of Evil." *Religious Studies* 27 (1991) 3–26.

Perszyk, Kenneth J. "Molinism and Compatibilism." *International Journal of Philosophy of Religion* 48 (2000) 11–33.

Plantinga, Alvin. *God, Freedom, and Evil*. Grand Rapids: Eerdmans, 1974.

Rowe, William. "The Problem of Evil and Some Varieties of Atheism." In *The Evidential Argument from Evil*, edited by Daniel Howard-Snyder, 1–11. Bloomington: Indiana University Press, 1996.

Stump, Eleonore. "The Problem of Evil." *Faith and Philosophy* 2 (1985) 392–423.

10

Demons, Idols, and Faith

RUSSELL HEMATI

How trustworthy is the mind? Are there honest and well-founded doubts about the inner workings of our own rationality? It is possible to ask these questions not skeptically, but devotionally. Rather than be clever at not-knowing, holding doubts about the trustworthiness of reason can serve a greater intellectual humility. In this chapter, I explore two forms of skeptical arguments, categorizing them into Demon-scenarios (inspired by Descartes) and Idol-scenarios (inspired by Francis Bacon). Then, through combining traits of each, and with some help from Friedrich Nietzsche, a new form of skepticism about reason can come into focus—what I will call Lesser Demon-scenarios—that can lead either to despair or faith. Following Augustine's analysis, I recommend faith.

THE DEMON

First, let us examine the most fantastical of skeptical arguments—Demon-scenarios. In Meditation I of his incomparable *Meditations on First Philosophy*, René Descartes attempts to destroy all his beliefs through showing that his two foundational commitments were subject to doubt. Those two commitments are that the senses are reliable and that reason is trustworthy. If those two commitments were to fall or to be subject to doubt, then all his other beliefs would topple with them. First, he gives the typical critiques of perception: The senses are unreliable at the edges, that is, when they report distant objects, faint sounds, and optical illusions. But, Descartes adds, not only are the senses unreliable at the edges, but they can also give fully fictitious reports in the rare cases of mental illness and delusions or the everyday cases of dreaming. Since no sense data can be used definitively to rule out the possibility of being in a delusion or dream, all sense data is thereby doubtful. This is different from observations based on optical illusions or distance, which can be corrected by changing one's perspective or using instrumentation to work around anomalies in human perception. Unlike optical illusions, any sense data used to confirm that one is not dreaming (pinching oneself, noting the continuity of one event with another, and so on) could easily take place within the dream; in fact, often dreams have elements in them that trick the dreamer into believing that what they are experiencing is real. Pop-culture has enjoyed this premise through a variety of imaginative scenarios: for example, being in a giant simulation (*The Matrix*) and being manipulated through dreams (*Inception*). Any evidence one uses to confirm the reality of what is being sensed could be generated by a delusory state of mind intent on protecting its own false perceptions.

Descartes wishes to push further: Even though this line of reasoning serves to make *all* sense experience less than certain, it does nothing to draw reason into its snare. After all, Descartes notes, even if he is dreaming, the basic truths of mathematics remain constant, as do various logical operations such as *modus ponens*. Being trapped in a dream world does nothing to shake one's commitments to reason, logic, and math. Triangles have three sides even if the triangle one sees is merely a figment of the imagination. Wishing to leave no stone unturned, Descartes continues. Showing that there was some cause for doubt concerning not only perception but also the operations of the mind, Descartes produces a fantastical objection to the trustworthiness of reason:

> And yet firmly rooted in my mind is the long-standing opinion that there is an omnipotent God who made me the kind of creature that I am. How do I know that he has not brought it about that there is no earth, no sky, no extended thing, no shape, no size, no place, while at the same time ensuring that all these things appear to me to exist just as they do now? What is more, just as I consider that others sometimes go astray in cases where they think they have the most perfect knowledge, how do

> I know that God has not brought it about that I too go wrong every time I add two and three or count the sides of a square, or in some even simpler matter, if that is imaginable?[1]

Note that this doubt has a different character than do dreams or hallucinations; those earlier arguments dealt only with the content of perception—I may doubt that I am here in my chair writing instead of still sleeping or that I really am in my home instead of in a simulation or an asylum. In this passage Descartes does more—he doubts the foundational building blocks of all knowledge and perception. What begins as an extension of the delusion/dream objection to the senses takes a disturbing turn. If God were a trickster, a being that Descartes will call "an evil genius" and "a supremely powerful deceiver," this being could not only cause him to perceive any number of things that were not there but could also cause him to have beliefs of whole categories that are fictitious (shape, size, location), and then what would prevent even the operations of one's own mind from becoming suspect? If there were no objects extended in space, or perhaps no space at all, no beliefs about the world could ever be certain. A being powerful enough to make him believe in a three-dimensional reality when no such reality exists would also be powerful enough to cause him to go wrong every time he counted to five or examined a square and noted its equal sides.

Later, in Meditation 3, Descartes downplays this cause for doubt, calling it "tenuous" and "metaphysical," attempting to couch this doubt in terms that make it seem like a merely theoretical rather than an actual concern. Yet this doubt has a power over the imagination not easy to dispel since it hides a more general objection to the reliability of one's own reason. While a Loki-like deity, the Cartesian Demon, could be the source of reason's downfall, there are other potential "demons" that could just as easily render the human mind incapable of finding the truth and thus prevent naive belief in math and logic. For lack of a better term, we can call skeptical doubts of this sort "Demon-scenarios."

The Demon-scenario is no ordinary hallucination; otherwise, it would bring doubt only to the senses, not to reason. Demon-scenarios can be identified by these four characteristics. First, the demon must have pervasive access to and control over every aspect of the mind. Second, the demon must be invisible to the person tormented. Third, the demon must lead the person away from the truth.[2] Fourth and final, the demon must be inescap-

---

1. Descartes, *Meditations on First Philosophy*, 14.
2. From an epistemological standpoint, being in a Demon-scenario with a benevolent demon may not be much better. Imagine a benevolent demon constantly altering a person's thoughts and beliefs in order to ensure that the tormented always had *true*

able. Descartes worries that such a being would be able to cause him to be deceived "every time I add two and three or count the sides of a square" *or something even simpler than these operations*. Counting and addition are so simple and foundational that it seems impossible to imagine anything simpler. Perhaps the work of the demon could obscure self-evident truths such that we could all be mistaken about the numbers 3 and 4 being different numbers at all, that the past is not subject to change, or that affirming the antecedent of a conditional statement necessarily implies its consequent.

Indeed, what would prevent the law of non-contradiction from being open to doubt? To see how this is possible, first consider how the demon would cause us to go wrong about the square. We see the diagram before us (whether real or hallucinatory) and start to count the sides, starting with the bottom one and going clockwise. "One, two, three, four," we recite to ourselves. Yet, while we were counting, the demon made us forget that we had counted one of the sides right after we counted it. A neutral observer would have heard us say, "One, two, three, three, four." The observer is puzzled by our repetition of one of the numbers, but we would not have noticed it at all since the demon would have conveniently erased from our memories our observation of one of the sides of the square. The demon might also give us the confident emotion that we often feel when we *know* that we have the correct answer to some problem. If the demon is capable of manipulating our memories and perceptions, it could also manipulate our emotions—making us feel confident about false things and doubtful about true things. If the demon can do all these things, then it seems arbitrary to protect the law of non-contradiction from this sort of attack. What is this law but a deep-seated feeling philosophers have that P and not-P cannot both be true or the fact that all propositions can be validly derived from a contradiction? No proof for this principle is possible without making use of the principle since it is axiomatic for all proofs. When we see "P & not-P" we see it as incorrect, an error, or absurd, but this declaration of the impossibility of "P & not-P" is itself a feeling—a feeling that the statement we are seeing cannot possibly be true. But then, how is this feeling to be safeguarded against the actions of the demon? Remember, this demon is already making us feel the same sort of disapproval when someone utters the statement, "Squares have five sides." As for all propositions being true if a contradiction holds, perhaps the belief that some propositions are false is due to demonic influence! There would be no way to tell which beliefs are the "control" beliefs that remain constant while other beliefs are tested. In a Demon-scenario, there are no principled reasons to find any idea more certain or more plausible than any other.

---

beliefs. What would be the justification for those beliefs?

Of course, the demon might cause us to go wrong about these "simpler" things in quite other ways. The preconditions for squares, counting, and logic might all be demonic fabrications. For example, the demon could be causing us to believe in numbers when none are real. The demon may be deceiving us about the nature of planes and solids when, in reality, the idea of a square is incoherent and its sides are necessarily uncountable. Or, most terrifying for philosophers, the demon might have arranged for us to think using propositions, yet that very structure is misleading. (Thus, there is no law of non-contradiction since there are no propositions that can contradict each other.) Descartes includes even simpler operations since, if there were a demon, no mental structure, scaffolding, or system would be safe from doubt. You could have no confidence in the pronouncements of your reason—each dictate just as open to doubt as any other, with no way to tell truth from error.

Descartes found the notion of being mentally tortured by the Demon to be so repulsive to his sense of morality that he could not imagine the existence of the Demon to be compatible with the existence of a good God. Later in the *Meditations*, after providing proof that a perfect being (God) does exist, Descartes moves straightforwardly into re-affirming those simpler operations. In the overall argument of the *Meditations,* the existence of God vanquishes doubt that we are in a Demon-scenario. Descartes was not merely trying to show that God was not the Demon but that, if there is a God, no Demon-scenario would be possible. A good God would never allow his creatures to be deceived in such a way, Descartes argues; so, once the existence of God was safeguarded by the idea of perfection and the confidence in clear and distinct ideas, Descartes can cast aside the possibility of the Demon and the associated doubts that come from it. In one stroke Descartes re-introduces the truths of math and logic (and a bit of theology for good measure) once the existence of a good God vouchsafes the operations of his mind.

IDOLS AND LESSER DEMONS

Descartes's declaration of victory seems premature. A demon of the sort Descartes imagines, with its active malevolence and supernatural power, may in fact be so morally outlandish that we may reasonably suppose that a good God would never allow *that* state of affairs to occur. But what if there are other, Lesser Demon-scenarios? What if we have the same degree of deception but without a malevolent trickster? Our moral intuitions may not recoil at a good God allowing pervasive deception without a *literal* demon doing the work.

A potential candidate for this pervasive deception comes from Francis Bacon's work that outlines a new form of scientific method, the *Novum Organum*. Bacon calls attention to four impediments to understanding, which he calls "Idols of the mind" due to their ability to block our understanding of nature.[3] Though we do not get malevolent, pervasive demons, as in Descartes, Bacon gives reasons to doubt our reason. He subdivides the Idols into the Cave, the Tribe, the Marketplace, and the Theater. First, we have no way of disconnecting our observations from ourselves. We see through a lens of our own preferences and observe only a very small portion of the world. Certain things will seem more reasonable to one person than another. For example, some people prefer old ideas to new ideas. They will become impressed by the antiquity of an opinion and give it greater credence than it deserves. Or, for myself, growing up in America has likely given me an overestimation of the values of representative democracy. Bacon calls these personal variations Idols of the Cave.

Second, we cannot separate our observations from our species. Humans have rather limited sense abilities (even compared to other animals) and have psychological traits that, while useful for survival, do not always lead toward truth about reality. We are, Bacon observes, a species that looks for connections. Our preference is to unify our observations into a whole even though that unity may not be supported by the phenomena. This quirk of the human species prevents us from seeing the world as it is. Bacon calls these species-general traits Idols of the Tribe.

Third, due to the need to communicate with each other, humans developed a system of signs called language. This system gives us confidence that, when we refer to something, we understand the reference, yet this confidence is misplaced. Unfortunately, our words often fail to respect the true taxonomy of the world. High-profile examples of this are outmoded medical diagnoses (such as Hysteria or Dropsy), circular scientific descriptions (such as force and matter), and political slogans (currently in vogue: labeling political enemies as "socialist" or "racist"). Bacon calls these failures Idols of the Marketplace.

Finally, and striking closest to home for me as a professor, Bacon calls attention to the mental-warping effect of education. Sitting in a class, being forced to memorize accepted theories, taking tests, being ranked in comparison to other students, learning to regurgitate the assumptions and conclusions of the past—this experience is more likely to prevent true and

---

3. Bacon, *New Organon*, 40. My gloss on Bacon begins at aphorism 39.

careful observation of nature than to aid it. Watching a teacher "prove" a theorem on a blackboard may look like knowledge, but it just as likely repeats and amplifies the mistakes of the past. Bacon classifies this effect as one of the Idols of the Theater.

Like Descartes, Bacon does not leave his audience in despair but attempts to find a way of escape. Naturally, their methods of escape are different. Descartes, with the active Demon preventing him from having knowledge (a Demon-scenario) needs an active God of greater power to vanquish his skepticism. Bacon, with the passive Idols structurally preventing him from acquiring truth about nature (an Idol-scenario), offers a new methodology (at least as powerful as the structure that the Idols give) that he believes will circumvent the knowledge-interrupting features of those Idols and allow nature, finally, to shine through. Bacon's early formulation of the scientific method is designed to compensate for these Idols by a comprehensive program of collective empirical induction. Unlike a demon, an idol can be cast aside once it is finally recognized as an idol. The task of designing a solution to avoid an Idol-scenario is not insurmountable.

GREATER IDOLS AND LESSER DEMONS

So far, we have seen two distinct classes of skeptical principles: demons, which actively thwart our knowledge and faculties, and idols, which passively interrupt our perception, transposing themselves in place of accurate observation. Are there mixtures of these two skeptical scenarios—passive (lesser) demons and active (greater) idols? A propaganda campaign seems like a plausible candidate for a greater idol. It would not be a demon, causing us to doubt even the most basic aspects of our own rationality, but it would (often successfully) interrupt and replace our experience of the world—exchanging observation for whatever the propagandists wish the public to believe. During the Second World War, propagandists represented the Allies' dedicated adversary, Japan, as deformed monsters with buck teeth and thick glasses who were kidnapping our women for their own perverse pleasures.[4] If successful, such propagandists can block our true observation of the enemy as a fellow human being. Even though the regrettable necessity of war causes us to do violence, we are all bound together in humanity. Instead, we see only the inhuman (or sub-human) that needs to be punished, perhaps eradicated. Anti-Semitic propaganda used by Germany during the same time had much the same effect. The Jews were not neighbors, not humans,

---

4. Thomas Bivins has collected some of the more striking examples for his course on media history. See Bivins, "Anti-Japanese Propaganda in WWII."

but a rapacious, envious sub-race not fit to exist.[5] This interruption of observation was accomplished with the help of illustrations, rhetoric, and even fraudulent "scientific" studies and papers. These systems acted as idols since they served merely to block or replace observation of nature and they can be overcome once recognized. But they were done purposefully and systematically. Propaganda, then, seems to be, at least potentially, a greater idol.

What of the reverse? Are there lesser demons? Two candidates seem ripe for analysis. The first is suggested by Nietzsche in *Twilight of the Idols*. In the chapter titled "Reason in Philosophy," Nietzsche expands Bacon's Idols of the Marketplace and points toward *language* as a kind of mental distortion. His primary critique is toward philosophers and their use of "Being" as both the most general abstract term and also as another name for the transcendent. "Being," Nietzsche argues, is the "last wisps of smoke from the evaporating end of reality,"[6] and the fact that philosophers worship it is evidence of their decadence and irrationality.

> Being is imagined into everything—*pushed under everything*—as a cause; the concept of "being" is only derived from the concept of "I." . . . In the beginning there was the great disaster of an error, the belief that the will is a thing with *causal efficacy*—that will is a *faculty*. . . . These days we know that it is just a word. . . . Much, much later, in a world more enlightened in thousands of ways, philosophers, to their great surprise, became conscious of a *certainty*, a subjecting *assurance* in the way the categories of reason were applied: they concluded that these categories could not have come from the empirical world,—in fact, the entirety of the empirical world stood opposed to them. *So where did they come from?* . . . In fact, nothing has ever had a more naive power of persuasion than the error of being, as formulated by the Eleatics, for example: after all, every word we say, every sentence we use, speaks in its favor!—Even the Eleatics' adversaries succumbed to the seduction of the Eleatic concept of being: Democritus, for instance, when he invented his *atom* . . . "Reason" in language: oh, what a deceptive old woman this is! I am afraid that we have not got rid of God because we still have faith in grammar.[7]

The error of "Being" is an easy one for humans to make since all of our language testifies to "Being" and causes us to encounter reality as a set of

---

5. Wikipedia, "Propaganda in Nazi Germany." There are almost too many resources for Nazi propaganda.

6. Nietzsche, *Twilight of the Idols*, 168.

7. Nietzsche, *Twilight of the Idols*, 169–70.

discrete objects with permanence. We say, for example, that a chair *is* over there or that the dog *is* asleep. The use of the word "is" causes us to imagine that the chair and the dog are real things with their own identity and history—that they can be preserved, carry meaning, and eventually go out of existence. But according to Nietzsche, this is all fiction. There are no objects distinct from other objects, no truth to the myth of "wholes with parts," nothing to be preserved. There is only nature in its ever-changing flux. Yet, we are bewitched by the word "is" into believing that the real things must be permanent and whole (since the word "is" makes existence seem to require permanence and unity to be real existence); thus, we make the only philosophical leap available to us. We would, like Socrates, start to imagine a world where those psychological desires of permanence and unity receive their final consummation. The Platonic world of the Forms (or its Christian mirror—the "Mind of God") is the next logical step.

As Nietzsche puts it: we cannot get rid of the idea of God because grammar itself leads us to think that only the existence of God can make sense of the reality that we experience. However, this experience is not an experience of reality *as it is*. We are experiencing reality mediated through language, through grammar, and thus with the ideas of unity and permanence superimposed onto our perceptions. Thus, the being of things, the properties of things, and the things we say about them are all suspect. The system of language, then, is a demon. Yet there is no supernatural Being causing us to go wrong; rather, there is a system of signs passively forcing us to believe in what we consider to be the most basic concepts of existence, identity, and rationality. But if rationality is merely a trick of grammar and if grammar is inescapable even in our thoughts, we have reason to doubt the inner workings of our own minds. Language places us in a Demon-scenario, but a passive, Lesser Demon-scenario.

I have often wondered if anyone reading Nietzsche actually develops language-foundational skepticism. The postmodern academic tradition of deconstruction, as Nietzsche's heir, engages in something like Nietzsche's skepticism concerning language, but it seems to stop short of Nietzsche's suggestion that we doubt being or existence as a fundamental and observational category. Rather, deconstruction seems to stop short of unmooring all concepts in favor of plucking the low-hanging fruit of culture and politics. To consider language a Cartesian Demon—that is a heavy charge Nietzsche places on grammar. Whether or not we deem Nietzsche's war on the copula, the being verb, a success—and it is up to each person to decide whether or not he or she is a skeptic of that sort—the suspicion that we *are in fact* in a Demon-scenario, but only due to the way that language developed, is intriguing for two reasons.

First, it provides a Demon-scenario that is resistant to Descartes's intuition that the existence of a good God is incompatible with a Demon-scenario. As Descartes argues, a good God would never allow us to be deceived in such a way that the basic foundations of our mind become suspect. Though Descartes's inference seems premature, since the existence of a good God would not rule out brainwashing or hypnotism, Nietzsche's language Demon gives us a further critique of Descartes's inference: A good God in no way rules out self-deception. As Nietzsche points out, our trust in language, though historically conditioned and taught to us from infancy, is part and parcel of human naivety. It is not the work of a supernatural deceiver but of ourselves. Also, language demons are not ruled out by the existence of God for theological reasons. Note that the confusion of languages at Babel was a divine judgment for human arrogance. Though that confusion may merely be that the vocabulary and syntax of each language became jumbled, the confusion from Babel may be deeper still. Perhaps belief in being, permanence, and unity are themselves divine judgments. Whether these are self-deceptions or divine punishment makes no difference—they are both compatible with the existence of God.

Second, Nietzsche's language Demon gives us conceptual space within which to search for other demons. We need not follow Descartes and posit malevolent spirit beings tricking us for their own demented pleasure. Rather, we can be on the hunt for self-deceptions that, like the structures of language, give us cause to doubt the most trusted structures of human reason. In order to qualify as Demon-scenarios, the deception would need to be pervasive and invisible. The demon must be able to muddy our clear thinking (or replace wholesale one thought with another) without being detectable to the person inside the scenario. And most important, unlike an Idol-scenario, there must be no means of escape from within the scenario. Neither can Nietzsche offer a form of language that does not try to make objects seem permanent or properties not universal, nor can he produce sentences without copulas. Perhaps someone can "peek" and, in a flash of insight, realize that one is in a Demon-scenario, but there would be no escape possible. Not without some sort of miraculous change.

THE LESSER DEMON OF SIN

St. Augustine's description in *Confessions* of the sin of pride seems very close to a passive Lesser Demon-scenario. Augustine recounts the many sins and indiscretions of his youth, among which are the many times in which he had plenty of evidence of the truth of Christianity but was unable to come to the correct conclusions due to his own arrogance. At the time, he was unaware of this, naturally. He was simply going to school, falling in love, and then later beginning his teaching career. At many points in his life, Augustine is given opportunities to convert but fails to do so because Christianity seemed unreasonable to him at the time: because he found the moral instruction from his mother to be boring, because he thought that the writing style of the Bible was unsophisticated, or because he enjoyed the ease of avoiding responsibility for his own actions. Manichean dualism and astrology proved potent distractions. For a time, his desire not to believe even prevented him from recognizing the existence of anything immaterial.

There was a point in his life where, by his own admission, Augustine *should have* understood the truth of Christianity. As he explored Neo-Platonism and even had a vision of the transcendence of the good and the nature of the divine being, he was filled with pride.

> I was sure that you (God) truly are, and are always the same; that you never become other or different in any part or by any movement of position, whereas all other things derive from you, as is proved by the fact that they exist. Of these conceptions I was certain; but to enjoy you I was too weak. I prattled on as if I were expert, but unless I had sought your way in Christ our Savior, I would have been not expert but expunged. I began to want to give myself airs as a wise person. I was full of my punishment, but I shed no tears of penitence. Worse still, I was puffed up with knowledge.[8]

Augustine cannot perceive the truth about himself, even after having a mystical vision where he is finally able to understand that evil is mere privation of good and that everything we value is a copy of one or another facet of the divine essence. Faith was impossible because of the sinful nature of his mind. Instead of having faith, he became *even more sinful*. In his mind, having the vision was now an *achievement*. He felt that now, finally, he was smarter, wiser, better than everyone else. This is a facet of sinfulness that Augustine revisits at other times in his works—the punishment for sin is often *more sin*.[9]

---

8. Augustine, *Confessions* 7.20 (130).

9. This is a curious feature of Augustine's theodicy. In *On Grace and Free Will* Augustine interprets passages such as Exodus 9:12 where God hardens Pharaoh's heart as punishment for prior sins. Pharaoh, then, is responsible for his heart's being hardened since it was a punishment for his disrespect of the God of Israel. Augustine reassures his readers—under no circumstances would God punish someone not already guilty. Pharaoh is judged by God guilty and his sentence is to commit even more sin, to his nation's ruin. While Pharaoh's hardening is performed by God as punishment, Augustine's

The inevitable result is that, once sinfulness has taken hold in someone's soul, he will continually victimize himself by becoming ever more sinful. The young Augustine was punished for his arrogance—the punishment was to receive a great philosophical and spiritual gift of insight yet have it make him a worse person. Under his own power, he is doomed to miss the point forever. And as the final capstone of despair, he "shed no tears of penitence" over his condition. He was being punished but could not realize it since the punishment brought on a kind of blindness. The truth was in front of him, but he could not respond to it in an appropriate way. All he had to offer was pride, pride, and more pride. His predicament had all the hallmarks of being in a Demon-scenario.

It may seem strange for Augustine, a vehemently anti-skeptical philosopher, to have a Demon-scenario in the *Confessions*. However, the blindness of his former condition is cause not for despair but for gratitude. The Sin Demon prevents us from recognizing the truth of Christianity, but Augustine does not believe that he had to find the truth on his own. Each stage of his spiritual autobiography includes the recognition that God was preparing him to be able to finally come to faith. He was not alone in trying to escape the Demon-scenario of his own making, but he was being led out gradually by a loving God. Realizing that God often leads people away from the Sin Demon through circuitous routes should give us all greater patience when engaging with those who ridicule the claims of Christianity and give us greater patience with ourselves as we are led step by step out of our own Demon-scenarios. None of us can know now which of our demons are still active, but through faith we can trust that God will eventually lead us from truth to truth, revealing himself as his gift.

BIBLIOGRAPHY

Augustine. *Confessions*. Translated by Henry Chadwick. Oxford: Oxford University Press, 1991.

———. *On the Free Choice of the Will, On Grace and Free Choice, and Other Writings*. Translated by Peter King. Cambridge: Cambridge University Press, 2010.

Bacon, Francis. *The New Organon*. Translated by Lisa Jardine and Michael Silverthorne. Cambridge: Cambridge University Press, 2000.

Bivins, Thomas. "Anti-Japanese Propaganda in WWII: Racism Takes an Uglier Turn." *J387: Media History*. http://j387mediahistory.weebly.com/anti-japanese-propaganda-in-wwii.html.

---

recounting of the experience of the epistemological effects of sin acts resembles a feedback loop. His punishment for his arrogance is being unable to see the truth when it would require him to be humble. He cannot recognize the truth even when he is directly confronted with it. As a result he finds plausible beliefs that are, in fact, ridiculous.

Descartes, René. *Meditations on First Philosophy with Selections from the Objections and Replies*. Translated by John Cottingham. Cambridge: Cambridge University Press, 1996.
Nietzsche, Friedrich. *The Anti-Christ, Ecce Homo, Twilight of the Idols, and Other Writings*. Translated by Aaron Ridley and Judith Norman. Cambridge: Cambridge University Press, 2007.
Wikipedia. "Propaganda in Nazi Germany." November 9, 2020. https://en.wikipedia.org/wiki/Propaganda_in_Nazi_Germany.

11

A Medievalist's Journey through Science and Faith

Adam D. Jones

Religion and science are both common passions, so it's frustrating to be told that we must choose between the two. If common rhetoric is to be believed, then we must eschew one to embrace the other, taking our place as either a bulwark of tradition or a champion of progress. Thankfully, some solace can be found when the debate is viewed through the eyes of a historian.

If we examine the worldview of earlier Christian leaders, we see something that is not obvious to the casual, modern observer: This antagonism between faith and science is a recent trend. Things were not always thus. Before our battle-hardened approach to this issue, influential thinkers embraced a much more reasonable philosophy, a philosophy I believe we should learn from.

An honest look at the past will reveal that scientific progress was held in high esteem by the medieval church leaders. These champions of thought and theology guided the faithful toward scientific understanding, not away from it, because doing so was, to them, part of their service to God. The startling truth that we find in the pages of history is that, rather than creating dissonance, reason and revelation have traditionally been a source of harmony.

Before we can set ourselves to learning from this older approach, we must dust away some stubborn cobwebs. Dispensing with the idea of medieval "flat earthers" will clear up a centuries-old misconception, but more important for our purposes, it will demonstrate the tenacity with which early Christians clung to scientific understanding. We will then see an in-depth example of this blending of faith and science in the person of Bede, a historical figure who, though he is hardly famous today, set the stage for scientific inquiry among Christian thinkers; his way of study is still a fine example for us.

Following his lead, Christian thinkers throughout the middle ages, exemplified eventually by Thomas Aquinas, embraced the sciences alongside their religion, demonstrating a robust worldview that, when placed alongside our own approaches, is sometimes a great deal more robust than our own. An important reason to study history is to learn about ourselves so that we can make better decisions, and understanding the traditional interaction between faith and science may not only show us how different we have become from our forefathers but also illuminate the way forward.

THE FLAT-EARTHERS WHO NEVER WERE

Assuming every pre-modern person in history believed he lived on a flat earth is among the most egregious examples of chronological snobbery, and doing away with this notion gives us a more honest look at the medieval mind while also preparing us to understand the examples we will discover in the likes of the Venerable Bede and Thomas Aquinas.

Most American schoolchildren, at some point, have been faced with a cartoonish version of Christopher Columbus standing before Queen Isabella while making a case that the earth was round, a fact that would enable his fantastic voyage. In these tales, Columbus is always confronted with jeerers and scoffers, the fifteenth-century version of the laughable, modern flat-earther. Reverberating through these lessons is the notion that man once thought the earth to be flat and that we ought to thank Columbus for his "discovery" to the contrary.

The frustratingly persistent notion of flat-earthers points to severe holes in our collective understanding of the past. Furthermore, this fallacy keeps us from understanding the people who came before us, giving us a distorted sense of their worldview. This sort of historical amnesia not only misrepresents the past, but it also completely misrepresents the present, fundamentally affecting our outlook.

The idea of a spherical earth is older than print in the Western world. Plato is well known among graduate students for his metaphysical speculations, but his contributions to science are equally important—even if they are not as well known to us. Martin Bernal, scholar of Ancient Science, has said that Plato and Eudoxos (a cosmologist and contemporary of Plato) were "those most responsible for the Greek view of the heavens as spinning spheres."[1]

Plato's view included an understanding of the earth as a sphere that rotated on its axis every day, of winter and summer solstices, of spring and fall equinoxes, and of the approximate paths of the moon and Mercury, Venus, Mars, Jupiter, and Saturn. In his cosmology, the stars were fixed to the great sphere that surrounded the earth. His view, while it contained metaphysical notions that did not last long beyond antiquity, became the dominant cosmological view.[2] Most notable is that Plato's entire view hinges on the spherical shape of the earth.

By the fourth century BC, the question of the earth's shape had been settled to the satisfaction of the Greek philosophers—so much so that they had moved on to other matters, considering this one closed.

Aristotle's heavenly observations include noticing that ships disappear prow-first, that certain lights in the sky are visible from one part of the world but not another, that shadows are shaped in ways that can only happen on spherical objects, and other basic observations that show us ancient philosophers were well aware of the planet's shape.

The shape of the world was not an issue for these thinkers; that problem had been long solved even though it is still unknown to us just who first worked this out. We often attribute the notion to Pythagoras, but, since his works are not extant, we have no way of knowing for sure. Either way, no matter how far back we look, we do not find flat-earthers informing our cosmology. To Aristotle, the shape of the earth was obvious:

> Its shape must necessarily be spherical. . . . If, on the one hand, there were a similar movement from each quarter of the extremity to the single centre, it is obvious that the resulting mass would be similar on every side. For if an equal amount is added on every side the extremity of the mass will be everywhere equidistant from its centre, i.e., the figure will be spherical.[3]

1. Bernal, "Animadversions on the Origins," 82.
2. Lindberg, *Beginnings of Western Science*, 41–43.
3. Aristotle, *On the Heavens* 2.14.

Clearly, not all of his assumptions have stood the test of time, but he has managed to demonstrate just how impressive these ancient minds really were. One need look no farther than the impressive Eratosthenes, a late-antiquity scientist who managed to measure the planet with remarkable accuracy. Eratosthenes studied in Athens, then later moved to Alexandria, where he became a librarian, a famous poet, and an associate of none other than Archimedes (who spoke very highly of him).[4]

Eratosthenes's most impressive contribution to the sciences came when he found a clever way to measure the circumference of the earth accurately using such simple tools as a sundial and a compass.[5] His computations led him to give the earth a circumference of 252,000 stadia. That figure leads us to a modern measurement of 25,000 miles, which is very accurate: We now know the earth to be 24,901.55 miles around the equator and 24,859.82 miles around the poles; Eratosthenes's figures were accurate within 1 percent of the actual measurement (assuming our methods are better than his).[6]

It's easy to see that the spherical earth was a popular point of view, not one merely observed by a few scientists. Centuries after Eratosthenes's calculations, the Roman poet Virgil penned the *Georgics,* which includes an understanding of Eratosthenes's cosmology that is displayed in the following passage:

> Therefore it is the golden sun, his course
> Into fixed parts dividing, rules his way
> Through the twelve constellations of the world.
> Five zones the heavens contain; whereof is one
> Aye red with flashing sunlight, fervent aye
> From fire; on either side to left and right
> Are traced the utmost twain, stiff with blue ice,
> And black with scowling storm-clouds, and betwixt
> These and the midmost, other twain there lie,
> By the Gods' grace to heart-sick mortals given,
> And a path cleft between them, where might wheel
> On sloping plane the system of the Signs.[7]

---

4. Archimedes, *Method,* preface.

5. Nicastro, *Circumference,* 24.

6. There is some question over the effectiveness of Eratosthenes's method. Since historians are not certain about the exact measurement of a *stadion,* it is possible that Eratosthenes did not come to the correct conclusion. However, since his method can be shown to work, he is generally granted success in this endeavor.

7. Virgil, *Georgics* 1.231–40.

Ovid, too, provided his readers with an understanding of the spherical earth in his poem, *Metamorphosis*.[8] Both of these poets enjoyed popularity throughout the middle ages, allowing medieval thinkers to see the spherical earth represented through famous art and science of the classical era.

Finally, we come to Ptolemy, whose ideas about the nature of the universe would reign until the time of Copernicus. While Ptolemy's rejection of heliocentrism is certainly a step in the wrong direction, we see his mathematical and rhetorical brilliance shine when he discusses the shape of the earth:

> If it were concave, the stars would be seen rising first by those more towards the west; if it were plane, they would rise and set simultaneously for everyone on earth; if it were triangular or square or any other polygonal shape, by a similar argument, they would rise and set simultaneously for all those living on the same plane surface. . . . Nor could it be cylindrical, with the curved surface in the east-west direction, and the flat sides towards the poles of the universe. . . . This is clear from the following: for those living on the curved surface none of the stars would be ever-visible, but either all stars would rise and set for all observers, or the same stars, for an equal [celestial] distance from each of the poles, would always be invisible for all observers. In fact, the further we travel toward the north, the more of the stars disappear and the more of the northern stars appear. Hence it is clear that here too the curvature of the earth cuts off [the heavenly bodies] in a regular fashion in a north-south direction, and proves the sphericity [of the earth] in all directions.[9]

In this passage, Ptolemy is tangling with alternative cosmological models; here, he is explaining specifically why the earth must be a sphere. Though some thinkers had put forth ideas of a flat earth, or a cylindrical one, Ptolemy, writing in late antiquity, dispenses with all of these notions and demonstrates, just as his predecessors had done, that the spherical earth is the only mathematical possibility.

There can be little doubt that the ancients believed they walked upon a round earth, and it's easy to see that the next generations of thinkers carried this idea with them. The tenacity with which the medieval minds held this view demonstrates an impressive devotion to the sciences in a time when few could afford to take up such a study.

---

8. Ovid, *Metamorphosis* 1.32–51.
9. Ptolemy, *Almagest* 1.7.

When the church fathers enter history's arena, their writings, understandably, are centered on theological matters rather than scientific ones, but their adherence to a spherical earth and ancient scientific achievement is plainly evident. The writings of Augustine, Origen, and even Basil the Great attest to their understanding of a spherical earth. Pope Sylvester II, who served the Vatican during the year 1000, enjoyed painting maps of the earth on wooden spheres as a hobby. Their knowledge of the spherical earth could be described as casual.

In the thirteenth century, a monk and mathematician named Sacrobosco (also known as John of Holliwood) wrote *De Sphaera Mundi*, a tract that detailed the shape of the earth and its place in the solar system. His writing became foundational to the medieval teachings on cosmology, influencing Albertus Magnus and eventually Thomas Aquinas, who spread Sacrobosco's methodology through his own writings. (Today, we can see a crater on the moon named after Sacrobosco.)

This casual study of medieval cosmology reveals that our predecessors from the middle ages were not the flat-earthers we have been told about. Not only did they understand more about the planet than we have often been led to assume, but this also tells us that their worldview held scientific understanding very highly. With this understanding firmly in place, we can look more closely at a few "traditional" Christian thinkers and see them in a new light.

CARRYING ARISTOTLE'S TORCH

European medieval history is dominated by the presence of the Catholic church, so much so that few influential rulers and writers are seen outside of its influence. After the slow collapse of the Roman organization of Europe, the church remained in place, creating a loose system of organization for culture to follow. Understandably, this time in history is commonly viewed as an era of religion and superstition, but the sciences were greatly upheld throughout.

Few medieval figures can demonstrate this more easily than the Venerable Bede, a seventh-century monastic scholar whose scholastic contributions are difficult to measure. While he may not be a household name like Augustine or Thomas Aquinas, Bede's influence on the medieval worldview is nothing short of profound. While his predecessors in Christianity wrote narrowly on the subject of theology, Bede seemed to believe that understanding world history and the workings of the universe were part and parcel of understanding God. His theological writings are extensive, but they are matched, if not exceeded, by his mundane studies. This approach may seem bifurcated to some, but for Bede there was a deeper reason why all of his studies were equally important. His approach is echoed throughout the middle ages by renowned thinkers, and studying his methods and his philosophy toward religion and science shows us a better way to harmonize these spheres.

The Venerable Bede was born near the monastery of Wearmouth-Jarrow and was placed in the care of the monks there when he was seven years old. Concerning his parents we know nothing, but his birth year was probably 673. Bede says he has observed the monastic rule and that he sang his part with the choir every day. He was ordained as a deacon at age nineteen and a priest at thirty, and he spent most of his time writing books.[10]

During his childhood, a plague swept through the surrounding area and devastated the population. This is detailed in Bede's *History of the Abbots* as well as the anonymous *Life of St. Ceolfrith*; however, the latter gives us a further detail. The author of Ceolfrith's story tells us that the sickness spread so severely that everyone in Jarrow who was capable of speaking or singing the monastic offices had been taken by the plague, leaving only Abbot Ceolfrith and one little boy to attend to the services. It goes on to say that this boy grew up to become a priest in Jarrow who recorded "Ceolfrith's laudable deeds by pen and by word." Scholars have often agreed that this child can be none other than Bede.[11]

The monastery boasted an impressive library, and scholars have found that Bede had access to more than two hundred fifty books.[12] As an example of his thorough education, it has been noted that Bede showed familiarity with eight different grammarians in his own book on the subject; he had copied from previous theologians the habit of assuming that an understanding of linguistics was necessary if one wanted to understand Christian teachings.[13]

The library must not have been limited to Christian writers because we see that he commanded the scientific and historical knowledge of the pagan authors who came before him. For Bede, these mundane, non-Christian academics were worthy of his time. He carried on their teachings and applied them to his own worldview. Like philosophers of old, Bede's mundane writings spanned the sciences, from mathematics and geography to weather patterns and temporal studies. No subject lay beyond his gaze.

---

10. Bede, *Historia Ecclesiastica* 5.24.
11. Blair, *World of Bede*, 178.
12. Brown, *Companion to Bede*, 11.
13. Blair, *World of Bede*, 245–51.

As a religious writer, Bede was prolific. He masterfully wrote historiographical surveys of the old testament, including thorough discussions of the tabernacle and commentaries on the prophets, and penned commentaries on new testament gospels, letters, and even apocryphal writings. No aspect of biblical commentary appears to have been left out of his work, and his output in theological studies is enough to convince any scholar that he was a powerhouse in that field.

But Bede was also prolific in the sciences. He managed to write extensively on chronology. His *De Temporibus* also includes an enlightening section on the medieval method of performing mathematical calculations involving large numbers without the use of paper and pen, using specific finger and hand stances to keep track of the sums. His *De natura rerum*, a book on natural science, is based on a similar work of Isidore of Seville, who, like Bede, was a religious leader who wrote passionately about science and mundane matters. (Isidore is considered the last of the church fathers.)

Bede's most famous work, the *Historia ecclesiastica gentis Anglorum* (Ecclesiastical History of the English People), opens with geographical information as he applies older scientific teachings to his own homeland, bringing England's natural history into the scientific canon.

Scholars have had different reactions to Bede's devotion to science. Was he a scientist? Bede certainly made observations and performed experiments, which, to some, is sufficient to warrant such a label. But others notice that his work is never entirely bereft of a spiritual component. As a monk who sang mass every single day, this is to be expected. But his scientific work does not appear to be dampened or harmed by the Christian dimension of his work, making it difficult for scholars to categorize Bede's work.

Here we find the importance of studying Bede. In the tension between his religious passion and his relentless pursuit of the mundane, we go nowhere when we seek to find resolution, for, to Bede, there was nothing to resolve. These two paths, faith and science, were not in opposition to one another. For Bede, the pursuit of wisdom reached in every possible direction.

Faith Wallis explains it well:

> For Bede, the natural and the providential can all but converge, so that all of nature becomes a miracle. [Bishop] Chad, he reports, prayed for divine mercy during *every* thunderstorm; and in his commentary on Ezra, Bede states that storms and droughts—*all* storms and droughts, apparently—are signs of God's wrath and impending judgement. When describing healing miracles, particularly in attributing a natural cause to the

illness, or in relating how the saint used the remedies and services of secular medicine.[14]

Wallis goes on to explain Bede's common "overlap" between sacred and mundane. Bede might refer to a cure as miraculous even while explaining the scientific properties of the remedy. For Bede, it appears the entire universe was a miracle, a miracle whose appearance was not sullied by natural study, and to intellectualize over the natural world was in no way, in his opinion, to turn his eye away from God.

Now that we understand the foundation upon which traditional Christianity built its scientific approach, we can explore how faith and science were woven together into a worldview that made plenty of room for both.

WHAT WE CAN LEARN FROM MEDIEVAL THINKERS

Bede, as we've discussed, is not a household name, so it might be surprising to the casual scholar that the tendrils of his work reached centuries ahead, setting the stage for scientific inquiry and informing the traditional Christian worldview. His work certainly became obsolete as scientific advancements marched on, but his mundane approach to the sciences is mirrored by thinkers throughout church history.

Once again, Faith Wallis has put it succinctly in a discussion where Bede's approach to science is referred to as *computus*:

> Bede's science is of a piece with the other learned activities he undertook in the cause of expounding and spreading the Christian faith.... Though he claimed to "seek for myself and for my people to better way of acting or speaking" than "to follow the sure judgement of the most revered fathers," he nonetheless substantially reshaped two crucial medieval scientific genres. He forced a systematic, forcefully argued and theologically imaginative vision of time out of the motley array of didactic texts and polemics that had hitherto constituted the literature of *computus*. But his most significant achievement may have an unintended one: to project through *computus* a vision of science as a problem-solving activity. Bede's writings made *computus* a core subject of clerical institution well into the scholastic period.[15]

---

14. Wallis, "*Si Naturem Quaeras*," 94–95.
15. Wallis, "*Si Naturem Quaeras*," 125.

Bede's intellectual journey set the stage for medieval thinkers who, like him, marched forward into scientific progress with their faith firmly in hand.

When we walk through the writings of the medieval church leaders, it becomes clear that there never was any antagonism between faith and science in traditional Christianity. Roger Bacon mused on the theological ramifications found in the garden of Eden story with as much passion as he used to promote empirical thinking. Hildegard of Bingen wove scientific understanding, such as the understanding of the spherical earth, into her complex mystical teachings. Copernicus's heliocentrism was celebrated by many in the church during his lifetime, and his successor, Galileo, found favor with the pope when he used his powerful telescope to prove Copernicus had been right.

Among the more famous theologians stands Thomas Aquinas, who takes us the rest of the way in this casual survey. In a lecture series titled *Reason and Revelation in the Middle Ages*, the renowned Thomist Etienne Gilson passionately demonstrated Aquinas's position on this issue.[16] Aquinas framed the science vs. faith conversation by first pointing out that revelation teaches us in a different way than reason does; thus, it would be improper to expect one to reason out what should come by revelation or to expect a revelation to help us understand something that ought to come by reasoning. To attempt to explain faith through logic would, according to Aquinas, make the Catholic faith appear foolish to non-believers.

While it may seem that Aquinas has firmly separated these two ideas, in truth, he has actually created a harmony. Just as Bede studied nature through reason and God through revelation, Aquinas sets up a worldview that allows both to inform one another, rather than spoiling one another. Gilson teaches us that once faith and objective knowledge are in their proper places, we are able to learn from our medieval counterparts and carry a healthy respect for reason and revelation as they both inform our worldview.

CONCLUSION

Thus, we find ourselves back at Bede, who, unlike Aquinas or more modern thinkers, simply performed his work without explaining his reasons. While Aquinas took it upon himself to detail the place of science in the life of a religious person, Bede was content simply to live it, to carry out his natural observations and experiments in between chants and prayers and monastic duties, seeing each of these activities as a way of understanding his Creator.

---

16. Gilson, *Reason and Revelation in the Middle Ages*.

It is fitting to end with an old tale about Albertus Magnus, a thirteenth-century monk and scientist who eventually became the patron saint of the sciences. The story goes that he was visited by the Devil disguised as a fellow monk, who claimed that Albert's scientific curiosity was taking too much of his attention from God. After Albert made a sign of the cross, the Devil vanished and Albert resumed his studies.

It is unlikely that anyone in the middle ages took this story to be true; instead, it served as a warning, intending to remind people that pursuing God and understanding the world were part of the same journey. While our medieval counterparts seem to have passed this test, one wonders how our modern churches would fare against the same devilish trickery.

BIBLIOGRAPHY

Bernal, Martin. "Animadversions on the Origins of Western Science." In *The Scientific Enterprise in Antiquity and the Middle Ages*, edited by Michael H. Shank, 72–83. Chicago: University of Chicago Press, 2000.

Blair, Peter Hunter. *The World of Bede*. Cambridge: Cambridge University Press, 1990.

DeGregorio, Scott, ed. *The Cambridge Companion to Bede*. Cambridge Companions to Literature and Classics. Cambridge: Cambridge University Press, 2010.

Gilson, Ettiene. *Reason and Revelation in the Middle Ages*. 1938. Reprint, New York: Scribner, 1952.

Lindberg, David C. *The Beginnings of Western Science: The European Scientific Tradition in Philosophical, Religious, and Institutional Context, 600 BC to AD 1450*. Chicago: University of Chicago Press, 1992.

Nicastro, Nicholas. *Circumference: Eratosthenes and the Ancient Quest to Measure the Globe*. New York: St. Martin's, 2008.

Ptolemy. *Almagest*. Translated by G. J. Toomer. London: Duckworth, 1984.

Virgil. *Georgics*. Online. http://www.gutenberg.org/files/232/232-h/232-h.htm.

Wallis, Faith. "*Si Naturem Quaeras*: Reframing Bede's 'Science.'" In *Innovation and Tradition in the Writings of the Venerable Bede*, edited by Scott DeGregorio, 65–99. Morgantown: West Virginia University Press, 2006.

12

The Christian Philosophical Worldview of St. Thomas Aquinas

Dax R. Bennington

INTRODUCTION[1]

My task for this paper is threefold. First, I'll discuss the notion of a Christian worldview, which David Naugle has aptly articulated and defended. I'll focus on the way in which a worldview in general is a systematic way of thinking and on how a Christian worldview, in particular, is structured in terms of the creation, fall, redemption, and consummation of all things. Second, I'll discuss Alvin Plantinga's advice to Christian philosophers in light of what has been said about developing a Christian worldview, in which discussion I'll focus on how developing a Christian worldview and the particular tasks of a Christian philosopher are uniquely and intricately linked. Third, I'll

1. Many thanks to Mark Boone for helpful comments on earlier drafts of this paper and Doc Rose Cothren for her helpful edits. I'd also like to thank Dr. David Naugle for being a model of a Christian philosopher to me. Additionally, I'd like to thank my confirmation saint, St. Thomas Aquinas, for his help and example. Last, and most importantly, I want to thank my Lord Jesus Christ for providing an opportunity to write on this topic.

discuss the life and work of St. Thomas Aquinas, who I'll argue provides a model for developing a Christian worldview and accomplishing the tasks of the Christian philosopher.

ON THE NATURE OF A CHRISTIAN WORLDVIEW

In this section, I'd like to articulate the notion of a worldview, in particular, a *Christian* worldview. I'll draw from what David Naugle has said concerning the nature of a worldview in general as well as what he thinks is the nature of a distinctively Christian worldview in particular.

On Worldviews in General

In *Worldview: The History of a Concept*, David Naugle understands a worldview in the following way:

> A worldview, then, is a semiotic system of narrative signs that creates the definitive symbolic universe which is responsible in the main for the shape of a variety of life-determining, human practices. It creates the channels in which the waters of reason flow. It establishes the horizons of an interpreter's point of view by which texts of all types are understood. It is that mental medium by which the world is known. The human heart is its home, and it provides a home for the human heart.[2]

Let's unpack Naugle's definition of a worldview by explicating each of the main concepts within the definition. First, consider the concept of a semiotic system. According to Naugle, a *semiotic system* is a set of signs made by humans. A semiotic system is an activity that humans engage in so that they can signify their "thoughts, feelings, and ideas as well as people, places, and things in the world. . . . By these primary semiotic activities, people have been able to parse the cosmos and create maps of reality."[3] So, according to Naugle, a worldview is a semiotic system insofar as humans are the kinds of creatures that make and manage signs, primarily in the form of words, either spoken or written, and humans use these signs to map the structure of reality.[4]

Second, consider the concept of a narrative sign. What exactly is a narrative sign? Naugle thinks that a narrative sign is a semiotic sign that is

---

2. See Naugle, *Worldview*, 329–30.
3. Naugle, *Worldview*, 292.
4. Naugle, *Worldview*, 291.

structured in the form of a story. Humans, as semiotic creatures, are specifically storytellers.[5] The way in which a worldview is structured is in terms of a network of stories that function as signs in order for humans to interpret and map the structure of reality.

Third, Naugle says that a semiotic system of narrative signs is the primary way in which a variety of life-determining human practices are decided. What exactly does this mean? The kind of life-determining human practices that Naugle takes a worldview to provide are the practices of human thinking, interpreting, and knowing.[6] A worldview, or a semiotic system of narrative signs, provides the foundation and groundwork for determining an individual's theory of rationality, hermeneutics, and epistemology. From these rational, hermeneutical, and epistemological human activities flows the praxis of daily human choices. Hence, a worldview, as this semiotic system of narrative signs that grounds the rational, hermeneutic, and epistemological framework for mapping reality provides a home for the heart of man. This is what Naugle refers to as the "kardioptical" nature of a worldview—the vision of the heart.[7]

On Christian Worldview in Particular

In developing an account of a Christian worldview, Naugle draws from the work of Brian Walsh and J. Richard Middleton.[8] Walsh and Middleton understand the unique structure of the Christian narrative as composed of three major events: creation, fall, and redemption.[9] Naugle, citing Walsh and Middleton's position, writes the following:

> These three biblical motifs [creation, fall, redemption] answer the four fundamental worldview questions that are at the heart of every worldview: "(1) *Who am I?* Or, what is the nature, task, and purpose of human beings? (2) *Where am I?* Or, what is the nature of the world and universe I live in? (3) *What's wrong?* Or, what is the basic problem or obstacle that keeps me from obtaining fulfillment? In other words, how do I understand evil? And (4) *What is the remedy?* Or, how is it possible to overcome

---

5. Naugle, *Worldview*, 291.
6. Naugle, *Worldview*, 291.
7. Naugle, *Worldview*, 291.
8. See Middleton and Walsh, *Truth Is Stranger Than It Used to Be*; *Transforming Vision*; Naugle, *Worldview*, 300, 302.
9. See Naugle, *Worldview*, 350–51; Walsh and Middleton, *Transforming Vision*.

this hindrance to my fulfillment? In other words, how do I find salvation?"[10]

According to Naugle, Walsh, and Middleton, the biblical worldview of creation, fall, and redemption provides the most coherent, comprehensive, and livable account of answers to the four fundamental worldview questions.[11]

Briefly, the biblical themes of creation, fall, and redemption answer the four fundamental worldview questions as follows. First, humans are created in the image and likeness of God and find their true fulfillment in adoring and worshiping their creator by being in intimate communion with him. Second, the world was created by God, who is the omnipotent, omniscient, omnibenevolent creator and sustainer of all things.[12] Third, humans fell from being in right relationship with God through sin, in particular, by disobeying God. The result of this fall was a severing of the relationship between God and man, man and his neighbor, and man and himself. Last, God provided a remedy for the restoration of all things. By becoming man, as the incarnate God-man, Jesus Christ, God made a way for man to become god, or to partake in the divine life.[13] God accomplished this primarily through the mysteries of his incarnation, life, death, resurrection, and ascension. Hence, the remedy to the problem of human sin, suffering, and evil is provided for by God through the works of his Son, Jesus Christ. Man is restored to right relationship with God and elevated to participating in God's very life.

Now that we have a grasp of what a worldview is in general and what a Christian worldview is in particular, let's look at what Alvin Plantinga has to say concerning the task of the Christian philosopher. We shall see that there is deep congruence with what Plantinga has to say and what we have seen from Naugle concerning the nature of a Christian worldview.

PLANTINGA'S ADVICE TO CHRISTIAN PHILOSOPHERS

In his paper "Advice to Christian Philosophers" (1984), Alvin Plantinga offers reflections on how Christians who are philosophers should engage

---

10. Naugle, *Worldview*, 350–51. See also Walsh and Middleton, *Transforming Vision*, 35.

11. Naugle, *Worldview*, 350–51.

12. I am reminded of being in the honors section of Dr. Naugle's "Developing a Christian Mind" course, in which he had us repeat after him *"ta panta"*—Greek for "all things." See also Col 1:16.

13. See Athanasius, *On the Incarnation* 54.3; 2 Peter 1:4.

in *doing* philosophy.[14] Plantinga offers the following general ideas of how Christians ought to practice philosophy. Plantinga writes,

> First, Christian philosophers and Christian intellectuals generally must display more autonomy—more independence of the rest of the philosophical world. Second, Christian philosophers must display more integrity—integrity in the sense of integral wholeness, or oneness, or unity, being all of one piece. Perhaps "integrality" would be the better word here. And necessary to these two is a third: Christian courage, or boldness, or strength, or perhaps Christian self-confidence.[15]

Plantinga thinks that Christian philosophers ought to display more autonomy, integrality, and courage. Let's turn to what he says about each of these three traits in more detail.

Christian Philosophers Ought to Display More Autonomy

Christian philosophers ought to display more autonomy. What does Plantinga mean by this? He gives the example of an undergraduate student who decides that studying philosophy is what he wants to do. Next, the student goes to graduate school at a top program in philosophy. The student learns how philosophy is done at the top level. Unfortunately, the questions asked by philosophers at the top universities are not always the same questions that are salient to the Christian community from which the student comes. Plantinga thinks that Christian philosophers ought to use their skills and gifts to serve the Christian community and address from a philosophical standpoint questions that matter to the *Christian* community. For example, Plantinga writes,

> Christian philosophers, however, are the philosophers of the Christian community; and it is part of their task as *Christian* philosophers to serve the Christian community. But the Christian community has its own questions, its own concerns, its own topics for investigation, its own agenda and its own research program.[16]

When Christian philosophers engage only in the questions that are of interest to the philosophical community, they are not exhibiting the kind of

---

14. See Plantinga, "Advice to Christian Philosophers," 253–71.
15. Plantinga, "Advice to Christian Philosophers," 254.
16. Plantinga, "Advice to Christian Philosophers," 255.

autonomy that they ought. For example, questions about different theories of reference in the philosophy of language, or the realism/anti-realism debate in the philosophy of science, or different analyses of the concept of knowledge in epistemology are all good things, but, says Plantinga, if Christian philosophers focus only on those questions and do not focus on questions the Christian community is concerned with, then they are not exhibiting the kind of independence or autonomy from the philosophical community that they ought. Plantinga thinks that Christian philosophers are called to do the philosophical work for their Christian community. When they don't do this, they are not fully living up to their vocation. For example, Plantinga says the following:

> Christian philosophers are the ones who must do the philosophical work involved. If they devote their best efforts to the topics fashionable in the non-Christian philosophical world, they will neglect a crucial and central part of their task as Christian philosophers. What is needed here is more independence, more autonomy with respect to the projects and concerns of the non-theistic philosophical world.[17]

Christian philosophers have a task to serve their Christian community with their gifts and skillset. Christian philosophers who don't exhibit autonomy from the philosophical community (which is largely non-theistic) and concern themselves only with questions from the non-theistic philosophical community do a disservice to their Christian community by not engaging in philosophical questions and research programs that are more salient to the *Christian* community.

Christian Philosophers Ought to Display More Integrity

In addition to arguing that Christian philosophers ought to display more autonomy in their work qua Christian philosophers, Plantinga argues that Christian philosophers ought to display more *integrality*. With respect to integrality, Plantinga has in mind the idea of wholeness or of being of one mind. He discusses the philosophy student who goes to graduate school and studies with a top-notch philosopher. The philosopher holds to a broadly naturalistic worldview that is fundamentally at odds with the student's Christian worldview. Plantinga thinks that the student, who is experiencing cognitive dissonance, should not resolve the cognitive dissonance by attempting to make his Christianity compatible with a philosophical

---

17. Plantinga, "Advice to Christian Philosophers," 255.

worldview that is deeply incompatible with Christianity. Concerning this notion of integrity and the student's relationship to his non-theistic professor, Plantinga writes,

> But his [the philosophy professor's] fundamental commitments, his fundamental projects and concerns, are wholly different from those of the Christian community—wholly different and, indeed, antithetical to them. And the result of attempting to graft Christian thought onto his basic view of the world will be at best an unintegral *pastiche*; at worst it will seriously compromise, or distort, or trivialize the claims of Christian theism. What is needed here is more wholeness, more integrality.[18]

Here, Plantinga cautions against an unintegral Christian philosophy that tries to be a cheap imitation of either of the incompatible worldviews or, even worse, could lead to a serious, even perverse distortion of the claims of Christianity. The Christian philosopher ought to be of one mind, not being tossed to and fro by the waves of what is philosophically in vogue (see Eph 4:14).

Christian Philosophers Ought to Display More Courage

Last, Plantinga advises that Christian philosophers ought to display more courage. What Plantinga has in mind here is something like intellectual self-confidence. Plantinga thinks that Christian philosophers are just as entitled to their pre-philosophical assumptions as their non-theistic colleagues and that Christian philosophers should not be intimidated by what others think about the plausibility or implausibility of their views.[19] Plantinga refers to an example of what not to do in his discussion of the relationship between verificationism and theism. Verificationism was a product of logical positivism that was prominent in early and mid-twentieth-century analytic philosophy. Part of verificationism was the thesis, known as the verifiability criterion of meaning, that a statement was meaningful only if it was either analytic or its truth or falsity could be verified by empirical methods.[20] Claims central to Christianity, such as "God loves you," were meaningless because these statements were neither analytic (e.g., all bachelors are unmarried males) nor verifiable via empirical methods. Plantinga discusses the response from

18. Plantinga, "Advice to Christian Philosophers," 256.
19. Plantinga, "Advice to Christian Philosophers," 269.
20. For more information on logical positivism, see Creath, "Logical Empiricism." The literature on this philosophical movement sometimes uses the term "positivism" and sometimes uses "empiricism." For our purposes, the distinction is not important.

theistic philosophers or those sympathetic to this view when verificationism was in vogue in the mid-twentieth century. He writes,

> Many philosophically inclined Christians were disturbed and perplexed and felt deeply threatened; could it really be true that linguistic philosophers had somehow discovered that the Christian's most cherished convictions were, in fact, just meaningless? There was a great deal of anxious hand wringing among philosophers, either themselves theists or sympathetic to theism. Some suggested, in the face of positivistic onslaught, that the thing for the Christian community to do was to fold up its tents and silently slink away, admitting that the verifiability criterion was probably true. Others conceded that strictly speaking, theism really *is* nonsense, but is *important* nonsense. Still others suggested that the sentences in question should be reinterpreted in such a way as not to give offense to the positivists; someone seriously suggested, for example, that Christians resolve, henceforth, to use the sentence "God exists" to mean "some men and women have had, and all may have, experiences called 'meeting God.'"[21]

In response to the verificationist attack on theism, many theists cowered and accommodated the pre-philosophical assumptions of the verificationists. Plantinga thinks that the theists should not have cowered so easily. They should have rolled up their intellectual sleeves and argued against the verificationists. They should have exhibited the intellectual virtues of courage and self-confidence in challenging the verificationists' presuppositions about the meaning of terms—which they generally assumed rather than argued for. Christian philosophers should not be so deferential and accommodating to what is currently philosophically in vogue; they should stand their ground and challenge pre-philosophical assumptions. Christians should have had the courage to insist that their convictions were meaningful even if a fashionable theory in philosophy of language said otherwise.[22] Christian philosophers should be bold and courageous (see Josh 1:9).

Now that we have discussed Plantinga's advice to Christian philosophers, let's turn to someone who I think is a Christian philosopher *par excellence*: St. Thomas Aquinas.

---

21. Plantinga, "Advice to Christian Philosophers," 257.
22. Thanks to Mark Boone for making this point to me.

ST. THOMAS AQUINAS: EXEMPLAR PAR EXCELLENCE

In this section, I'll argue that St. Thomas Aquinas is the Christian philosopher *par excellence*. My reason for thinking this claim is true is two-fold. First, Aquinas's theological magnum opus, the *Summa Theologica*, is structured according to the essence of a biblical worldview: creation, fall, and redemption. Man's coming from God, falling away from God, and God's returning to man. Hence, Aquinas does philosophy from a distinctively Christian worldview.

Second, Aquinas does what Plantinga says a Christian philosopher ought to do. In the second part of this section, I'll elucidate how Aquinas is an exemplar of what Plantinga takes to be a Christian philosopher.

St. Thomas's Work Is Structured as a Christian Worldview

My goal is to demonstrate, by discussing the contents of St. Thomas's *Summa*, how Aquinas's thought comports with the nature of a Christian worldview as articulated by Naugle, Walsh, and Middleton. Let's begin this task by looking at the details of Aquinas's *Summa*.

In his theological magnum opus, the *Summa Theologica*, St. Thomas Aquinas provides a systematic theology for the Christian religion.[23] Concerning the structure of the *Summa*, Peter Kreeft writes the following:

> The structural outline of the *Summa Theologica* is a mirror of the structural order of reality. It begins in God, Who is "in the beginning." It then proceeds to the act of creation and a consideration of creatures, centering on man, who alone is created in the image of God. Then it moves to man's return to God through his life of moral and religious choice, and culminates in the way or means to that end: Christ and his church. Thus the overall scheme of the *Summa*, like that of the universe, is an *exitus-redditus*, an exit from and return to God, Who is both Alpha and Omega. God is the ontological heart that pumps the blood of being through the arteries of creation into the body of the universe, which wears a human face, and receives it back through the veins of man's life of love and will. The structure of the *Summa*, and of the universe, is dynamic. It is not like information in a library, but like blood in a body.[24]

---

23. See Thomas Aquinas, *Summa Theologica*.
24. See Kreeft, *Summa of the "Summa."*

We can see that St. Thomas's systematic theology is structured in the same way that Naugle, Walsh, and Middleton think that a Christian worldview ought to be structured. In its most general outline, Aquinas's *Summa* is structured as follows.

First, there are three main parts. Part one, or the *prima pars*, discusses the nature of God in himself and the treatise on creation. This includes the act of creation of things in general and angels, the physical world, man, and the divine government in particular.

Second, the second part, or *secunda pars*, is divided into the *prima secundae*, or the first part of the second part, and the *secunda secundae*, or the second part of the second part. The *prima secundae* focuses on man's final end, the treatise on habits, and the treatise on law.[25] The *secunda secundae* focuses on the virtues. This includes the treatise on prudence and justice, the treatise on fortitude and temperance, and the actions of some particular men.

Third, the third and final part of the *Summa* is the *tertia pars*, or the third part. In this part of the *Summa*, Aquinas discusses the nature and purpose of Christ's incarnation; the nature of Christ's mother, the blessed Virgin Mary; Christ's passion and resurrection; and the nature and purpose of the sacraments, to name a few things.

With this brief outline of the *Summa* in hand, let's look at each of the parts in greater detail, keeping an eye on how they follow the same pattern of the nature of a Christian worldview articulated by Naugle, Walsh, and Middleton.

First, Aquinas begins the *Summa* reflecting on the nature of God, the author, creator, and sustainer of all that is, also understood as *ipsum esse subsistens*, or the sheer act of being itself.[26] For example, in the *Summa Theologica*, after explaining the nature and extent of sacred doctrine, St. Thomas discusses the existence and nature of God at length.[27]

Second, after discussing the nature of God, Aquinas proceeds by discussing the nature of creation in general and the nature of man in particular. Within this section of the *Summa*, Aquinas subdivides his account of creation into five distinct treatises: the treatise on the creation, the treatise on the angels, the treatise on the work of the six days, the treatise on man, and the treatise on the divine government.[28]

---

25. Aquinas, *Summa Theologica* IIa, Iae, QQ1–114.
26. See Barron, *Catholicism*, 228.
27. Aquinas, *Summa Theologica* Ia, QQ1–43.
28. Aquinas, *Summa Theologica* Ia, QQ44–119.

Third, after detailing his treatise on creation, Aquinas, in the first part of the second part of the *Summa*, moves to the end or purpose of man. Aquinas begins by outlining man's nature and purpose. He then discusses the habits of man, or virtues and vices. Next, he moves on to discuss the nature of law and how man relates to his neighbor and the city of man and the city of God. Additionally, Aquinas discusses the nature of grace and the order of grace in terms of man's end or destiny.

Fourth, Aquinas, in the second part of the second part of the *Summa*, continues to discuss the various actions of man, including his natural actions (i.e., the cardinal virtues) as well as the supernatural actions, such as the gift of faith.

Fifth, Aquinas, in part three of the *Summa*, discusses the nature of the incarnation, crucifixion, atonement, resurrection, and ascension. He also discusses the nature and effects of the sacraments.

To conclude, it is evident that Aquinas's thought is thoroughly in line with what Naugle, Walsh, and Middleton take to be a Christian worldview. In the last section of this essay, we shall see that Aquinas does, though preemptively, take Plantinga's advice for Christian philosophers.

Aquinas Takes Plantinga's Advice

In section two of this essay, we considered what Plantinga had to say concerning advice for Christian philosophers. In this section, I'll argue that Aquinas takes Plantinga's advice. Setting aside the fact that Aquinas lived around seven hundred years before Plantinga, we can see that St. Thomas fulfilled the advice that Plantinga gives to Christian philosophers.

Aquinas Displays Autonomy

St. Thomas Aquinas displayed autonomy as a Christian philosopher in the following way. During the medieval period, Christianity had not yet fully embraced the works of Aristotle. Many Christian philosophers and theologians were skeptical or wary of Aristotelianism. Moreover, Aquinas's works were not immediately accepted by the Catholic Church. Yet, this did not prevent St. Thomas from developing a systematic theology and philosophical worldview that incorporated Aristotelian notions such as act and potency, form and matter, substance and accident.

Aquinas Displays Integrality

St. Thomas also displayed integrality. He was of one mind. Aquinas was known as the great synthesizer because he was able to integrate a number of positions that seemed to be in fundamental tension with each other. For example, Aquinas was able to provide deeply robust accounts of the relationship between conceptual pairs that are difficult to reconcile, integrate, or synthesize. Some of these pairs are the relationships between faith and reason, grace and nature, special revelation and natural revelation, and Platonism and Aristotelianism. Concerning this point, Peter Kreeft writes,

> [Aquinas] fulfilled more than anyone else the essential medieval program of a marriage of faith and reason, revelation and philosophy, the Biblical and the classical inheritances. . . . Not only does St. Thomas represent a unity of ingredients that were later to separate, but also a unity of ingredients that existed separately before him. In reading St. Thomas you meet Thales, Parmenides, Heraclitus, Socrates, Plato, Aristotle, Plotinus, Proclus, Justin, Clement, Augustine, Boëthius, Dionysius, Anselm, Abelard, Albert, Maimonides, and Avicenna. For one brief, Camelot-like moment it seemed that a synthesis was possible.[29]

Moreover, a primary way in which St. Thomas displayed integrality was through his commitment to Christian orthodoxy. He does this by explaining and defending Christian dogmas as well as citing scripture and the church fathers as authorities to support his arguments.

Aquinas Displays Courage

Aquinas demonstrated intellectual courage. G. K. Chesterton, in his biography of St. Thomas Aquinas, tells a story about St. Thomas when he was dining with St. Louis of France. During the meal, St. Thomas, lost in thought, loudly exclaimed, "And that will settle the Manichees!"[30] The Manichees were a heretical sect of Christianity that St. Dominic, the founder of the Dominican order, and his friars, which included St. Thomas, combated in the streets of France. St. Thomas was not afraid to boldly proclaim the gospel in a rational and deliberate way. Hence, he exhibited Christian intellectual virtue.

---

29. Kreeft, *Summa of the "Summa,"* 13.
30. See Chesterton, *Saint Thomas Aquinas*, 79.

CONCLUSION

Assuming that Naugle and Plantinga are correct in what they say a Christian philosopher ought to be, then, as I've argued, St. Thomas Aquinas is a Christian philosopher *par excellence*.[31] My reasons in support of this claim consisted in the facts that Aquinas's thinking was structured in accordance with a Christian worldview and that he did what a Christian philosopher ought to do. I elaborated on the nature of worldviews in general and of a Christian worldview in particular by drawing from the work of David Naugle. Additionally, I discussed the task of the Christian philosopher outlined by Alvin Plantinga. I tied together these two ideas from Naugle and Plantinga by giving the example of the life and work of Aquinas. Aquinas provides an example of how to do philosophy as a Christian. In my view, we should also add Naugle and Plantinga to the list of exemplars.

BIBLIOGRAPHY

Athanasius. *On the Incarnation*. http://www.newadvent.org/fathers/2802.htm.
Barron, Robert. *Catholicism: A Journey to the Heart of the Faith*. New York: Random, 2011.
Chesterton, G. K. *Saint Thomas Aquinas: The Dumb Ox*. New York: Doubleday, 2001.
Creath, Richard. "Logical Empiricism." In *Stanford Encyclopedia of Philosophy*, April 5, 2017. https://plato.stanford.edu/entries/logical-empiricism.
Kreeft, Peter. *A Summa of the "Summa": The Essential Philosophical Passages of St. Thomas Aquinas's "Summa Theologica" Edited and Explained for Beginners*. San Francisco: Ignatius, 1990.
Middleton, Richard J., and Brian Walsh. *The Transforming Vision: Shaping a Christian Worldview*. Downers Grove, IL: InterVarsity, 1984.
———. *Truth Is Stranger Than It Used to Be: Biblical Faith in a Postmodern Age*. Downers Grove, IL: InterVarsity, 1995.
Naugle, David K. *Worldview: The History of a Concept*. Grand Rapids: Eerdmans, 2002.
Plantinga, Alvin. "Advice to Christian Philosophers." *Faith and Philosophy* 1 (1984) 253–71.
Thomas Aquinas. *Summa Theologica*. Translated by Fathers of the English Dominican Province. Benziger Bros. ed. 1947. https://aquinas101.thomisticinstitute.org/st-index.

---

31. Thanks to Mark Boone for pointing this out to me.

13

From Evidence to Total Commitment

Two Ways Faith Goes beyond Reason

MARK J. BOONE

We all know that faith and reason are not exactly the same thing. What exactly is the difference, and how are they related? A good orthodox Christian answer is that faith transcends reason, for at least two reasons. First, the doctrines of orthodox Christian theology are beyond comprehension. Second, faith requires a total commitment when reason can provide only partial evidence. We cannot act meaningfully if we act only halfway. If evidence produces a 95-percent probability that a certain conclusion is true, sometimes 100 percent is still the only way to act on it; commitment to Christ must lead all the way (perhaps unto death).

After a look at some definitions, some distinctions, and an illustration, I will consider what Immanuel Kant, Augustine of Hippo, William James, and Søren Kierkegaard have said about how faith goes beyond reason.[1] Kant thinks faith goes beyond reason as a matter of necessity given the nature of morality and human knowledge. Augustine thinks faith goes beyond reason, but this is not a permanent thing; with sufficient mental training and

---

1. For a more detailed analysis of a different but overlapping set of thinkers, see Evans, *Faith Beyond Reason*. For a more detailed look at Augustine and James on faith and reason, see Boone, "Augustine and William James."

contemplation, we may hope to achieve knowledge of God. James concurs, save that he looks to future experience rather than contemplation. Finally, Kierkegaard thinks Christian faith must always by nature go beyond reason; neither philosophical contemplation nor any experience in this life will change this; faith cannot be fully understood by reason and requires a commitment beyond what the evidence alone guarantees.

FAITH, REASON, TRANSCENDENCE, AND COMMITMENT

"Faith" means trust. This is true of the English term and also its precursors, *pistis* in Greek and *fides* in Latin. *Fides* unites the related concepts of religious belief, trust, and economic credit. Religious faith may be taken merely as trust that such belief is true although it would be more appropriate to take it as trust in the *source* of those beliefs—biblically speaking, trust in the authority of scripture (Acts 17:11), trust in Jesus the Messiah to deal with our sins (Matt 1:21; Acts 16:30–31), or trust in God to keep his promises (2 Cor 5:5–7). Credit in the fiscal or economic sense is also trust: the hotel trusts the credit card corporation to pay it for my stay, the credit card corporation trusts me to pay them in turn, and so on.

Trust may even be understood as action without explicit reference to belief. Suppose that I am on a small volcanic island and that the volcano is erupting! I could wait it out, hoping the lava does not get to me. I might try swimming, hoping to make it to safer shores before exhaustion—or a shark—claims me. Instead, I decide to rely on the rickety old airplane that happens to be on the island, hoping that both it and its drunken charter pilot will do their jobs properly. As I, trembling with fear, fasten my seat belt, I reflect on the fact that I am putting my faith in this old aircraft and yet am not quite sure I actually believe that it will not crash.[2] Biblically speaking, I know that I am a sinner (Rom 3:23). In desperate need of help, I trust Jesus to take care of my sin problem rather than try to save myself (Acts 4:12). I know that the requirement for faith involves following Jesus (Matt 16:24), but I am not sure I am never allowed to doubt.[3]

So we should beware of thinking of faith simply in terms of belief; still less should we think of faith simply in terms of irrational belief or belief

---

2. Daniel Howard-Snyder is helpful on the active aspect of faith. See Howard-Snyder, "Propositional Faith," 357–72.

3. Although Mark 11:23 appears to speak of belief without any doubt, the Greek word *diakrino* can also be translated as "waver" and may refer to wavering in our commitment to Christ, not to the entertaining of doubts.

without evidence. Trust is the main point of faith. Trust may be rational or irrational, evidenced or not, within or without the bounds of reason. It typically involves belief and, biblically speaking, always requires obedience.[4]

Now let us consider our second key term, "reason." First, the most broad sense would be something along the lines of proper thinking, the correct operating of our minds, or being in our right minds. More specifically, and second, "reason" may refer to one or more of the things we do when our minds are operating properly. For example, belief based on evidence is a paradigmatic function of reason, a normal and important way of using our minds to know the truth. After all, reason involves logic—the weighing of evidence to see how well it supports a particular conclusion. A third sense of "reason" is full comprehension or complete understanding, the ability to wrap our brains around a matter and fully grasp it, to know it for ourselves and not by relying on any authoritative testimony.

Now in what senses of the term "reason" does faith go beyond it? Not the broadest sense. At least according to orthodox Christianity, Christian faith is believing and following the truth, especially the truth about God and us. There could be no more proper operation of the mind than this. Indeed, some truths about himself God has made known to us by natural means (Rom 1:18–20). Others he has made known by means of prophecy, miracles, and scripture. (See, for example, John 20:30–31; John 21:24; Acts 17:31; Heb 1:1–2; 2 Pet 1:19–21.)

Even in the second sense of the term, it is difficult to say that faith transcends reason. At any rate, insofar as testimony is a legitimate source of evidence, it is bad theology to say that faith transcends reason in the sense of belief based on evidence. God can be trusted to keep his promises (Josh 23:14–15; Heb 6:18; 2 Cor 1:20). Jesus can be trusted (John 14:1). The Bible can be trusted (2 Tim 3:15–16). The apostolic witness (Gal 1:11–12) and the prophetic witness (2 Pet 1:16–21) can be trusted. Christian faith based in these trustworthy sources is faith based on good testimonial evidence.

It is in our third sense of the term that faith can best be said to go beyond reason. Certain Christian doctrines are rightly said to be mysteries: their full comprehension is beyond us. We should not expect anytime soon fully to grasp either the infinite goodness of God or the doctrines of the Incarnation and the Trinity. Nor to know firsthand the glories of the eschaton in this life, for what we do know of this we know by faith rather than sight—by trusting in the apostolic testimony and in God's promises accompanied by the down-payment of the Holy Spirit (2 Cor 5:1–5). Although the

---

4. A helpful related analysis may be found in chapter 1 of Evans, *Faith Beyond Reason*.

New Testament does teach that we know the gospel and, more generally, the truths of Christianity, this knowledge is largely secondhand and based on trust. It is not knowledge borne of full comprehension.

How best to characterize this relationship between faith and reason? As transcendence. This faith is not contrary to reason. *Un*reasonable faith is not biblical, no matter how often people may refer to the alleged absurdity of faith. Nor should faith be understood as simply separate from reason and having nothing to do with it. Then there would be no relevance of the evidence for faith such as we have recently considered. The entire tradition of academic theology and apologetics would be a contradiction in terms. From Augustine to C. S. Lewis, from William Lane Craig to Alvin Plantinga, the whole enterprise would be based on a delusion if, indeed, reason is not even relevant to faith.

So faith, Christianly conceived, is neither in conflict with reason nor totally cut off from it. Nor is it fully within the jurisdiction of reason defined as full comprehension. Were that the case, Christianity would be a matter of reason alone and would not require trust. Faith, Christianly conceived, transcends reason: It is something to which reason is relevant, yet which is outside of the jurisdiction of reason. In this unconventional Venn diagram,[5] faith occupies the outermost circle alone. All unreasonable things are within the jurisdiction of reason, but not vice versa; all things within the jurisdiction of reason are things to which reason is relevant, but not vice versa. That is one important sense in which faith may be said to go beyond reason. Let's look at another.

Say a young man (call him Mark if you like) is in love with a young lady (you could call her Shonda). He is seriously thinking about putting a ring on her finger. Suppose he were to sit down with a pen and paper to analyze his situation and were to estimate the probability that this course of action will lead to years of marital bliss (stipulating that he is the kind of nerd who might actually do this). He is not going to end up with a result of 100 percent. There is always the tiny, tiny chance that she is secretly a witch, an alien, or a robot. More likely, perhaps personality differences that have already become evident hint at years of communication problems and marital fights. Optimistically, the young man would be pretty lucky to be able to estimate a probability of around 95 percent.

But what young lady wants 95 percent of a ring?

The fact of the matter is simple: His action ought to be either 100 percent or zero percent.

---

5. In a standard Venn diagram in a logic course, all three circles bisect each other.

Of course, the conclusion of the matter may be a 100-percent matter. Given pretty good odds that they are meant to be together, it is reasonable to say that there is only one right course of action. What right action avoids all possible risk of a bad outcome? And that is another way of making the main point: Even an action which is certainly right may be based on uncertain evidence. In any case, the action must be either done, or not: He must give his lady friend a ring, or not. Similarly, she must agree to be his wife, or not; if she is less than fully convinced about it, she cannot act accordingly by becoming less than fully a wife, for there is no such thing, and if there were he is not asking her for it.

Faith is like that. It involves a commitment, not only of belief but of life. There is no faith without repentance (Acts 17:30–31) or without works (Jas 2:14–26). There is no faith without following Jesus, who says, "If anyone would come after me, let him deny himself and take up his cross and follow me" (Matt 16:24 ESV). This commitment is meant to be total; we do not get to keep 10 percent of our idols or 10 percent of our sins, and follow Jesus carrying 90 percent of a cross if a good study of apologetics leads us to assess the probability that Jesus is the Messiah at just 90 percent. The evidence is not binary, but the action is: We do it, or not.

Now, as it happens, I think the evidence is pretty good. (In fact, at the time of the initial composition of this paragraph, I am on Hong Kong Island to do my bit to teach part of a course on the evidences for Christianity for the Hong Kong Center for Christian Apologetics.) Still, I have to admit that the evidence is, technically, uncertain. My commitment to Christ must be 100 percent precisely. My decision to follow him when I was nine years old was between two choices—yes and no. But my evidence is not binary; it is only very good, but less than 100 percent.

In other words, the evidence is best understood probabilistically. Let's look at this a bit more closely.

It is relevant that some arguments for God's existence are inductive; in other words, their premises are not designed to render their conclusions certain, but merely probable. Such, for example, would be a typical teleological argument, such as an argument from evidences for design in nature. Another typical kind of argument for God's existence is the cosmological, such as the *Kalam* cosmological argument: Whatever begins to exist has a cause for its beginning; the universe began to exist; so there is a cause for the universe's beginning to exist, which is God. This is a deductive rather than an inductive argument; its premises are meant to guarantee the conclusion. But this argument, like the teleological arguments, works best after experience. There may, for example, be some good evidence from physics for the theory that the universe had a beginning. However, it is always possible that future physicists will find evidence to the contrary. The argument ultimately relies on probabilistic reasoning.[6]

Perhaps the infamous ontological argument establishes God's existence with certainty. Okay. But only if the argument works. I, like most, think that the original argument is not quite right.[7] Alvin Plantinga's analysis, if correct, shows that the argument works only given that the existence of God is a metaphysical possibility.[8] It might well depend on a probabilistic argument to prove *this*, however. Passing over other attempts to demonstrate God deductively,[9] let us note one limitation of such arguments. If they work, they demonstrate a higher power or even the greatest possible being Anselm wanted to prove—no small accomplishment. But they do not prove Christianity as such. The major religions have their specific doctrines; even those that teach a god, gods, or God (which Buddhism, for example, tends not to do) teach more than that he exists. The Abrahamic religions teach specific claims about historical events, miracles, and verbal revelation. The gospel is central to Christianity, and it consists of historical claims about the Messiah—about his birth, life, death, burial, and resurrection—and fulfilled prophecies (1 Cor 15:3–8). You can't prove this sort of thing with just an *a priori* argument—one not derived from experience. It also takes a historical argument, which is to say—an empirical and probabilistic one.

Even an unreasonable doubt ensures that the evidence for Christianity is only partial. As a Star Trek nerd, I can easily imagine an alternative account of the events surrounding the resurrection of Jesus the Messiah, without which (as Paul says in 1 Cor 15) my theology is so much fanciful error.

Stipulate that the best evidence from history, archaeology, and so on supports the Resurrection.[10] It is still possible that things are not what they seem. Suppose dishonest but otherwise benevolent otherworldly visitors came to Palestine at the time—perhaps extraterrestrials or even time-traveling humans from the future. Using holographic images, they rescued

---

6. This is actually a bit of an oversimplification of the *Kalam* argument; on the plausibility of *a priori* arguments that the universe had a beginning, see chapter 2 in Loke, *God and Ultimate Origins*.

7. See chapters 2–3 in Anselm, *Proslogion*. Roughly, the argument is: God is a perfect being, and non-existence is an imperfection; so if God does not exist, then a perfect being has an imperfection, which is impossible; therefore God exists. But if God does *not* exist then there is no being such that he is a perfect being. If, using some Anselmian language, God only exists in our minds, then he is *not* a perfect being.

8. Plantinga, *Nature of Necessity*, chapter 10.

9. For example, see the arguments of the third and fifth meditations in Descartes's *Meditations on First Philosophy*.

10. On this topic, the interested reader might consult the likes of Baukham, *Jesus and the Eyewitnesses*; Wright, *Resurrection*; Craig, *Assessing the New Testament Evidence*.

Jesus, faked his crucifixion, and had a good long talk with him aboard their cloaked spaceship. Meanwhile, Joseph of Arimathea mournfully buried a corpse the visitors had surgically altered and placed on the cross before switching off their holographic device. By Sunday morning, they had persuaded Jesus that it was necessary to fake his death and resurrection as an inspiration to his followers to teach his moral principles and spread them throughout the world. Bolstering the ruse with plastic surgery to give him the appearance of having been crucified, they returned Jesus to the tomb after rolling away the stone with a tractor beam and dazzling the guards with more holographic imagery. One or two stayed around long enough to impersonate some angels when the women arrived at the tomb. After Jesus had made enough appearances, the visitors drew him into the clouds before the Apostles' eyes. After arranging his meetings with Paul a little bit later, they conveyed him to South America, where he later died at a ripe old age.

Is all of this likely? No. But is it possible? As far as I know. Thinking about it actually makes me uncomfortable: I am facing the possibility that my faith relies on such a ruse.

But it is pretty unlikely, so I follow the evidence as well as I can understand it: I remain a Christian, a believer in the historical events that constitute the gospel—that Jesus the Messiah died for our sins in accordance with the scriptures, was buried, and was raised miraculously to life on the third day. I commit to this my whole life, for the most part leaving such doubts behind. The evidence is good enough to convince me that I ought to go beyond the evidence, for my Lord Jesus Christ does not ask me for a 90-something-percent commitment corresponding to my 90-something-percent evidence.

KANT

We are considering two reasons faith may be said to transcend reason—that the teachings of faith are less than fully comprehensible to the human mind and that the commitment required by faith is a total commitment of one's entire life whereas reason cannot guarantee the truth of religious beliefs. Let's look at some great thinkers who concur.[11] First up is Kant. As Stephen Evans summarizes Kant's perspective, "there are some truths that reason,

---

11. Much has been written on these matters. The interested reader might consult Evans, other sources cited below, or relevant articles in the Stanford and Internet Encyclopedias of Philosophy as paths into the secondary literature.

in its theoretical employment, can say nothing about, but which can and should be accepted by faith."[12]

In Kant's view, some putative realities are beyond our ability to learn about. When reason tries to demonstrate the truth about them, it ends up confused and contradicting itself. Kant attempts to show that an attempt to uncover the truth about these matters will end up proving both sides of the question—we will have solid arguments both for and against the proposition concerned. These are Kant's (in)famous antinomies of reason,[13] the pairing of contrary arguments in order to show that reason and argument have certain limits. They must work within these limits, rather than try to demonstrate anything about realities beyond them. Such is God, outside the limits of reason. Trying to understand God using reason will end up in confusion. Considering the venerable strategy of using cosmological arguments to prove that God exists, Kant argues that we can actually prove both sides of the question of a supreme being—we can prove both that a First Cause exists and that it does not. On the one hand, the changes we observe in the world must have a necessary first cause, or else there is no explanation for the fact that there are effects. On the other hand, the cause must be within time, for a cause always precedes its effect within time. Thus, the first cause must be either the first link in the chain of causes, or else the chain must itself be a necessary being and the first cause. But everything within time, as we observe from experience, is subject to cause and not merely a cause in itself; so we cannot consider the first link in the chain to be a first cause. Nor can the whole chain itself be a necessary being, since it is made of all its parts, and nothing made of parts is a necessary being if none of its parts are necessary beings. In short, we have solid arguments both for and against the existence of God.[14] So there is no knowledge of God; to the contrary, Kant says, "Thus I had to deny knowledge in order to make room for faith."[15]

Now the point is not only to keep reason from straying out of its own proper sphere but also to free it to operate within that sphere. Something similar is the case with Kant's metaphysics and epistemology. We cannot prove that we exist in three-dimensional space and do not need to. Kant does a bit of philosophical psychology and finds that this belief does not

12. Evans, *Faith Beyond Reason*, 65.

13. Or, as Kant himself refers to them, apparently considering them as a whole, the antinomy of reason. My gratitude to Stephen Palmquist for pointing this out.

14. To study the antinomy in more detail, see Kant, *Critique of Pure Reason*, second part, division 2, book 2, chapter 2, section 2. On the origins of Kant's idea of the antinomy and its influence on his philosophy, the interested reader might consult Al-Azm, *Origins of Kant's Arguments*.

15. Kant, *Critique of Pure Reason*, 117.

come from experience. The mind applies it to sensory experience in order to make sense of sensory experience. For example, take a few moments to search the internet for a picture of Victoria Falls and to think about what you're looking at when you look at that picture—perhaps some rocks or trees as well as the waterfall itself. What you're looking at is actually just a two-dimensional image; however, your mind knows how to apply the idea of three dimensions to it, so you can perceive that the rocks are behind the water, the trees are in the foreground, and so on.

But all you ever really see with the eyes (unaided by the mind) is, like this image, no more than an arrangement of shades and colors, which the eyes by themselves cannot tell you involve any three-dimensional objects. Depth-perception is not the gift of the eyes to the mind, but the mind's gift to what the eyes see in order to make sense of it.

So we do not need to prove that we exist in space. Rather, we should accept what we cannot help thinking—that the world as we know it is structured in three dimensions—and get on with the work that proceeds from that assumption, doing science to learn about that world. What is true of our concept of space is true of time and other matters, as Kant explains in the *Critique of Pure Reason*.[16]

Similarly, reason has no business proving God. However, moral reasoning requires us to believe in God.

Why is this? Well, Kant is a great ethicist, with a very influential and insightful analysis of the requirements of moral obligation. A proper analysis of this would make for a long digression.[17] For our purposes we need to make only a few observations. Kant's view is that the requirements of morality can be known by pure reason; we do not need to learn them from experience or from an authority.[18] We can always be sure of following the requirements of morality if we test our actions by what Kant calls the "Categorical Imperative"—the test of whether our choices are consistent with moral law. Kant proposes three[19] formulations of the Categorical Impera-

---

16. Kant employs a similar analysis for other beliefs, including the belief that we exist in time, the belief that there are substances underlying the properties of objects, and the belief in cause and effect. In fact, the concept of time also structures our perceptions of the waterfall. As Stephen Palmquist put it to me, "We *know* the water is moving, yet there's no actual movement in the pictures. When we think 'Victoria Falls,' the object is schematized insofar as we think the whole space-time body of water that runs over the rocks, down the cliff, and between the trees."

17. The interested reader might seek an introduction in Johnson, "Kant's Moral Philosophy."

18. On this topic I suggest Palmquist, *Comprehensive Commentary*, 8–9.

19. Or four. Kant presents the third one in two different ways, and the second way looks like a fourth to some readers.

tive. But all this is only enough to know what morality requires of us. Actually *living* by morality is another matter, for frail beings such as we are easily tempted by the flesh. Kant thinks we need religious hope to properly inspire us to always act morally. Specifically, he thinks we need to believe that God will eventually make circumstances line up with the requirements of morality. In our experience, moral goodness does not always correlate with happiness, but we understand that it should. God can make this happen, and a belief that he exists and will ultimately do so helps us live morally, looking with hope toward that end, and sticking with morality even when things are tough, believing that morality will be worth it.[20]

So, although faith is necessary, the defense of faith is not based on evidence for its truth but on evidence for its practicality.[21] Faith is a matter of reason, to be sure, but of reason acting in its capacity as a guide to conduct rather than a guide to truth. The putative facts about God and about life after death remain beyond our understanding. This is a permanent fixture of the human condition: We cannot have knowledge of God, and we must act, for the sake of morality and despite our lack of theological knowledge, as if God exists. Kant even claims that the moral theology he is developing is more reliable than speculative theology.[22] He goes on to explain what are the different modes of taking a proposition to be true: *Opinion*, where we are neither 100 percent committed to a theory nor persuaded by logical proof, is the weakest; *knowledge*, where both of these things are the case, is the strongest form of belief.[23] Between these is *belief*, in which state we are entirely committed but lack proof. Faith in God and in his final justice is found in this middle ground.

Note that what we have in Kant does not fit the transcendence model of the relationship between faith and reason quite so well as it fits a separation model. Although it is true, in Kant's view, that the content of faith is not known by reason and that a moral life requires action beyond what the evidence can justify, he is not in favor of all aspects of the account overviewed in the previous section of this chapter.[24]

---

20. Again, Palmquist is helpful. See Palmquist, *Comprehensive Commentary*, 14–15, 21.

21. Note that Kant is not opposed to attempts to understand the truth about God. Systematic theology from a biblical perspective is okay by Kant's lights; see Palmquist, *Comprehensive Commentary*, 28–30.

22. Kant, *Critique of Pure Reason*, Doctrine of Method, chapter 2, section 2.

23. Kant, *Critique of Pure Reason*, section 3. My gratitude to Stephen Palmquist for pointing me to this passage in connection with this topic.

24. In my analysis a necessary condition for X transcending Y is that Y have some relevance to X—not merely about what we should think about X. In Kant's analysis

AUGUSTINE

Augustine points to both reasons faith may be said to transcend reason; in his way of thinking, this is largely a temporary situation. In the future, sufficient mental and moral training may give us the ability to see God and know firsthand his existence and nature, and then of course this knowledge will be fully justified and will fully justify a total commitment to following Christ. (This is a perspective drawn largely from the early writings; his later writings, in which I have spent less time, are likely to be less optimistic about reason.)

Although these matters appear in many of his books, a brief look at three will suffice. In his first surviving writing, *Contra Academicos* or *Against the Academics*, we read the following:

> Moreover, no one doubts that we are urged on to learn by the twin weight of authority (*auctoritas*) and reason (*ratio*). Therefore, I am determined not to depart ever, in any way, from the authority of Christ. . . . But what should be pursued by a most subtle reason (*sublitissima ratio*)—for I am now of such a mind that I impatiently long to apprehend what is true not only through believing (from *credo*), but also through understanding (from *intelligo*)—I am confident that in the meantime I shall find among the Platonists, and that it won't be incompatible with our sacred [teachings].[25]

Closely related and written in the same year (386 AD) at the same place (Cassiciacum, near Milan), we read in *De Ordine, On Order*:

> Twofold is the path we follow when we are moved by the obscurity of things: either reason (*ratio*), or at least authority (*auctoritas*). Philosophy promises reason but it barely frees a very few. Nevertheless, it drives them not only not to disdain those mysteries, but to understand them alone, as they should be understood.[26]

Philosophy here means the neo-Platonic tradition's insights into non-physical reality. And, as he goes on to explain, it teaches that God exists, but authority teaches the Christian mysteries of the Incarnation and the Trinity.

---

reason can tell us we should have faith, but does not give any evidence for the truth of the religious doctrines in question. So faith may only be said to transcend reason in a looser sense, such as that used by Evans, *Faith Beyond Reason*, 66.

25. Augustine, *Against the Academics* 3.20.43. Foley notes that Augustine later regretted his overstatement concerning the overlap of Christianity and neo-Platonism.

26. Augustine, *On Order* 2.5.16.

In a letter to his old friend Honoratus, whom he aims to free from the Manichean heresy as he had formerly led him into it, Augustine explains that to believe by trust is different from *intellegere*, to understand, or *discere*, to know.[27] However, both are important. We must seek the truth in both ways. First, we must seek by faith in orthodox Christianity.[28] Later, we seek by means of reason added to faith—a reason for which our minds have been trained by faith.[29] In his own words,

> When you do not have the ability to appreciate the arguments, it is very healthy to believe without knowing the reasons (*ratio*) and by that belief (*fides*) to cultivate the mind and allow the seeds of truth to be sown. Moreover, for minds that are ill this is absolutely essential, if they are to be restored to health.[30]

In short, according to Augustine's usual way of talking, faith and reason are not the same thing. Although faith is rational and useful, reason requires first-hand understanding, and faith necessarily involves trust. Trust must go beyond what reason alone can guarantee. This is the case with respect to action, for we must trust Christ, the Bible, and the church; trust involves obeying their commands and reordering our lives and our loves around them. It is also true with respect to evidence, for this trust is in truths that we find ourselves incapable of knowing for ourselves. Yet, hopefully, this is a temporary situation, not a permanent feature of the human condition. We may, in time, come to understand these truths by means of contemplating the nature of immaterial reality with minds trained by neo-Platonic insight.

JAMES

William James, like Augustine, thinks of faith as going beyond reason both in terms of full comprehension and in terms of action. James gives a particularly interesting analysis of action as that which must go beyond mere reason—in other spheres of life as well as religion. Also like Augustine, he thinks of this as a temporary situation. Knowledge may come in the future after—indeed as a result of—faith. One difference between the two is that James is more empirical than Augustine; the knowledge he hopes to add to faith he hopes to gain from experience—not, as in Augustine, from

---

27. Augustine, *Advantage of Believing* 11.25.
28. Augustine, *Advantage of Believing* 8.20.
29. Augustine, *Advantage of Believing* 17.35.
30. Augustine, *Advantage of Believing* 14.31.

contemplation. For our purposes, a brief look at James's most famous work, his essay "The Will to Believe," should be sufficient.

In James's view, knowledge of God must come from experience. As an empiricist, James thinks knowledge comes "by systematically continuing to roll up experiences and think."[31] James is, moreover, a member of the tradition of American Pragmatism in philosophy. In other words, he is an intellectual descendant but not a member of the tradition of British Empiricism. These British Empiricists (such as Hobbes, Locke, and Hume) held that knowledge comes from sensory experience alone. James's Pragmatism considers experience in broader terms. Knowledge comes from experience, and religious experience counts. James's *The Varieties of Religious Experience* is a long and systematic look at the past data of religious experience in hopes of getting a feel for how strong might be the evidence for God or some other spiritual reality.

In "The Will To Believe," James is considering something different—the rationality of belief in God when that evidence from experience is, for the present at least, inconclusive. He thinks it is, and his arguments to that effect are practical ones. There are two.

First, we each face an unavoidable decision whether to be religious or not. We can avoid choosing between being Southern Baptist or Roman Catholic by opting to be Presbyterians, materialistic atheists, or Confucians. But we cannot avoid deciding whether to have either no religious beliefs or at least one; that decision is forced on us. Moreover, the decision has a big effect on our lives. Not only does it change how we live, but religion also alleges that there are significant positive effects even in this life, promising that we will benefit from believing that the eternal things are the more valuable ones. Now, although some of us may not be able to be atheist even if we were to try—or to be religious—some of us really could go either way. For such, the decision is what James calls live, forced, and momentous: We could go either way, we must go one way, and there are big consequences.

In the absence of convincing evidence, we have the right to make such decisions not based on evidence alone. People normally do make such decisions in this way, and no one has a problem with it—Do I marry? Whom? How many kids do we want to have? Shall I become a philosopher or a dentist? Anyway, what choice do we have but to—make the choice? When the evidence is lacking and the decision is live, forced, and momentous, deciding not based on convincing evidence is all we can do. Moreover, James thinks we have a right to take into consideration the possible good consequences promised by religion. In deciding whether to have a religious

---

31. James, "Will to Believe."

belief, we decide between two risks. If we believe and are wrong, we will be in error. If we do not believe, we will avoid that error but also avoid any possible good results of believing any religious truths there may be. We have a right, James says, to decide for ourselves whether we prefer the risk of not believing a religious truth or the risk of believing a religious falsehood.

Second, James draws an analogy from human relationships to the divine:

> We feel, too, as if the appeal of religion to us were made to our own active good-will, as if evidence might be forever withheld from us unless we met the hypothesis half-way. To take a trivial illustration: just as a man who in a company of gentlemen made no advances, asked a warrant for every concession, and believed no one's word without proof, would cut himself off by such churlishness from all the social rewards that a more trusting spirit would earn,—so here, one who should shut himself up in snarling logicality and try to make the gods extort his recognition willy-nilly, or not get it at all, might cut himself off forever from his only opportunity of making the gods' acquaintance.[32]

There is a decent chance that, if there is a God, our major religions are right in thinking that this God is a person (or three). It is also likely that the divine person is like human persons in that he will not provide proof of his existence and good intentions prior to any willingness on our part to trust him. In the kind of relationships with which we are most familiar—the human-human variety—evidence of goodwill frequently comes after, not before, trust. Perhaps God exists after all, but the evidence for God's existence may come about after—even because of—our faith.

In sum, James thinks religious knowledge based on experience is a possibility. Given this knowledge, religious faith would be a matter of reason. In the present, however, many of us face the decision whether to believe in God. It is like other decisions along life's way—decisions we all recognize as rational despite their being based on incomplete evidence. Moreover, if indeed God is personal, it is likely that his making himself known to us will depend on our willingness to believe, and in this respect faith in God is much like the faith we regularly place in human persons—prior to the evidence, and (when all goes well) leading to confirmation later that our faith was well-placed. Faith, thus, goes beyond reason in both senses. Faith is belief in religious propositions not currently proven. It is also an activity of life, a practical commitment beyond what the currently available evidence

---

32. James, "Will to Believe."

warrants. Faith transcends reason in these two ways, but temporarily—until future experience brings about the right evidence.

KIERKEGAARD

C. Stephen Evans says, "Søren Kierkegaard is often cited in textbooks as a prime example of irrational fideism."[33] Chapters 6 and 7 of Evans's *Faith Beyond Reason* are very helpful in explaining that Kierkegaard is actually "a responsible fideist": he thinks faith is not contained within reason, but his views "do not imply any repudiation of reason."[34] Kierkegaard is adamant that Christian faith transcends reason and cannot be made to answer to its standards. This does not make faith *against* reason—just a little bit *beyond* it. We might say, rather, that reason goes against faith sometimes—when reason gets a little uppity and oversteps its bounds. Unlike Augustine and James, Kierkegaard thinks reason will never quite catch up to faith in this life. In what follows, I will consider Kierkegaard's analysis in *Fear and Trembling* of Christian faith as that which goes beyond full comprehension. Then I will consider his analysis in *Philosophical Fragments* of Christian faith as requiring a leap of total commitment.

Fear and Trembling is probably Kierkegaard's most intoxicating book. The reflections on Abraham's act of faith in Genesis 22 may leave us speechless, breathless, or in tears. Yet this book is easily misunderstood. We should not presume that it is simply written by Kierkegaard. We could just as easily say that it is a piece of fiction written by Johannes de Silentio (John the Silent), the fictional character Kierkegaard made up to write it! To be a bit more precise, *Fear and Trembling* is one of Kierkegaard's pseudonymous works, and it is not quite right to say that what de Silentio says is what Kierkegaard says. Rather, de Silentio must be understood as representing a position Kierkegaard wants us to understand and to take seriously.[35]

As I understand him, de Silentio is under the influence of Enlightenment and post-Enlightenment philosophical concepts of reason. His worldview is more-or-less Hegelian. Hegel is one of the great philosophers of the late modern era of philosophy—the next truly great German philosopher after Kant. He is an influential character in the history of process theology—theology based on the idea that God grows and develops. In Hegelian

33. Evans, *Faith Beyond Reason*, 78.
34. Evans, *Faith Beyond Reason*, 78.
35. For guidance on reading Kierkegaard's pseudonyms, see Evans, *Faith Beyond Reason*, 78–79, as well as Evans's longer analysis in chapter 1 of *Kierkegaard's "Fragments" and "Postscript."*

thought, it is not easy to say, "In the beginning God created the heavens and the earth," because God in his final form was not there in the beginning. God emerges over time through the experiences and growth of the human race. That growth is moral, but also rational. The human race increases in knowledge and reason. The perfectly rational and moral consciousness to emerge at the end of history—that is God. So God does not on his own authority lay down for us commands we must follow or propositions we must believe. God himself (in his final form) is largely the product of human reason. God is not above reason. All theology must submit to the requirements of reason, and human reason itself must grow as the human race works together to increase in understanding until it encompasses all reality.

Now de Silentio frankly admits that he is not a man of faith and cannot understand Abraham's faith. Yet he can understand what it is *not*, and it is not Hegelian. His central claim is that faith is absurd. This claim is made from a Hegelian perspective; if we have a different perspective, we may reject it. Too much under the influence of Hegelianism, de Silentio has no choice but to view faith as absurd. Kierkegaard himself, who is actually Hegel's biggest critic, can and does think otherwise.

Why is faith absurd from a Hegelian perspective? Abraham's faith is exemplified by his willingness in Genesis 22 to obey God and sacrifice his son. Hegelian reason can understand sacrificing one's child for the good of the community—as Agamemnon and Jeptha do. The Hegelian conception of reason recognizes the superiority of the community to the individual, considers that even destructive actions may be justified by their higher ends, and judges actions by the standard of the universal community. For the good of the many, the one may be sacrificed, as Spock says in *Star Trek II: The Wrath of Khan*.

But Isaac is Abraham's heir, the heart of the Hebrew community. There is no sacrificing him *for* the community: Sacrificing him *is* sacrificing the community. Hegelian ethics can understand no higher end in Abraham's action. Abraham is the lone individual receiving instructions from God; there is no universal communal standard that can evaluate this.

Now, Kierkegaard is writing in a time of confusion. Practically everyone in Denmark in the 1800s assumes that practically everyone in Denmark is a Christian. Yet the majority of Denmark's intellectuals are Hegelians! As Hamlet opines, something is rotten here. Christianity and Hegelianism are not compatible, but most people do not realize that, and many fancy themselves to be both. Even those who are not intellectuals studying Hegelianism at the university typically have many of the same ideas—particularly that human reason can ultimately prove everything that is true and justify everything that is just.

If that is the case, what do we make of Abraham? Kierkegaard's goal in writing *Fear and Trembling* is to help people see that there is an inconsistency between Christian theology, based on Abrahamic faith, and these widespread Hegelian principles. The main lesson from *Fear and Trembling* is this argument: If Hegelianism is right, then Abraham has attempted murder and his actions are absurd; Abraham has not attempted murder, and his actions are not absurd; so Hegelianism is wrong.

Having said that, the main thing is to understand the inconsistency—to understand the if-then premise. Kierkegaard would be delighted if people would follow through on the whole argument, renounce Hegelianism, and be faithful Christians. He would still be somewhat pleased with those who admit the if-then premise and proceed as honest Hegelians who admit that they are not Christians.

Johannes de Silentio is like that. He can see the first premise of the argument above, but he can't quite accept the second. In other words, he can see the conflict between Hegelian conceptions of reason and Christian faith, but he is not prepared to reject Hegel and accept Christian faith. More generally, de Silentio can see the tension between biblical faith and any standard of reason that insists that everything we believe submit to the full comprehension of the human intellect. He admires this faith but is not prepared to abandon his prejudice in favor of the ultimate authority of reason.

In short, faith is absurd when measured by the standards of comprehensive post-Enlightenment reason. It goes beyond full comprehension, and it requires trust in God's pronouncements and commands instead of perfect understanding.

Another pseudonymous character invented by Kierkegaard is Johannes Climacus, the author of *Philosophical Fragments* (or *Philosophical Crumbs*) and *Concluding Unscientific Postscript to the Philosophical Fragments* (*Crumbs*). The main point of Climacus's writing, as I understand it, is that the doctrine of the Incarnation cannot be understood by those Enlightenment standards of reason culminating in Hegelianism. The Incarnation goes beyond the limits of human reason. It is, in Climacus's recurring words, an "absolute paradox." It is the paradox that God became man, or, in Climacus's words, "The eternal truth has come into existence in time. That is the paradox."[36] This can be believed, but not understood. The result of making it understandable can only be that the doctrine loses its significance for life.

The only way to make the Incarnation understandable is to abolish it, as Hegelian philosophical theology has done. It has not always done so explicitly or even knowingly. The typical Hegelian distances himself from

---

36. Kierkegaard, *Concluding Unscientific Postscript*, 209.

the "modern mythical allegorizing trend" of denying the truth of Christianity, swearing his friendliness to the doctrine of the Incarnation. Climacus's reply is biting. The allegorizers are at least "forthright" in their rejection of Christian doctrine, but "The friendship of speculative thought" is different: "Speculative thought . . . accepts the paradox, but it does not stop with it."[37] With friends like speculative thought, who needs enemies? It goes on to explain the Incarnation, thus disarming its paradoxical nature. Ultimately, the explanation is just an audacious correction.[38] The correction goes something like this: According to the carnal understanding of Christians from an earlier era, there was a paradox, but now that theology and speculative philosophy have come of age, we can look at the Incarnation from a better perspective, that of speculation. From this vantage point, there is no paradox—only the truth that God and man are ultimately one. We can even imagine that, when everyone learns to be more speculative, "Christianity will have ceased to be a paradox."[39]

But the doctrine that God became a human like us does not admit of explanation. Christianity never ceases to be a paradox. The amended doctrine of the Incarnation is without significance, but the historical doctrine has enormous significance for my life and yours. God became a human like you and me and lived a life like yours and mine; the significance of the doctrine is for everyday life. The claim of speculative thought removes the Incarnation from human existence, establishing it as the ideal unity of God and man, a doctrine far removed from the real world where the Incarnation has its significance. Climacus says this "is an explanation not for existing individuals but for the absentminded."[40] These Hegelians explain the doctrine only by denying its significance. These are the consequences of insisting that the true meaning of the Incarnation is accessible to human understanding.

From God's perspective, the Incarnation is no contradiction. In fact, Kierkegaard regularly lambasts Hegelian thought for giving up the principle of noncontradiction.[41] Speculative thought's mistake is, rather, that it claims to be able to view the Incarnation from God's perspective. We do not have any access to this perspective. One would have to become God to have the intellectual capacity for understanding the Incarnation.[42] Modern

37. Kierkegaard, *Concluding Unscientific Postscript*, 218.
38. Kierkegaard, *Concluding Unscientific Postscript*, 219.
39. Kierkegaard, *Concluding Unscientific Postscript*, 221.
40. Kierkegaard, *Concluding Unscientific Postscript*, 221.
41. See, for instance, Kierkegaard, *Concluding Unscientific Postscript*, 304–5. I am indebted to a comment from Dan Johnson for the insight that Kierkegaard's defense of noncontradiction is significant for his view of the Incarnation.
42. Kierkegaard, *Concluding Unscientific Postscript*, 217–18.

intellect has gotten big-headed. Moreover, speculation removes itself from the context in which the doctrine is significant. The Incarnation presents itself to us as a momentous change in the meaning of our own lives. It does not call any person to become God so as to understand theology—only to do what God did as a man and become a different kind of person.

What must we do with this doctrine, according to Climacus? The correct response to the Incarnation is not primarily intellectual: We approach the truth of the Incarnation with passion rather than speculation.[43] We must take a leap of faith, a decision of total commitment.

The truth of Christianity would preclude that everyone has access to the truth; only those in right relation to Christ have access to the truth. The Incarnation spurs us more to live our lives in response to it, less to speculate in hopes of understanding it. The doctrine takes its stand in everyday human existence. God became a person and lived a human life; it is in the context of our own lives that we must respond to this fact. We realize the significance of the Incarnation by living. It begins with a decision. As Climacus says at the beginning of *Postscript*, the issue of Christianity is not whether speculation can make sense of the Incarnation, but "the issue is rooted specifically in decision."[44] The decision cannot be delayed indefinitely. The worst one can do is spend all his time speculating about the paradox and so never come to a decision.[45] Even rejecting Christ outright is better than thinking he does not demand decisive action.

The decision is decisive and absolute. A good analogy is the decision required by erotic love. Listen to Climacus: "Much that is strange has been said about erotic love, much that is lamentable, much that is outrageous, but the most obtuse thing of all said about it is that it is to a certain degree."[46] Imagine our young man from earlier telling his girlfriend that he has great affection for her, estimates the odds that she is the girl for him at 95 percent, and is prepared to offer her 95 percent of the rest of his life, keeping the last 5 percent for whatever else may come up later. If a self-respecting girl prefers 100 percent, how much more so Christ, who says "any one of you who does not renounce all that he has cannot be my disciple" (Luke 14:33 ESV)? Climacus observes: "What does it mean to assert that a decision is to

---

43. As J. I. Packer said, "We shall be wise . . . to shun speculation and contentedly to adore" (Packer, *Knowing God*, 58).
44. Kierkegaard, *Concluding Unscientific Postscript*, 21.
45. See part 1 in Kierkegaard, *Concluding Unscientific Postscript*.
46. Kierkegaard, *Concluding Unscientific Postscript*, 229.

a certain degree? It means to deny decision. Decision is designed specifically to put an end to that perpetual prattle about 'to a certain degree.'"[47]

The absolute decision for Christ brings one into relationship with God. In this relationship one knows the truth. Ethics and religion are for practice. A person becomes ethical by striving to bring her life into concordance with the demands of ethics; so also for the demands of religion. Climacus calls this striving knowledge: "all ethical and all ethical-religious knowing is essentially a relating to the existing of the knower."[48] We know the requirements of ethics and religion by expressing them in our lives. Christ requires that we follow him; we know him by relating this requirement to our lives. Expressing the truth of the Incarnation in our lives is holistic. No part of our lives can escape it. It is at least as passionate as it is intellectual.[49] The truth must fill up every corner of our lives.

CONCLUSION

What does the Christian worldview say about faith and reason? Quite a lot. Faith is beyond reason, at least according to the terms of Christian theology, and philosophers of religion help us to understand how and why this is the case. There are two ways in which we can say that faith transcends reason. Faith requires belief in that which reason has not first comprehended perfectly and proven to be true. Faith also involves action that reason has not proven to be correct. Kant, Augustine, James, and Kierkegaard concur on these matters although they differ on the permanence of this arrangement this side of the grave—Kant and Kierkegaard being for it, Augustine and James being against. They differ in how we might add reason to faith if we can—James being more empirical than Augustine. They even differ in their Christianity—Kant and James, by my understanding, lacking Christian theology altogether! Yet they help to give us a clear picture of how faith may be beyond reason—in more ways than one—yet still be rational and necessary. "Of making many books there is no end," even of books about faith and reason. But one of the points of these books is well made: We are justified in having faith; with or without reason, it's only reasonable.

---

47. Kierkegaard, *Concluding Unscientific Postscript*, 221.
48. Kierkegaard, *Concluding Unscientific Postscript*, 198.
49. Kierkegaard, *Concluding Unscientific Postscript*, section II, chapter 2.

BIBLIOGRAPHY

Al-Azm, Sadiq J. *The Origins of Kant's Arguments in the Antinomies*. Oxford: Oxford University Press, 1972.

Augustine. "The Advantage of Believing." In *On Christian Belief*, edited by Boniface Ramsey, 116–48. Translated by Ray Kearney. Notes by Michael Fiedrowicz. Vol. 8 of *The Works of Saint Augustine: A Translation for the Twenty-First Century, Part I–Books*. Hyde Park, NY: New City, 2005.

———. *Against the Academics*. Vol. 1 of *St. Augustine's Cassiciacum Dialogues*. Translated by Michael P. Foley. New Haven: Yale University Press, 2019.

———. *On Order*. Vol. 3 of *St. Augustine's Cassiciacum Dialogues*. Translated by Michael P. Foley. New Haven: Yale University Press, forthcoming.

Baukham, Richard. *Jesus and the Eyewitnesses: The Gospel as Eyewitness Testimony*. Grand Rapids: Eerdmans, 2006.

Boone, Mark J. "Augustine and William James on the Rationality of Faith." *Heythrop Journal* 61 (2020) 648–59. https://onlinelibrary.wiley.com/doi/10.1111/heyj.13123.

Craig, William Lane. *Assessing the New Testament Evidence for the Historicity of the Resurrection of Jesus*. Lewiston, NY: Mellen, 1989.

Evans, C. Stephen. *Faith Beyond Reason: A Kierkegaardian Account*. Grand Rapids: Eerdmans, 1998.

———. *Kierkegaard's "Fragments" and "Postscript": The Religious Philosophy of Johannes Climacus*. Amherst, NY: Prometheus, 1983.

Howard-Snyder, Daniel. "Propositional Faith: What It Is and What It Is Not." *American Philosophical Quarterly* 50 (2013) 357–72.

James, William. "The Will to Believe." In *The Will to Believe and Other Essays in Popular Philosophy*. New York: Longmans, Green, and Co., 1912. Online. https://www.gutenberg.org/files/26659/26659-h/26659-h.htm.

Johnson, Robert. "Kant's Moral Philosophy." In *Stanford Encyclopedia of Philosophy*, July 7, 2016. https://plato.stanford.edu/entries/kant-moral.

Kierkegaard, Søren. *Concluding Unscientific Postscript to Philosophical Fragments*. Translated and edited by Howard V. Hong and Edna H. Hong. Kierkegaard's Writings 12. Princeton: Princeton University Press, 1992.

Kant, Immanuel. *The Critique of Pure Reason*. Translated by Paul Guyer and Allen W. Wood. Cambridge: Cambridge University Press, 1998.

Loke, Andrew Ter Ern. *God and Ultimate Origins: A Novel Cosmological Argument*. London: Palgrave Macmillan, 2017.

Packer, J. I. *Knowing God*. Downers Grove, IL: InterVarsity, 1973.

Palmquist, Stephen R. *Comprehensive Commentary on Kant's "Religion Within the Bounds of Bare Reason."* Malden, MA: Wiley Blackwell, 2016.

Plantinga, Alvin. *The Nature of Necessity*. New York: Oxford University Press, 1974.

Wright, N. T. *The Resurrection of the Son of God*. Minneapolis: Fortress, 2003.

Part 3

The Beautiful

14

Three Poems

SARA TRIANA MITCHELL[1]

THE WACO PLANT

Willie Jean took a cutting from
inside the courtyard
of the limestone Waco church
after photos around bride and groom
clustered clicked and concluded.

Half the people wouldn't exist
without her, not the bride
not the bride's father
not without the quiet living room, the garden
not without her weekly call.

---

1. These poems previously appeared in my self-published chapbook, *Poppy Seeds*.

She slipped the smarting stem
into cool water, a Styrofoam cup
in her car hardly cooling
in the scorch of late August
before the reception. She never had

grown that flower before:
leaves like mimosa and a spray
of red and gold blooms, not so deep
a red as the Episcopal carpeting
where every sound sank in a holy hush.

Not so gold as the stole wrapped
around the almost-lovers hands.
Her granddaughter swishing in a white
skirt swinging fuller with the petticoat
she, Willie Jean, had made was promising forever.

Now, the intertwining, the cake slicing,
the revelers dancing while the wilting
leaves hurtled home with Willie Jean
alone as the Saturday sun settled.
She'll make up for the missed mass tomorrow.

In the morning, the first morning,
gingerly adjusting, peeking out
at a garden of pines, ivy and hibiscus
the Waco flower stretches out.
Tender new roots say

this day is eternal.
She thought it might be nice
to let the promising, the reveling
the intertwining, the blooming
have a chance at forever

no matter how short it ends up.
You never know. She didn't know
how soon she wouldn't need a plus one.
Sometimes forever is a cutting
you didn't expect, rooting back

to the beginning of all things.

IF POEMS ARE FLOWERS

If poems are flowers,
then this one is
a silent pop
a burst of baby's breath
or the tiny yellow blooms
woven in the weeds
outside
running down the sides
of sidewalks
in the in between

A flower just for today.
A flower marking time.

If this poem
is the white egret
swooping by my back window
gliding over the greenbelt
watching for fish
then I just barely
caught sight of it.

One quiet moment of awe
of looking out and looking in.

Before the hum of all
the everything else
turns up loud again.

THE DAY YOU ONLY SURVIVED

The day you only survived
the day of nightmare news
and decimated heart
and lungs without a breath.

The day whose silent growl
you never heard approach,
whose prowl alerted
the hairs along your neck too late.

When you walked through the fire.
When every springy, shiny part of you
became smoke, became ash
and all you could think was

THIS IS NOT RIGHT.
NOTHING ABOUT THIS IS RIGHT.

We called you strong.
We named you brave
and spoke of grace and mercy.
But the only true thing is

you had to keep moving.
You could not choose
to stop, to switch places
to be the one upon the cross.

to gift your heartbeat
to be the one detained, deported.
You would have slipped the diagnosis
around your own neck

but that's not how it works.
You are still here.
You are still here.
You are still here and you are different now
      but you don't get an out, you just
      have to keep waking up, slicing tomatoes
      and checking the mail and you
      even laugh at jokes now and you
      even make plans.

And we will call that strong,
and speak of grace and mercy,
because there really is no good word
for living with part of you

just gone.

15

Or Whither Shall I Flee?

Mark J. Boone

This chapter develops my best idea ever for a story. The story has come a long way since I first experimented with it in high school. Above all, it has taken on a good bit more Augustine and C. S. Lewis. Now, as it happens, I actually agree with Augustine and Lewis on God and time. In this particular piece of fiction, however, Augustine and Lewis are wrong about God and time. They are apparently right about everything else, but I leave it to the reader—or, if necessary, to myself at some later date—to trace these connections.

Strictly as a matter of citation, I feel I must here clarify one thing: The philosopher to whom the angel refers is Max Black; the bridge world in this story is inspired by the world of Castor and Pollux in Black's famous article, "The Identity of Indiscernibles."

VOID

They say time is the fourth dimension, but they don't say what happens to a time traveler if our universe passes through the timefield only once.

The first travelers who went the wrong way in time found a past that was *almost* nothing, but not *quite*. It was just enough of *something* to be even worse than nothing.

They had christened the timeship the *Virgil*.

Because the time-engines required speeds not possible in the terrestrial sphere, the *Virgil* was also a spaceship. Its mission was to travel exactly five minutes into the past and to return five minutes later to its point of origin.

In one respect, the maiden voyage was a smashing success: It confirmed that travel into the past was possible. The problem was where the *Virgil* did *not* take them—for the place to which they went was more like no place at all than any other place.

The mission began without a hitch. The *Virgil* hurtled through space at faster speeds than man had before attained, the crew activated the time-engines, and the *Virgil* hurtled backward in time. It reached five minutes ago—and stopped.

The Captain sat on the bridge. His eyes were dark green, almost black; he had just enough silver hair on his temples for it to look dignified; he was a man who made a point of never slouching in front of anyone, not even a quarter-inch. Dressed in his uniform and sitting in his fancy chair, he looked every bit the master of some grand spaceship from a science fiction television show.

The Captain looked through the viewscreen into the world of the past.

But there was no world.

Emptiness.

Blackness.

Ink.

He checked the readings on his console. The precise temporal location of the *Virgil* was five minutes ago, plus the past few seconds.

Their spatial location was impossible to determine. The *Virgil* should have been orbiting the sun. But there was no sun, nor any Earth or anything else to orbit.

The Captain glanced out the viewscreen again.

Nothing.

Emptiness. Blackness. Ink. Depth. Void.

No sun, no star by which to chart their location.

The Captain saw that his befuddled crew were looking to him for guidance; they were being very professional about it, of course—minding their duties and waiting for orders. The First Officer stood at attention just within his peripheral vision—dutifully waiting for an order to pass on.

This void was rather a disappointment after humanity's first successful journey back in time. The Captain decided that the first order of business was simply to keep up morale.

"Well done, crew!" he said, casting a glance at his First Officer, and shifting to a slightly more comfortable position in his chair to indicate that, wherever they had gone, their Captain considered that all was well.

At that moment the intercom crackled on from Engineering. The *Virgil* shuddered around them as through the intercom came screams and the sound of tearing metal.

WHERE IN HELL?

About two minutes later, with most of the crew busy with repairs, the Captain gathered with his chief officers in the Operations Room. It was assumed that the explosion had been the result of some technical malfunction. The Captain had said some extremely brief yet lovely words about the casualties. More information would be forthcoming. Meanwhile, the explosion had evidently damaged the time-engines, which now could run at only about half-power.

The Captain paused to gather his thoughts. There had also been two or three minor malfunctions reported. A piston giving out here, an electrical failure there. Nothing dangerous.

Probably a few technical problems were just the downside of making the first successful time journey in history.

The problem of where the *Virgil* had gone seemed more pressing.

A yard or so from where he sat, the eerie nothingness still waited outside.

"Now: Where the hell *are* we?" asked the Captain.

Surprisingly, most of the officers had nothing to say. Even the three physicists were silent. They were obviously thinking very hard; one was scribbling models and equations in a notebook.

It was, unexpectedly, the ship's Chaplain who spoke first. He was a man in his forties with a slightly pointy nose, curved a bit downwards like an eagle's beak. His bald spot had seized some new territory from his graying black hair over the last few months. "It's a bit unsettling," he said, staring at the nothingness through a porthole. "I had hoped my books would be right about the past."

Lacking anyone better to talk to, the Captain engaged: "I wasn't aware that they taught physics in seminary."

"Hardly. I hoped to see the past because I used to read that God sees everything in the past as an eternal present. It's in Boethius, Augustine, Lewis. I had hoped they might actually be right."

"Well," said the Captain, "that's ... one perspective." Turning to an Airman who was standing at attention ready to do menial work such as answer such questions, he asked, "*When* the hell are we?"

"1:59 p.m., Sir. Same day, same year. About one minute before we, uh, left."

"We've been here for four minutes then?"

"Yes, Sir."

"Well, let's wait until we left and see if we see us. At 2 p.m., if nothing interesting happens, I'll ask again, where the hell are we?"

A minute solemnly filed past.

"Where the hell are we?" said the Captain.

An Airman burst into the room. Between deep breaths, he stammered, "Captain—Sir!—You need to see this, Sir!"

The Airman held out a tablet computer on which had been loaded some sort of video. The Captain received it, nodded to the Airman, set it on the table where his officers could see it, and played the video. It turned out to be a slow-motion replay of the explosion in engineering.

The Captain and his offers watched as a semi-sphere of fire worked its way out from a wall. The blast wave caught a computer console, ripped it from its desk, and smashed it into the head of an engineer.

The console carried the head clean off the body.

Spinning slightly, the head sailed alongside the console. A moment later, both head and body vanished. A spurt of blood continued to sail through the air with the console before the blast wave finally killed the camera.

"Dear God ..." said the Chaplain, who was praying.

"My God ..." said the Captain, who was not.

The First Officer referred to something as holy that was not.

"Where in hell did he go?"

In the Chaplain's mind, a strange new idea shifted into view.

Turning the eye of his mind to gaze on it, he was astonished. He muttered under his breath: "Maybe that was where he *didn't* go. Chief Master Sergeant Cortez: We knew his faith by his works. He's not *supposed* to go *there*. Yet he wasn't able to stay *here*. Dear God! Please, *not that*!"

Louder, the Chaplain said, "Something strange has just occurred to me, Captain. I think I may have an idea where we are."

"And where in hell is that, Chaplain?"

"Captain, I wish you would stop saying that."

THE COUNCIL

Shortly afterwards, the Chaplain listened as the physicist most blessed with the ability to communicate with mere mortals tried to explain things: "Our universe is a three-dimensional object moving through time, which is a *four*-dimensional field. We can illustrate this by taking everything down one dimension."

Taking up a piece of paper and balancing it on his hand, he pronounced, "This is a two-dimensional representation of our *three*-dimensional universe. Not *exactly* two dimensions, but close enough." Still balancing the paper on it, he slowly raised his hand.

"And our three-dimensional universe is moving forward in time."

"Now," he continued while tearing a small piece from one corner of the paper. "*Suppose* a piece of our universe is separated from the rest of it and goes the other way!"

He dropped the shred, which fluttered to the floor while the sheet of paper continued to rise. More loudly, the physicist said: "What does our small piece of the universe find when it goes backwards in time?"

A second physicist said impatiently, "Yes, yes! We can see that it finds nothing."

"You mean it finds nothing *familiar*," put in the third physicist. "In our case, we have found an entire *universe* moving through time behind our own!"

The Captain leaned toward the second physicist. "*You're* saying that the past does not exist." Shifting towards the third, he added, "And *you* say that it does, only our world is not in it."

The first physicist answered: "It does and it doesn't. It depends what you mean by 'the past.' The past of *our universe* does not exist anymore because our universe is not there, but *the timefield through which our universe traveled in its past is still there, and there is another universe in it!*"

During a brief silence, the Chaplain was heard muttering just a little too loudly, "I'm beginning to understand."

Glancing around to find everyone looking at him, the Chaplain pointed to the second of the physicists. "*You* said there is nothing in the past." To the third, he said, "*You* said there *is* something in the past. I am afraid you may both be right." Finding that all were still looking at him, the Chaplain saw nothing to do but continue: "If Plato, for example, is correct, and science explores only a dreamland, then we have reached the place where rocks go in their dreams."

More puzzled looks.

"We have reached Nothing," said the Chaplain.

As if it were perfectly obvious to any thinking person, he added: "We have reached the very edge of reality."

Puzzled looks.

"I wouldn't be surprised if that were prime matter out there, not just empty space."

Puzzled looks.

"What the hell is prime matter?" someone asked.

In response, the Chaplain snapped, "*Please* stop saying such things!"

The unusual hint of anger from their Chaplain caused a moment of surprised silence from the crew, during which the Chaplain rose to his feet to make an announcement.

"Ladies and gentlemen, I believe we are in Hell."

Slowly, silently he took his seat.

Hell? Like hell! thought the Captain as he had earlier when first the Chaplain had drawn him aside to present his wild theory. Aloud he said, though he feared it was a bad idea to encourage him, "Would you care to . . . explain your hypothesis, Chaplain?"

"Sir, all I can give you is my theory as to where we are. I think we have made a more significant, if less pleasant, discovery than that the past does not exist. As if the old, broad way were not enough, we have charted a new course to destruction. Captain, I believe we have taken the *Virgil* to Hell."

Through another long moment of silence, the Chaplain managed not even to blink, and the Captain nearly managed to keep the grimace off of his face.

The Chaplain continued the amazing feat of not blinking as the First Officer chuckled and said through a sneer, "You think we have discovered *Hell*?"

"That discovery was made long ago. We have merely charted a new course. And . . . one more thing, Captain. There are some other things we should be doing while we are here. We should each be praying and repenting."

"Of *what*, Chaplain?" queried the Captain.

"Of anything we can think of, Captain, as long as there is time left to do it in."

At that moment an intercom burbled on and conveyed a message to the Captain from Engineering: No progress with the time-engines. They couldn't even figure out what was wrong with them.

The Captain acknowledged the report and nodded to his officers to resume.

"Well, here is what we *have* discovered," said the first physicist. "*Our* past does not exist."

"And it's even better than that!" said the second. "The past timefield *does* exist, only without our being in it! Instead we've found that it's full of other realities, other worlds if you will. Other *universes* exist in the past! It's the discovery of the millennium!"

"Well, I hope you're working on a way of getting back to report it," said the Captain.

"Sir, with our time-engines damaged, we cannot travel directly back to our universe. But we might try something else."

CHANGE OF DIRECTION

"To make the time jump, we have to run the time-engines at *full* power. If we run them at *half*-power, it alters the direction we're *pointing* in time, not the direction we're *moving* in time."

"And what good is that?"

"Think of it in three dimensions. If you lift the front of an automobile off the ground so it's pointing into the air, that doesn't make it go *into* the air. It just keeps moving straight ahead with its front wheels spinning. But if you give those wheels something to get some traction on, a ramp or something, it can start going up."

"Okay."

"Well, say there's another three-dimensional universe intersecting this one. We could normally go right through it and never notice because it would be curved just like ours is. Just like two interlocked spheres."

"Slowly now, please."

"Okay, let's start with two interlocking circles, like a Venn diagram."

"Okay."

"But *perfect* circles, you understand? Curved lines having no width. Now if you were a one-dimensional being living on one of these circles who could see only forward or backward on the circle but not *into* or *out* of your circle, then you could travel *right through* the other circle where it intersects *your* circle, and never know it."

"Okay. I think I'm with you."

"Now a circle is a straight line, a one-dimensional object, curved in a two-dimensional area. Now imagine a *two*-dimensional object, curved in *three*-dimensional space. Say you live on the surface of a sphere and you can travel along the surface in any direction except in or out. And say there's another sphere intersecting *yours*. You could travel right through the other sphere and never know it."

"Okay. Wait a minute, wait a minute. Okay, go on!"

"Now, take everything up one *more* dimension. Imagine our three-dimensional universe is curved in a four-dimensional field."

"So if you keep traveling in one direction you get back to where you started."

"Yes, although it would take a long time."

"And our three-dimensional universe is like this?"

"Well, close enough. Probably. The point is that another three-dimensional universe might intersect it and we'd never know."

"We could be walking through other worlds all the time without knowing it?"

"Yes, I think so. And what we're hoping is that *this* world is one of them! All we need to get back to *our* world is a way to *not* walk through it but *into it*."

"Okay . . ."

"And a change in direction ought to do it. If we cruise long enough with the time-engines at half-power, we should just move straight into the next universe we come across."

"And what if it's not ours?"

The third physicist chimed in: "Sir, if I may?"

At that moment an Airman arrived with a printed report detailing some more malfunctions. Broken CO_2 scrubbers in Sick Bay, etc., etc. The Captain skimmed it, wondered if it were a portent of worse things to come, resolved to look into it later, and set the file down.

"Proceed, Lieutenant."

"It might *not* be ours. What we're hoping is that *this* universe is curved in time and just five minutes behind our own. If we change direction in time but keep moving in space, we have a good chance of intersecting our own universe . . . eventually."

"Just a chance?"

"Yes, Sir. But it's a chance. And, Sir, it's the *only* chance unless we can fix the time-engines."

"And right now we can't even find out what's wrong with them, so you're thinking we might as well try?"

"Yes, Sir. We can always jump ahead five minutes *if* we can fix them and if this *doesn't* work."

The Captain mused silently for a moment on the finitude of the *Virgil*'s reserves of fuel, food, and oxygen.

"All right, I want you three to spend the next two hours thinking of any better ideas or of *any* ways this could go wrong that are even worse than hanging out in this creepy joint any longer. If you've got nothing in two hours and there's no improvement with the time-engines, we'll try it. The rest of you, to your posts—clean up after these malfunctions, keep things on this ship shipshape. Ladies and gentlemen, *dismissed!*"

"How fitting," muttered the Chaplain. "A change of direction. It almost sounds like repentance!"

He retired to his quarters, hoping to get some prayers in. That was *his* post, after all.

And maybe, God willing, a quick nap. He felt as if he had not slept in days.

THE MESSENGER

Awaking at his tiny desk an hour later, the Chaplain saw a man standing in his quarters, incomprehensibly clothed in a partially unbuttoned Hawaiian shirt, black dress pants, and flip-flops with surprisingly bright yellow socks. The man was looking at him with a puzzled expression.

"What's it like, having that on all the time?" said the other.

Out of sheer good upbringing, the befuddled Chaplain managed to say, "Pardon?"

In a desperate attempt to make some sense of things, he added, "I'm usually in full uniform. I don't dress like this all the time."

The other replied, "No, no. Not the clothes. The matter, the what-do-you-call-it, the body, you know! The bit of matter occupying a tiny region of time and space. I know all about occupying bits of time and space, you know. I've been doing it for millennia, off and on. This is my first time occupying space and time with *matter* in it. It's a strange feeling."

The Chaplain gazed at the stranger for a moment after which, in a desperate attempt to make sense of *something*, he asked the stranger to "Wait, please, just a moment," and donned his coat.

Now, standing to attention and beginning to remember his rank and responsibilities, he snapped, "Name and rank, Airman!"

Tilting his head a bit, the stranger said, "My name is Aljin. By "airman," you mean a kind of soldier, I think. I am here only as a messenger today."

The Chaplain simply stared.

"I have things to show you. May we begin now?" asked the stranger.

The Chaplain tried to say something sensible, muttered something unintelligible, felt the stranger seize his wrist, and blinked in surprise as the room and the entire timeship disappeared.

THE VOICE IN THE DARK

He tried not to panic. He closed his eyes to feel more at home with the blackness. It didn't help.

The Chaplain reached out and felt nothing.

Not even a breath of air. Nor the stranger who had grabbed him.

From the darkness came a voice.

The Chaplain tried to blow onto his hand just to feel some movement of air. He felt nothing.

The Voice came again.

His mind froze in terror. Mid-freeze, it suddenly became aware of the meaning of the words he had just heard:

"I am taking you deeper into Hell. But do not worry. I will keep you safe. You will not need air, but maybe I can provide some if breathing makes you more comfortable."

The mind-freeze continued.

"You do not need to talk either. I can read your mind. In fact, it seems like you are experiencing considerable distress. Oh, dear me. Just a moment."

Suddenly the Chaplain felt a breath of wind on his face. He breathed. He gulped down the air like water.

"I am terribly sorry about that. I should have known better. I can take the matter, the what-do-you-call-it, the body, on and off. It's not *part of me* like it's part of *you*. I have to concentrate to remember to keep things comfortable for you."

The Chaplain felt hairs on top of his feet trying to stand on end inside his socks.

The Voice was still droning. Was there any point in reasoning with it? Which question should he ask first? And when would it shut up for a bit?

"SHUT! UP! SHUT UP! SHUT UP!"

During a momentary silence, he realized that the scream had been his.

"I am sorry, again. You are wondering many things, I see. I am not much of an explainer, am I?"

"*Who* are you?" asked the Chaplain in the low growl he normally reserved for persistently misbehaving children. "*What* are you? *Where* are you? And *where* am *I*?"

"I told you. I am Aljin, and I am a messenger. I am what you usually call an 'angel.' And I am here with you. And you are in Hell—but a little deeper than your friends back on the ship."

Hell.

The Chaplain could feel hairs he'd never known he'd had standing on end.

"If it helps, I will put on a makeshift body again; there's plenty of—what do you call it?—matter lying around, not very well organized, of course, but that only makes it easier. Just a moment. There."

The Chaplain blinked in the emptiness and still saw only emptiness.

"If it helps, I can provide some light."

Two tannish triangular smudges appeared. The Chaplain realized it was the tip of his nose, seen from the different angles of his two eyes.

"Do not be frightened. I am here. Look to your right."

And there at last was the stranger.

THE UPPER HELLS

"Al . . . Alger . . ."

"My name is Aljin. I've been sent to show you a little more of Hell."

"Just what I've always wanted," mumbled the Chaplain.

"It *is*, though, isn't it? You volunteered for this voyage. You said you wanted to serve your country and mankind. But what you told *God* was that you wanted to gain some wisdom for yourself."

"How did you know that? Oh, of course: You said you're an *angel*."

"And what you couldn't even tell *yourself* was that you wanted a bigger wisdom that made better sense of all the little ones. You'd grown dissatisfied with the philosophy and theology you used to study, and you thought mankind's maiden voyage backward in time might somehow help you find that wisdom."

"What do you mean I couldn't tell *myself*?"

"You wanted a wisdom that set you apart. You wanted it like Solomon taught you to—for its own sake, and for the sake of others. But you also wanted it so that it would be *you* that has it. Your wants were half-wrong, half-right, all wrapped up in one big desire. Very typical *human* behavior, I would say! And now you get what you want."

"I didn't exactly ask for a guided tour of Hell."

"But this is what you *needed*. You will soon be a little wiser. I am afraid it will be somewhat unpleasant. That is the discipline for your pride."

"Oh, goody."

"Are you ready to go?"

"Wait. If you're an angel, shouldn't you be *dressed* as an angel?"

"Oh, you mean with white robes? Would it make you more comfortable?"

"What would make me *comfortable* is knowing what's going on."

"That is easy to explain to someone who has traveled the wrong way through time. The precise location of Hell's outer circle is, in relation to Earth, five minutes ago."

"Oh, so *that's* what 'easy to explain' means now. I see. So: I'm in Hell, and the *Virgil* is in Hell, and you're supposed to be an *angel*—but also in Hell."

"I go where I am sent."

"And my ship?"

"It's where we left it—in the outermost circle of Hell. I have taken you deeper. Only the *outermost* circle is five minutes within your world. There are many others."

"You're talking about matter curved in time?"

"Yes, the four-dimensional equivalent of a sphere. Your world is one. Each circle of Hell is one."

"You mean Hell actually has *circles*? Like in *Dante*?"

"Dante? What is that? Do you mind if I just read it?"

"Well, sure! Did you bring a copy?"

"I mean in your mind. Yes, I see. Nice literature, is it? Well, it's a bit like that. Hell is a large number of distinct concentric four-dimensional equivalents of spheres. Your ship landed in the outermost shell. Not a pleasant place to be, but it gets worse farther in."

"Do these . . . Hells . . . intersect our world, like they were saying back on the ship?"

"No. The whole set of Hells is within the circle of your world. One Hell for each person."

"Just one?"

"Just one, but all uninhabited for now."

"They're all empty?"

"I said no one *lives* there. The angels travel through them at times—both the fallen and the unfallen."

"Why isn't anyone there?"

"The judgment comes first, and then the punishment."

"And the resurrection of the dead comes before the judgment?"

"Yes."

"So where are they now—all the . . . people who will be here?"

"Not all mysteries are to be revealed to you."

After a pause, Aljin spoke again, more slowly. "The fallen ones are there now. With your ship. Your shipmates may find that they are being visited by . . . old friends."

The Chaplain's silence seemed to elicit further explanation. "Back on Earth, these demons mainly tempted and deceived surreptitiously. That is how they work with people in your modern technological world. Here, where they feel more at home, I am afraid they are getting bolder. They have already damaged your ship, and killed."

After another pause, Aljin continued. "I talked with Robert Cortez on his way up. I was happy for him; he had a lucky escape. You were right, you know, about him not being able to remain here although you didn't fully understand why.

"In any case, my fallen brothers are still there. They are toying with you. You humans like to think of yourselves as those feline creatures you have on your planet. And of the universe as a great big rodent creature for you to play with. If your father Adam had stuck to his post, the truth might have been something like that—although kittens would make a better metaphor than rodents.

"As things are now, the opposite is not far from the truth. However, we will speak of this situation again when it is time. As you can see, they are not *here*. There are no men or angels in the circles of Hell we visit today—save us."

"Okay, whatever you say. And we're near the *outer* edge now?"

"Yes. The outermost Hell's radius is only five minutes smaller than your world. Your Earth is on the leading edge, the very *front* of that universe in its movement through time. That's why you had to go *back* to go down into Hell."

"Dear God. That means . . . we can't get back just by crossing over, can we? We'll have to *jump!*"

"You may cross over. There are . . . other worlds, just as your shipmates suspected. The right one will lead you back to your own. There is one rather small one nearby that should work nicely; it intersects both the outer circles of Hell and your own world. One of your human philosophers once imagined it nearly accurately. But you will not be permitted to travel *outward*. You cannot ascend to any larger worlds on this voyage."

"Okay, let's just pretend I understand all that as well as could possibly be expected. Now can you *please* tell me why I can't see anything besides the two of us?"

"Oh, there is light everywhere here. For hundreds of miles—for light-years."

"So why can't I *see* it?"

"There is nothing to see *by* it."

"So it's just pure emptiness for light-years? No lava, then? No fire? Smoke?"

"The emptiness is worse. It consumes the *soul*."

The Chaplain thought of the nothing behind him, felt hairs on his neck stand up as if the nothing were rubbing them—which, he supposed, it was. He imagined the blackness as an enormous monster ready to devour him. He turned his head to see behind him. But there was nothing to see.

"I suppose . . . it *is* pretty bad."

And the Chaplain stared. He stared and he tried to think.

But there was nothing here to think *about*.

Suddenly, he wondered how long he had been thinking nothing at all.

"About one minute," Aljin informed him.

"The mind could go empty out here."

"It will, when there is a mind here, for centuries at a time."

"Will that be a relief for them? For . . . the damned?"

"In a way. But your minds were not made for emptiness. It hurts. There will always be a spark of awareness. The mind's eye sees that there's nothing in it, like the eye in your face sees that there is nothing to see. In its way, it also burns."

"And that's why it's Hell."

"That is one reason. Better yet, it's one of many ways to describe what Hell *isn't*. It's actually *nothing*—as close to nothing as man can get without *quite* being nothing himself."

"Didn't you say there was *matter* here?"

"After a fashion. You can't see it. It's what-do-you-call it—oh, I see you have a name for it because you read it in a book! It is *prime* matter. Or very nearly so, since it does have extension in space. Perhaps you could call it *secondary* matter?"

"Nothing to breathe but prime matter. And this is . . . God's *justice*, is it?"

"Yes."

"Isn't it a bit worse than anything anyone ever did to God?"

"Well, of course your sin never *hurt* God—until the Cross. But the punishment *does* fit the crime's . . . effrontery. Well, that is the best word I can find in your language. We have a better word in mine."

He continued: "But what I want you to see is that this punishment is what the damned *ask* for. They turn away from light, and find themselves in darkness. They turn away from Reality, and find themselves nowhere."

The Chaplain was trying to think through this when Aljin seized his wrist and announced, "We are going deeper now!"

He tried to protest—to say "No, wait!" But they were gone before he had the chance.

THE LOWER HELLS

The Chaplain wondered whether anything *had* really changed. He tried wiggling his wrist and felt the resistance of the other's hand.

"We are in much deeper now. Behold: one of the lower circles of Hell!"

Then, once again, he saw the little triangles of his nose. There was a slight glisten from the light reflecting off his companion's face.

"There," said Aljin. "In the distance. Look!"

The Chaplain looked, and saw . . .

"*Two?* Two damned men in one circle? I thought you said they got one Hell apiece."

"They do, or rather they *will*."

"Yeah, I thought no one was supposed to be here yet. Okay, those two aren't . . . *going* anywhere, are they?"

"Not before you are ready."

"Okay, that's also confusing, but one problem at a time. Why . . . why won't they ever run out of Hells?"

"One Hell for each of billions. Each one is an entire universe. It only has to be smaller than the next one by a single unit of space."

"And how small is that?"

"Small enough. So there will be room for everyone."

"Oh, terrific. Now my *third* confusion is why those two aren't going anywhere without *me* being ready. And my *second* is: *Why are there two people over there? Shouldn't there be no one? Am I looking at two . . . demons?* I thought you said they weren't going to be here either."

"No. Point to them. Then you will understand."

The Chaplain complied.

A twinge of nausea in his innards accompanied his sudden comprehension.

"Yes. They are *we*," said Aljin. "This Hell is very small. It is such a small circle that you can see *yourself* from a distance."

"And I thought it was creepy enough that my feet weren't standing on anything. But which one am I—the one over here or the one over there?"

"Don't forget the one behind you."

The Chaplain turned and, with a shudder, saw his own front some distance away—head turned back, with Aljin's hand clasping his, Aljin's face showing what almost looked like a smile.

"It is spherical," came the voice of Aljin right at his side, even as he saw the mouth of Aljin moving in the distance. "Well, the four-dimensional equivalent."

"You mean I'm . . . I'm . . . all around me?"

The Chaplain looked down and thought he could make out, below, his own head.

"Shouldn't I be able to see myself in *any* direction I look? In *every* direction?"

"Yes. That illustration you are thinking of will do nicely—the insect on the basketball. Its line of vision curves along the surface, and it can see nothing but itself no matter where it looks. It should have the appearance of being entirely ringed in by itself. You are correct. I have been meddling with your perception so you do not get too confused."

"Don't worry, I'm already as confused as I possibly could be."

The Chaplain thought he would try something, and called out into the blackness: "Hey!" His voice returned from a thousand directions as from so many echoes, all calling in to the center.

"The mind can fall apart out here. It's like I'm . . . in pieces."

"That is another reason it is Hell. The self is not a monad. It lives on reality. If it turns away from reality, it becomes *less*. Very nearly a monad. And yet a fragmented one."

"It's a state of madness."

"Yes. And it is time to go deeper."

"*More* deeper?"

"Yes. I will not meddle with your perceptions there. I will provide a little light. There will be no room for me to take shape there, but you will be able to hear my voice. Brace yourself."

Instantly, the Chaplain felt the angel's grip tighten and disappear along with the light.

THE EGGSHELL PRISON

And, again, darkness.

And, again, the feel of fingers brushing up against his hand, his left hand, but without grabbing on. Simultaneously the feel of *another* hand, felt with his own right.

There were *two* of them, he realized, a sudden warmth of shivers running the length of his body.

Two of *them*.

Whatever *they* were.

Their hands were both moving around, fidgeting, stroking, grabbing. Desperately he tried to fend them off, perhaps to grab them—

—and just as he seized one in his *right* hand, the enemy hand to the *left* grabbed his *own*.

There followed a frantic period of tugging, gripping, yanking—the right hand nearly crushing the hand in *its* grip while the *left* flailed about trying to escape. Meanwhile the enemy hand to the *left* only gripped more strongly, and the enemy hand to the *right* struggled ferociously.

He heard himself screaming in the dark, and the sound reverberated from all around, pounding into his head like a thousand tiny hammers.

Finally, he fainted.

When he awoke, seconds later—or minutes, or hours, or days for all the difference time made in this emptiness—his hands were hanging unchallenged by his side. Imagining what might be lurking unfelt nearby, he feared to move and find out.

Aljin's voice was giving instructions: "Do not panic. Breathe."

The Chaplain's voice was a mere croak: "Will you . . . please . . . bring back . . . the light."

"The light will only make it worse. But it will help you to understand and so to leave this place the sooner. But first try reaching ahead. Gently."

Gently, the Chaplain did so. To his horror, he found the soft flesh of *another* one *in front of him*.

And there was another *behind*!

Its hand was resting on his own back!

A sort of prayer came out through sobs and choking—"Dear God. Dear *God* in Heaven."

"And now I shall provide light," said Aljin.

There appeared shades of brown and green and tan and black. All mere inches away from him, enclosing him like the inside of a huge eggshell. It was ugly, and he hated it.

"In these lower levels the Hells are more like ovals than circles," explained Aljin. "They have only enough room for one person. Since it all curves back on itself, the result is particularly unpleasant."

The Chaplain's hand was drawn to a curious smear of whitish-tan before him—set in a mess of silver and black.

He felt cold fingers on the back of his head.

He threw his hands back to fend them off, waving and scratching.

Long, thin protrusions shot out of the eggshell-wall and tore at the skin of his forehead.

"BE STILL!" commanded Aljin.

The Chaplain did his best to comply, though with many a shudder and much blinking.

"You understand?" asked the angel.

He managed a feeble nod.

The whitish-tan smudge was his own bald spot.

The protrusions had been his own fingers.

All the hands had been his own.

The eggshell-wall was a hideous inversion of his own skin and hair and clothing.

Aljin spoke: "The space around you is filled with *you*. This is the eternity chosen by one who most persistently chooses himself without God. He flees from Reality and becomes his own reality—his own universe filled with himself where he dwells forever stuck inside himself, just as he desired."

The Chaplain saw himself surrounded by himself.

For one terrible, terrible moment he thought he understood that, in this tiny, tiny universe, *he* was the eggshell—the horrible inversion of his own skin looking in on himself.

For some incomprehensible reason, Aljin was droning on: "—now return you. After walking straight into the cat's lair, your little mouse is nearly eaten: The demons have almost destroyed your ship. You *must* remember one thing. You may yet return home in the way your comrades are attempting. The other world I mentioned will serve as a bridge back to yours. But you must keep the time-engines running. Do not let them turn them off. *Keep the time-engines running. Keep them running.*"

For one sickening moment the Chaplain thought he could *see* himself from the perspective of the wall—the ugly eggshell wall looking in on the pitiful little body trapped inside.

"*Keep them running. Keep them running.*"

He felt himself retching, and all went dark.

TO HELL AND BACK

More slowly this time, hazy light crept back into his eyes, the soft hum of the *Virgil* into his ears. Fearing to feel nothing, the Chaplain extended his fingers and felt—

—his desk.

He broke into a shudder of relief and of recollected terror. He whimpered in his chair.

The intercom beeped. "Chaplain, report!"

The intercom was on the desk next to a tiny mirror. In it, the Chaplain could make out nail scratches on his forehead. He could smell some vomit somewhere. He couldn't see any on his shirt. He thought—with an additional shudder—that it might have ended up on the back of his head.

He checked in via the intercom.

The intercom crackled, "Chaplain, report to the bridge NOW. And get your bio-monitor checked out later. It wasn't responding for about an hour back there."

Minutes later, on the Bridge, the Chaplain was slowly coming to grips with the situation.

The *Virgil* was descending into chaos. There were malfunctions in every system. There were explosions, electrical fires, and hull breaches. People were dying, their bodies disappearing.

There were eerie reports of alien boarders—luminous humanoids who were teleporting about the ship and wreaking havoc. Other reports spoke more confusingly of enormous snakelike, locust-like, or feline things.

The time-engines were still running at half-power. Life support was failing.

"That's it, Sir," an Airman informed the Captain. "We're about to lose life support if we don't cut the time-engines."

"Captain," said a physicist, "we have no idea if our own universe intersects this one ten miles from here or ten light-years. If we keep going like this, there's every chance it won't do any good."

The Captain glanced at another physicist, who nodded in agreement.

"Captain, we must cut the time-engines NOW!"

As if from a dream, the angel's voice echoed in the Chaplain's mind: "*Keep them running. Keep them running. Keep them running.*"

The Captain was giving the order: "Airman, cut—"

The Chaplain turned to look back at the Captain. "*No, Sir!*" he cried. "*Keep them running! Keep them running!*"

The Captain paused, his mouth hung open, looking at the strange little Chaplain with a Lieutenant's rank, something gross in his hair, dried blood on his forehead, and a strangely compelling sense of urgency.

The *Virgil* shuddered again. A console showed the entire stern going up in flame. An additional klaxon blared. Lights winked out. Airmen screamed.

The Captain shouted the order: "AIRMAN, CUT THE—"

His console exploded, throwing him out of his chair.

On the viewscreen, in place of the void, a vast expanse of soft, golden light popped into existence.

It was space, a whole new universe of it.

In it were suspended two enormous, shimmering, golden spheres—the size of dwarf stars, a mere planet's width apart, and each exactly like the other.

The one remaining time-engine strained.

The *Virgil* listed in the sea of light.

The spheres vanished.

There was a flash of blue, a surge of green, a great thud, and silence.

THE SEVERED TIMESHIP

"Captain. Captain! Can you see me?"

"No . . . Chaplain. I can't see a damned thing."

"Your face is badly burned, Captain. Your eyes got the worst of it. And you may have a concussion. But you'll live."

"Who else will live, Chaplain?"

"There are twenty other survivors, last I heard. We've lost the rest."

"Help me up, Chaplain. I have to command my ship. Are we still in that hellhole of a universe?"

"We are out of Hell, Sir. Captain, we are home."

"Home?"

"Earth. Commander Blackburn is commanding. We landed about five minutes ago. My orders are to look after you and to not let *you* give any orders. You need to rest until we can get you to a doctor. Ours are gone. Sick Bay was in the stern. Half the ship is gone, Sir. Sheared off."

"Explain."

"The *Virgil* was exploding, Captain. The explosion began in the stern. It was working up toward the bridge. One of our physicists will probably explain it better than I could, but I think as much of the ship as changed directions before the explosion hit it made it through."

"And the enemy? The . . . aliens?"

"The . . . creatures are . . . nowhere to be seen, Captain."

"And where am I, Chaplain? Where's this heat coming from?"

"From the sun, Captain. We've carried you outside. What's left of the ship is unstable."

"And where did we land?"

"I don't know for certain, Captain. Perhaps we're in Kansas?"

The Captain pondered this for a moment, trying to decide whether it made him angry. "That isn't funny," he finally said.

"I am serious, Captain. I see cornfields."

"Cornfields?"

"Cornfields, Captain. The corn is very close."

"Show me."

The bright, green stalks were at arm's length. The Chaplain tore off a long leaf. He held it in his hands, admiring the wonderful greenness, the fact that it was solid, that you could *touch* it with your hands.

He placed it reverently in the Captain's outstretched hand. He himself stroked another leaf of corn.

He remembered what he had learned about its insides long ago: Within those tiny ridges were millions of cells filled with chloroplast, mitochondria, and hydrogen ions obediently filing through the gateways in their phospholipid bilayers undergoing chemiosmotic phosphorylation. Inside *them*, billions of atoms held trillions of smaller wonders, obediently spinning and dancing around each other.

Most impressive of all was that they *existed*.

A moment later the Chaplain spoke: "It's children, Captain. Little boys and girls."

"Yes, Chaplain. I can hear them."

The Chaplain closed his eyes. "Have you ever heard anything so wonderful in all your life?"

"No, I suppose not," admitted the other. Then he added, "That doesn't sound like English."

"No. It's a pity I didn't study Swahili in college."

"Are they speaking Swahili?"

"I don't know. If I had studied it, maybe I would."

"Are they *laughing* at us?" asked the Captain incredulously.

"Yes," said the Chaplain. "The children are laughing at us. I suppose we must look ridiculous, sitting here next to half of a spaceship in the middle of a cornfield. Isn't it wonderful, though?"

The Captain answered, "Sure, Chaplain. Whatever you say."

With a slight smile, the Chaplain said, "Captain, there are some things I need to tell you about our voyage on the *Virgil*."

EPILOGUE

Even in rural Zimbabwe, some kids have smartphones.

Almost instantly after a photo of what was left of the *Virgil* had been posted to social media, the US government knew about it through software it had set to patrol the internet for any information about its missing timeship.

For a situation of this magnitude, all resources were made available. International complications were quickly and expensively smoothed over, leaving endless future conversations for the diplomats—and mountains of future paperwork for the accountants.

But, in the end, it was only a matter of minutes before the helicopters were under way from an aircraft carrier in the Indian Ocean.

While other personnel and choppers set to work transporting the remains of the ship itself, the twenty-two survivors of the damned maiden voyage of the *Virgil* were immediately airlifted to the carrier.

Physicians and a psychiatrist kept close tabs on them, but for the most part each was kept in seclusion. No details of the mission were to be revealed to anyone until top men could meet with them in person.

The Chaplain sat in his cabin for hours each morning staring through the porthole.

Sometimes he would whisper, "Whither shall I go from thy spirit? or whither shall I flee from thy presence? If I ascend up into Heaven, thou art there. If I make my bed in Hell, behold, thou art there. Even there shall thy hand lead me, and thy right hand shall hold me."

16

Beauty, Bad Guys, and Art in God's Good World[1]

Dustin Messer

> But if you confess that the world once was beautiful, but by the curse has become undone, and by a final catastrophe is to pass to its full state of glory, excelling even the beautiful of paradise, then art has the mystical task of reminding us in its productions of the beautiful that was lost and of anticipating its perfect coming luster.
>
> —Abraham Kuyper[2]

"What character would I eliminate if I wrote this?" That's a question I ask myself after finishing every book. When I first started asking this question, villains came to mind: Grendel's mother, Claudius, Sauron—the bad guys.

Of course, the older I get the more I realize how boring fiction would be without antagonists. Who would read Harry Potter were it not for

---

1. Originally published on the blog for the Institute for Faith, Work, and Economics. My thanks to the Institute for allowing this reprint.
2. Kuyper, *Lectures on Calvinism*, 93.

Voldemort, after all? The answers I give to that question have shifted from those who create the most conflict in the story to those who create the least: bit characters, vanilla sidekicks.

While it may seem silly, this exercise actually develops a necessary skill for the evaluation of any piece of art, written or otherwise: the ability to identify and appreciate tension. Beauty, especially beauty seen in the arts, is the result of tension of one kind or another. Obviously, the kind of tension that typically comes to mind is that between good and bad, right and wrong: Aslan and the White Witch. Christianity gives a full-throated voice to this tension as I will explain below with reference first to the tension between good and evil, second with respect to the doctrine of the Trinity, and third with respect to the power of art to point us to the transcendent.

While the world was created good, it has fallen—which is to say it's both broken and rebellious—but Christ has come to restore and redeem creation. In other words, Christ has come to resolve this tension. As David Naugle has argued throughout his storied career, the epic of creation, fall, and redemption permeates the scriptures, and because the scriptures tell the true story of this world, creation, fall, and redemption permeate our experience as well. Thus, for art to be affirmed by the Christian worldview, it can—and must—touch on these themes.

Granted, each and every piece of art won't include each and every theme each and every time. A work that reflects the pain and depravity of creation is no less true than a work that points to the world's inherent dignity and goodness or a work that alludes to the balm and remedy brought by Christ, for that matter. The fact that beauty is a result of tension and that the tension between good and evil is resolvable poses an interesting and important question vis-à-vis the Christian aesthetic; namely, "is beauty eternal?"

The answer is more complex than one might first expect. The tension between good and bad is contingent upon evil, which is finite. Obviously, before the fall and after the second coming of Christ, there is no such tension. This tension has a beginning (Genesis 3) and an end (Revelation 21).

At least the three major Abrahamic religions (Christianity, Judaism, and Islam) agree on this point: Evil is not eternal. It has a beginning and an end. This tension will be resolved. But the Christian faith has a unique claim on beauty specifically.

Before the fall, indeed before creation, God lived in perfect love, peace, joy, and relationship. The Father, the Son, and the Spirit were one, yet three. Were God only one—were he a mono-personal being—there would be no tension in eternity past, let alone in the perfect world to come.

God is not such a being. While we can affirm the oneness of God's essence, we can also affirm the various personalities of the Trinity. This tension between Father, Son, and Spirit is irresolvable. It is the governing reality of the cosmos. Of course, this reality is why we can say that love is eternal. There has always been love, a lover, and a beloved.

This is also why Christians can say that beauty is eternal. Before the creation of the world, God was not stagnant. He was in a complex and textured relationship with his trinitarian self. Tension is eternal because of the eternality of the Trinity.

David Skeel alludes to this very matter in his book *True Paradox*. As trinitarians, Skeel argues, we can heartily acknowledge that there are more tensions in the world than those between good and bad. When we look at a truly beautiful painting, we appreciate the tension not only between right and wrong but also between colors, shades, fabrics, etc. These tensions—those that exist apart from sin—allude to the complexity found in the Godhead.

Art has a transcendent effect on the viewer for this reason: In viewing beauty, as with experiencing love, the connoisseur is coming in contact with something that lacks a beginning and an end. At its best, this is what art does. Art makes us worship—not the object, of course, but the reality that lies beyond the object: the triune God of the universe.

It's no wonder, then, that the arts have always been a key means of spiritual formation and renewal in the church. Art beckons us to look higher, to look deeper—to recognize the transcendent in items as ordinary as canvas and clay. This transcendent experience poses its own dilemma that is a sort of counterpoint to the dilemma of evil.

Just as evil causes us to ask, "How could this exist if there's a God?" the goodness and order we see in art causes us to ask, "How could this exist if there isn't a God?" Indeed, we'll be able to make sense of the world's ugliness in moments of crisis only if we first try to make sense of the world's beauty in moments of transcendent joy. Dealing with the problem of pleasure will prepare us for dealing with the problem of pain. The great conductor and composer Leonard Bernstein put it beautifully:

> Beethoven turned out pieces of breathtaking rightness. Rightness—that's the word! . . . Our boy has the real goods, the stuff from heaven, the power to make you feel at the finish: something is right in the world. There is something that checks throughout, that follows its own law consistently: something we can trust, that will never let us down.[3]

In the Christian account of the world, creation is sacramental: It points beyond itself. But if we haven't trained our eyes to look for order and

---

3. Bernstein, *Joy of Music*, 105.

meaning in the symphony, we won't be likely to see with eyes of faith in the midst of tragedy. So, be it a piece of music, a painting, a sculpture—all art should lead our eyes beyond the immediate and to the infinite, beyond the creation itself to the Creator himself. This is a point C. S. Lewis makes in *The Weight of Glory*:

> The books or the music in which we thought the beauty was located will betray us if we trust to them; it was not in them, it only came through them, and what came through them was longing. These things—the beauty, the memory of our own past—are good images of what we really desire; but if they are mistaken for the thing itself they turn into dumb idols, breaking the hearts of their worshipers. For they are not the thing itself; they are only the scent of a flower we have not found, the echo of a tune we have not heard, news from a country we have never yet visited.[4]

After a sabbatical in Oxford during which he stayed in the very room in which Lewis died, David Naugle penned perhaps the most powerful expositions of Lewis's understanding of art. "[Lewis] saw divinely ordained, objective beauty embedded in ordinary things of everyday life," wrote Naugle. "Life was sacred, sacramental, holy. The challenge, for him and us, is to represent this artistically and aesthetically."[5]

In the secular, de-mythologized West, our eyes are taught to look *at* and *in*, but never *through* and certainly not *up*. Whatever you call this cultural phenomenon—objectivism, scientism, utilitarianism—its effects are palpable: We're habituated to see *creation* as mere *nature*, an end in itself, an object for dissection but certainly not delight.

In such a culture, appreciating art takes more discipline and effort than ever before. At first, the clay appears to be just that: a lump of dirt. Yet, if you make it your practice to stop by the same sculpture each time you visit the museum, over the months and years you will find the clay transforms into something different. It takes on new meaning and significance. But of course, it is not the object itself that changes—it's how you see it. The seeing is changed not by the *seen* but by the *see-er*.

To see more than a lump of dirt in a sculpture takes a patience that is rarer and rarer in our fast-paced age. The thing is, *seeing* well takes intentionality, especially in our distracted age. But if we as Christ's followers want to honor God's beautiful creation (including the creations of his image-bearers), we need to cultivate this patient mode of seeing.

4. Lewis, *Weight of Glory*, 4–5.
5. Naugle, "With Their Christianity Latent."

The conditions that make art appreciation difficult are the same conditions that make reckoning with the problem of evil difficult. The same eyes that see only a lump of clay in a sculpture will see only discoloration and scars when looking in the mirror after a major surgery. Conversely, eyes trained to see meaning and beauty while sitting on the museum bench will be able to recognize the handiwork of God while lying in the hospital bed, even as they yet see through a glass, dimly.

This is not to say we will *always* discover meaning by looking at something hard enough. Meaning in art, as in suffering, is sometimes elusive or even inaccessible. The death of a loved one or relentless hardship can often feel senseless, absurd, devoid of meaning. Some overly artsy music or films can feel the same way. But the extremes do not detract from the broader principle. The more we cultivate intentional, observant viewing of art, the more we'll be able to make sense of all of reality.

The arts are crucial in recovering the skills necessary to regain a right disposition toward reality. They can help us see order and cohesion in the good, the true, and the beautiful. Not only can a deep familiarity with the beautiful give us the standard by which we recognize and name the ugly, but once we've become accustomed to looking for meaning in moments of joy, perhaps we can also see with eyes of faith in moments of despair. We might say it this way: The problem of pain becomes more manageable if we've already reckoned with the problem of pleasure.

BIBLIOGRAPHY

Bernstein, Leonard. *The Joy of Music*. 1959. Reprint, Lanham, MD: Amadeus, 2004.
Kuyper, Abraham. *Lectures on Calvinism*. Lafayette, IN: Sovereign Grace, 2001.
Lewis, C. S. *The Weight of Glory and Other Addresses*. New York: Macmillan, 1949.
Naugle, David K. "With Their Christianity Latent: C. S. Lewis on the Arts." *Official Website of C. S. Lewis*, June 3, 2012. https://www.cslewis.com/with-their-christianity-latent-c-s-lewis-on-the-arts.
Skeel, David. *True Paradox: How Christianity Makes Sense of Our Complex World*. Downers Grove, IL: InterVarsity, 2014.

17

A Hot Coal in My Mouth

My Personal Journey with "The Last Temptation of Christ"

Kevin C. Neece

This piece was originally written for the annual spring conference of Dr. Naugle's Paideia College Society at Dallas Baptist University in 2009. I felt I was taking a major risk presenting a paper lauding The Last Temptation of Christ *at a Baptist university at which I hoped to teach that summer. But Dr. Naugle always made it feel safe to take risks. And since his teaching had so revolutionized my worldview, it seemed fitting that I should present a paper about a film that had changed my life in a similar way. I did get hired that summer, and I've never regretted presenting the paper. Like much of what I wrote for those conferences, it is among my favorites of my own works. I present it here in a longer, updated form, created for this volume.*

  I wrote my first real research paper in the eighth grade. I'll never forget sitting in a temporary classroom on my junior high campus, listening as my English teacher, Mr. Womack, along with our librarian, explained the assignment. We would be learning to use the periodical section of the library, the periodical reference books, and something I'd never heard of before that sounded very advanced and scary called "parenthetical notation." I confess I was a little intimidated. I was fourteen years old.

The assignment was to think of a controversial topic, look up periodical sources on it, do research—making photocopies of articles and proper notation on index cards—and come up with a position on the issue. We were then to hand-write a five-page paper (an unheard-of length) explaining both sides and defending our own position.

Later, in the library, we were led to a small room along the back wall that was crammed floor to ceiling with boxes upon boxes of magazines. Just outside the room, a line began forming in front of the librarian, who stood near a rolling metal book cart that held large green books, indexed by topic, in which we were to find our periodical references.

At this point, I had no idea what to write about. I had already become fascinated with the topic of Jesus films and had determined that I would not only see every one of them but also would have them all in my personal library. If I was going to do heavy research, I wanted to write about that subject. But what was controversial about Jesus films?

I was just learning how to spell the word "controversy," let alone what it meant. But I did remember something—a radio ad I had heard once when I was about ten years old, warning against a scandalous new film about Jesus. I remembered being immediately interested in the movie. I'd seen a few other references to it since and I'd probably even seen it in the video store. What was it called? It was that one that Christians were never, ever supposed to see but that I would have to own one day because of my Jesus film commitment. Of course, I would have to wait until I was older to buy it because it was rated "R." This was great. I knew all sorts of details except the title!

I can see myself standing there in the library, trying to shut out the noise of the room. I was already becoming bored and annoyed by school (a state that would only increase through high school), but here was something interesting—a real assignment! If I could recall this one film title, I could turn it into an opportunity to research and write about something I was really interested in (a skill I would continue to develop all the way through college). Why could I not think of it? I remember feeling as though I was squeezing my brain to make it bleed the words. "Tempt... Temptations..."

That was it! *The Last Temptation of Jesus Christ*! Okay, so I was one word off. But that moment, digging that title out of my mind, would later become one of the most important moments of my life because the paper I was about to write (however poorly) would begin a journey for me that would continue into my adult years. It would be a journey with a film that would cause me to think more deeply about the nature of Christ and the meaning of his sacrifice than any other film I would ever see. It was to be my personal journey with *The Last Temptation of Christ*.

As far back as I could remember, I'd always wanted to be a filmmaker. There was something about the cinematic arts that had always made a deep impression on me and something about the people who made movies that I felt I could understand and relate to. I loved getting to see how they worked, what they looked like, how they talked and moved; and I especially loved listening to the stories they told about the process of making films. From Steven Spielberg to Disney animators, it was always a special experience to get a glimpse into their world. It was a world I felt at home in, to the degree that I hoped—even planned—to become a filmmaker myself.

The first image I saw of director Martin Scorsese was in the August 8, 1988, issue of *People* magazine. He was on the right-hand page, looking through an out-of-frame window to the left. His hand rested on the wall next to the window and his eyebrows were bent with stress, sending ripples through his forehead. A juxtaposed photograph on the left-hand page showed a close-up image of people protesting *The Last Temptation of Christ*. A woman's hand held up a thick wooden crucifix above what looked to be a vast blanket of fellow protesters. Behind her, another protester's homemade sign was legible, though slightly out of focus. It read, "LAST TEMPTATION FIRST DECEPTION." Above this image was the article's title: "In the Name of Jesus."

I knew it was skillful layout that was creating the illusion that Scorsese was looking out his window to the people protesting below, but the idea conveyed in that image seemed to ring true. These people were ridiculing something Scorsese cared about—and he was hurt by it. Something in that image haunted me. Perhaps more unsettling was the title. I wasn't sure this looked like the kind of action that ought to be carried out "In the Name of Jesus." The image of the raised crucifix frightened me somewhat. It looked like a weapon. The cross, I thought, is not a weapon—at least not one we should use on each other.

As I read this and the other articles I was photocopying, though, I was disturbed by some of the things I was hearing described about the film: Jesus thinks he might be following Satan, Jesus only reluctantly fulfills his role as Messiah, Mary Magdalene is the ex-girlfriend of Jesus. These things seemed like they could not be part of a serious Jesus film. My interest in the genre was fueled by the concept of historical accuracy. To me, the goal of every Jesus film ever made was to try to reflect Jesus and his world as accurately as possible, based on the best historical and archaeological information at hand. I was, therefore, extremely dubious about what I was hearing described.

In the pages of these magazine articles, I read that many pastors and Christian leaders reacted to the film as though it showed a wild, insane, sex-crazed Jesus and mocked everything Christ stood for. Even the novel on which the film was based, they said, had almost gotten its author, Nikos Kazantzakis, excommunicated from the Greek Orthodox Church. Then other reverends and bishops and the like would say it was a wonderful film, full of deep theology that would "help people understand their own commitment to Jesus."[1] Further, there were Scorsese's own words regarding his Catholic faith and his sincerity of purpose in making the film. "It's the last battle between God and Satan," Scorsese had said, "and God wins."[2] And again, "This film for me is like a prayer. It is my way of worshiping."[3]

The extreme contrast between these viewpoints was perplexing. I didn't take a position in my paper. How could I? I could see no clear evidence for either side of the story and I wasn't about to make a judgment about a film I hadn't even seen yet. The film, I said, "will have to wait to be proven right or wrong."

So, I waited. I kept all my note cards and all my photocopied articles, re-reading them often and wondering at the drastic extremes presented within them, with almost no middle ground. The film was out either to destroy faith or to preserve it. It was either interminably boring and clumsy or skillfully made and riveting. It seemed to depend on whom one asked. One bit of nuance I learned as I read more closely was that it often also depended on whether the person speaking had actually seen the film. "Ninety-Nine percent of the people who are complaining," Scorsese had said, "have not seen the picture."[4] In my later studies, I would find that this statement, however approximate, was barely an exaggeration, if it was one at all.[5]

By the age of sixteen, I decided it was finally time to see *The Last Temptation of Christ*. I had seen one or two R-rated movies by then and I doubted a film about Jesus could be any worse than *Robocop*. So, with some money I'd gotten as a gift, probably for Christmas or my birthday, I decided to make my first big purchase of Jesus films. My dad drove me to the mall and we went to Suncoast Motion Picture Company, then my favorite store in the world. I had spent so much time memorizing where everything was in the store that I went right to them—VHS copies of *The Greatest Story Ever Told*, *King of Kings*, and *The Last Temptation of Christ*. As I was still too young

1. Lacayo, "Days of Ire and Brimstone."
2. Grogan et al., "In the Name of Jesus."
3. Grogan et al., "In the Name of Jesus."
4. Lee, "Holy Furor."
5. Lindlof, *Hollywood Under Siege*.

to purchase an R-rated film without parental consent, I had spoken with my parents about my intentions and they had agreed that I could buy *Last Temptation*. My dad told the clerk at the counter that I had his permission and I went home with a fat stack of very expensive movies and a huge sense of satisfaction.

I watched the film for the first time by myself. By this time I'd seen my first Scorsese film, *The Age of Innocence*, and from that picture alone, I had become an enormous fan. I greatly admired Scorsese's lyrical camera movements and his unusual pacing, which could be surprising, but nonetheless flowed seamlessly from moment to moment. The simple wonder of the rhythm of the cutting he did with his editor, Thelma Schoonmaker, left me in awe. It was so precise, yet so organic. The balance was an amazing thing to watch.

I knew already, then, that many outspoken objectors to *The Last Temptation of Christ* were wrong. Scorsese was no Hollywood hack, carelessly producing films with his eyes on nothing but money. He was a sincere and talented filmmaker whose work was honest. By that, I knew that he would not have misrepresented himself. He was clearly a director of great sensitivity who would not apologize for his artistic vision. This told me that when I read all those things he had said in interviews about his faith and the worshipful act of making *Last Temptation*, I could only take him at his word. Of course, if his theology was as deeply flawed as I feared it might be, I thought, his sincerity didn't matter. The film could still be the blasphemy so many had claimed it to be.

Well, this would settle it. I carefully slid the tape into the player, sat down very quietly in the dark (as I always did when viewing a film), and waited for the truth to reveal itself.

Two hours and forty-three minutes later, I was perhaps more confused than I had been when I started. But at least I could be confused about the thing itself and not simply the idea of it as presented by others. That, at least, was satisfying. No doubt the film was stunningly beautiful. I loved every image, every cut, right from the start. The craft of the film—somewhat rough-hewn though it was on its slender budget and tightly constrained production schedule—was excellent. But I wasn't sure about the story.

I was a very binary person then. In many respects, I saw the world in two-toned glory. I had written in my research paper about the film being proven "right or wrong." This was something I had believed would be a point of fact—definable, quantifiable, and provable. I honestly expected to see this film and know right away what it was all about. In reality, however, I had viewed the film and still didn't really have a clue.

Another part of my binary reality at that time was the chasm between history and fiction. It was impossible, I felt, to successfully blend the two—especially when it came to Jesus. I felt a great deal of tension in the film because of that—as if Scorsese were trying to braid two magnetically opposed cords into a single rope. For me, that just didn't work. I didn't like the tension. A Jesus film should be clear, I thought. Still, I could not deny the beauty and power of this confounding piece of cinema. My verdict for the moment was that, at the very least, despite my puzzlement regarding its theology, I was utterly in love with most of the film. Its craft was beautiful, but I was also drawn to its sense of authenticity. This feeling was derived less from meticulous attention to historical detail and more from the film's emotional honesty and the admission (for all I knew, for the first time in Jesus film history) of the existence of dirt in ancient Israel and its ability to cling even to the robes of Jesus. This, I thought, was beautiful. There was a layer of dust on everything and everyone for most of the film. If I ever made a film about Christ, I determined, I wanted it to be this immediate, this unflinching and real.

Most of the things that had bothered me about the film in the reports I'd read didn't hold true. They were poorly reported exaggerations. I was glad for that, but I was still challenged by other aspects of the film, particularly the image of Christ struggling to understand and accept his calling. I puzzled over this for years. Eventually, I decided to augment my old research. I was fascinated by the film, challenged and unsettled by it, and I wanted to understand it better. I was also intrigued to learn more about the equally unsettling events surrounding its release. I spent years slowly collecting every book I could find, gathering things like the Criterion Collection DVD, the score CD, back issues of all the magazines I'd dug out of the library, newspaper articles, booklets and newsletters written in protest, and even an original production screenplay from the first attempted making of the film at Paramount in 1983.

Ultimately, it was the book *Scorsese: A Journey* by Mary Pat Kelly that helped me really unpack the film. I read it voraciously on my lunch breaks while working at the largest Christian bookstore in America. Through interviews with actors, writers, and producers involved in the film, I saw where Scorsese and screenwriter Paul Schrader were coming from. I'd learned long before that the accusations against the content of the film were largely based on misconceptions, and it was obvious that allegations of malicious, anti-Christian intent on the part of Universal Studios or Scorsese were pure mythology. These things fueled my interest in how Christians engage the broader culture. But there was another element to my research that elevated this film from a beautiful piece of cinema to my favorite film of all time: It started to expand my Christology.

I have always been deeply interested in the historical person of Jesus as reflected in the Scriptures and in the meaning of his sacrifice. What I was reading in this book about a director and his movies were some of the most amazing concepts I'd ever encountered—among them, the idea that we all struggle as humans and that, if Jesus was fully human and fully divine, his struggle must have been profound. If Jesus came, not to be *like* one of us, but to actually *be* one of us, then he had to struggle, just as I was struggling.

He came to be offensive, to tear down one world and build a new one in its place. He came to shake people, to rattle their teeth with his fury and his love. Perhaps some of the ways in which the film was off-putting to me were just a reminder that Jesus himself could be off-putting. Just like *The Last Temptation of Christ*, Jesus both attracted and repelled. He said, "Come to me, all you who are weary and burdened" (Matt 11:28 NIV) and also, "You snakes! You brood of vipers! How will you escape being condemned to hell?" (Matt 23:33 NIV). Now, through Schrader's dialogue, the words of Jesus were landing on my ears as blisteringly as they would have landed on first-century ears as he lambasted religious leaders in the temple, yelling, "You think God belongs only to you? He doesn't. God's an immortal spirit who belongs to everybody! To the whole world! You think you're special? God is not an Israelite!"[6]

Such lines were difficult for a young conservative Evangelical Christian to hear from the mouth of a toothy, sinewy Christ, his neck bulging with fury as he spat out the words. Surely, actor Willem Dafoe's Jesus was also capable of great gentleness and compassion, carefully and protectively leading a huddled and crying Mary Magdalene away from the crowd that had wanted to stone her and tenderly explaining to Judas why the Messiah had to die, to be the sacrifice that would "bring God and man together." But there is nothing easy about the script or Dafoe's performance. *The Last Temptation of Christ*—at times violent, at times esoteric—can be uncomfortable and upsetting for audiences in many ways, but that ability to cause discomfort is perhaps the film's most sacred quality.

I entitled this piece "A Hot Coal in My Mouth" for two reasons. First, the title is an illustration of the kind of misunderstanding of the film that characterized the response of Christian critics in 1988 and the assumptions on which those misunderstandings were based. The phrase comes from a line that appeared in at least two early drafts of the script but which ultimately did not end up in the final screenplay or in the film.

---

6. Scorsese, *Last Temptation of Christ*.

At some point just prior to the film's release and at the height of protest demonstrations and public outcry from conservative Christians, a 1982 draft of the script—a very early version that Martin Scorsese had said was not even ready to be used to pitch the film to a studio—was leaked. It fell into the hands of Donald Wildmon of the American Family Association, who quickly distributed photocopies to dozens of pastors and Christian leaders across the country. Touted as a "new version" of the script, several lines from this very early draft were quoted as representing the "shocking truth" about the film in numerous mailers, fliers, and pamphlets distributed in protest across the nation.[7]

Most of the lines quoted and scenes described were not even part of the script as early as 1983,[8] and almost none of them appear in the finished film. Those that do appear in the film show themselves to be grossly misinterpreted. The particular example on which my title is based comes from a much ballyhooed moment in which John the Baptist kisses Jesus on the lips. The line, spoken by Jesus in narration, was to have been, "His tongue felt like a hot coal in my mouth."[9] This was immediately seized upon by detractors as a salacious depiction of Jesus engaged in a homosexual liaison.

The kiss between the two men remains in the film without the narration, but in the context of the scene, it takes on quite a different appearance. Jesus and the Baptist are sitting by a fire, arguing over what it is that God demands of us. Is it merely love and kindness, or is it also anger? The Baptist argues the latter.

> Jesus implores, "But isn't love enough?"
> "No! Look at the world," the Baptist insists, "Look around you. Plague, war, corruption, false prophets, false idols, worship of gold. Nothing is of value! The tree is rotten! You have to take the ax and cut it down."
> Jesus is unconvinced. "That's not the answer."
> The Baptist challenges, "Then what is the answer?"
> Jesus confesses, "I don't know."[10]

After this heartfelt and somewhat heated exchange, the Baptist recommends that Jesus go to the desert to see what God has to say. Jesus agrees, thanks the Baptist, and the two men kiss and embrace one another. There is no use of tongue in the kiss and it does not indicate romantic sentiment. Rather, the two are expressing brotherly love despite their differences, giving each

---

7. Lindlof, *Hollywood Under Siege*.
8. Schrader, *Last Temptation of Christ*.
9. Schrader, *Last Temptation of Christ*.
10. Scorsese, *Last Temptation of Christ*.

other what the Scriptures call "a holy kiss" (1 Thess 5:26; Rom 16:16; 1 Cor 16:20; 2 Cor 13:12) in an age and culture in which affection between men was more readily accepted as something other than an expression of sexual attraction or romantic interest.

In this context, it would seem that the original line likely neither referred to the Baptist's literal tongue entering the mouth of Jesus nor to the heat of sexual passion. Rather, it more plausibly referred to the experience of kissing the lips of a fiery prophet, especially a prophet whose words are currently singeing one's own assumptions. The image of the hot coal recalls the biblical image of Isaiah, whose speech was purified when an angel touched a burning coal to his lips (Isa 6:6–7). The prophet Isaiah (played by Scorsese) is important to the film, as he is invoked by Jesus at the resurrection of Lazarus and appears to Jesus in a vision or a dream. "He had a prophecy," Jesus tells Judas of the encounter, "I saw it written. It said: 'He has borne our faults. He was wounded for our transgressions, yet he opened not his mouth. Despised and rejected by all, he went forward without resisting, like a lamb led to the slaughter.'" Jesus then tells Judas, "I have to die on the cross and I have to die willingly." When Judas asks what happens after that, Jesus replies, "I come back to judge the living and the dead."[11]

Similarly, a burning tongue foreshadows the tongues of fire representing the coming of the Holy Spirit on the day of Pentecost (Acts 2:3). Unfortunately, this interpretation of the moment, though much more in keeping with the context presented in even the earliest script and similarly representative of the tone and intent of the film, was lost on Christian critics who at the time seemed more intent on finding scandal than on finding substance.

While I can hardly claim this interpretation as definitive or authoritative, others have noted, while admitting the potential homoerotic implications, that the line and the kiss "can be seen as a sign of the Baptist's blessing."[12] Certainly, this is true of the kiss in the finished film. Further, since the line does not appear in the film, the outcry it caused, according to one scholar, "problematizes even further a ritual of spectatorship that censures a director for the musings of a screenwriter whose literary notions aren't even produced cinematically."[13] In any case, the consternation over this and other moments in the early script is an example of overzealous Christians objecting loudly to something they simply do not understand, the production of which, quite frankly, needed neither their approval nor their permission.

11. Scorsese, *Last Temptation of Christ*.
12. Cutara, *Wicked Cinema*, 176.
13. Allen, "Word Made Cinematic," 120.

I chose this line as my title, second, because it represents to me my own experience of *The Last Temptation of Christ*. It has been uncomfortable, sometimes painful. My initial response was to reject the film, to spit it out of my mouth (Rev 3:16). But something about the burning felt good. It felt clean and pure and, over time, started to bring more clarity to the gospel and to my Christology than I had found in a long time. I decided to bring the fire inside, to let it burn in my belly. The fire of discomfort soon became a fire of faith, and I found a renewed passion and love for Jesus that has become one of the greatest gifts of my life.

Like a strong, dark, French roast coffee, *The Last Temptation of Christ* was at first off-putting, shocking, and difficult for my unaccustomed palate to accept. But as I took sip after sip, unpacking one bit here, exploring another bit there, I came to find that it was not bitter, not acidic. Rather, it was well-rounded, robust, and unapologetically packed with more than a mere cupful of flavor.

The film is intended to challenge, to unsettle, to provoke—but not for the purpose of defaming Christ or demeaning faith in him. Rather, it is so disorienting in order to cause us to reexamine our comfortably held assumptions, to contemplate the full, frightening impact of God in the flesh, and to recognize Jesus as a man who struggled just as we do, except for one remarkable difference: He won!

He won a victory over something stronger than political oppression or religious conflict; he conquered the deep desires of his own human nature. If Jesus was not just fully divine but also fully human, the film proposes, then it seems only natural that he would have loved his human life as much as any of us and would not have wanted to give it up, at least on anything but his own terms. But, by surrendering his human body and his human will to the will of God, he won the victory over death. He won by letting God win.

This was not a victory of the force of will, but of the strength of submission. The film emphasizes this point through a fictional event that highlights the dramatic difference between the expectations of the Messiah—a political revolutionary—and the reality—a sacrificial lamb. Jesus and his followers attempt to lead a revolution in Jerusalem, marching in with torches and raising the people into a frenzy, with Jesus shouting, "I'm going to baptize everybody with fire!"

But suddenly, Jesus hesitates, waiting for a sign from God that he is on the right path. "Give me an ax, not the cross," he pleads in an internal dialogue with God, "Let me die like this." But blood begins running from his palms like the stigmata and he becomes weak, leaning on Judas for support as he is whisked away from the rioting crowd, upon whom soldiers are descending. When they are alone, Jesus tells Judas, "I wish there was another way. I'm sorry, but there isn't. I have to die on the cross."[14]

While extra-biblical, this event highlights the need for Jesus to surrender his own will, to take the harder way of releasing control. The fact that such a submission was required and that such a battle had to be fought is an idea that can make us uncomfortable. We're much happier with the notion of Jesus being ready, willing, and fully prepared to be the lion to our lamb. We love to see him flex his muscles, stand up tall, and show himself as the pillar of self-assured strength. But then the Garden of Gethsemane comes to haunt our perfect picture.

The image of Jesus surrendering through struggle then becomes an example for our own faith and life as, through pain and sorrow, through stubbornness and surrender, we must ultimately give ourselves over completely to the things God has in store for us, whether we want them or not. Encountering the hard truth of the necessity for submission before God even for Jesus himself, and therefore especially for us, may be offensive to our tender egos and fragile plans, but it is the way in which we must go, even as our human arrogance doesn't want to submit. It is the way in which Christ went, even though he could have shown the kind of force of will that our arrogance pretends.

Jesus came to shake the foundations of comfortably accepted religion in his day. It seems, at least to me, that it only makes sense that a film about him should be able to have the same kind of impact on our own religion today. Indeed, if we are not allowing Jesus to overturn the tables of our temples, to rattle the cages of our sense of understanding, we are doing him the dishonor of asking the lion to be tame. Like C. S. Lewis's Aslan, we must constantly be reminded that he is good, but he is not safe.[15]

Faith in Christ demands something of us. In my experience, however, our films about him rarely do. What *The Last Temptation of Christ* dares to realize is that our familiarity with the trappings of the Gospel story is what often keeps us from experiencing the full, challenging freshness of the Christ presented in that story. The film, therefore, takes the audacious, even dangerous, approach of finding new language for that story and inventing new narrative for its protagonist. In so doing, it paints an image that is not concerned with presenting an accurate picture of a history we already know as much as it is with creating a provoking portrait that causes us to ask deeper theological questions about a Christ who surpasses our

---

14. Scorsese, *Last Temptation of Christ*.
15. Lewis, *Lion, the Witch, and the Wardrobe*, 75–76.

understanding and who, at least on this side of eternity, we can know only in part (1 Cor 13:9–12).

It is that partial knowing, that view "through a glass darkly" in which *The Last Temptation of Christ* stubbornly resides. It asks more questions than it answers, indicates more than it tells, and prefigures a resurrection that does not appear on screen. Far more than a biblical epic, it is an exploration of human spiritual struggle. In stark contrast to the grand pageantry of most Jesus films and the simple emotional pattern of tragedy leading to triumph that provides the underpinnings of the greater majority of the genre, *The Last Temptation of Christ* instead chooses to focus on the significance of Christ's sacrifice and to contemplate what it really means for him to be both fully human and fully divine.

That is what my journey has been about so far—embracing the struggle, accepting the mystery, and finding beauty in the paradoxical. A simple, one-sided Jesus could not be Lord over a complex, confusing world, so I had simplified my world to match. But, just as the world was growing out of the black-and-white clothes I'd made for it, Jesus began to show himself to be ever more complex, ever more mysterious, and therefore ever more powerful than anything I could come against in this world. If Jesus could let the villains of his day mow him down and still win the victory, then perhaps when I am looking out my own window and seeing weapons raised against me, when I am hurt and broken by the world, it doesn't matter so much anymore if I am defeated for the moment. I can take courage. Jesus has indeed overcome the world. I don't have to try to do it anymore.

> A wild, indomitable joy took possession of him. No, no he was not a coward, a deserter, a traitor. No, he was nailed to the cross. He had stood his ground honorably to the very end; he had kept his word. . . . He uttered a triumphant cry: IT IS ACCOMPLISHED! And it was as though he had said: Everything has begun.[16]

BIBLIOGRAPHY

Allen, Gregory Kahlil Kareem. "The Word Made Cinematic: The Representation of Jesus in Cinema." PhD diss., University of Pittsburgh, 2008.
Cutara, Daniel S. *Wicked Cinema: Sex and Religion on Screen.* Austin: University of Texas Press, 2014.
Grogan, David, et al. "In the Name of Jesus." *People*, August 8, 1988.

---

16. Kazantzakis, *Last Temptation of Christ*, 496.

Kazantzakis, Nikos. *The Last Temptation of Christ*. Translated by P. A. Bien. 1960. Reprint, New York: Simon & Schuster, 1988.

Lacayo, Richard. "Days of Ire and Brimstone." *Time*, July 25, 1988.

Lee, John. "A Holy Furor." *Time*, August 15, 1988.

Lewis, C. S. *The Lion, the Witch, and the Wardrobe*. 1950. Reprint, New York: Macmillan, 1978.

Lindlof, Thomas R. *Hollywood under Siege: Martin Scorsese, the Religious Right, and the Culture Wars*. Lexington: University Press of Kentucky, 2008.

Neece, Kevin. "The Last Temptation of Christ." Unpublished manuscript.

Schrader, Paul. *The Last Temptation of Christ*. Original Production Screenplay. Los Angeles, CA: Tisch/Avnet Productions, 1983.

Scorsese, Martin. *The Last Temptation of Christ*. Universal City, CA: Universal Pictures, 1988.

18

Worship Made Flesh

How Modern Worship Songs Incarnate Meaning

CHRISTINE HAND JONES

In my senior year at Dallas Baptist University, I did something that now seems like a bright, flashing arrow pointing the way toward my future in academia: I wrote and presented a paper just for the fun of it. The occasion was our annual Paideia College Society Conference, and the paper's title was "From the Beatles to Britney: Can Pop Music Be Redeemed?" This question was personal for twenty-one-year-old me, an aspiring singer-songwriter who wanted, more than anything, to write music that would draw every listener toward the beauty of God. Fifteen years later, I am an active singer-songwriter, but what pays my bills is my work as a professor who specializes in the intersections of music and literature. In my own songs and in my explorations of the songs of others, I have never stopped asking the question "Can pop music be redeemed?" alongside a related question: "How can Christians be the vehicle of that redemption?"

In searching for an answer to that question, I've come to realize one truth: good songs express meaning through a coherent union of words and music. Attempting to separate the form from the content does violence to both. Too often, Christian musicians have elevated content above form, not seeing how the two are inextricably linked. In my own work on Bob Dylan, I've witnessed the way Dylan scholars have split his songs among the various compartments of academia, with musicologists, historians, and literary critics all weighing in separately but with very few scholars attempting to analyze his songs as cohesive unions of words and music. However, when he won the Nobel Prize in Literature in 2016, Bob Dylan won not for his prose or poetry, but for his *songs*, leaving literary scholars and critics with the task of figuring out how to engage song as a legitimate literary form. If Dylan's Nobel signals the inclusion of popular song in the literary canon, scholars and critics must learn how to approach song holistically. One must take the sonic elements of a song seriously to a degree that has perhaps been only incidental in other explorations of poetic prosody.

For the contemporary literary critic, taking music seriously as part of the total literary work can create an uncomfortable problem, for music can illuminate the mysterious or ineffable parts of poetic expression that modern attempts at literary criticism rarely admit to. In his comprehensive work on lyric poetry, *Theory of the Lyric*, Jonathan Culler attempts to engage Gerard Manley Hopkins's over-the-top sonic sensuousness in the poem "The Leaden Echo and the Golden Echo," explaining, "For secular readers the poem is embarrassing because it depends so utterly on a hyperbolic version of the Resurrection of the Body, which cannot seem anything but wishful."[1] But Culler goes on to say that "the hyperbolic literalization of claims in the poem" lifts the poem above mere sentiment, bringing a radical vision of literal resurrection into being through "language and its *surprising incarnational effects*, so dramatically staged by the linguistic patterning."[2] For Culler, the sonic effects of language somehow transform word into flesh, making the supernatural, illogical concept of resurrection into a felt experience for even the jaded secular critic. If the sonic elements of words alone are able to transform the sentimental into the sacramental, then how much more might music add to that experience? In what follows, I want to explore the "surprising incarnational effects" inherent in song form, particularly for modern Christian worship music. How does song bring into being an experience of its poetic content in a unique way, and what are the implications of that incarnation for Christian music?

My text for this analysis will be the top songs in today's worship music as defined by Christian Copyright Licensing International (CCLI), an organization that exists to license worship lyrics for display in Christian worship

---

1. Culler, *Theory of the Lyric*, 178–79.
2. Culler, *Theory of the Lyric*, 179 (emphasis added).

services. The "CCLI Top 100" list ranks worship songs by their use in worship services, thus providing a clear picture of the most popular modern worship songs today. I will explore patterns among these popular Christian songs with a focus on elements that I believe have particularly incarnational effects. Strong poets and songwriters employ image and metaphor, structure and repetition, and melody and harmony to plant in their works seeds of life that good interpreters cultivate. All these elements work together to bring the lyrics' meaning into being in a more concrete way than literal prose can accomplish on its own. Metaphor engages not only our mind but also our senses, while rhyme, meter, repetition, music, harmony, and other sonic elements of poetry and song engage our ears and even our bodies in a physical manifestation of their content. While much has been written on the importance of sound theology in church music, I am less interested in the doctrinal details of modern worship than I am in the ways image, metaphor, song form, harmony, and melody flesh out those doctrines, contributing to our current Christian culture in ways that may get overlooked when we elevate literal meaning above poetic experience.

METAPHOR

One important way that both poetry and song connect the physical to the metaphysical is through metaphor. Metaphor, by its nature, connects abstract to concrete. In the study of poetry, the abstract part of a metaphor, which the metaphor itself attempts to define or describe, is called the "tenor," and the more concrete part of the metaphor, to which the tenor is compared, is called the "vehicle." The tenor represents some concept whose nature defies an exact prose description or formula. Love, death, eternity, justice, and other such ineffable qualities often take on the role of the tenor in a given metaphor because those concepts can be difficult to define or discuss. The vehicle of a metaphor carries that far-off idea to the more familiar shores of our senses. In the metaphor "love is a flame," "love" is the tenor and "flame" is the vehicle, helping us to understand some concrete reality about the abstraction "love." The most effective metaphors work by bridging the gap between the abstract and the concrete, helping us to feel in our bodies the realities of something beyond the body. But metaphor is more than an intellectual exercise in connecting fuzzy concepts to solid objects. Recent findings in neuroscience suggest that metaphor engages not only the mind but our emotions and our bodies as well. Neuroimaging studies have shown that, although it reacts to literal or abstract language using the parts of the brain traditionally associated with information and language processing, the brain reacts to metaphors differently, using parts of the brain that are normally reserved for the actual experience being described.[3]

For example, a February 2016 study led by Francesca Citron used neuroimaging to discover the difference in the brain's reaction when subjects read conventional metaphors, such as "that's so sweet," and when they read those phrases' literal counterparts, such as "that's so kind." Whenever the subjects read the metaphors, the amygdala, a part of the brain that processes emotionally meaningful experiences, became active. According to the researchers, these results "suggest that when participants read for comprehension, metaphorical formulations are more emotionally engaging than literal paraphrases."[4] In other words, if I call Jesus "the light," I will have a stronger emotional association than if I call Him "good," even if the two words are used interchangeably. Metaphors, then, fulfill an important task in connecting our emotions, as well as our intellects, to God.

But even when emotions induce physical reactions in us, they may still fall into the realm of the abstract. If it engages only our minds and emotions, metaphor still may not go so far as to incarnate truth, as I have claimed it does. Here is where the neuroscience gets interesting. Metaphor—particularly when it employs concrete, sensory imagery—affects the reader's brain in the same way that physical sensations do. Annie Murphy Paul expertly explains some of these findings in her *New York Times* piece "Your Brain on Fiction." She reports that a 2006 study showed that "Words like 'lavender,' 'cinnamon,' and 'soap' . . . elicit a response not only from the language-processing areas of our brains, but also those devoted to dealing with smells." Paul also cites a similar study from Emory University in 2012 that showed that texture metaphors activated subjects' sensory cortex. She explains, "Metaphors like 'The singer had a velvet voice' and 'He had leathery hands' roused the sensory cortex, while phrases matched for meaning, like 'The singer had a pleasing voice' and 'He had strong hands,' did not." It seems that, when our brains encounter metaphors, they react as though they have encountered life.

Still other studies, such as one published in *NeuroImage* in July 2013, have shown activation of the sensory-motor areas of the brain whenever people read language related to action, including action metaphors.[5] When a reader encounters action verbs involving arms and legs, the arm and leg receptors and the part of the brain associated with performing that action

---

3. Paul, "Your Brain on Fiction."
4. Citron et al., "Conventional Metaphors in Longer Passages," 219.
5. Desai et al., "Piece of the Action."

become active in a process called "somatopic activation."[6] So, presumably, when a congregant sings about Jesus's climbing mountains and kicking down doors, as in the popular worship song "Reckless Love," the parts of our bodies associated with climbing and kicking also activate.[7] Of course, congregational singing is already a full-body activity, so adding apt physical descriptions and metaphors to worship songs can only enhance the whole-person engagement of a worship service. The metaphors of our modern worship songs engage mind, emotion, and body all at once so that, in a sense, these metaphors truly incarnate some aspect of theological meaning.

In order to find out what the most common metaphors in modern worship are, I consulted CCLI for the top fifty worship songs at the time of this writing and analyzed them for trends and patterns.[8] I then fed the song lyrics of the top twenty-five CCLI songs into a web-based text analysis tool.[9] The general scan of the top fifty titles and the more detailed analysis of the top twenty-five songs revealed similar patterns. For example, when worship songs use animal metaphors for God, they use Lamb and Lion most often, with Lamb receiving slightly more references. Out of the top twenty-five songs, the word "Lion" was used in four unique lines, with a total of seven repetitions, and the word "Lamb" five unique times, but with eleven total repetitions. When it comes to the experience of Christian life, trust, and salvation, a quick scan of the lyrics of the top fifty songs reveals two dominant metaphors. The first uses chains, slavery, and freedom as metaphors for forgiveness and victorious living. The second dominant metaphor employs water, storms, oceans, and other related concepts as metaphors for life's troubles, and compares God's help, mercy, and presence to either salvation from those storms or a full plunge into mysterious deeps. In closer analysis of the top twenty-five songs, these metaphors continue to rise to the top.

"Who You Say I Am," by Hillsong Worship, is the number-one song at the time of this writing, and it depends on the slavery-freedom metaphor for its celebration of Christian adoption.[10] The line beginning "Free at last" and announcing that one has been ransomed evokes not only general slavery but also American slavery with its evocation of the well-known Negro Spiritual, "Free At Last," which none other than Dr. Martin Luther King Jr. used to express his hopes for future racial equality.[11] But the next

6. Desai et al., "Piece of the Action," 862.
7. Asbury, "Reckless Love."
8. "CCLI Top 100."
9. "Textalyser."
10. Hillsong Worship, "Who You Say I Am."
11. King, "I Have a Dream."

few lines turn toward the more abstract notion of having been "a slave to sin." Having established the slave metaphor in the verses, the chorus makes explicit the contrast between slavery and sonship, with a reference to the words of Christ: "If the Son sets you free, you will be free indeed" (John 8:36 NIV). As the number-one worship song in CCLI's records, "Who You Say I Am" is a strong representative of the slavery-freedom metaphor trend throughout the other top worship songs. Not counting repetition of exact lines or refrains, the words "free" and "freedom" occur nine times in the top twenty-five worship songs. If repetitions are included, the terms occur sixteen times in only twenty-five songs. The words "ransom" and "ransomed" occur three times, always referring to Jesus; on a related note, Christ's blood purchases forgiveness and "breaks the chains." Speaking of chains, versions of the word "chain" occur five times, and the word "slave" or "captive" appears three separate times, for a total of eight references to enslavement offered in contrast to Christ's freedom. These trends suggest that the primary way modern evangelicals talk about the salvation and sanctification experience is through the slavery-freedom metaphor. Despite the recurrence of "ransom," the predominant atonement theory in these metaphors appears not to be the ransom theory but the substitutionary atonement theory. And though the metaphors are borrowed from Paul's biblical language of being free from sin and a slave to Christ, most of the songs have adapted the metaphor to fit a more fluid version of freedom.

Nautical, storm, or rain metaphors also dominate the top worship songs. Six different times in the top twenty-five songs, the difficulties of life are compared with storms, gales, or waves, and four different times, God is the source of stability or navigation as both the "wind inside my sails" and "the anchor in the waves."[12] Two different times in these top songs, God brings thunder, and on four separate occasions, God's grace, peace, or presence is characterized as "deep." In these metaphors, God is both storm and safety, both fathomless ocean and calm shore. This pattern continues when expanding the analysis to the top fifty songs, which include the Hillsong United hit, "Oceans," in which the oceans represent both the "great unknown," where one stumbles, and "the mystery," wherein one encounters God.[13] In John Mark McMillan's "How He Loves," popularized by the David Crowder Band, God's love and mercy are characterized first as wind and then as a hurricane.[14] In "Open up the Heavens" by Meredith Andrews, God's presence is "a mighty river" that Christians may access by asking God

---

12. McMillan et al., "King of My Heart."
13. Hillsong United, "Oceans."
14. David Crowder Band, "How He Loves."

to "open up the floodgates." In all these songs, the dominant image is that of being awed and overwhelmed. Drowning is imminent, but where one might, in other circumstances, cling fervently to Christ as the navigator and anchor, in these songs one instead submits to the waves of God's presence and calling. To drown in Christ is, apparently, a consummation devoutly to be wished.

So what do these commonly used metaphors have to do with an "incarnation" of meaning? First, any casual observer of a body of believers engaged in singing these songs could probably attest to the emotional impact of these metaphors on those proclaiming them. The affective result of metaphor applies even to conventional metaphors, as the previously cited study shows, so worship participants will experience a heightened emotional response to those chain and ocean metaphors, regardless of how often they have heard them. The physical response is more difficult to make claims about, however. Without neurological scans of actual worshippers, we cannot know for sure, but one might assume that the brain would register a physical state of freedom of movement when singing about the dramatic removal of chains or a sensation of plunging or being covered when singing about God's oceanic love. But since these metaphors are so common, the neurological response is more complicated because the brain reacts differently to idioms than it does to fresh metaphors. In a 2013 study, researchers studied the activation of sensory-motor areas of the brain whenever it was exposed to action-oriented language on a four-point scale.[15] The scale began with literal descriptions of physical actions, then metaphors using figurative action verbs, then common idioms using action words in a figurative way, and ended with abstract phrases using verbs that had "relatively low association with actions."[16] The results? As abstraction increases, the level of sensory-motor brain involvement decreases.[17] In other words, the closer a metaphor moves to conventional, idiomatic status, the less engaged our bodies become in processing it.

One indicator that these common worship metaphors may be moving into the realm of idiom may be the ease with which writers mix and match them at will, often without regard for the metaphor's internal integrity. For example, in the previously mentioned song, "Open Up The Heavens," God's glory is figured mostly as a flood, but the metaphor gets mixed up when, in one verse, God's glory is a fire that will "burn our hearts with truth."[18] Are

---

15. See Desai et al., "Piece of the Action."
16. Desai et al., "Piece of the Action," 865.
17. Desai et al., "Piece of the Action," 865.
18. Andrews, "Open Up the Heavens."

the congregants asking God to quench that glorious fire with His equally glorious flood? It's hard to be sure. Similar confusion occurs in Chris Tomlin's popular rewrite of the hymn "Amazing Grace," which also appears in the top twenty-five songs.[19] That song presents a chain metaphor, referring to chains as "gone," as worshippers proclaim themselves to have been "set free" and "ransomed" by God. In the very next phrase, however, the song shifts to a water metaphor, describing God's mercy as "a flood," that "reigns." The singer is simultaneously free from chains yet submerged in a mercy so overwhelming that it now rules and reigns. It does not "rain" as one would expect, given the flood metaphor, and as the lyric is indeed sometimes misquoted when used in worship services. These metaphorical inconsistencies may indicate more than poetic laziness; they may be a sign that these popular metaphors are becoming so overused as to lose their effectiveness as metaphors. As these metaphors move toward idiom (as many of them already have in Christian circles), they will engage our bodies less and less, allowing for a kind of groundless, disembodied worship experience. By contrast, the metaphors most likely to engage the whole person—mind, emotions, and body—in worship are the freshest, most logically consistent ones that rely on specific, sensory details that are not so unfamiliar as to distract the worshipper, but not so familiar as to have no physical effect at all.

STRUCTURE AND REPETITION

So far, I have examined only one poetic element common to both poetry and song, and I have promised to look at both words and music. But before we can move on to melody and harmony, we must focus on an aspect of both poetry and song in which music influences and intertwines with words: structure and repetition. Poetic form already contains the musical elements of rhythm and sonic patterning. Terms like "meter," shared between music and poetry, reveal this poetic-musical connection. When it comes to popular worship music, we can examine the overall structure of the songs, with its ordering of parts and patterns of repetition and contrast, as well as rhyme and the patterns of stresses within the lyrics. The difference between song and poetry when it comes to structure and form is that, in song, the lyrics tend to subordinate themselves to the melody rather than to a set poetic meter, so I will save analysis of the patterns of lines themselves for the section on melody. For now, I will focus on trends among song structures and trends in repetition, for the two are almost always related.

19. Tomlin, "Amazing Grace."

The most common song form by far among the top fifty worship songs uses two verses, a chorus, and a bridge in the following order: verse-chorus-verse-chorus-bridge-chorus. The second most common is a variant of the same: a verse-chorus-verse-chorus form, often with a third verse included where the bridge might typically go. In fact, out of the top fifty worship songs at the time of this writing, only two used the traditional strophic hymn form (similar to the ballad form in poetry), which features three or four different verses using the same melody. Surprisingly, those two songs are not old hymns. Though a few older hymns did make it into the CCLI top fifty, those hymns used verse-chorus format. The two strophic songs in the top fifty, "In Christ Alone" by Keith Getty and Stuart Townend and "How Deep the Father's Love for Us" by Stuart Townend, were released in 2001 and 1997, respectively.[20]

In itself, this information is not surprising or especially enlightening. It's normal for all popular music to follow the trends and patterns of the surrounding culture. Check the top forty pop songs, and you'll find similar patterns. Hymns from our past also followed the trends and traditions of their times. What is perhaps more interesting is how consistent the patterns within the verse-chorus-bridge structures are. For example, when I took a closer look at the top twenty-five worship songs, I found that every song with a bridge used a similar format: two to four short lines, usually employing only two short melodic phrases, alternating and repeating at increasing intensity over the course of several repetitions. This pattern is so ubiquitous that providing examples from every song that employs it would prove tedious. One excellent representative example is the bridge of Phil Wickham's "This Is Amazing Grace," which simply repeats two almost identical lines extolling the worthiness of Christ.[21] Another example is the Big Daddy Weave hit, "Lion and the Lamb," which repeats a single line over and over again.[22] Chris Tomlin's song, "Good Good Father" uses this approach as well, repeating, a single line proclaiming God "perfect" in all of his actions three times before adding the prepositional phrase "to us" to the third refrain of the line.[23] In these songs, the repetitive bridge functions as a kind of meditation on the theme already set up in the verses and choruses of the songs.

In other worship songs, the bridge serves less as a new spin on the song's theme and more as the thematic focal point. In fact, I would argue

20. Townend, "How Deep the Father's Love."
21. Wickham, "This Is Amazing Grace."
22. Big Daddy Weave, "Lion and the Lamb."
23. Tomlin, "Good Good Father."

that, in today's worship songs, the bridge serves as the song's "thesis statement." Where a bold statement of theme would ordinarily occur only in the song's chorus, today's worship songs often restate the thesis in the bridge after already having done so in the chorus. One example is found in the All Sons and Daughters song "Great Are You Lord," which at the time of writing sits at number five on the CCLI charts.[24] The bridge features two lines, sung in such quick succession so as to feel like a single phrase, despite the two lines' natural syntactic separation, followed by a third, short line ("Great are you, Lord!") with a new melody. The song then repeats this short phrase several times before returning to the chorus. Housefires's "Build My Life," withholds the song's thesis entirely until the bridge.[25] Its bridge uses only two lines, identical in melody, expressing the worshippers' resolution to trust only in the sure foundation of Christ's love. The bridge repeats as many times as the worship leader desires. The title of the song provides the clue to the song's thesis, for in no place but the bridge is the phrase "build my life" to be found, though one might expect it to occur in the song's chorus.

What makes this pattern worth noting? Well, the medium, as they say, is the message. Song structure provides a framework for expressing or thinking about the issues a song brings up. This marriage of form and content is a key component in understanding formal poetry. For example, the "volta" in a sonnet or the repetition with a difference in the structure of a villanelle both create an expectation in the reader for a particular way of thinking about the content of the poem. One noticeable structural element that arises naturally from a verse-chorus-bridge structure or from a verse-chorus structure with three verses is the tripartite form that a song's argument naturally takes to fit into those sections. The three-point sermon is practically an Evangelical trope, much like the three-point, five-paragraph student essay so common to young writers. The three-point structure demands clear three-point thematic movement. In Housefires's song "Build My Life," for example, the verses declare the worthiness of God, the choruses ask God to reveal his goodness and holiness, and the bridge commits to an action: building one's life upon God's love in response to God's character and worthiness. Like a good sermon, the three parts of many worship songs first explain or describe, then exhort or praise, and finally, encourage practical application or response.

These tripartite worship songs contrast with traditional strophic hymns, which almost always use four verses. A good hymn writer employs these four stanzas to follow key points of Christian faith: sometimes creation,

---

24. All Sons and Daughters, "Great Are You Lord."
25. Housefires, "Build My Life."

fall, redemption, and restoration; sometimes sin, confession, salvation, and glorification. The modern hymn "In Christ Alone" uses its four verses to make a general statement of theme in verse one and then to meditate on Christ's birth, death, and resurrection as various components of that hope.[26] That four-point pattern creates a different mental journey for members of a congregation—not necessarily a superior one, but an important one that may be overlooked in an overreliance on a single type of song structure. Strophic structures excel at supporting more robust theologies in a way that three-part modern worship songs, with their reliance on repetition, cannot easily accommodate. However, modern worship songs have different strengths. When the bridge functions as the focal point for congregants' worshipping energies, the structure and repetition combine to point the worshipper not only to a moment of praise or to a statement of doctrine, but to a whole life of worship, as the "response" portion of the song is repeated time and again.

This discussion of song structure leads naturally to a discussion of repetition. As I have already observed, the locus of most repetition in many worship songs is the bridge, and the most repeated ideas are often those phrases that hope to move the Christian to active response toward God. The second most popular site of repetition is, of course, the chorus. Repetition is expected in the chorus because it usually contains the song's hook and title. The chorus's job is to repeat the title and main idea and sear it into the singer or listener's mind with enough supporting lines to make sense of that main idea. Berklee College of Music songwriting instructor Andrea Stolpe identifies the patterns in most choruses as consisting of alternating "title" lines—which, as one might expect, contain the song's title and theme—and "developmental" lines, which provide support.[27] For example, Matt Maher's "Lord, I Need You," adapted from the hymn of the same name, contains three variants of a title line, with only one development line, expounding on the nature of defenseless, sinful humanity's need for Christ.[28]

Chris Tomlin's "Good Good Father" has a similar pattern. Line one of the chorus is essentially the title, calling God a "good good Father," followed by three development lines proclaiming repeatedly that this good Father is who God is and that the singer is loved by God. Such repetition shows that not all repetition in choruses establishes the title or hook. In cases like "Good Good Father" or John Mark and Sarah McMillan's "King of My Heart," which also repeats the word "good" multiple times, repetition

26. Getty, "In Christ Alone."
27. Stolpe, *Beginning Songwriting*, 96–98.
28. Maher, "Lord, I Need You."

is primarily a tool for emphasis. In my analysis of the top twenty-five Christian worship songs, only two words repeat immediately after one another in more than one song: One is the word "good." Apparently, one "good" is simply not enough to express God's goodness. (On a related note, the hit song, "Reckless Love," repeats not "good," but "so," in the line, describing God as "*so, so* good.")[29] All these cases favor enthusiasm over erudition—God's goodness is so overwhelming that excited repetition is the only way to express it. The other serially repeated word, "holy," frequently gets not two, but three iterations in a row, with biblical precedent from the books of Isaiah (6:3) and Revelation (4:8). Like goodness, holiness is an aspect of God's eternal character that can be difficult to comprehend fully. In these songs, repetition fills in the gap of comprehension with a simple restatement of truth.

Why does this matter and how does repetition serve to incarnate ideas? For starters, repetition is one way in which we can literally change our brains. Repetition has long been an important educational tool, even before neuroscience introduced the idea of neuroplasticity, the brain's ability to adapt and change based on experiences. According to Manfred Spitzer, learning happens when "neural networks digest . . . new input with every repetition, thereby changing the weights of the [brain's] synaptic connections."[30] So repetition is valuable in itself because it helps to carve truth into our minds, making it easier to recall that truth in times of doubt, fear, and uncertainty. While these repetitions may often feel like overkill or lazy writing—and at times, perhaps, they are—they are also useful tools for memory, for brain building, and for literal neurological transformation.

HARMONY AND MELODY

Metaphor, structure, and repetition are all common to both song and poetry, though the kinds of structures and patterns vary between poetry and song. Music, however, plays a more explicit role in song than in poetry. While poetry benefits from the rhythms of meter and the sonorities of rhyme or alliteration to some musical effect, song lyrics do not fully come alive without melody and harmony. Western worship songs like those I have examined are rooted firmly in western harmony. While some of the songs employ a five-note pentatonic scale, most are diatonic—that is, a standard, western seven-note scale using only notes and harmony that occur naturally within that key. Out of the top twenty-five songs, none stray from their key, and almost

---

29. Asbury, "Reckless Love."
30. Spitzer, *Mind Within the Net*, 204.

all of the top fifty songs use simple chord progressions built around the I, IV, V, and vi chords of a major scale. (For the non-musician, those are chords built around the first, fourth, fifth, or sixth notes of the scale. Upper-case Roman numerals denote major chords, while lower-case Roman numerals denote minor chords.) As with the song structures noted earlier, these patterns simply reflect the larger culture. According to a popular music theory website, Hooktheory, I-V-vi-IV is the most popular chord progression in western pop music at this time.[31] In the small sample of worship songs I analyzed, I-IV-vi-IV, a slight variation on that popular pattern, seemed to be the most common, but further analysis could reveal closer adherence to the larger cultural trend for pop harmony. All the top twenty-five songs are in major keys—even those that begin with minor chords use major diatonic melodies—and always resolve to major harmony by the song's end.

At this point, a brief primer on western harmony may help demonstrate how harmony and melody can flesh out certain meanings or feelings. Harmony works through the tensions produced in a scale. Certain notes "want" to resolve to other notes because of their musical relationships. Like an inhale followed by an exhale, the seventh note of the scale cannot release its tension until it is followed by the first note of the scale. Because of that tug from the seventh note to the first one, the strongest harmonic pull in western harmony is from the V chord, also called the dominant chord, to the I chord, also called the tonic chord. That is a movement of a fourth, so western pop songs tend to move either by fourths or between chords that approximate fourths because of the ways certain chords are able to substitute for others due to shared notes and close relationships. The second strongest pull is between the IV chord, or the subdominant, and the dominant V. The entire project of western harmony has been to exploit these notes' magnetism by increasing harmonic tension until the music can do nothing but resolve, thus making that resolution all the sweeter. In their simple way, modern worship songs participate in a long tradition of tried-and-true harmonic progressions, all designed to create the sensation of tension and release so that the listener is carried through a physical and emotional journey by the harmony.

For the most part, these worship songs succeed in these attempts to build and resolve tension through common harmonic progressions. Take the aforementioned All Sons and Daughters song, "Great Are You Lord," for example. It uses only four chords: I, IV, vi, and V. The verses and chorus consist entirely of repetitions of IV, vi, and V. The effect of that simple progression is to suspend the participant in a cycle: the pull of IV to V is

---

31. "Popular Chord Progressions."

interrupted, and thus heightened, by the detour to the minor vi chord. When that V returns to the IV instead of resolving to I, the song's overall tension grows. You may recall the earlier structural pattern that showed that, in modern worship songs, the bridge marks the height of emotional as well as thematic intensity, and "Great Are You Lord" is no exception as it uses its bridge to restate the song's thesis and broaden its application from the individual worshipper to the entire creation. Therefore, it is only fitting that the song delays resolution from V to I until that dramatic bridge. Using only four chords, the songwriters carry the participants through an emotional journey, culminating in all creation's cry of worship to God.

Country music writer Harlan Howard, writer of Patsy Cline's hit "I Fall to Pieces," held as his songwriting motto that a good country song is comprised of "three chords and the truth,"[32] and perhaps one could make the same claim for modern worship. For that reason, I hesitate to criticize the limited harmonic palette that we observe in modern worship music. However, two potential problems stand out in observing these patterns. The first is the total absence of minor keys. While some of the songs have a minor "feel" in parts of verses, none of the top songs uses completely minor keys, thus limiting the emotional expressiveness available. The Psalms contain laments, but our Sunday services have not even carved out the appropriate musical space within which to accommodate them. The second problem with these trends is the way they ignore a rich heritage of older church music that has painted with many harmonic colors throughout history. Just as we should be careful not to toss out the rich truths and lyrics of many of the older hymns, we should also not neglect the musical vocabulary they provide.

That musical vocabulary affects song melodies as well, for melodies cannot follow where harmonic progressions do not lead. When one listens to the top fifty CCLI worship songs, four broad trends stand out. First, most of the songs keep their melodies within an octave, give or take a couple of notes. Because these songs are meant to be sung by congregations, not by trained vocalists, the limited range is wise. Second, while conventional songwriting wisdom would call for a bridge to be either much lower or much higher than the choruses, modern worship song bridges tend not to exceed whatever range was established in either the chorus or the verses. Again, this trend has mostly to do with accommodating congregational vocal ranges, though for my taste, many worship songs could still benefit from more melodic variety. The final trend is closely related to the first two: what I am calling the "octave jump" trend, in which a melody is introduced at

---

32. "Harlan Howard."

one octave and then repeated later on in the song at the next octave up, for dramatic effect. This way, the worship leader and the more vocally gifted congregants can indulge in greater emotional and musical dynamics while keeping the melody on the same notes, so that the rest of the congregation can still technically sing it.

A final melodic trend common to most modern worship songs is melodic fragmentation. Rather than feature longer melodic lines that carry a musical idea across an entire phrase, most modern worship songs build melodies around short melodic motifs, which are then repeated, with slight variations, and alternated with other motifs. This melodic trend is common to much popular songwriting today. In a book I use for my introductory songwriting classes, Andrea Stolpe encourages this style of writing, especially for beginners who may struggle to demystify the process of melody writing. She calls the motif "the most important characteristic of a melody . . . like the fingerprint of the song"; she explains that, since they point the listener to the song's main musical message, repeated motifs are powerful because "the repetition helps you to remember the song melody."[33] Stolpe's observation rings especially true for modern worship music, which needs to be instantly memorable in order for congregations to sing along without the aid of printed music, once so common when the use of church hymnals was more prevalent.

While these fragmented melody lines are useful and even necessary in our world of screen-projected lyrics and rapidly changing digital music releases, it is still worth considering how these disconnected melodies contribute to the content of these songs. Anglican theologian N. T. Wright has commented on this trend, relating fragmented melodies to fragmented doctrines:

> I like to challenge Christians . . . to think about the songs they sing and the music they use. . . . I do think that some of the things we use at the moment have . . . capitulated totally to postmodernity in terms of destroying the narrative structure both of the words and of the music. The repetition of a few musical phrases, and the tossing together of words which are vaguely Christian devotional words, but which don't actually produce a narrative of any sort—I think we need to be awfully careful about going there.[34]

---

33. Stolpe and Stolpe, *Beginning Songwriting*, 50–51.
34. Wright and Walt, "N. T. Wright Interview."

In other words, for Wright, a through-line melody leads to a through-line theology—theology that has narrative cohesion—whereas a disjointed melody leads to disjointed doctrine.

Wright's critique may come across as curmudgeonly, but his caution deserves attention. Where enjambment can create interesting poetic effects for poetry on the page, the line in a song is governed by the ear. Those short, musical phrases limit the writer to short grammatical phrases, which cannot help but have an effect on the expression of theology. For example, "Build My Life" by Housefires builds its verse on a series of sentence fragments that speak of worthiness and the name of Jesus. The fragments make sense in context of the overall song and the worship service, but on their own, they fall apart. Who is worthy, and why? And just what are we saying about Jesus—that his name is above all other names, or something else yet to be added in a follow-up phrase? Add to the musical fragmentation the trend of projecting only one line at a time onto the church lyrics display, and it is easy to see why N. T. Wright might be concerned. Narrative and theological coherence are at least related to grammatical and musical coherence, if not directly affected by it.

SONG AS INCARNATE WORD

I began this study in the hopes that I might discover some principles for the redemption of modern worship music by analyzing the ways in which popular worship songs engage the full person—mind, soul, and body—in an act of worship, thereby incarnating some aspect of their message. Because sound waves are physical; because congregants raise their voices and move their bodies; and because metaphor, structure, repetition, and music engage our minds at intellectual, emotional, and physical levels; all worship services have an incarnational component. Through song, we can rewrite our brain's memories, create and release emotional tension, and even build frameworks for theological understanding. The form is not incidental or secondary to the content. The form, in many cases, determines the content, and it certainly determines what congregants experience and remember of that content.

In truth, I had also hoped for a revelation of the sort Jonathan Culler spoke of in reading Hopkins's poetry. In looking for the "incarnational effects" of song, I hoped that some of these worship songs would appear more meaningful after closer analysis than they do on the surface. While some songs have surprised and encouraged me, I've mostly come away with the sense that songs *do* exercise a power far beyond their lyrical content and that

Christian artists have a responsibility to wield that power well. Certainly, the ability of harmonic movement to facilitate emotional movement or the effectiveness of a single fresh metaphor in a sea of familiar ones has reenergized my commitment to creating music that will draw listeners to God's beauty. Culler posits that "the historical connection of lyric [poetry] with song might provide a salutary corrective model" for engaging lyric poetry,[35] but my analysis has convinced me that the same historical connection might provide a "corrective model" for worship songwriters to approach their work from within the framework of lyric poetry. For Culler, the lyric poem is very near to a kind of liturgy because of its "ritualistic dimensions," including the "lyric address and invocation, and sound patterning of all kinds."[36] Culler goes so far as to say that lyric poetry evokes something like the supernatural because it presupposes "the enchantment of the world—a world inhabited by sentient forces, a world before the flight of the gods."[37] Christians, of course, already believe in such a world, a world that Alexander Schmemann called "shot through with the presence of God."[38]

When I first read Schmemann's words as a student in David Naugle's Christian Worldview class, my perspective of the universe shifted. I saw God's presence shining through every bit of creation, and nowhere did this affect me more profoundly than in my studies of literature and music. Through these two art forms, I came to understand beauty as an apologetic, for through the superfluous joy found in form and sound, I gained a glimpse of God's superfluous love and saw evidence of an artistic Creator's hand at work. For me, reuniting music and poetry is akin to uniting body and soul or wine and blood. When we engage song as a poetic whole, we cannot ignore the ineffable qualities of a musical experience and the deeper truths those qualities imply. Indeed, we may find ourselves encountering a world "shot through" with God's presence. Let that be a challenge to all Christian songwriters, but especially to those who create music for congregational worship. Songs, perhaps more than any other art form, illuminate metaphysical mysteries by transforming word into flesh in an almost sacramental fashion. Christian artists must faithfully steward that priestly duty.

---

35. Culler, *Theory of the Lyric*, 353.
36. Culler, *Theory of the Lyric*, 350.
37. Culler, *Theory of the Lyric*, 351.
38. Schmemann, *For the Life of the World*, 16.

BIBLIOGRAPHY

"CCLI Top 100." *Song Select by CCLI*. 2020. https://songselect.ccli.com/search/results?List=top100&CurrentPage=1&PageSize=100.

Citron, Francesca M. M., et al. "Conventional Metaphors in Longer Passages Evoke Affective Brain Response." *NeuroImage* 139 (2016) 218–30.

Culler, Jonathan D. *Theory of the Lyric*. 2015. Reprint, Cambridge: Harvard University Press, 2017.

Desai, Rutvik H., et al. "A Piece of the Action: Modulation of Sensory-Motor Regions by Action Idioms and Metaphors." *NeuroImage* 83 (2013) 862–69.

"Harlan Howard." *Songwriters Hall of Fame*. https://www.songhall.org/profile/Harlan_Howard.

King, Martin Luther, Jr. "I Have A Dream." Washington, DC: US National Archives and Records Administration, 1963.

Paul, Annie Murphy. "Your Brain on Fiction." *New York Times*, March 17, 2012. http://www.nytimes.com/2012/03/18/opinion/sunday/the-neuroscience-of-your-brain-on-fiction.html.

"Popular Chord Progressions." *Hooktheory*. https://www.hooktheory.com/theorytab/common-chord-progressions.

Schmemann, Alexander. *For the Life of the World: Sacraments and Orthodoxy*. 1963. Reprint, Crestwood, NY: St. Vladimir's Seminary, 2004.

Spitzer, Manfred. *The Mind within the Net: Models of Learning, Thinking, and Acting*. Cambridge, MA: MIT Press, 2000.

Stolpe, Andrea, and Jan Stolpe. *Beginning Songwriting: Writing Your Own Lyrics, Melodies, and Chords*. Boston: Berklee, 2015.

"Textalyser: Keyword Analysis, Content Optimization, and Word Count Tool." *SEOScout*. http://textalyser.net/index.php?lang=en#analysis.

Wright, N. T., and J. D. Walt. "N. T. Wright Interview on Worship, Baptism, Justification, and Atheism." *Seedbed*, October 10, 2016. http://www.seedbed.com/n-t-wright-interview-worship-baptism-justification-atheism.

DISCOGRAPHY

All Sons and Daughters. "Great Are You Lord." MP3 audio. Track 4 on *Live*, Integrity, 2013.

Andrews, Meredith. "Open Up the Heavens." MP3 audio. Track 1 on *Worth it All*, Word, 2013.

Asbury, Cory. "Reckless Love." MP3 audio. Track 1 on *Reckless Love*, Bethel Music, 2017.

Big Daddy Weave. "The Lion and the Lamb." MP3 audio. Track 5 on *Beautiful Offerings*, Word, 2015.

David Crowder Band. "How He Loves." MP3 audio. Track 10 on *Church Music*, Sixsteps Records, 2009.

Getty, Keith, and Kristyn Getty. "In Christ Alone." MP3 audio. Track 4 on *In Christ Alone*, Getty Music, 2007.

Hillsong United. "Oceans (Where Feet May Fail)." MP3 audio. Track 4 on *Zion*, Hillsong Music and Capitol CMG, 2013.

Hillsong Worship. "Who You Say I Am." MP3 audio. Track 1 on *There Is More*, Hillsong Music and Capitol CMG, 2017.

Housefires. "Build My Life." MP3 audio. Track 8 on *Housefires III*, Housefires, 2016.

McMillan, John Mark, and Sarah McMillan. "King of My Heart." MP3 audio. Track 3 on *You Are the Avalanche*, Lionhawk, 2015.

Maher, Matt. "Lord, I Need You." MP3 audio. Track 4 on *All the People Said Amen*, Essential, 2013.

Tomlin, Chris. "Amazing Grace (My Chains Are Gone)." MP3 audio. Track 11 on *See the Morning*, Sparrow and Sixsteps Records, 2006.

———. "Good Good Father." MP3 audio. Track 1 on *Never Lose Sight*, Sixsteps Records, 2015.

Townend, Stuart. "How Deep the Father's Love for Us." MP3 audio. Track 9 on *Say the Word*, Integrity, 1997.

Wickham, Phil. "This Is Amazing Grace." MP3 audio. Track 4 on *The Ascension*, Warner Chappell, 2013.

19

Transcendent Aesthetics

Training Our Spiritual Senses with St. Augustine

TAVNER THREATT

Delight of the sense is one thing; delight through the sense is something else.[1]
—St. Augustine

Formal philosophical study pairs well with being a specialty coffee trainer, a sommelier, and a teacher, at least in my experience. It might be an easy assumption that the service industry serves a merely utilitarian function during college and graduate studies. However, no accident of circumstance accounts for how much time and energy I have devoted to the qualities and nuances of taste. I'd like my parents to know once and for all that this is St. Augustine's fault. By the transitive property, it is also the fault of the teacher who first introduced me to St. Augustine—Professor David Naugle. Together they taught me that the human heart is full of the energy of desire and God created the world in an ordered way, as a sign pointing back to

---

1. Augustine, *Divine Providence and the Problem*, 139.

himself.[2] The philosophical journey, according to St. Augustine, consists of learning to direct our affection toward what is most worthy. Philosophy, Socrates tells us, begins in wonder. For St. Augustine, wonder—transcendent desire—is excited by encounters with beauty. Through the senses we are drawn beyond the sensory. Sadly, we tend to miss the opportunity because of misplaced desire and its consequences. When we confuse that which presents beauty with Beauty itself, we are left with a lingering sense of emptiness. Wisdom means training our minds to discern the difference and training our hearts to follow. We often, however, overlook the part our senses play. St. Augustine admits he learned these things from experience. He opens his *Confessions* with the prayerful words, "You stir man to take pleasure in praising you, because you have made us for yourself, and our heart is restless until it rests in you."[3] Implied in this elegant phrase is a journey marked by misplaced desires and unsatisfied longing due to the misuse of the bodily senses. The chapters that follow this prayer are his way of saying to us, *I know how your disappointment feels because I've been there too. Come with me and I will show you the way out.* For St. Augustine, beauty beckons beneath the surface of sensory experience and illuminates the path to true joy by giving spiritual delight.

The power of beauty cuts straight to the heart. It reaches into the core of who we are and transforms us. For St. Augustine, gaining wisdom is an exercise of the mind and the heart together, as we learn to exercise right judgment to order our desires according to what is most satisfying. In the opening line of book 6 of his treatise *On Music*, St. Augustine advises, "We must not hate what is below us, but rather with God's help put it in its right place, setting in right order what is below us, ourselves, and what is above us, and not being offended by the lower, but delighting only in the higher."[4] Just judgments of value are a prerequisite of true enjoyment. We don't take an active enough role in the aesthetic judgment of our experiences because we misunderstand the depth of our desire. If all we want is a little entertainment, we can't expect to be happy. The result of our failure to judge rightly what is better and worse is that we make a mess of love.[5] St. Augustine teaches us to order our love according to what is most worthy by understanding and ordering our delight.

---

2. In many ways the essay that follows could be summarized as a closer look at the aesthetic dimension of the book by David Naugle, *Reordered Love, Reordered Lives.*

3. Augustine, *Confessions* 1.1.1.

4. Augustine, *De Musica* 6.10.29.

5. From Dr. Naugle's precedent, I hear the ringing phrase from Switchfoot, "Ammunition."

UNDERSTANDING GOODNESS

> *You must change your life.*
> Rainer Maria Rilke, "The Archaic Torso of Apollo"[6]

For St. Augustine, we don't fall in love—we are formed to love. The thought that we are merely passive in our loves is a romantic and modern notion—or is it? Our innate capacity for loving is immense, and we are all too eager. No matter how bad we are at evaluating what is worthy, our lives take the shape of what we desire. If only we could see more clearly what is most worthy of our love, we might be able to find what we are looking for. The result of blindness—sometimes willful—is that we mistake what is able to satisfy our deep desire and end up feeling empty. St. Augustine is no stranger to this experience, as he tells in his timeless *Confessions*. He shows us that it is through learning, both from experience and from reason—under the influence of ever-present grace—what is most worthy of our desire that we become able to love well. Love is a natural and proportionate value response to that which is seen as worthy.[7] The problem isn't the energy of our love but the orientation of our hearts, which is influenced by the degree of clarity of our minds. The reason we love lesser things is either that we haven't experienced greater things or that, for a variety of reasons, we haven't seen them adequately for what they are. Paying attention takes conscious effort. Do we even know where to look? We often mistake what will be able to satisfy our desire because we do not understand what we want. For instance, we admit "beauty is fleeting," but lurking beneath that sentiment is the fact that we don't want it to be. What is it then? Socrates tells us, "love is wanting to possess the good forever."[8] Abiding goodness is what we are searching for when we look for happiness.

Aristotle opens his *Nicomachean Ethics* with "Every art and every inquiry, and similarly every action and pursuit, is thought to aim at some good; and for this reason the good has rightly been declared to be that at which all things aim."[9] Goodness is what we are seeking in all our pursuits, and beauty entices us toward the good. Conversely, the abiding character of goodness, it could be said, is the true "tell" of beauty. Learning to perceive that tell is paramount. Goodness, like beauty, is experienced through the senses and understood first by intuition, but it can and should be evaluated

---

6. Rilke, "Archaic Torso of Apollo," in Wood, *Nature, Artforms*, 91.
7. See Hildebrand, *Heart*; *Aesthetics*.
8. Plato, *Symposium* 206a; 204d–e.
9. Aristotle, *Nicomachean Ethics* 1.1.1–3 (935).

rationally by honest reflection. How else could we know that our value judgments—which we often make intuitively, in the moment—are actually *good* judgments?

Value judgments happen so frequently and instinctively in the interaction between our hearts and minds that we forget it is a rational skill we can intentionally cultivate. The stakes are high because the results of these subtle evaluations guide nearly all our decisions. Making appropriate value judgments is how we keep ourselves from disappointment, how we keep our love safe from waste and misuse. Therefore, it is important not only to pay attention to what we experience but also to how, and why, we respond the way we do. We often cultivate bias unknowingly, out of this self-preservation. We cling to our judgments because they inform what we love.[10] Yet, if our previous judgments were wrong, then we come to each new experience predisposed to judge badly. We can trap ourselves in a cycle of disappointment.

How can we determine what goods are greater or lesser than others? Through the reciprocal motion of experience and rational reflection. The unmistakable quality of splendor, which the truth alone possesses, is difficult to impersonate. We build on our knowledge of the good with each new experience of it. The trick is seeking joy instead of hollow pleasure. We should be motivated because, while shallow pleasure tends to quickly leave the bitter taste of disappointment in our mouths, enduring delight comes from experiencing what is truly good. By learning to rationally understand the enduring character of goodness as it presents itself in aesthetic experience, we can train ourselves to love only what is most worthy.

St. Augustine offers as much insight and eloquence on the topic of aesthetic experience as anyone in the Western tradition. In fact, he is a fountain of inspiration for thinkers even into the twentieth century.[11] As it turns out, philosophers do have hearts. His *Confessions* testifies that a life of chasing sensory pleasures and worldly power—with remarkable achievement, I might add—continually fails to satisfy the heart's deepest longings. As a successful academic, he warns against the dangers of such ambition. Becoming a successful expert does not necessarily mean one knows oneself. In his eventual encounter with Christ in the ancient Catholic tradition, St.

---

10. Unsurprisingly, it is an Augustinian maxim that *to know is to love*. See *On Christian Doctrine* and *The Teacher*, among many other places. The inverse of this maxim is revealing: we can have no true knowledge of that which we hate.

11. In phenomenology especially, through his explicit influence on Martin Heidegger and company—Gabriel Marcel, Jean-Paul Sartre, Albert Camus, Jacques Derrida, and Jean-Luc Marion, among others. See Smith, *On the Road with Saint Augustine*; Caputo and Scanion, *God, the Gift, and Postmodernism*; Paulo, *Influence of Augustine on Heidegger*; Smith, *Speech and Theology*.

Augustine finally finds satisfying answers for both his head and his heart. When St. Augustine famously says, "You stir man to take pleasure in praising you, because you have made us for yourself, and our heart is restless until it rests in you,"[12] he recognizes that all goodness is God's goodness. This epiphany proved fitting to his energetic quest for happiness. The timeless popularity of *Confessions* indicates that his experience is not unique.

To rightly understand where St. Augustine arrived, we must look at where he came from. Before finding his way to the church under the influence of St. Ambrose, St. Augustine was convinced of the teachings of the philosophical-religious sect called Manicheism—a movement condemned as heretical because it denied the humanity of Christ. The Manicheans prioritized immaterial, spiritual insight, condemning physical, bodily reality as evil. St. Augustine eventually left because he couldn't deny that it was through tangible experience he was drawn beyond the mere material in the first place.[13] On the one hand, St. Augustine could not reconcile a philosophy that minimized the value of bodily experience with the desires that drove him most deeply. On the other, even the greatest exploits of pleasure offered only fleeting, pseudo-resolution to the inner drama of his heart. To resonate with his experience, materiality and immateriality needed to exist in an ordered relation. As beings composed of both spirit and matter, perhaps it is only our limited self-understanding that creates such divisions in the first place.

St. Augustine soon found that the solution lay in taking the sensory experiences of goodness not as terminating in themselves but as an opening to transcendence of the temporal and spatial. Perceiving this dilemma of the human condition, many other traditions recommend differing solutions, often emphasizing one aspect and avoiding the other. St. Augustine first found some truth in a tradition that maximized the invisible, or spiritual, and minimized the role of the body along with the whole physical realm.

---

12. Saint Augustine, *Confessions* 1.1.1.

13. See the admonition of St. Paul in Colossians 2:16–23. Often ironically, systems of thought that devalue the physical realm tend to also lead to practices that divorce spiritual dignity from human experience, creating a kind of confirmation bias. If the body doesn't matter, why not get drunk, take psychedelic drugs, and sleep around? When the motive for putting moral parameters around physical behavior disappears, ironically, the potential spiritual richness of those experiences also fades away. Hence. St. Augustine's existential disappointment with sex and ambition. When we forget that the natural end of the physical senses is spiritual experience, we may then feel morally obligated to condemn the pleasures of the senses entirely, rather than rightly ordering them toward their natural end of spiritual dignity. St. Augustine's ordered delight provides the solution to escape the cycle.

However, that felt dishonest.[14] Equally dissatisfying are other traditions that simply reduce the concept of man to something more manageable. By either aiming to sacralize bodily desire or to ignore our innate capacity to experience spiritual joy through the bodily senses, all alternatives that articulate a reduction of the dual nature of human desire have an air of inauthenticity. If in our weakness we succumb to the lusts of the body, this does not mean that matter itself is evil or that desire is evil. It means something more subtle about the capability of our will to be corrupted by ignorance and deceit (Rom 1:24–25 ESV).

For St. Augustine, it was finally the Christian tradition, which teaches the divinely given dignity of matter, that reconciled the issue. Christianity neither worships the physical nor attempts to merely get beyond it. The Christian story claims that God created the world and called it "good." Then he himself entered into it, after its purity became marred by the corruption of man's will by sin, to reconcile all creation to himself. Therefore, only in Christ do all things hold together (Col 1:17). This story proved finally compelling for the wandering St. Augustine. Sin accounted for the unsatisfying result of disordered material desire, for his frustrated longing for the spiritual. Enduring wonder accompanies the mystery of the Incarnation and its implications.[15] In *On Christian Doctrine*, St. Augustine writes, "by means of corporal and temporal things we may comprehend the eternal and spiritual."[16] God's nature can be known through creation,[17] but without Christ he remains inaccessibly transcendent. When he brings the Real Presence (Image/"Icon") of the Father into our sensible experience,[18] we can not only know but also participate in his divine life. Against the Manicheans, without the divine descent, we can never truly ascend.

Some have alleged that traces of Platonic dualism can still be seen in St. Augustine's Christian synthesis. This allegation is based on false assumptions about both schools of thought. Generally speaking, while St. Augustine does owe much of his intellectual formation to the Neoplatonic tradition, he finally saw its deficits completed by Christ. In book 7 of *Confessions*, St.

---

14. "Superior things are self-evidently better than inferior. Yet with a sounder judgment I held that all things taken together are better than superior things by themselves" (Augustine, *Confessions*, 7.13.19).

15. See Athanasius, *On the Incarnation*.

16. Augustine, *On Christian Doctrine* 1.4.4., which includes references to 2 Cor 5:6 and Rom 1:20.

17. "For his invisible attributes, namely his eternal power and divine nature, have been clearly perceived, ever since the creation of the world, in the things that have been made" (Rom 1:20 ESV).

18. "He is the image of the invisible God" (Col 1:15 ESV).

Augustine lists the various places of similarity and distinction between the "books of the Platonists" and Holy Scripture, namely with regard to the doctrine of the Incarnation.[19] St. Augustine was by no means an uncritical recipient of the Neoplatonic tradition, but he saw the revelation of God in Christ as essential.

In his *Placing Aesthetics*, Robert E. Wood has offered a history of aesthetics that gives context to the Platonic lineage of St. Augustine's thought. Against the standard interpretation of Platonic dualism, for Plotinus, who was a prime influence on St. Augustine, "it is as Beauty that the One is a Real Presence in sensorily given things, healing the *chorismos*, the gap between the Forms and the sensory appearance."[20] In the Neoplatonic understanding, Beauty itself is manifest to the bodily senses. Furthermore, Plato's theory of beauty is clearly the source for the Neoplatonic understanding. In *Phaedrus*, Plato says that beauty alone has the privilege of being visible, which makes it the most loved of the Forms.[21] *Phaedrus* and *Symposium* both articulate that Beauty is the means and the end to which the philosophical mind ascends to wisdom following an erotic desire for the Good. It is by the ordered ascent of love from beautiful things to Beauty itself that knowledge culminates in a kind of aesthetic mystical vision.[22] When we see beauty, we are given new eyes, so to speak.

Wood explains,

> For Plotinus, following Diotima in Plato's *Symposium*, this One radiates itself in all things as Beauty, as coherence, the harmony of each and all. The initially experienced intoxication associated with sensory surface is suffused with a sense of the ultimate expressivity. . . . The sensory surface is therefore not simply color and pattern, but colored pattern illuminated by an underlying depth. For Plotinus there is nothing beautiful that does not express something more than beautiful.[23]

This "underlying depth" is precisely what radiates from particular beautiful forms, giving them a transcendent character. The truly beautiful is never mere surface or mere object. When we see something beautiful, Beauty looks back at us. We may not realize it at first, but encountering Beauty evokes our transcendent love and raises us to its Splendor. Wood remarks on the progressive nature of aesthetic experience in the Platonic tradition,

---

19. Augustine, *Confessions* 7.9.13–10.16.
20. Wood, *Placing Aesthetics*, 97.
21. Plato, *Phaedrus* 250d–e.
22. See Socrates's climatic speech in Plato, *Symposium*, 484–94, esp. 210–12.
23. Wood, *Placing Aesthetics*, 97–98.

saying, "one cannot expect to reach the higher levels of contemplation unless one learns to contemplate the beauties given through sensation."[24] There is a hierarchical nature to the encounter with beauty, a gradual attunement of our hearts that allows us to see. This is adapted in St. Augustine's thought in the form of *ordered delight*. For example, it may be difficult for someone who has little intensity of experience with the beauty of nature or art or love to understand what is meant by the language of transcendent experience. Encountering beauty transforms us because it directs what we love, and what we love shapes our life.

Wood makes sure to indicate that St. Augustine is clear about where Platonic thought is incomplete. In *Confessions*, St. Augustine states that "very much of Christianity was in the Neoplatonists. . . . But . . . that there is one central omission: that the Logos became flesh."[25] For Platonism, the encounter with Beauty causes a contemplative ascent to the Forms. The line between the ideal realm and physical experience is perforated by beauty but the ascent is intellectual. For Christianity, the divine descended fully into human nature, meaning the Christian story is nothing if not a case against dualism.[26] The similarities between the Platonic tradition and the Christian one are worth noting but so is the central difference. The similarities between Platonic articulation of the transformative experience of manifest Beauty and the Christian understanding of "real presence" in the sacraments is uncanny. This is hermeneutically important for understanding both the Platonic tradition and the history of Christian theology, since both are often falsely reduced to metaphysical dualism.[27] While some Platonic texts are used to construct a contradicting view,[28] the important thing hermeneutically is how they are assembled into one unified whole by Plato's central notion of love.[29] In Christianity, however, there is no place for mere

---

24. Wood, *Placing Aesthetics*, 99.

25. Wood, *Placing Aesthetics*, 102; cf. Augustine, *Confessions* 7.9.

26. Students of Dr. Naugle will easily recall this theme from his course "Developing the Christian Mind."

27. The side of dualism has probably gotten the most airtime in philosophical history by thinkers like Nietzsche (who also loved to chide Christianity for alleged dualism). Yet, along with Wood, there seems to be a renaissance advocating that Plato's thought actually sets forth a more holistic view, usually emphasizing the central role of *eros*. See Pickstock, *After Writing*; Milbank et al., "Introduction"; Pabst, *Metaphysics*; and, again, Wood, "Art and Truth."

28. See Smith, *Speech and Theology*, 170–76.

29. Plato himself promotes a vision of "the Whole" as the aim of inquiry. For example, "anyone who can achieve a unified vision is dialectical, and anyone who can't isn't" (Plato, *Republic*, 537c). For the central notion of orienting philosophical *eros* in *Republic*, see 4.436; 5.458–59, 474c–76, 479–80. Once seen, it's seen everywhere.

cognitive ascent. Divine hospitality in the Incarnation and the cross invites us into participation in the divine life initiated by the Word-made-flesh, God-with-us (see John 1:1–34).[30]

TRANSCENDENT DESIRE: ORDERING LOVE BY ORDERING DELIGHT

> *Glory be to God for dappled things-*
> *For skies of couple-color as a brinded cow;*
> *... And all trades, their gear and tackle and trim*
> *... He fathers-forth whose beauty is past change:*
> *Praise him.*
>
> Gerard Manley Hopkins, "Pied Beauty"[31]

Following his baptism by St. Ambrose in Milan, St. Augustine developed a massive repertoire of philosophical and theological writing that has influenced the West as much as any other thinker. Though his writings and their influence are vast, they could perhaps all be said to center around one key idea: *ordered delight*. This concept could, and should, function as the unitive, interpretative key to everything from his metaphysics to his epistemology, his ethics, and his aesthetics. It is precisely from the vantage of aesthetics that St. Augustine frames his other modes of thought. Beauty opens transcendent goodness and truth to us and draws us beyond ourselves to experience and to know reality. The quantity, elegance, and devotion of his words on beauty help us to keep in view the irreducible relationship between his aesthetics and his metaphysics. Examination of his thought through the lens of ordered delight yields layers of substantial insight that prove continual relevance.

The opening of St. Augustine's work called *On Christian Teaching* serves as a simple introduction to this thought as a whole. While the aim of the work is to demonstrate training in Christianity, the paradigm has far-reaching philosophical import. He begins the project by setting up a fundamental contrast between *use* and *enjoyment*. It is best to employ his own words:

> Some things are to be enjoyed, others to be used, and there are others which are to be enjoyed and used. Those things which are to be enjoyed make us blessed. Those things which are to

---

30. See also Boersma, *Heavenly Participation; Violence, Hospitality, and the Cross.*
31. Hopkins, *Poems*, 28.

TRANSCENDENT AESTHETICS   269

> be used help and, as it were, sustain us as we move toward blessedness in order that we may gain and cling to those things which make us blessed. If we who enjoy and use things, being placed in the midst of things of both kinds, wish to enjoy those things which should be used, our course will be impeded and sometimes deflected, so that we are hindered in obtaining those things which are to be enjoyed, or even prevented altogether, shackled by an inferior love.[32]

Here, he articulates a hierarchical structure of our experience of the world, which directly influences our happiness. Our ultimate happiness depends on ordering our affections and actions according to what is most deserving, meaning that, in St. Augustine's terms, our state of blessedness, or deep happiness, turns on delight.[33] He is setting up a rich, trinitarian system with ethics implying epistemology and depending upon aesthetics.

His words are meant to motivate and to warn. He advises enjoying, loving, and delighting in things that will lead to deep thriving, and he warns against the real dangers to happiness and well-being that originate in loving or trying to delight in the wrong things. Now, one might expect from a thinker with Platonic sensibilities that he would advise turning away from the world of sensory pleasures and the desires associated with them for the sake of higher contemplation. However, his refusal to turn away from, and instead utilize, the sensory demonstrates his particular Christian genius; that is, he does not make the move that so many other traditions and systems of thought do at this point. Instead, he advises a hierarchical system of enjoyment that, incorporating the material and immaterial aspects of reality, implies the wholeness of human experience. For St. Augustine, this means that the bodily senses, contemplative reason, and moral goodness must work together in unity. His account may seem complex at first, but the more it is explored the more remarkably intuitive it reveals itself to be in accordance with experience. He defines his terms:

> To enjoy something is to cling to it with love for its own sake. To use something, however, is to employ it in obtaining that which you love, provided that it is worthy of love. For an illicit use should be called rather a waste or an abuse.[34]

---

32. Augustine, *On Christian Doctrine* 1.3.3.
33. "For where your treasure is, there your heart will be also" (Matt 6:21 ESV); inversely apt are the lines from a song by Jon Foreman, "Caroline."
34. Augustine, *On Christian Doctrine* 1.4.4.

Here he maps the philosophical reasons for unhappiness,[35] what for Christians is meant by sin. Sin separates creature from Creator by human idolatry. Loving created things for their sake alone—reducing or rejecting transcendent joy for fleeting pleasure—violates the purpose of nature to reveal transcendence. It is often a product of self-deception or willful ignorance (see Rom 1).[36] What St. Augustine means is that aesthetic objects ought not be loved in themselves. Rather, beautiful things ought to be embraced as vehicles of transcendence. Directly put, it is through rightly using beautiful things that we are able to know, experience, and delight in God. Delight in God is the state that represents our greatest good. This is the Hebraic idea of living in *shalom*, ultimate metaphysical wholeness, or deep happiness.[37] For St. Augustine, we miss wholeness because we abuse, and waste, the natural good toward which the world points. The true question behind orienting our desire is: Do we truly want to be happy?[38]

TRANSCENDENT AESTHETIC PERCEPTION

> *Eyes and ears are bad witnesses to people if they have barbarian souls.*
> Heraclitus, B107[39]

Beneath this discussion resides the problem of perception. For St. Augustine, the ground or condition for perceiving the transcendent is *purity of heart*.[40] Purifying the heart from the improper use of things is the primary way we tune our spiritual senses toward being able to see and enjoy God—Beauty Himself. How is this accomplished? As we have already covered, this happens, first, by opening oneself to the possibility of encountering

---

35. Jean-Luc Marion picks up on St. Augustine's distinction here and develops it for the language of philosophical icons and idols. "In the idol, the gaze of man is frozen in its mirror; in the icon, the gaze of man is lost in the invisible gaze that visibly envisages him.... In this sense, the icon makes visible only by giving rise to an infinite gaze.... The essential in the icon—the intention that envisages—comes to it from elsewhere, or comes to it as that elsewhere whose invisible strangeness saturates the visibility of the face with meaning" (Marion, *God Without Being*, 20–24).

36. See also Augustine, *On Christian Doctrine* 3.10.15.

37. See Naugle, *Reordered Love, Reordered Lives*, 18–29.

38. A variation of Jesus's question to the man lame for thirty-eight years: "Do you want to be healed?" (John 5:6 ESV). Also, C. S. Lewis reminds us, "It would seem Our Lord finds our desires not too strong, but too weak . . . like an ignorant child who wants to go on making mud pies in a slum because he cannot imagine what is meant by the offer of a holiday at the sea. We are far too easily pleased" (Lewis, *Weight of Glory*, 26).

39. Curd, *Presocratics Reader*, 42.

40. "Blessed are the pure in heart, for they shall see God" (Matt 5:8 ESV).

the transcendent. This means aiming to align oneself with the transcendent intention for all of nature, even human nature itself. Classically, this is called virtue. The state of virtue is characterized by cultivating the seven cardinal virtues and avoiding the seven deadly sins. Seeing nature properly involves living in accordance with our own moral nature. In short, if we want to be able to see beauty, then we must position ourselves with humility with regard to our place within the transcendent cosmos. We must practice courage, justice, self-control, and practical wisdom along with faith, hope, and love. Also, we must avoid pride, lust, greed, wrath, envy, sloth, and gluttony. The latter traits will lead to misuse or abuse of others, the self, and the world, effectively enclosing one's vantage in an ever-constricting noose of self-exaltation. We make terrible gods, but, like Adam and Eve, we want to try transcending human nature. Making habits of virtue will open one up to greater freedom and the possibility of encountering the transcendent, including transcendent presence in the immanent. Put another way, what we see seems to require the consent of our hearts.[41]

Humility stands archetypically for all virtue since all virtue depends upon it. Cultivating humility allows us to see what is given, which is hidden by pride. St. Augustine agrees with the classical position that practicing the virtues provides clarity for the mind, as is indicated by the speech on the effects of the virtues which precedes his discussion of the criteria for aesthetic judgment in book 6 of *On Music*.[42] Yet is St. Augustine equating moral purity with the recognition of beauty? Not exactly. The Christian vision of human flourishing depends on grace initiated by God; by this the redeemed mind will be truly humbled and purified. With one's vision transformed, the eyes become clear to witness greater revelation of the divine. St. Augustine, the Doctor of Grace, says, "Although to the healthy and pure internal eye He is everywhere present, He saw fit to appear to those whose eye is weak and impure, and even to fleshly eyes."[43] Moral purity—summarized by humility—would be impossible if not for the activity of grace. On the other hand, as long as we have life, we are never totally incapable of experiencing beauty—praise God! So we always have grace, and we always need more. We can willingly turn our eyes away from beauty or we can exercise humility and care, cultivating purity of heart and the proper attention of the mind. We are then able to experience beauty in increasing measure. In one of the

---

41. This is picked up in the twentieth century by Heidegger in his concept of *care*, which he admits originated in reading St. Augustine. See Heidegger, *History of the Concept of Time*, 302. For a deeper look, see Engelland, "Augustinian Elements," 263–75.

42. See Augustine, *On Music* 6.14.48–58.

43. Augustine, *On Christian Doctrine* 1.12.11.

most memorable passages in *Confessions*, St. Augustine nearly sings a prayer demonstrating purity of heart:

> But when I love you, what do I love? It is not physical beauty nor temporal glory nor the brightness of light dear to earthly eyes, nor the sweet melodies of all kinds of songs, nor the gentle odor of flowers and ointments and perfumes, nor manna or honey, nor limbs welcoming the embraces of the flesh; it is not these I love when I love my God. Yet there is a light I love, and a food, and a kind of embrace when I love my God—a light, voice, odor, food, embrace of my inner man, where my soul is floodlit by light which space cannot contain, where there is sound that time cannot seize, where there is a perfume which no breeze disperses, where there is a taste for food no amount of eating can lessen, and where there is a bond of union that no satiety can part. That is what I love when I love my God.[44]

Does it seem that he is saying the flesh and the senses do not matter? No, he is saying that they give beyond their physical capacity: They are a gateway to the soul.[45] In fact, they are the necessary pointers to the source of their own meaning. In a sense, he is sanctifying the classical tradition by integrating fully the Christian mystery of the Incarnation. The point is that St. Augustine advocates aiming our love at only what can measure up to the soul's deep yearning. The aroma of a rose fades. An open bottle of wine spoils. Though we have come to expect change, we are naturally disappointed by it. Knowledge of death, even contentment with it, does not prevent us from shedding tears at a funeral. Our experience of beauty convinces us that temporality is permeable; it reminds us that we were made for the eternal.

If the heart is pure—if our disposition toward the beautiful is untainted by vice—sensory pleasure offers potential for an experience of beauty beyond itself. It creates the potential for greater *use*, in St. Augustine's sense of the word. This means also that there is potential danger if the heart is not pure. Metaphysical beauty inevitably involves dangers of various kinds.[46] Perhaps, the greater the beauty the greater the danger, especially from misuse or abuse. More glory brings greater potential for idolatry. Does virtue

---

44. Augustine, *Confessions* 10.6.8.

45. See Aristotle's *On the Soul*, where Aristotle asserts the necessity of the body for thought.

46. One might think of many examples from the ocean to the vulnerability of love. A scene from *The Chronicles of Narnia* comes to mind. Young Susan and Lucy express they are nervous about meeting Aslan, the lion. Mr. Beaver reassures them, "Safe? . . . Who said anything about safe? 'Course he isn't safe. But he's good" (Lewis, *Lion, the Witch, and the Wardrobe*, 80).

then require avoidance of the greatest sensory goods? By no means! Instead, they require greater care and protection.[47] In fact, the danger must remain for virtue to be possible.[48] St. Augustine's aesthetics employ an incarnational vision that rejects the Manichean mistake. He sees all good things as having their source in God and their purpose as revealing him. He teaches us how to see potential idols as icons instead.[49]

TRANSCENDENT AESTHETIC JUDGMENT

> *To what serve mortal beauty . . .*
> *See: it does this: keeps warm*
> *Men's wits to the things that are*
> Gerard Manley Hopkins, "To What Serves Mortal Beauty?"[50]

St. Augustine's aesthetics are based on the ability to recognize greater or lesser goodness as a greater or lesser revelation of God. He calls this an object's *usefulness*. Beauty gives transcendent presence in accordance with its sensibility in an aesthetic object. Yet, all is ordered according to God's design. Beauty delights us, but ugliness rightly repulses because it dissatisfies the heart's yearning for delight in the beautiful; it points us back to the beautiful. Our reactions to the beautiful and the ugly are instinctual and, in specific objects, are conditioned by perception. We can misjudge if we fail to be humble and if we become apathetic in our anticipation of the beautiful. If we let our transcendent desire grow cold, our aesthetic sensibility also dims. Through training ourselves to recognize beauty, we learn more clearly what we truly desire because we experience greater delight.

Some experiences seem to lend themselves to aesthetic contemplation more readily. Glorious sunsets, majestic vistas, and grand symphonies all rightly move us and evoke our affection. Yet beauty also appears in ordinary places where we might not expect it. In one of St. Augustine's eloquent arguments against the material-hating Manicheans, he lists food and drink as carrying potential usefulness for delight in God—so long as they are not

---

47. For a rich defense of the biblical value and theological aesthetics of wine, see Kreglinger, *Spirituality of Wine*.

48. A classic example is that courage only exists in the presence of fear—the greater potential for fear, the greater potential for courage.

49. "If physical objects give you pleasure, praise God for them and return love to their Maker. . . . 'Him we love; he made these things and is not far distant.' For he did not create and then depart; the things derived from him and have their being in him" (Augustine, *Confessions* 4.12.18).

50. Hopkins, *Poems*, 51.

immoderately used. (This certainly makes the daily grind and mundane pay in an excellent restaurant or a coffee shop more endurable!) He goes on to employ his famous concept of evil as having no real essence to justify the potential of all nature for bearing beauty. The condition for beauty's appearance, again, is virtue, for the "concealment of the use of things is itself either an exercise of our humility or a leveling of our pride; for no nature at all is evil, and this is a name for nothing but the want of good."[51] It is because all that exists derives its existence from God that all is capable of partaking in his goodness. If a thing appears bad instead of good, it's because it is a corruption of its own nature. It is not fulfilling the end toward which its nature aims. Promiscuity distorts the unitive and generative ends of human sexuality. Faithful marriage preserves both these ends. However, our failure to perceive the natural end of something can also account for its negative appearance.[52] For example, either it is true that all coffee is hopelessly bitter and unpleasant or that bitter coffee twists the nature of what coffee is—the seed of a fruit, which should show the natural sweetness and acidity of its nature.[53] St. Augustine acknowledges also that not all things will be equal in their capacity to reveal goodness when he concludes, "from things earthly to things heavenly, from the visible to the invisible, there are some things better than others; and for this purpose are they unequal, in order that they might all exist. Now, God is such a great worker in great things that He is not less in little things."[54] Existing things bear goodness according to the capacity with which they were designed. My son's colored sketch can truly be beautiful yet possess a lesser capacity for beauty than a painting by Cezanne. Like varying containers can all be full yet unequal in size, the variety of existing things can be beautiful yet unequal in their capacity to reveal beauty. The quality of goodness is not strained[55] because it is given by an infinite Source to all according to natural creative diversity ordained by divine providence.

For St. Augustine, there even seems to be a moral obligation to judgment. St. Augustine advises us not to insult divine providence but to carefully evaluate the potential revelatory power of the goodness of each thing,

---

51. Augustine, *City of God* 11.22.

52. This implies without jest that many seemingly ordinary occupations, like the sommelier, have a priestly function to steward and protect what may carry divine presence.

53. No doubt we are all familiar with the burnt or stale taste of over-roasted or pre-ground coffee sold by popular chains or in tins at the grocery store. Drinking freshly-roasted, freshly-ground coffee from a local provider is a revelatory experience.

54. Augustine, *City of God* 11.22.

55. As Shakespeare's Portia tells Shylock, "The quality of mercy is not strain'd" (Shakespeare, *Merchant of Venice* 4.1.182). Goodness and mercy are infinitely abundant and variously applicable because they are divine attributes.

great or small. It's one thing to make the most of one's own garden; it's another to fail to admire the grandeur of the vineyard. He says that goodness may be hidden from us by pride and that it's the process of looking for the goodness of God in things that makes us humble. No learning of any kind happens without humility, without recognizing first that we do not know something. Humility enables us to see what pride conceals. The continual search for goodness hones our ability to perceive it. If we are not careful to protect our metaphysical sense of beauty, our physical senses will also shrink in perceptive capacity. Indiscretion or gluttony hides the revelatory nature of good food and drink. St. Augustine confirms the moral dimension of judgment in *On Christian Doctrine*, where he says, "He lives in justice and sanctity who is an unprejudiced assessor of the intrinsic value of things."[56] Thus, there is a dual aspect to the moral dimension of judgment: One must be unprejudiced (pure of heart) and just (in accord with reason). He further summarizes this condition with this explanation: "He is a man who has an ordinate love: he neither loves what should not be loved nor fails to love what should be loved; he neither loves more what should be loved less, loves equally what should be loved less or more, nor loves less or more what should be loved equally."[57] Our love should swell in proportion to the rightly judged worth of the object of our love.

St. Augustine offers practical tools of reason, found most directly in *On Music*, to help us to evaluate aesthetic objects. Evaluation helps us discover the reason for each object's sensory delight and, even more, its potential transcendent value. In *On Music*, as well as in other texts, St. Augustine references several values of aesthetic judgment, including *unity, balance, harmony, proportion,* and *order*. Each of these is, for St. Augustine, a sensory manifestation of metaphysical truth. Music stands as the archetypal art for the discussion because music "holds in balance time and space under transcendence,"[58] the potential for perfect harmony between sense and spirit.

A brief sketch of examples of St. Augustine's principles for aesthetic evaluation will prove useful. For instance, to demonstrate what he means by unity, in *On Genesis: A Refutation of the Manichees*, St. Augustine uses the example of the body: "If by contrast a beautiful hand, which in the body was admired even on its own, is separated from the body, not only does the hand itself forfeit its own proper grace, but the other parts are also rendered

---

56. Augustine, *On Christian Doctrine* 1.27.28.
57. Augustine, *On Christian Doctrine* 1.27.28.
58. See Pickstock, "Soul, City, and Cosmos," 243–77; Marcel, "Music According to St. Augustine," 117–24

unsightly without it."⁵⁹ Unity is a foundational criterion for the aesthetic quality of goodness because without it the object cannot be truly known. Plato saw all dialectic aimed at a vision of "the Whole." For St. Augustine, unity reflects the relational oneness of the Trinity—the source of being itself—and all objects within the universe reflect their cause. Unity is a core trait of all beautiful things as they radiate the splendor of Beauty itself.

Another example of a foundational aesthetic value is symmetry, proportion, or balance. In *On True Religion*, he gives a keen architectural example:

> We must indeed inquire what is the cause of our being dissatisfied if two windows are placed not one above the other but side by side, and one of them is greater or less than the other, for they ought to have been equal; while, if they are placed one directly above the other, even though they are unlike, the inequality does not offend us in the same way.⁶⁰

Balance serves as a core quality for aesthetic evaluation, even if the balance is not simply expressed—as is the case with asymmetrical balance. Even a small deviation can make an aesthetic object seem unbalanced and less than excellent. St. Augustine gives a humorous example following the previously cited passage in *City of God* when he writes,

> In the visible appearance of a man, if one eyebrow be shaved off, how nearly nothing is taken from the body, but how much from the beauty!⁶¹

Clearly St. Augustine is not speaking of balanced asymmetry here. He is making the case that the traits of beauty exist in everyday experience with which we can all identify, by which we all make judgments. On the ever-presence of symmetry in beautiful things, St. Augustine says, "In all the arts it is symmetry that gives pleasure, preserving unity and making the whole beautiful. Symmetry demands unity and equality, the similarity of like parts, or graded arrangements of parts which are dissimilar."⁶² This is true in the evaluation of any art. In the evaluation of specialty coffee or wine, a harmony of the various dimensions of flavor—such as acidity and sweetness, body, texture, and finish—represents higher quality. Too much acidity or sweetness can overshadow the other characteristics, but a lingering sense of balance brings delight to the palate. Likewise, when a film or a work of

---

59. Augustine, *On Genesis* 60
60. Augustine, *Of True Religion* 30.54.
61. Augustine, *City of God* 11.22.
62. Augustine, *Of True Religion* 30.54.

literature returns in the end to where it began, it causes the sense of internal development to resonate.⁶³

The similitude of the aesthetic object within itself bears a resemblance to what we can rationally know of beauty or goodness as metaphysical values. In a particularly helpful comment St. Augustine says,

> As it is, we use the absolute standard of squareness to judge the squareness of a market-place, a stone, a table or a gem. . . . The standard of all the arts is absolutely unchangeable, but the human mind, which is given the power to see the standard, can suffer the mutability of error. Clearly, then, the standard which is called truth is higher than our minds.⁶⁴

For St. Augustine, the fact that we cannot escape making aesthetic judgments based on a "standard" is revelatory. An object is seen as beautiful because it radiates beauty, as the existence of an object is an extension of Being. We desire goodness and often speak as if it is the standard of value by which we judge. When we recognize a thing as "good," it is from an internal source within us—a source that transcends us—recognizing itself. We intuitively respond to what is good with delight. St. Augustine roots this capacity for aesthetic judgment in our being made in *imago Dei*. We are creatures made by God, and we recognize the family resemblance of our Father in his creation.⁶⁵ Where we see his likeness, we respond with joy; we rightly follow his precedent in deeming things "good."⁶⁶

Innate standards of aesthetic or moral judgment represent the basis by which we exercise intellect. Appealing to a criterion like "goodness" implies a judgment of the mind. In articulating these standards of measurement, St. Augustine is defining the values for judgment common throughout the ancient and medieval eras. It is only in the modern age that innate standards of judgment have been obscured and forgotten in the effort to exercise a faulty notion of individual freedom. By its own nature, aesthetic judgment cannot be merely a matter of subjective taste. No one who hears Mozart's

---

63. One recalls *Four Quartets*, T. S. Eliot's Pulitzer-Prize-winning poem, concluding with the stanza from "Little Gidding," beginning with the lines: "We shall not cease from exploration / And the end of all our exploring / Will be to arrive where we started / And to know the place for the first time" (Eliot, *Four Quartets*, 59).

64. Augustine, *Of True Religion* 30.56.

65. Recall St. Paul speaking to the philosophers in Athens: "What therefore you worship as unknown, this I proclaim to you. The God who made the world and everything in it . . . is actually not far from each one of us, for, 'In him we live and move and have our being'" (Acts 17:23-24, 27-28 ESV).

66. See Genesis 1, which sets a divine precedent for the liturgical habit of praise as proper recognition of the quality of goodness.

Requiem is tempted to respond with a whimsical folk dance. Certainly, taste exists as a mode of perception, but the question is how it corresponds with the nature of reality.

For those tempted toward radical subjectivism in matters of aesthetic judgment—mere "beauty in the eye of the beholder"—St. Augustine reminds us to embrace our distinct humanness, meaning our intellect and will. Certainly perception, and even judgment, has a subjective element. Perception works according to the formation of prior experience as well as natural capacity, both of which may vary.[67] The fact remains that our physical senses can only facilitate an incomplete experience. When aided by reason, the perceptive capacity of the physical senses can grow to become more acute. The palate can become trained to perceive nuance. Aesthetic sensitivity must be intentionally cultivated within a given field of awareness. Coffee and wine are both said to be acquired tastes, and it takes years of thoughtful practice and learning to develop a sharp enough palate to understand why things taste the way they do. Pleasure comes through the bodily senses; then the mind judges the goodness and the heart takes delight. Without rationality to interpret the quality of a given experience, the content of the senses is emptied of its value. The human aesthetic experience is reduced to that of an animal stimulus response. St. Augustine describes this to be a waste of the natural purpose of a thing to show forth its value, the willful effect of sin. This is the reason that St. Augustine equates the exercise of reason to an antidote for vice.[68] Our hearts desire goodness, and by reason we can protect our hearts from false goods. We encounter objective beauty subjectively—by our own perceptions seasoned by our own experiences. Each new experience grows our capacity for the next. Depth of knowledge and experience take time to develop. The question is whether our standards of goodness are rational, just, and capable of bringing a deep sense of delight or whether they merely serve disordered appetites and fleeting animal pleasures. For St. Augustine, the Holy Trinity constitutes the foundation of all reality, the

---

67. "Not everyone can attend to the deepest expressiveness of sensory surface. This is transparently clear in relation to the written and spoken word. But it is also the case with regard to the immediacy of sensuous form, whether visual or audible. In high art, the sensuous togetherness of form plays in relation to the depth of its capacity to express the profundity of things apprehended and given shape by the artist for the properly integrated receptivity of the perceiver" (Wood, *Placing Aesthetics*, 99). I owe the image of containers of varying size to Anthony Esolen's exposition of the idea of perceptive capacity in Canto III of Dante's *Paradise* (Dante, *Paradise* 3.66n406). The souls in the lowest of the heavenly spheres know others are more blessed but they themselves feel no lack of blessedness. Dante's own capacity to perceive the presence and glory of God grows as he ascends.

68. Augustine, *Confessions* 10.31.43–33.50.

one thing to be enjoyed for its own sake.[69] Therefore, it is unsurprising that, being made in the image of God, the human experience of Beauty will be trinitarian in form—requiring a harmonious interworking of the body, the intellect, and the heart.

St. Augustine's aesthetics consist of ordered delight, made possible by purity of heart, and of right judgment by the intellect. In particular, he suggests humility and openness when considering possible aesthetic objects, paired with exercising the intellectual work to determine the degree of *usefulness* an object might possess. St. Augustine asserts that all good things derive their goodness from their origin in God. Part of trusting in the goodness of God is being willing to see goodness revealed in the world since his creation reflects his own nature. Sin taints our ability to perceive goodness clearly. Therefore, there is an ethical mandate to order one's love according to wise judgment. Ultimately, we delight most fully in God, in whose image we are beautifully created. Therefore, beauty merits our love through an aesthetic object's revelatory capacity. The greater beauty things have, the greater potential they have to reveal God to us through their presence if we could only recognize it. Determining this potential is the natural impulse of every aesthetic judgment. Whether we do it well or poorly is determined by our own self-knowledge, our field of awareness, and our sensory attunement. We are rewarded by the joyful delight we most deeply desire for willfully training our affections and our senses according to right judgment. Tuning our spiritual senses widens our capacity to experience the presence of Beauty all around us and gives us a satisfying sense of gratitude for the gift of life in an enchanted world (see Gen 2:15).[70]

EPILOGUE: TRANSCENDENT AESTHETIC VISION

> *To see a World in a Grain of Sand*
> *And a Heaven in a Wild Flower,*
> *Hold Infinity in the palm of your hand*
> *And Eternity in an hour.*
> William Blake, "Auguries of Innocence"[71]

---

69. "The things which are to be enjoyed are the Father, the Son, and the Holy Spirit, a single Trinity, a certain supreme thing common to all who enjoy it" (Augustine, *On Christian Doctrine* 1.5.5).

70. There is here, by implication, a robust Christian ecological ethic and vision. See also Wirzba, *From Nature to Creation*.

71. Blake, *Selected Poetry*, 147.

All up to this point is leading to a new type of vision and beyond into a way of participation.[72] Seeing the world around us, even life itself, as a gift allows us to commune gratefully with our Creator, whose shared presence is the source of our ultimate happiness.[73] I have long feared that many Christians forget that Christ came as an apocalypse—a veil lifted on reality, a curtain torn between the transcendent and the immanent—to bring the Kingdom of Heaven to earth. When we neglect the divine movement toward the physical, we show that we have forgotten that our faith is based in Incarnation. Modernity's division of mind and body makes it easy for us to fall back into thinking and acting in ways that mimic the early Christian heresies that wrongly separated what the Incarnation holds together.[74] Against these misunderstandings of Christ stand the prolific writings of early Christian theologians, like St. Augustine. If we heed their words, our vision will be fully *incarnational*.[75]

David Naugle teaches us well in *Reordered Love, Reordered Lives*:

> In Christianity, the happy life is the sacramental life. . . . Thus, if we refer all our human activities and experiences to God in love—work, marriage, sexuality, children, family, friendship, food, rest, recreation, place, and anything else you can think of—then we discover contentment, satisfaction, fulfillment, joy, and happiness in life, all summed up in the word *shalom*. If God is the proper reference point for all aspects and things in life, then God gives them their true meaning and puts them in the proper order in our lives. This grand union of God, ourselves, and the whole cosmos in a sacred synthesis of rightly ordered love constitutes the deep meaning of happiness.[76]

We ought to evaluate every aspect of our human experience for its ability to reveal God to us by the activity of Christ, to uncover more and more reasons to gratefully praise God, and to give us a deeper sense of wonder and happiness.[77] Perceiving beauty sacramentally around us preserves the world as a gift. Our own nature as divine image-bearers privileges us to act

---

72. See Boersma, *Seeing God; Nouvelle Theologie & Sacramental Ontology*.

73. Schmemann, *For the Life of the World*. No influence has been greater for my thinking on this topic than this text. If one referenced title sticks, let it be this one.

74. A whole intellectual history of modernity is implied here. For a concise treatment, see Taylor, *Poetic Knowledge*. For something more in-depth, see Dupre, *Passage to Modernity*.

75. See the ancient Apostles' and Nicene Creeds.

76. Naugle, *Reordered Love, Reordered Lives*, 22–23.

77. "So, whether you eat or drink, or whatever you do, do all to the glory of God" (1 Cor 10:31 ESV).

justly in aesthetic judgment and to delight in what is most worthy: For "God saw everything that he had made, and behold, it was very good" (Gen 1:31 ESV). We are blessed when we humbly see and justly love God as he is revealed.[78] We gaze westward in the evening with renewed eyes, lift a glass with a reflective mind, and sit at the dinner table with a deeper sense of gratitude.

> The heavens declare the glory of God and the sky above proclaims his handiwork. Day to day pours out speech, and night to night reveals knowledge. —Psalm 19:1–2 ESV

> Although to the healthy and pure internal eye He is everywhere present, He saw fit to appear to those whose eye is weak and impure, and even to fleshly eyes. . . . He came to a place where He was already, for He was in the World, and the World was made by him. But since men were made conformable to this world by a desire to enjoy creatures instead of their creator, whence they are most aptly called "the world" they did not know Him so that the Evangelist says, "the world knew him not." . . . How did He come except that "the Word was made flesh, and dwelt among us." —Augustine, *On Christian Doctrine*[79]

> All that exists is God's gift to man, and it all exists to make God known to man, to make man's life communion with God.[80] —Alexander Schmemann, *For the Life of the World*.

> Oh, taste and see that the Lord is good! Blessed is the man who takes refuge in Him. —Psalm 34:8 ESV

BIBLIOGRAPHY

Aristotle. *Nicomachean Ethics*. Translated by W. D. Ross. In *The Basic Works of Aristotle*, edited by Richard McKeon, 935–1112. New York: Random, 1941.

---

78. Again, see Romans 1, which indicates that only unrighteousness and, eventually, God's wrath, come from refusing to acknowledge, honor, and give thanks to God who is revealed "in the things that have been made" (Rom 1:20 ESV). For philosophical souls, explore Jean-Luc Marion's phenomenological notion of *saturated givenness*. For the literary, let Dante Alighieri be your guide. For the theologically inclined, study the church fathers, especially St. Irenaeus, St. Athanasius, St. Gregory of Nyssa, St. Cyril, St. Maximus the Confessor, etc. Or, for a brilliant recent voice, listen to Hans Urs von Balthasar.

79. Augustine, *On Christian Doctrine* 1.12.11–12.

80. Schmemann, *Life of the World*, 14.

———. *On the Soul*. Translated by J. A. Smith. In *The Basic Works of Aristotle*, edited by Richard McKeon, 535–603. New York: Random, 1941.
Athanasius. *On the Incarnation*. Translated by a Religious of CSMV. Crestwood, NY: St. Vladimir's Seminary, 1977.
Augustine. *Against the Academicians and The Teacher*. Translated by Peter King. Indianapolis: Hackett, 1995.
———. *City of God*. Translated by Marcus Dods. New York: Random, 1978.
———. *Confessions*. Translated by Henry Chadwick. Oxford: Oxford University Press, 1991.
———. *Divine Providence And The Problem of Evil: A Translation of St. Augustine's De Ordine*. Translated by Robert P. Russell. New York: Helenson, 1942.
———. *Of True Religion*. Translated by J. H. S. Burleigh. Philadelphia: Westminster, 1953.
———. *On Christian Doctrine*. Translated by D. W. Robertson Jr. Upper Saddle River, NJ: Prentice Hall, 1958.
———. *On Genesis*. Translated by Edmund Hill. Hyde Park, NY: New City, 2002.
———. *On Music*. Translated by W. F. Jackson Knight in *Philosophies of Art and Beauty*. Edited by Albert Hofstadter and Richard Kuhns. Chicago: University of Chicago Press, 1964.
Boersma, Hans. *Heavenly Participation: The Weaving of a Sacramental Tapestry*. Grand Rapids: Eerdmans, 2011.
———. *Nouvelle Theologie & Sacramental Ontology: A Return to Mystery*. Oxford: Oxford University Press, 2009.
———. *Seeing God: The Beatific Vision in the Christian Tradition*. Grand Rapids: Eerdmans, 2018.
———. *Violence, Hospitality, and the Cross: Reappropriating the Atonement Tradition*. Grand Rapids: Baker, 2004.
Caputo, John D., and Michael J. Scanion, eds. *God, the Gift, and Postmodernism*. Bloomington: Indiana University Press, 1999.
Curd, Patricia, ed. *A Presocratics Reader: Selected Fragments and Testimonia*. Translated by Richard D. McKirahan and Patricia Curd. Indianapolis: Hackett, 2011.
Dante. *Paradise*. Translated by Anthony Esolen. New York: Random, 2004.
Dupre, Louis. *Passage to Modernity*. New Haven: Yale University Press, 1993.
Eliot, T. S. *Four Quartets*. New York: Houghton Mifflin Harcourt, 1943.
Engelland, Chad. "Augustinian Elements in Heidegger's Philosophical Anthropology." *Proceedings of the American Catholic Philosophical Association* 78 (2004) 263–75.
Foreman, Jon. "Caroline." Track 4 on *The Wonderlands: Sunlight*, Lowercase People Records, 2015.
Heidegger, Martin. *History of the Concept of Time*. Translated by Theodore Kisiel. Bloomington: Indiana University Press, 1986.
Hildebrand, Dietrich von. *Aesthetics*. Vol. 1. Edited by John F. Crosby. Translated by Brian McNeil. Steubenville, OH: Hildebrand Project, 2016.
———. *The Heart: An Analysis of Human and Divine Affectivity*. South Bend, IN: St. Augustine's, 2007.
Hopkins, Gerard Manley. *The Poems of Gerard Manley Hopkins*. Overland Park, KS: Digireads.com, 2018.
Kreglinger, Gisela H. *The Spirituality of Wine*. Grand Rapids: Eerdmans, 2013.
Lewis, C. S. *The Lion, the Witch, and the Wardrobe*. New York: HarperCollins, 1994.

———. *The Weight of Glory.* New York: HarperCollins, 2001.
Marcel, Gabriel. "Music According to St. Augustine." In *Music and Philosophy*, by Gabriel Marcel, 117–23. Translated by Stephen Maddux and Robert E. Wood. Milwaukee: Marquette University Press, 2005.
Marion, Jean-Luc. *God Without Being.* Translated by Thomas A. Carlson. 2nd ed. Chicago: University of Chicago Press, 2012.
Milbank, John, et al. "Introduction: Suspending the Material." In *Radical Orthodoxy: A New Theology*, edited by John Milbank et al., 1–20. New York: Routledge, 1999.
Naugle, David. *Reordered Love, Reordered Lives: Learning the Deep Meaning of Happiness.* Grand Rapids: Eerdmans, 2008.
Pabst, Adrian. *Metaphysics: The Creation of Hierarchy.* Grand Rapids: Eerdmans, 2012.
Paulo, Craig de, ed. *The Influence of Augustine on Heidegger.* Lewiston, NY: Mellen, 2006.
Pickstock, Catherine. *After Writing.* Oxford: Blackwell, 1998.
———. "Soul, City, and Cosmos After Augustine." In *Radical Orthodoxy: A New Theology*, edited by John Milbank et al., 243–77. New York: Routledge, 1999.
Plato. *Phaedrus.* In *Plato: Complete Works*, edited by John M. Cooper, 506–96. Translated by Alexander Nehamas and Paul Woodruff. Indianapolis: Hackett, 1997.
———. *Republic.* In *Plato: Complete Works*, edited by John M. Cooper, 971–1223. Translated by G. M. A. Grube. Indianapolis: Hackett, 1997.
———. *Symposium.* In *Plato: Complete Works*, edited by John M. Cooper, 457–505. Translated by Alexander Nehamas and Paul Woodruff. Indianapolis: Hackett, 1997.
Schmemann, Alexander. *For the Life of the World.* Crestwood, NY: St. Vladimir's Seminary, 1963.
Shakespeare, William. *The Merchant of Venice.* Oxford: Oxford University Press, 1979.
Smith, James K. A. *On The Road With Saint Augustine.* Grand Rapids: Brazos, 2019
———. *Speech and Theology: Language and the Logic of Incarnation.* New York: Routledge, 2002.
Switchfoot. "Ammunition." Track 4 on *The Beautiful Letdown*, Columbia Records, 2003.
Taylor, James S. *Poetic Knowledge: The Recovery of Education.* Albany: State University of New York Press, 1998.
Wirzba, Norman. *From Nature to Creation: A Christian Vision for Understanding and Loving Our World.* Grand Rapids: Baker Academic, 2015.
Wood, Robert E. "Art and Truth: Plato, Nietzsche, and Heidegger." In *The Beautiful, the True, and the Good: Studies in the History of Thought*, by Robert E. Wood, 107–53. Washington, DC: Catholic University of America Press, 2013.
———. *Nature, Artforms, and the World Around Us: An Introduction to the Regions of Aesthetic Experience.* Cham, Switzerland: Palgrave Macmillan, 2017.
———. *Placing Aesthetics.* Athens: Ohio University Press, 1999.

20

Evangelism through Beauty

DAVID DALLAS MILLER[1]

"[Lord,] you have made us for yourself,
and our heart is restless until it rests in you."[2]

St. Augustine wrote these words long ago, but they are as true today as they have ever been. A contemporary version of St. Augustine's words is Bruce Springsteen's song, "Hungry Heart."[3] The two men are getting at the same truth: we are hardwired for God and the only way to find fulfillment is

---

1. My thanks to Mark Boone for several crucial suggestions he made along the way to completing this essay.

2. Augustine, *Confessions*, 3. This classic Christian text, as well as its author, was unknown to me before I met Dr. Naugle (or Davey as he is affectionately known to many). The thesis of this essay, as well as its supporting arguments, can in some form or fashion be traced back to having Davey first as a professor and then as a mentor and dear friend. Davey and Deemie exemplify the beauty of Christ Jesus at work in marriage, friendship, work, and recreation.

3. Springsteen, "Hungry Heart."

through him. Nothing else in our lives, no matter how significant or good it may be, can fulfill the yearning, the restless desire that is inside all of us.

Many evangelical Christians have expressed our restless or hungry hearts in this way. "We are created," they say, "with a God-shaped hole, and until he fills it we will always be trying to fill it with something else." In other words, we try to scratch the divine itch through filling our lives with temporal goods like relationships or wealth. This is what the Bible calls idolatry. Addiction is a modern term that comes close to the biblical view of idolatry. Pleasure, wealth, power, knowledge, and relationships are temporal goods, and there is nothing wrong with them. God created us to seek after them as a means to an end, but not as an end in and of themselves. When we do that, we are trying to fill our God-shaped hole with them. And we soon discover they promise far more than they deliver.

Once the buzz wears off, we are forced to seek more pleasure, more wealth, more power, more knowledge, or another relationship to satisfy us. But do we find ultimate fulfillment in these things? No, we do not. In the end, these temporal goods disappoint us. And if we do not turn from them to find fulfillment in something else—or, better put, someone else—they break our hearts in the end. Generation after generation illustrates this truth. If our pursuit of temporary goods teaches us anything, it teaches us that we have an insatiable hunger for that which transcends our material existence.

The ancient Greek philosophers knew that temporal goods do not slake our soul's thirst. That is why they believed that human happiness or fulfillment was essentially grounded in three transcendentals: goodness, truth, and beauty. Plato knew that material things, at their best, were fingers pointing to something better. The Catholic Church embraced this teaching and added to it. Catholic teaching says that God is goodness, truth, and beauty itself.[4] To know that which is true is to know something about God. Likewise, to live in conformity to that truth is to participate in God's goodness, and to have a genuine experience of beauty is to have an experience with the truth and goodness of God. In other words, since God is goodness, truth, and beauty itself, there is no way of having a genuine experience of beauty that leaves us isolated from goodness and truth. We cannot experience beauty without seeing that which is both good and true.[5]

The purpose of this essay is to make an argument for a method of evangelism best described as evangelism through beauty.[6] But that is not to

4. Navone, *Toward a Theology of Beauty*.

5. This is what Christian theologians call the doctrine of divine simplicity. I was exposed to this doctrine in John Navone's book, *Toward a Theology of Beauty*, which I was assigned to read in one of Davey's classes.

6. I credit this idea to Catholic theologian Robert Barron. Bishop Barron is currently

say that goodness and truth are jettisoned in favor of the beautiful. Evangelism through beauty means that, as Christians, we are prepared to give an account of the good news of Jesus Christ through leading with the beauty of Christianity. After leading with beauty, we move to the moral demands or the goodness of Christianity, and finally we set forth the truth claims of Christianity.

In this essay I will consider why I think prioritizing truth and goodness over beauty is not the most effective way for Christians to evangelize. Then I will give a brief account of how the expression of Christianity through the use of icons, symbols, and art was defended and, in large part, saved by a fifth-century monk. Following that, I will tell the stories of two influential twentieth-century Christians who were converted through beauty. Those stories lead into a discussion of the instinctive desire we all share for beauty as well as its objective qualities. The final and longest section of this essay will be about the one who is goodness, truth, and beauty itself, namely, Jesus Christ, the Son of God. I will do this by presenting Jesus as the paradigmatic representative of beauty as beauty is defined by St. Thomas Aquinas.

Why should we consider giving priority to the beautiful when evangelizing? Given the state of postmodern culture, with its prevailing claim that the only truth is that there is no meta-truth or absolute truth, I believe we will find it hard slogging to evangelize leading with truth. Since the mantra these days is "My truth is as real or sacred as your truth," many of today's non-Christians respond to the Christian claim, "Jesus is the truth!" with the question, "What right do you have to say that?" As Zadie Smith likes to say, "In the end, your past is not my past and your truth is not my truth and your solution—is not my solution."[7] If this is the pervading claim of today's predominantly secular society—and I believe there is substantial evidence to prove that it is—I believe we are better off leading with either goodness or beauty.

I am aware that my approach differs from that of Francis Schaeffer, one of the twentieth-century's greatest Christian apologists. Schaeffer was firmly committed to leading with truth when making his argument that the Christian worldview illuminates both mind and heart to understand the world and human beings as they truly are.[8] He understood that an enormous intellectual and cultural shift had taken place that called into question previously held ideas of truth, as well as its discovery and application. He therefore

---

one of the auxiliary bishops of the Catholic Diocese of Los Angeles.

7. Zadie Smith is a contemporary English novelist, essayist, and short-story writer. This line apparently derives from Smith, *White Teeth*, 150.

8. For an excellent introduction to the thought and writings of Francis Schaeffer, see Kappelman, "Need to Read Francis Schaeffer."

argued that Christians could no longer take for granted that non-Christians understood even the rudimentary truth claims of Christianity. As a solution to this problem, Schaeffer outlined the decline of objective truth claims in theology, philosophy, and the arts. In doing so, he sought to awaken both Christians and non-Christians alike to the disastrous consequences this jettisoning of truth would have on human life, morality, and meaning.[9]

I am not gainsaying Schaeffer's argument. I fully agree that, if objective truth is ditched for a subjective substitute, it will have a deteriorating effect on our institutions of learning, churches, and the culture as a whole. Our present day is proof that Schaeffer was right, is it not? Because Schaeffer's fear has come to fruition, I believe it is better for Christians to emphasize beauty before truth.

The moral argument for Christianity also seems to be on shaky ground these days. Because today's culture places excessive stress on individual rights, freedom, and self-determination, we will shut the door of opportunity if we take our stand on the moral high ground: "The way that you are living your life is wrong. You need to live your life in accord with the truth!" Heaven knows this argument is hard enough to make within the household of faith. It is even more difficult to make to non-Christians enmeshed in a culture that has enshrined the individual as the sole determiner of goodness and truth.

Just as there is no objective truth, there is also no objective goodness, says today's culture. Even so, I believe our culture has maintained a sensitivity toward goodness. Many Americans, and this seems to be especially true of millennials, are strongly attracted to the Mother Theresas of the world, and they want to do their part to make the world a better place.[10] On the whole, however, our culture seems to be as skeptical of biblical claims of objective goodness as it is of biblical claims of objective truth.[11] Given the decades-long church sex-abuse scandal, can we blame them? Besides, no one likes to be told their choices are immoral or what they are doing is wrong. If we evangelize by leading with the good, I am afraid we will discover that we are sawing off the limb on which we stand.

I realize that this claim puts me at odds, or at least seems to, with the person I consider to be the greatest Christian apologist of the latter half of the twentieth century, Clive Staples Lewis.

Lewis's defense of Christianity is contained in his classic text on apologetics, *Mere Christianity*. Far from making an argument for God's existence

---

9. Follis, *Truth with Love*, 31–65.
10. Lamb, "People Believe They Can Make a Positive Difference."
11. Barna, "Americans Are Most Likely to Base Truth on Feelings."

from beauty, Lewis spends the entire first section of the book making a moral argument for it.[12] In the third section, he describes how Christians ought to behave.[13] It is indeed a compelling and masterfully crafted argument. But I wonder if Lewis's fictional works like *The Chronicles of Narnia* and *Till We Have Faces* have had an even greater impact on evangelizing non-Christians and nominal Christians alike. His fiction sets the imagination ablaze with the beauty of Christian-themed storytelling in a way that *Mere Christianity* does not. However, it is beyond the scope of this essay to make an argument in favor of Lewis's fiction. Let us therefore proceed with beauty as an effective starting place for evangelism.

To begin from the place of beauty is to begin from a magical or enchanted place. It is the place of whimsy but also the place of seriousness. Just listen to the music of Brahms, Beethoven, or Bach. Look at a waterfall, the Mona Lisa, or the Sistine Chapel. Without being told what to do or what to think, just look at these things. Beauty goes beyond words and touches a person at the level of the soul. It is, in fact, hard to underestimate the power of the beautiful to draw the observer into its orbit. There is an inherent power in beauty to win someone's heart and soul without telling her what to think or how to behave.[14]

But is there ancient precedent for this? Can we as Christians point to a time in our history when we said "Yes" to beauty as a model for evangelism? I believe there is. Let us consider for a moment the life and times of St. John of Damascus.[15] John Damascene, as he is also known, was a Syrian monk and priest born in the latter half of the fifth century CE. He lived in a time when many Christians were questioning the use of icons as an appropriate part of their worship. The iconoclasts (i.e., icon smashers) were a group of Christians who were, as their name indicates, dead set against the use of icons. They stated their case mostly through the use of Old Testament texts that made explicit the prohibition of graven images:

> You shall not make for yourself an image in the form of anything in heaven above or on the earth beneath or in the waters below. You shall not bow down to them or worship them; for I, the LORD your God, am a jealous God, punishing the children for the sin of the parents to the third and fourth generation of those who hate me, but showing love to a thousand generations

---

12. Lewis, *Mere Christianity*, 17–36.
13. Lewis, *Mere Christianity*, 69–126.
14. Barron, "Catholicism and Beauty."
15. St. John of Damascus is considered such a pivotal player in the life of the church that he is one of only thirty-six saints to receive the title Doctor of the Church.

of those who love me and keep my commandments. (Exod 20:4–6)[16]

At the same time and in the same part of the world, Islam was beginning to emerge as a force to be reckoned with. Islam, of course, has a very strong belief in the transcendence of Allah and the inappropriateness of ever using iconography to depict the image of God. Into this perfect storm steps John Damascene. His defense of depicting God and the saints through art is simple but true. He draws upon the letter of St. Paul to the Colossians to make his argument. St. Paul writes,

> [Jesus] is the image of the invisible God, the firstborn of all creation; for in him all things in heaven and on earth were created, things visible and invisible, whether thrones or dominions or rulers or powers—all things have been created through him and for him. He himself is before all things, and in him all things hold together. He is the head of the body, the church; he is the beginning, the firstborn from the dead, so that he might come to have first place in everything. (Col 1:15–18 NRSV)

John Damascene does not refute that God in his essence is beyond all knowing and specification; however, he argues that because God makes an image of himself in the person of Jesus, God himself is an iconographer. If it pleases God to make an icon of himself, it should also please us to make icons of the Holy Trinity and the saints, he says. His point is simple and clear. To participate in making art that depicts the richness and beauty of Christianity is to participate in the life of God as primordial iconographer.[17]

This may not seem like a compelling reason for evangelism through beauty, but we should reconsider. Without John Damascene there may never have been Chartres Cathedral, Michelangelo, the Sistine Chapel, or Leonardo da Vinci. Because of this fifth-century monk, much of premodern, modern, and postmodern Christianity is spread through the use of iconography, stained glass, sculptures, and cinematic art.

There is, however, little evidence of the early Christians making use of art to spread their message. But that has more to do with the tremendous persecution the early church faced than it does with their reticence toward images and icons to illustrate the good news of Jesus Christ. Seeking to keep them under the imperial thumb, Rome put the early Christians on the run. There were concentrated efforts to keep this fledgling group of Jesus-followers from gaining traction. Christians were under constant threat of

---

16. All biblical passages in this chapter are from NIV unless otherwise stated.
17. Barron, "Catholicism and Beauty."

having their property seized, being thrown into jail, flung to wild animals, or burned as human torches. In such an adverse environment, Christians could hardly think of expressing their faith through art. In spite of this, the *Ichthys*, which is one of the most recognizable Christian symbols, comes from this early period, as do the paintings in the catacombs.[18]

Of course, all of this changed under the Emperor Constantine. During his reign, Christianity became the recognized religion of the Roman Empire. Christians suddenly found themselves free to practice their faith. There ensued an explosion of Christian art that has continued to this very day. Whether it was the early Christians hiding their art because of state-sponsored persecution, John Damascene defending the use of icons to depict the faith, or Christian artists working freely, the church has always defended the role of beauty as a means of spreading the faith.

But do people really have conversion experiences through an encounter with beauty? The best way to answer that question is to highlight the stories of people who became Christians as a result of their encounters with beauty. With that in mind, let's consider the lives of two men who were converted in just that way.

The first is Aaron Jean-Marie Lustiger, a French Cardinal of the Catholic Church who served as Archbishop of Paris from 1981 until 2005. He is remembered for giving beautiful sermons in French. His sermons typically drew extensively on the history of Israel, which was only natural given that Jean-Marie was a converted Jew.[19]

Jean-Marie came of age during Hitler's reign of terror. His mother was sent to Auschwitz and died there. For his protection, Jean-Marie was sent to live with a Christian family. It was with this family that he began to read the New Testament for the first time. As he did, his mind began to be filled with Christian ideas. Nonetheless, reading this was not enough to convince Jean-Marie of the truth of the gospel.[20]

The decisive moment of conversion came when, at about age thirteen, he walked into a cathedral. While standing in the cathedral, it was neither the truth claims of Christian doctrine nor listening to a sermon on the goodness of God that converted Jean-Marie. Though these things played a role, they did not convert him. It was as he stood in the beauty of the cathedral, amid the beauty of liturgy, stained glass, and incense, that he was enchanted and touched at the level of his soul. Jean-Marie experienced a

---

18. The *Ichthys* (i.e., the Jesus fish) was a secret code or symbol of faith for the early Christians.

19. Barron, "Catholicism and Beauty."

20. Barron, "Catholicism and Beauty."

transformation that compelled him to say, "I believe this is the truth."[21] The beauty of the cathedral and liturgy opened the door for Jean-Marie to accept the goodness and truth of Jesus Christ.

I have already mentioned the second man: C. S. Lewis. In *Surprised by Joy*, Lewis writes the following about his conversion:

> You must picture me alone in that room at Magdalen, night after night, feeling, whenever my mind lifted even for a second from my work, the steady, unrelenting approach of Him whom I so earnestly desired not to meet. That which I greatly feared had at last come upon me. In the Trinity Term of 1929 I gave in, and admitted that God was God, and knelt and prayed: perhaps, that night, the most dejected and reluctant convert in all England.[22]

Given his own testimony, how can we say that Lewis's conversion was an experience with beauty? He states plainly that he was miserable at the moment of his conversion. Nevertheless, that does not gainsay the significant role beauty played in Lewis's acceptance of the goodness and truth of Jesus Christ.

Even as a young boy, Lewis was strongly attracted to the beauty of the natural world. It gave him his first experience with joy:

> The first [experience of joy] is itself the memory of a memory. As I stood beside a flowering currant bush on a summer day there suddenly arose in me without warning, and as if from a depth not of years but of centuries, the memory of that earlier morning at the Old House when my brother had brought his toy garden into the nursery. It is difficult to find words strong enough for the sensation which came over me; Milton's "enormous bliss" of Eden (giving the full, ancient meaning to 'enormous') comes somewhere near it. It was a sensation, of course, of desire; but desire for what? . . . and before I knew what I desired, the desire itself was gone, the whole glimpse withdrawn, the world turned commonplace again, or only stirred by a longing for the longing that had just ceased.[23]

Lewis had two other childhood experiences with joy. One came through reading *Squirrel Nutkin* by Beatrix Potter and the other while reading Longfellow's *Tegner's Drapa*.[24] The latter two experiences were identi-

---

21. Barron, "Catholicism and Beauty."
22. Lewis, *Surprised by Joy*, 266.
23. Lewis, *Surprised by Joy*, 13.
24. Lewis, *Surprised by Joy*, 13–14.

cal to his first experience of joy. It is Lewis's pursuit to understand joy that dominated his early life and culminated in his becoming a Christian. What I find fascinating about Lewis's experiences of joy is that they were mediated through beauty. The first experience of joy was mediated through an experience with the beauty of nature. The second and third experiences of joy were mediated through the beautiful and enchanting world of prose and poetry.

Jean-Marie and Lewis are just two examples of men who were converted through profound experiences with beauty. Again, this does not mean that goodness and truth are not part of their conversion stories. I am not attempting to jettison either from their narratives. On the contrary, both Jean-Marie and Lewis had strong convictions about morality before their conversions. They were undoubtedly attracted to what they rightly perceived to be the goodness of Christianity. And after their conversions, they were men who used words, and a lot of them, to argue for the truth of Christianity. Nevertheless, it was beauty that moved these men toward goodness and truth. Their conversion stories, as well as the subsequent shape of their lives, demonstrate that a true experience with beauty carries with it both goodness and truth.

The conversions of Jean-Marie and C. S. Lewis—as well as of everyone who is converted to Christ through a genuine experience with beauty—illustrate that our experiences with beauty are not isolated from goodness and truth; rather, they open the door for them to come into our lives. In other words, beauty, goodness, and truth are a package deal because they are an integral part of who Jesus Christ is. Since he is God in the flesh, Jesus *is* goodness, truth, and beauty itself. Opening the door for beauty means that we are opening the door for goodness and truth as well: "Behold, I [Jesus] stand at the door and knock. If anyone hears my voice and opens the door, I will come in to him and eat with him, and he with me" (Rev 3:20 ESV).

Of course, there is no way of knowing how many people have been converted to Christ through experiences with beauty, but if anthropological studies have taught us anything, it's that we place a high premium on replicating the beauty we see around us. Does this mean there is evidence that every person has an innate desire for beauty? Scientists are increasingly answering that question in the affirmative. In fact, they are providing more evidence than ever that our brains are hard-wired for beauty and that people are fashioned to recognize beauty when they see it.[25] From a theological and biblical perspective, we know we have an innate desire for beauty because we are made in the image and likeness of God: "So God created mankind in his own image, in the image of God he created them; male and female he

---

25. Choi, "Sense of Beauty Partly Innate."

created them" (Gen 1:27). Since everyone is created in the image and likeness of God, everyone has an innate desire for goodness, truth, and beauty.

Making an argument for the inherent desire we all have for goodness, truth, and beauty is not simply a glorification of our subjective likes and dislikes. To like the music of Johann Sebastian Bach over the music of Ludwig van Beethoven is a subjective experience. We all have our likes and dislikes that dictate the music we listen to, the food we eat, the clothes we wear, etc., and this subjectiveness may tempt us to say, "Well, beauty is ultimately in the eyes of the beholder."

However, Dietrich von Hildebrand, a twentieth-century Catholic philosopher and theologian, says that these things are merely subjectively satisfying and should not be confused with the objectively valuable.[26] The objectively valuable, says Hildebrand, is beautiful whether or not we ever put our stamp of approval on it. What's more, once we experience that which is truly beautiful, it is something so overwhelming in its value that it rearranges our subjectivity, and then it changes our subjectivity.

Hans Urs von Balthasar, another twentieth-century Catholic philosopher and theologian, says that the beautiful chooses us, elects us, and then sends us on mission.[27] A subjectively satisfying experience does not have the power to change us. For instance, to have a fondness for Indian cuisine over American cuisine does not have the power to transform us and to send us on mission. It is when we encounter the objectively beautiful that our lives are upended, our plans are rearranged, and we are sent on a mission that is greater than ourselves.

St. Thomas Aquinas says the beautiful occurs at the intersection of wholeness, harmony, and radiance. For Aquinas, when something is whole it has integrity. It is completely what it is without distortion. By harmony, he means there is balance. And by radiance, he means it is glorious to behold.[28] Whether it is a stunning sunset or a remarkable performance or a lovely piece of music or the life of a saint, beauty is present in these things because wholeness, harmony, and radiance have come together.[29]

The perfect coming together of wholeness, harmony, and radiance happened in Jesus Christ. Jesus was completely whole because he did not miss the mark in relationship to God. That is, Jesus was without sin: "He committed no sin, and no deceit was found in his mouth" (1 Pet 2:22). And "we do not have a high priest who is unable to empathize with our weaknesses, but

26. Barron, "Catholicism and Beauty."
27. Barron, "Catholicism and Beauty."
28. Barron, "Catholicism and Beauty."
29. Barron, "Catholicism and Beauty."

we have one who has been tempted in every way, just as we are—yet he did not sin" (Heb 4:15).

The perfect harmony of Jesus was revealed through his two natures. He was both fully human and fully divine. The gospels bear witness to his true humanity. For instance, Jesus was born of a human mother: "[Mary] gave birth to her firstborn, a son. She wrapped him in cloths and placed him in a manger, because there was no guest room available for them" (Luke 2:7; cf. Matt 1:18–25). Jesus's human nature was also illustrated through his experience of thirst, hunger, and fatigue. He once stopped to rest at Jacob's well because he was tired and thirsty from his journey. While he rested, his disciples went into town to buy food to eat, and, having returned with the food, they urged Jesus to eat (John 4:6–8; 31). Another time he was apparently so exhausted from the demands of ministry that he was found sleeping through a bad storm at sea (Matt 8:23–27; Mark 4:35–41; Luke 8:22–25).

Jesus also displayed a full range of human emotions. There were times, as in the healing of the officer's servant, when he was amazed by the faith of other people (Matt 8:5–13; Luke 7:1–10). Conversely, there were times when he was amazed at people's lack of faith (Mark 6:1–6). Then there were times when he was angry: "Jesus entered the temple courts and drove out all who were buying and selling there. He overturned the tables of the money changers and the benches of those selling doves. 'It is written,' he said to them, 'My house will be called a house of prayer,' but you are making it 'a den of robbers'" (Matt 21:12–13; cf. Mark 11:15–17; John 2:13–17). There are also times when he was filled with joy and with sorrow (Matt 26:36–46; Mark 14:34–42; Luke 10:21; John 11:32–35). Throughout his entire life, the gospels demonstrate that Jesus was a human being just like the rest of us.

Just as the gospels bear witness to Jesus's humanity, they also bear witness to his divinity. He was indeed born of a human mother, but the context and manner of his conception were utterly divine:

> In the sixth month of Elizabeth's pregnancy, God sent the angel Gabriel to Nazareth, a town in Galilee, to a virgin pledged to be married to a man named Joseph, a descendant of David. The virgin's name was Mary. The angel went to her and said, "Greetings, you who are highly favored! The Lord is with you." Mary was greatly troubled at his words and wondered what kind of greeting this might be. But the angel said to her, "Do not be afraid, Mary; you have found favor with God. You will conceive and give birth to a son, and you are to call him Jesus. He will be great and will be called the Son of the Most High. The Lord God will give him the throne of his father David, and he will reign over Jacob's descendants forever; his kingdom will never end."

"How will this be," Mary asked the angel, "since I am a virgin?" The angel answered, "The Holy Spirit will come on you, and the power of the Most High will overshadow you. So the holy one to be born will be called the Son of God. (Luke 1:26–35)

Likewise, Jesus sat at Jacob's well to rest because he was tired, but there was also a divine purpose in going to that well. There he waited for, and met with, a Samaritan woman. He knew the sordid details of her life and revealed his divine identity to her as well (John 4:4–26).

And it is true that Jesus slept in the back of the boat during a storm, but he also did something no human being could do. By simply speaking a word, he calmed the storm (Matt 8:23–27; Mark 4:35–41; Luke 8:22–25). Sally Lloyd-Jones retells this story for children. It is simply magnificent and is good reading for children and adults alike. She writes,

> Now Jesus's friends had been fishermen all their lives, but in all their years fishing on this lake they had never once seen a storm like this one.... "HELP!" They screamed. "Wake up! Quick, Jesus!" Jesus opened his eyes. "Rescue us! Save us!" they shrieked. "Don't you care?" (Of course Jesus cared, and this was the very reason he had come—to rescue them and to save them.) Jesus stood up and spoke to the storm. "Hush!" he said. That's all. And the strangest thing happened. The wind and the waves recognized Jesus's voice. (They had heard it before, of course—it was the same voice that made them, in the very beginning). They listened to Jesus and they did what he said. Immediately the wind stopped. The water calmed down. It glittered innocently in the moonlight and lapped quietly against the side of the boat, as if nothing had happened. The little boat bobbed gently up and down. There was a deep stillness and a great quiet all around. ... "Why were you scared?" [Jesus] asked. "Did you forget who I Am? Did you believe your fears, instead of me?" Jesus's friends were quiet. As quiet as the wind and the waves. And into their hearts came a different kind of storm. "What kind of man is this?" they asked themselves anxiously. "Even the winds and the waves obey him!"[30]

Lloyd-Jones's detail of the wind and waves recognizing Jesus's voice is marvelous. Of course, she is right. John's gospel describes Jesus as the *Logos* or Word of God who was with God in the beginning: "In the beginning was the Word, and the Word was with God, and the Word was God. He was with God in the beginning. Through him all things were made; without him

---

30. Lloyd-Jones, *Jesus Storybook Bible*, 239–42.

nothing was made that has been made" (John 1:1–3). So, Jesus is not only a man sleeping in the boat; he is also God in the flesh ruling over the wind and the waves.

We know that Jesus experienced the joys and sorrows of life like we all do, but as God incarnate he suffered in a unique way. Jesus's suffering was not the result of his own sin or wrongdoing, but it was the result of his bearing our sins in his body (1 Pet 2:24). Still, Jesus was tempted to sin as we are because he was human. Yet, he did not sin because he was divine (Heb 4:15). In the First Epistle of John, we read that Jesus's suffering took away our sin precisely because he was not a sinner: "But you know that he appeared so that he might take away our sins. And in him is no sin" (1 John 3:5).

The New Testament authors testify that Jesus is the Son of God,[31] and, because he is God's son, there is a unique quality to his suffering. For instance, through his suffering we are healed (1 Pet 2:24). Moreover, he is also the fitting instrument to cleanse us from all sin: "If we confess our sins, he is faithful and just and will forgive us our sins and purify us from all unrighteousness" (1 John 1:9).

Jesus's suffering and death were not simply a gross miscarriage of justice. Nor were they a regrettable coincidence of random circumstances. Rather, they were part of God's mysterious plan.[32] St. Peter explains this to the Jews in his sermon on Pentecost. Speaking about Jesus, he says, "This man was handed over to you by God's deliberate plan and foreknowledge; and you, with the help of wicked men, put him to death by nailing him to the cross" (Acts 2:23). The mysterious plan of God was fulfilled through Jesus, the one who suffered and died for our salvation.

This divine and mysterious plan of salvation was foretold in the Scriptures. It is most notably seen in Isaiah's vision of the suffering servant:

> For he grew up before him like a young plant, and like a root out of dry ground; he had no form or majesty that we should look at him, and no beauty that we should desire him. He was despised and rejected by men, a man of sorrows and acquainted with grief; and as one from whom men hide their faces he was despised, and we esteemed him not. Surely he has borne our griefs and carried our sorrows; yet we esteemed him stricken, smitten by God, and afflicted. But he was pierced for our transgressions; he was crushed for our iniquities; upon him was the chastisement that brought us peace, and with his wounds we are healed. All we like sheep have gone astray; we have turned—every

---

31. See Matt 3:17; Mark 1:1; Luke 3:23; 9:35; John 5:19; Acts 13:33; Rom 1:4; 1 Cor 15:28; Heb 1:8; 5:5; 2 Pet 1:17; 1 John 5:9.

32. *Catechism of the Catholic Church*, 599.

one—to his own way; and the Lord has laid on him the iniquity of us all. He was oppressed, and he was afflicted, yet he opened not his mouth; like a lamb that is led to the slaughter, and like a sheep that before its shearers is silent, so he opened not his mouth. By oppression and judgment he was taken away; and as for his generation, who considered that he was cut off out of the land of the living, stricken for the transgression of my people? And they made his grave with the wicked and with a rich man in his death, although he had done no violence, and there was no deceit in his mouth. (Isa 53:2–9 ESV)

Jesus himself explained the purpose of his suffering and death in light of Isaiah's prophecy (Matt 20:28). Furthermore, after his resurrection, Jesus joined Cleopas and his companion and said to them, "'How foolish you are, and how slow to believe all that the prophets have spoken! Did not the Messiah have to suffer these things and then enter his glory?' And beginning with Moses and all the Prophets, he explained to them what was said in all the Scriptures concerning himself" (Luke 24:25–27). He also did the same thing for his disciples (Luke 24:44–45). And, to the Christians at Corinth, St. Paul confirmed that "Christ died for our sins according to the Scriptures" (1 Cor 15:3).

For clarity's sake, let's recall Aquinas's definition of beauty: it is the correlation of wholeness, harmony, and radiance. Thus far I have endeavored to explain that Jesus is the epitome of wholeness and harmony. He was completely whole because there was no sin in him. His life was harmonious because his human and divine natures co-existed perfectly within him. But what about radiance? Did Jesus's life show forth the kind of radiance that equaled his wholeness and harmony? I believe it did in three extraordinary events: his transfiguration, his resurrection, and his glorified appearance to Saul.

The first remarkable event is his transfiguration: "After six days Jesus took with him Peter, James and John the brother of James, and led them up a high mountain by themselves. There he was transfigured before them. His face shone like the sun, and his clothes became as white as the light. Just then there appeared before them Moses and Elijah, talking with Jesus" (Matt 17:1–3).

Aquinas believed Jesus's transfiguration was the greatest of his miracles because it both honored his baptism and illuminated the greater life of heaven.[33] In other words, Jesus's transfiguration confirmed his Father's word at his baptism: "This is my Son, whom I love; with him I am well

---

33. Healy, *Thomas Aquinas*, 100.

pleased" (Matt 3:17; cf. Mark 9:7). Likewise, the radiance of Jesus, as well as the appearance of Moses and Elijah, revealed that heaven is a realm of glory existing at a higher pitch of perfection than earth. Jesus's divine nature overwhelmed his disciples because their earthliness could not take in his heavenly glory. This was not so with Jesus. His earthly body was transformed and radiated his heavenly glory precisely because he is the connecting point between the temporal and the eternal. He is the bridge between heaven and earth.[34]

The second extraordinary event is Jesus's resurrection:

> Now Mary stood outside the tomb crying. As she wept, she bent over to look into the tomb and saw two angels in white, seated where Jesus's body had been, one at the head and the other at the foot. They asked her, "Woman, why are you crying?" "They have taken my Lord away," she said, "and I don't know where they have put him." At this, she turned around and saw Jesus standing there, but she did not realize that it was Jesus. He asked her, "Woman, why are you crying? Who is it you are looking for?" Thinking he was the gardener, she said, "Sir, if you have carried him away, tell me where you have put him, and I will get him." Jesus said to her, "Mary." She turned toward him and cried out in Aramaic, "Rabboni!" (which means "Teacher"). Jesus said, "Do not hold on to me, for I have not yet ascended to the Father. Go instead to my brothers and tell them, 'I am ascending to my Father and your Father, to my God and your God.'" (John 20:11–17)

Of the seminal events in history, there are four that are at the top of the list and they all have to do with Jesus. They are his birth, death, resurrection, and ascension. (Of course, Jesus will return to earth again, but I believe that event will be the end of time and history as we know it.) The linchpin of these four events is the resurrection. Without Jesus's resurrection there is no ascension, and though his birth and death would still have some historical significance, his life would have no transformative power: "And if Christ has not been raised, your faith is futile; you are still in your sins. Then those also who have fallen asleep in Christ are lost. If only for this life we have hope in Christ, we are of all people most to be pitied" (1 Cor 15:17–19).

Of course, Jesus has been raised from the dead! He is what St. Paul calls the "firstfruits" of those who have died, which means that Jesus is the first who has risen from the dead and that all who put their trust in him will also be raised to eternal life (1 Cor 15:21–23; 2 Cor 4:14). Jesus's resurrection is

---

34. Lee, *Transfiguration*, 2.

by no means a mere resuscitation to the old physical life. Lazarus is an example of that (John 11:38–44). Rather, Jesus's bodily resurrection ushers in a new creation. It is a transformed body powered by the Spirit.[35] Incidentally, Jesus's transfiguration was a precursor to his resurrection. Both display his radiance, and his resurrection is our guarantee that we too will be resurrected victorious over death (1 Cor 15:20–58).

The third amazing event is the appearance of the glorified Christ to Saul on the road to Damascus: "Now as he went on his way, he approached Damascus, and suddenly a light from heaven shone around him. And falling to the ground, he heard a voice saying to him, 'Saul, Saul, why are you persecuting me?' And he said, 'Who are you, Lord?' And he said, 'I am Jesus, whom you are persecuting'" (Acts 9:3–5 ESV).

Jesus's presence was so radiant that it overwhelmed Saul. His encounter with Jesus was life-changing. Saul, the persecutor and a murderer of Christians, became St. Paul, missionary and evangelist to the Gentile world. Once an up-and-coming star among the Pharisees, he joined the new Christian community as one of its apostles.[36]

Balthasar's words about beauty choosing, electing, and sending us on mission could not apply better to anyone than St. Paul. When he met the resurrected and glorified Christ, his life was completely upended. What he thought he knew about God's kingdom was shattered. He was forced to rethink his theology.[37] He grew to understand that he was God's chosen instrument sent on mission to carry the gospel first to the Israelites and then to the Gentiles (Acts 9:15). In the end, St. Paul became what he once despised and tried to destroy. That's the transformative power of an authentic encounter with Jesus Christ, i.e., with beauty itself.

In this essay I have undertaken, albeit briefly, to make a case for evangelism through beauty. I do not believe this discards goodness and truth, far from it. Leading with beauty is meant to enchant the senses and to baptize the imagination so as to open the door for goodness and truth to enter.

Two of the last century's greatest apologists, namely, Francis Schaeffer and C. S. Lewis, took a different approach. Schaeffer evangelized leading with truth, and Lewis did so leading with goodness. I think the case can be made that Lewis, through his fiction, also evangelized leading with beauty. Nonetheless, the fact is that *Mere Chrsitianity*, which makes a moral argument for God's existence, stands as a classic in Christian apologetics.

---

35. Wright, *Resurrection of the Son of God*, 272.
36. Wright, *Paul and the Faithfulness of God*, 1397.
37. Schreiner, *Paul, Apostle of God's Glory in Christ*, 208.

But I wonder whether Schaeffer and Lewis would still be committed to these traditional styles of evangelism if they were alive today. We are living in a different ideological world than they. Personally, I think they would recognize the difference and make necessary adjustments. Would it be enough to convince Schaeffer and Lewis to do apologetics and evangelism in a different way? We will never know. All the same, I believe we are wise to at least consider doing evangelism through beauty.

In conclusion, I end where I began. With St. Augustine's *Confessions* and perhaps its most sublime prayer. It says that goodness and truth are found in the beauty of one person, Jesus Christ. In loving him, we always feel that we have arrived late; that we have, without ceasing, explored the world and discovered that we have come home "and know the place for the first time."[38] So, on bended knee, let's say this prayer to the one who is goodness, truth, and beauty itself:

> Late have I loved Thee, O Beauty so ancient and so new; late have I loved Thee! For behold Thou were within me, and I outside; and I sought Thee outside and in my unloveliness fell upon those lovely things that Thou hast made. Thou were with me and I was not with Thee. I was kept from Thee by those things, yet had they not been in Thee, they would not have been at all. Thou didst call and cry to me and break open my deafness: and Thou didst send forth Thy beams and shine upon me and chase away my blindness: Thou didst breathe fragrance upon me, and I drew in my breath and do now pant for Thee: I tasted Thee, and now hunger and thirst for Thee: Thou didst touch me, and I have burned for Thy peace.[39]

BIBLIOGRAPHY

Augustine. *Confessions*. Translated by Henry Chadwick. New York: Oxford University Press, 2008.

———. *The Confessions of St. Augustine*. Translated by F. J. Sheed. New York: Sheed & Ward, 1943.

Barna. "Americans Are Most Likely to Base Truth on Feelings." *Barna*, February 12, 2002. https://www.barna.com/research/americans-are-most-likely-to-base-truth-on-feelings.

Barron, Robert. "Catholicism and Beauty." Lecture delivered at the Religious Education Congress, Los Angeles, CA, March, 26, 2018. YouTube video, 1:01:42. https://youtu.be/iUBNTNiqn6o.

---

38. Eliot, *T. S. Eliot*, 209–10.

39. Augustine, *Confessions*, 236.

Catechism of the Catholic Church. 2nd ed. Washington, DC: United States Catholic Conference, 2000.

Choi, Charles Q. "Sense of Beauty Partly Innate, Study Suggests." *Live Science*, November 21, 2007. https://www.livescience.com/7389-sense-beauty-partly-innate-study-suggests.html.

Eliot, T. S. *T. S. Eliot: Collected Poems 1909–1962*. Orlando: Harcourt, 1991.

Follis, Bryan A. *Truth with Love: The Apologetics of Francis Schaeffer*. Wheaton, IL: Crossway, 2006.

Healy, Nicholas M. *Thomas Aquinas: Theologian of the Christian Life*. New York: Routledge, 2017.

Kappelman, Todd. "The Need to Read Francis Schaeffer." *Probe Ministries*, May 27, 1999. https://probe.org/the-need-to-read-francis-schaeffer.

Lamb, Gregory M. "People Believe They Can Make a Positive Difference, Poll Says." *Christian Science Monitor*, September 27, 2011. https://www.csmonitor.com/World/Making-a-difference/Change-Agent/2011/0927/People-believe-they-can-make-a-positive-difference-poll-says.

Lee, Dorothy. *Transfiguration*. New York: Continuum, 2004.

Lewis, C. S. *Mere Christianity*. New York: McMillan, 1977.

———. *Surprised by Joy*. New York: HarperCollins, 2017.

Lloyd-Jones, Sally. *The Jesus Storybook Bible*. Grand Rapids: Zondervan, 2009.

Navone, John. *Toward a Theology of Beauty*. Collegeville, MN: Liturgical, 1996.

Schreiner, Thomas R. *Paul, Apostle of God's Glory in Christ*. Downers Grove, IL: InterVarsity, 2020.

Smith, Zadie. *White Teeth: A Novel*. New York: Random, 2000.

Springsteen, Bruce. "Hungry Heart." Track 1 on *The River*, Columbia Records, 1980.

Wright, N. T. *Paul and the Faithfulness of God*. Minneapolis: Fortress, 2013.

———. *The Resurrection of the Son of God*. Minneapolis: Fortress, 2003.

21

In Defense of Beauty

How Gardens Manifest the Unity of Truth and Prescribe a Life-Preserving Posture of Submission

Mary Flickner

Were you to visit Freundschaftsinsel in Potsdam, Germany, you might notice clusters of grasses tipped with burnt red plumes. Come back in the dead of winter and the grasses would still be there, frosted with ice and glistening in sunlight like giant sticks of white rock candy. A little later still and the grasses would be sending up fresh green shoots from the root ball, eager to start the seasonal show again. You would be looking at Foerster's feather reed grass (*Calamagrostis acutiflora*). This is an award-winning perennial that provides structure and seasonal silhouettes to gardens around the world. The grasses deliver seasonal beauty without much fuss. Karl Foerster developed this cultivar. He was not tipped with red feathers, much preferring his signature beret, but he was long-lasting, undemanding, part gardener and part philosopher. Foerster did not merely set plants in the ground: He observed nature, noted her patterns, and joined her in what she was already doing. After his 1903 start in the plant business, Foerster developed a natural approach to gardening with perennials and grasses such that the gardener works in tune with nature. Foerster's ideas organically birthed a movement still in full force today. Noel Kingsbury and Piet Oudolf, both contemporary subscribers to Foerster's naturalistic approach, emphasize in their book, *Hummelo,* that "his mission was to grow a selection of plants from the contemporary 'chaos' of cultivars, and to combine beauty with reliability."[1] Foerster bred around three hundred seventy new plant varieties and developed his style in the midst of two wars and communist rule in his native East Germany. While he did not live to see reunification, his gardens did. Freundschaftsinsel is his legacy. This public garden "is today one of the most notable and well-labeled collections of perennials in Germany, and a true survivor—it was commissioned during the Nazi regime, maintained by the communist one, and restored after reunification."[2] Imagine that. Germany's soil witnessed trench warfare, Hitler's punishing steamroll through Western Europe, and communism's smash of all things free and creative. But the gardens survived.

Nature's enduring quality is profound. In the end, the age-old debate of whether or not a falling tree makes a sound when no one is around pales in comparison to this fact—a falling tree collapses to the forest floor and unleashes biological systems that create new life. The space created by its descent allows sunlight to reach plants once shaded, nurturing their growth upward. The ground beneath the tree claims new nutrients as it decomposes. Insects and animals reproduce in its hollow. Given time, the once-great tree is unrecognizable on the forest floor. Where has it gone? It has gone the way of nature, absorbed by the *logos* governing plant life. It has submitted to and participated in the resonance of the forest. Do we fault the tree for its submission? Or do we admire the bio-logic that organizes the generative forest and appraise the beauty of the great tree as it participates in that logic? Human experience with the natural world answers this question. We admire the beauty and find ourselves braced by it.

If ever your soul has thrilled while hiking through a forest or listening to birdsong in a meadow, come along on this brief journey into a garden's magical world that conveys deep truth for wise living. As famed neurologist Oliver Sacks and Oxford don C. S. Lewis will teach us, gardens evoke deep longing and spiritual awakening. The High Line garden in New York City will further demonstrate how participating in a garden's beauty requires us to learn and submit to her logic. Ultimately, the Christian worldview will find cosmological patterns for human flourishing in a garden. Christian faith is, in fact, rooted in garden imagery that profoundly directs human

---

1. Kingsbury and Oudolf, *Hummelo,* 60.
2. Kingsbury and Oudolf, *Hummelo,* 61.

life in the world. Human life begins in a garden—Eden. Human life is re-purposed to its original task of generative submission in a garden—Gethsemane. Human life finds its ultimate security and fullest expression in a garden—before a tree whose life source is a river flowing from the throne of God. A garden's beauty speaks of an absolute truth—there is a logic for life that cannot be transgressed without consequences. However, for the one willing to seek out this life-logic and submit to its norms, life awaits. When a Christian recites, "I believe in God the Father, maker of heaven and earth," the Christian articulates a most fundamental creed: Human life is best lived in submission to an all-encompassing logic that produces ever-expanding life and beauty. The garden shows us how.

Oliver Sacks practiced neurology in New York for decades. He also wrote extensively about swimming, about gardens, and about his patients, earning him the title, "The Poet-Laureate of Medicine." In a posthumous collection of essays, Dr. Sacks gives anecdotal evidence for a garden's nurturing capacities:

> I cannot say exactly how nature exerts its calming and organizing effects on our brains, but I have seen in my patients the restorative and healing powers of nature and gardens, even for those who are deeply disabled neurologically. In many cases, gardens and nature are more powerful than any medication. . . .
>
> I have a number of patients with very advanced dementia or Alzheimer's disease, who may have very little sense of orientation to their surroundings. They have forgotten, or cannot access, how to tie their shoes or handle cooking implements. But put them in front of a flower bed with some seedlings, and they will know exactly what to do—I have never seen such a patient plant something upside down. . . .
>
> Clearly, nature calls to something very deep in us. Biophilia, the love of nature and living things is an essential part of the human condition. Hortophilia, the desire to interact with, manage and tend nature, is also deeply instilled in us. . . . The effects of nature's qualities on health are not only spiritual and emotional but physical and neuro-logical. I have no doubt that they reflect deep changes in the brain's physiology, and perhaps even its structure.[3]

Writing some sixty years before Sacks, Oxford don C. S. Lewis shares his first encounter with a garden's beauty. Lewis was young, shut up inside

---

3. Sacks, *Everything*, 245–47.

with sickness, when his brother "brought into the nursery the lid of a biscuit tin which he had covered with moss and garnished with twigs and flowers so as to make it a toy garden or a toy forest."[4] Lewis explains an awakening: The garden "made me aware of nature—not, indeed, as a storehouse of forms and colours but as something cool, dewy, fresh, exuberant."[5] The awakening is furthered by the view outside his nursery window of the Castlereagh Hills. These hills, he writes, "made me for good or ill, and before I was six years old, a votary of the Blue Flower."[6] Lewis claims the toy garden and the green hills awakened *sehnsucht,* longing to grasp all that is infinitely beautiful, enduring, and true.

Sacks and Lewis both indicate that something happens when a human being perceives beauty in the natural world. More specifically, a garden provides sensory context for human encounters with physical forms that transcend the physical. Sacks praises the garden because of its power to organize the neurological function of otherwise disordered minds. A tangible garden administers intangible effects. This famed neurologist admits that, though scientifically unproven, experientially he has witnessed that gardens heal. Human beings interact with gardens and sense their resonance. They exist in material form but somehow elicit an immaterial force. Lewis makes a similar observation, stating that the toy garden was *more than* its particular form. Writing in his mid-fifties, Lewis looks back at his sixth year as the beginning of a journey toward an organizing Absolute that structures reality. The garden alerted him to beauty, and beauty alerted him to an ideal that existed outside of the physical form it took.

Like Lewis, G. K. Chesterton speaks of physical forms alerting him to something transcendent. He outlines his own first steps toward an Absolute in *Orthodoxy*:

> I felt in my bones; first, that this world does not explain itself. ... The thing is magic, true or false.
> Second, I came to feel as if magic must have a meaning, and meaning must have some one to mean it. There was something personal in the world, as in a work of art. ...
> Third, I thought this purpose beautiful in its old design, in spite of its defects. ...
> Fourth, that the proper form of thanks to it is some form of humility and restraint.

---

4. Lewis, *Surprised by Joy*, 6.
5. Lewis, *Surprised by Joy*, 6.
6. Lewis, *Surprised by Joy*, 6.

> ... And last, and strangest, there had come into my mind a vague and vast impression that in some way all good was a remnant to be stored and held sacred out of some primordial ruin.[7]

Chesterton outlines a fascinating philosophical journey activated by encounters with "trees and planets," "the Matterhorn," and "this cosmos . . . without peer and without price."[8] The sensory intake comes first, creating a spark of delight, an appraisal of beauty, and a longing. This is Lewis's *sehnsucht*. What the eyes see, ears hear, and skin feels is beautiful beyond mere shape and sound and texture. Beauty has no quantifiable proof. But do not "all men by nature desire to know?"[9] Chesterton himself says that "thinking means connecting things, and stops if they cannot be connected."[10] *Sehnsucht* instigates a search for the proof, the logic, the root that produces the beauty. But if a logic exists, submission will be required. Here is the strange turn Chesterton notes: Submission to beauty's logic is not stagnant admiration, but life-preserving participation. Lewis echoes this sentiment, writing, "The Desirable . . . cares only for temples building and not at all for temples built."[11] Beauty creates longing. Longing searches out logic. Beauty's logic requires submission. Submission enables participation.

Gardens embody this journey from beauty to generative participation. The High Line in New York City can serve as a case study. Once an elevated train line transporting foodstuffs from the Meatpacking District of the city, the line fell silent by the 1980s. Much of the structure was removed and new real estate developed. In the late Nineties, many urged complete demolition of the remaining section. It was, after all, a simple case of city blight, an unsightly remnant of a former Industrial Age. Before leaving office, Mayor Rudy Giuliani signed the order for demolition. Yet a 2002 *New York Times* article headlines: "On West Side, Rail Plan Is Up and Walking."[12] A local group, Friends of the High Line, had been lobbying behind the scenes for the railway to be repurposed as a public space. David Dunlap writes in the *New York Times* piece that a public space "is not easy to envision while standing in the dark shadow of the viaduct. . . . But it becomes clearer on the deck, where trees, weeds and wildflowers among rusting tracks and switches create a verdant swath through Hell's Kitchen, Chelsea and the Gansevoort

---

7. Chesterton, *Orthodoxy*, 63.
8. Chesterton, *Orthodoxy*, 63.
9. Aristotle, *Metaphysica*, 980.
10. Chesterton, *Orthodoxy*, 31.
11. Lewis, *Surprised by Joy*, 205.
12. Dunlap, "On West Side."

Meat Market."[13] Founders of the Friends, Joshua David and Robert Hammond, had been "inspired by the beauty of this hidden landscape."[14] The lobbying succeeded. A newly elected Mayor Bloomberg enacted protections for the railway and discussions commenced on how best to cultivate the space. Beauty was at work.

Just like the railway that prescribed a patterned path for movement, beauty's work has a pattern. David and Hammond happened upon an urban meadow of sorts in the midst of the derelict tracks. Native plant species, scattered and planted by wind and rain, had subscribed to the same bio-logic as the great tree in the forest. The seeds had landed in soil, been watered by rain, and called upward by sunlight. Developed plants had run their seasonal course, released seeds from their dried-out flowers, and fallen to the ground to generously return nutrients to the soil, building up organic biomass thirty feet above the concrete below. Birds, insects, and pollinators assisted in this process. Some non-native plant species even found expression in this spontaneous garden although how they got there is a mystery. One can only imagine the resulting *sehnsucht* produced by this scene. Beauty called to neighborhood residents who knew about this hidden garden, and they answered with a generative project. Today, the High Line is a world-renowned urban perennial garden, where visitors are instructed "to appreciate nature's remarkable ability to heal the scars of dereliction."[15]

Yet beauty's path from *sehnsucht* to generative participation has some stops in between. Dutch garden designer Piet Oudolf can testify to those stops. Following in Karl Foerster's footsteps, Oudolf has garnered a reputation in his native Netherlands and beyond for "a deep knowledge of plants and an appreciation of plant diversity."[16] Recognizing that "knowledge creates freedom," Oudolf has spent a lifetime studying, propagating, and combining perennials and grasses to create natural landscapes in wide open spaces and tight urban centers.[17] As any serious gardener knows, creating a natural landscape requires deep knowledge of how landscapes work. A gardener cannot violate soil, sunlight, water, and space needs. The logic governing how plants interact with one another and their environment is fixed. The best gardeners learn this logic and submit to it. Creative expression is not dampened by submission to bio-logic. Creative expression is magnified. When Oudolf was selected to design the High Line gardens, his task was to

13. Dunlap, "On West Side."
14. Friends of the High Line, "History."
15. Kingsbury and Oudolf, *Hummelo*, 327.
16. Kingsbury and Oudolf, *Hummelo*, 17.
17. Kingsbury and Oudolf, *Hummelo*, 18.

mimic the wild landscape that first inspired David and Hammond to save the railway. When beauty calls to the human spirit, she can be joined only by those who will learn her ways and submit to her logic. Kingsbury notes in her book with Oudolf that "the visual challenge in creating a planting scheme for the High Line was . . . unlike anything Piet has had to cope with in his career."[18] What prepared him for this challenge was his past "intensive research into North American native plants" and his personal experience with many of those plants in his private gardens at Hummelo.[19] Oudolf had studied the logic of these plants. Knowledge of and submission to that logic enabled him to participate in what nature had already done on the High Line. Today, *sehnsucht* is heightened and multiplied. What used to be a hidden garden in the midst of an otherwise blighted stretch of track is now a vibrant community space generating life from the microbes in the soil to the human connections made on the walkways. Quite appropriately, Foerster's feather reed grass grows there.

To visit the High Line is to be nurtured. As Oliver Saks observed in his neurology patients, human beings heal and awaken when in contact with the natural world. In many ways, gardens tune us, recalibrating our attention to what is enduring and beautiful. Though humans are willful creatures who have freedom to select value-rubrics for their lives, a garden provides this tangible lesson: You must choose in accordance with beauty's logic if your life is to be caught up in her resonance. As seen already in both Lewis and Chesterton, the Christian belief is that beauty's logic is in fact the Absolute logic for the universe. It is the Logos that organizes all reality, seen and unseen. This Absolute transforms willful submission into generative participation. This belief stands in stark contrast to post-Enlightenment philosophical thought. The place of divergence centers on ideas of truth. Is truth unified, set down by the divine Logos, or is truth bifurcated?

Nancy Pearcey writes extensively about bifurcated truth in *Saving Leonardo: A Call to Resist the Secular Assault on Mind, Morals, and Meaning*. As a student of Francis Schaeffer and former resident of L'Abri, Pearcey explores historical examples of a foundational Schaefferian premise: Beginning with the Reformation and continuing through the Enlightenment and beyond, truth is functionally divided between facts and values. This dualism has profound consequences on the way humans view themselves, the world, and their place in it. Pearcey explains that scientific facts "are held to be empirically testable and universally valid" while values, "things like morality, theology, and aesthetics . . . are now regarded as subjective and culturally

---

18. Kingsbury and Oudolf, *Hummelo*, 328.
19. Kingsbury and Oudolf, *Hummelo*, 328.

relative."[20] This means that "humans can have genuine knowledge only in the realm of empirical facts."[21] Or stated in another way, humans can have confidence only in empirical facts. We can only build consensual agreements based on empirical facts. What then happens to all truth claims in the realm of values? Claims of morality, theology, and aesthetics become subjective. Pearcey summarizes the dilemma:

> What this means is that most people live fragmented lives. In the private world of home, church, and friendships, they operate on a view of truth (subjective values) that is completely contrary to the one they employ in the public world of work, business, and politics (objective facts). The opposition between facts and values has become the main obstacle to living as whole persons with a consistent, coherent philosophy of life.[22]

Like the Roman god Janus, our Western outlook has two different faces, viewing two different realities and prescribing two different rubrics for living. There is no governing logic over all life, thus compromising preservation of that life. Consistency and coherence dwindle, and generative participation with a larger world is compromised.

In his 1943 University of Durham Riddell Memorial Lecture series, now published as *The Abolition of Man*, Lewis critiques the spread of this fact/value split in education and imagines the frightful world that will emerge if this approach to truth runs its course. In his first lecture, "Men Without Chests," he accuses modern educators of propagating the fact/value split. These educators indoctrinate their pupils "in the belief that all emotions aroused by local association are in themselves contrary to reason and contemptible."[23] According to their aberrant way of thinking, Coleridge before the waterfall was not actually appraising the scene as sublime—because who could logically prove that? What is felt cannot be reasoned with because it is not factual. It is relative. Lewis notes that this recent "progress" of human reason runs contrary to a rather long philosophical tradition: "Aristotle says that the aim of education is to make the pupil like and dislike what he ought."[24] The aim of education is actually to develop "the Chest—Magnanimity—Sentiment—these are the indispensable liaison officers between cerebral man and visceral man."[25] Writing several decades later in *The*

20. Pearcey, *Saving Leonardo*, 26.
21. Pearcey, *Saving Leonardo*, 2.
22. Pearcey, *Saving Leonardo*, 29.
23. Lewis, "Abolition of Man," 431.
24. Lewis, "Abolition of Man," 434.
25. Lewis, "Abolition of Man," 437.

Closing of the American Mind, Allan Bloom laments that "the quest begun by Odysseus and continued over three millennia has come to an end with the observation that there is nothing to seek."[26] The "ought" has been removed. Value creation replaces value discovery. Both Lewis and Bloom observe the consequences: If you do not train a student to value what he ought, he will in the end be highly vulnerable to an irrational and incoherent life. Lewis claims that all students must be trained to recognize and submit to the *Tao*—"the doctrine of objective value, the belief that certain attitudes are really true, and others really false, to the kind of thing the universe is, and the kind of things we are."[27] Only in this way can one develop into the participatory creature he essentially is. Lewis explains in the second lecture, "The Way," that two alternative choices arise by modern man's challenge of objective value: either exist in a constant state of internal incoherence, denying the presence of the *Tao* while loving the order and justice the *Tao* provides, or—go the way of Nietzsche and kill God.

In his final lecture, "The Abolition of Man," Lewis explores a world where the *Tao* is rejected and the only organizing principle for human beings is that of power wielded via scientific knowledge. Nature no longer makes tangible the invisible but true *Tao*. Nature, as empirically studied and manipulated by man, becomes the *Tao*. Here we see the footprint of Nietzsche's Overman. Without an unseen, but discoverable, value-logic governing the universe and man, and man in the midst of the universe, submission is replaced by power. In particular, submission is replaced by the power of scientific knowledge unregulated by an Absolute. Science becomes the only rubric by which man lives and makes his way in the world. Yet without an overarching value-logic, Lewis cautions that "Whatever *Tao* there is will be the product, not the motive, of education."[28] Bloom observes that "the value-creating man" is posited as "a plausible substitute for a good man."[29] In the real world, this cannot work. Lewis exposes the great fault of Overman. Without the *Tao*, life is consumed by defining, enacting, and solidifying one's own meaning. Human life is devoured by human choice until it is no longer human at all. Here Lewis explains the lecture's title: "Stepping outside the *Tao*, they have stepped into the void. Nor are their subjects necessarily unhappy men. They are not men at all: they are artefacts. Man's final conquest has proved to be the abolition of Man."[30] In

26. Bloom, *Closing of the American Mind*, 143.
27. Lewis, "Abolition of Man," 435.
28. Lewis, "Abolition of Man," 451.
29. Bloom, *Closing*, 144.
30. Lewis, "Abolition of Man," 453.

his lecture, Lewis attempts to expose the folly of structuring life solely in accordance with what is seen, measured, and scientific. Without an unseen value-logic that governs all, humanity utterly loses its humanness.

G. K. Chesterton also analyzes the effects of denying objective value in *Orthodoxy*. He illustrates the weakening effect of such a denial. A human being cut off from a unified truth is equally cut off from generative participation in the world. Chesterton says, "the wild worship of lawlessness and the materialist worship of law end in the same void."[31] He uses Tolstoy and Nietzsche as particular examples. When values are subjective, some choose to hold their hands open in a refusal to assign meaning (Tolstoy). Others are compelled to accept everything (Nietzsche). In his witty, yet biting prose, Chesterton continues:

> The Tolstoyan's will is frozen by a Buddhist instinct that all special actions are evil. But the Nietzscheite's will is quite equally frozen by his view that all special actions are good; for if all special actions are good, none of them are special. They stand at the cross-roads, and one hates all the roads and the other likes all the roads. The result is—well, some things are not hard to calculate. They stand at the cross-roads.[32]

This, Chesterton says, is an example of "using mental activity so as to reach mental helplessness."[33] His final blow comes as a woman dressed in men's clothing. Chesterton exclaims, "Joan of Arc was not stuck at the cross-roads. . . . She chose a path, and went down it like a thunderbolt. . . . She was a perfectly practical person who did something, while they are wild speculators who do nothing."[34] There you have it: Life devoid of an objective value is consumed by deliberation and fails at its generative task while life submitted to an objective value can act with coherence and confidence in the midst of the world.

It is not an overgeneralization to say that we all stand at the crossroads. Each of us lives in accordance with a selected direction. Christian philosopher Arthur Holmes explains personhood in *The Idea of a Christian College* as reflective, valuing, and responsible. Reflective and valuing capacities make a person who she is and thus prescribe the particular ways said person interacts with the surrounding world via her responsibilities. Humans cannot help but interact with the world around them, causing fundamental changes based on that interaction. At the most basic level of interaction,

31. Chesterton, *Orthodoxy*, 40.
32. Chesterton, *Orthodoxy*, 39.
33. Chesterton, *Orthodoxy*, 40.
34. Chesterton, *Orthodoxy*, 41.

humans are much like the plants growing on New York City's High Line. We breathe and cause changes in the oxygen-carbon dioxide cycle. We drink and participate in the water cycle. We eat and join the food cycle. We have specific air, water, and nutrient needs that cannot be transgressed if life is to flourish. Bio-logic is as binding to a human being as it is to a plant. But unlike the perennials and grasses, we make choices about our value-logic. We stand at a metaphorical crossroads and decide what truth will direct us in the world. The perspective of the fact/value split acknowledges the binding nature of bio-logic; this is an empirical logic, rational and quantifiable. But value selection is not binding: Each individual must be free from all extraneous absolutes in order to exercise unique human capacities to choose one's own meaning. Allan Bloom observes in *The Closing of the American Mind* that viewing the value realm as relative means, "There are no absolutes. Freedom is absolute."[35]

The Christian view of truth stands in sharp contrast to this relativity. The Christian worldview acknowledges the religious choice given to every human being and even finds in this religious choice an argument for human distinctiveness. Brian Walsh and Richard Middleton argue in *The Transforming Vision* that religious choice, along with dominion, is what it means to be created *Imago Dei*.[36] Yet here is where the Christian view radically diverges from adherents to value relativity—value selections are freely made, yet they issue predetermined ends. Yes, a human being stands at a crossroads and freely selects which road to take. But the ultimate end of each direction is set and cannot be altered. Christianity is indisputably teleological (see Rom 6:20–23).

When he first encountered beauty in the biscuit-tin garden, C. S. Lewis was awakened to something desirable and permanent in the world. For decades, this awakened *sehnsucht* compelled Lewis to chase beauty and the joy she elicited so that he could satisfy his longing. But Lewis came to see that beauty and joy were signposts guiding him along a worthy road. They were not, in fact, the destination. Lewis writes that joy "was valuable only as a pointer to something other and outer."[37] Beauty had worked on Lewis's view of reality: "I had always wanted, above all things, not to be 'interfered with.' I had wanted (mad wish) 'to call my soul my own.' . . . Total surrender, the absolute leap in the dark, were demanded. The reality with which no treaty can be made was upon me."[38] Lewis was free to select which road

---

35. Bloom, *Closing*, 28.
36. Walsh and Middleton, *Transforming Vision*, 53.
37. Lewis, *Surprised by Joy*, 291.
38. Lewis, *Surprised by Joy*, 278–79.

to travel, but if he wanted beauty's road, he would have to go her way. Here is Christian truth: "You show me the path of life. In your presence there is fullness of joy; in your right hand are pleasures forevermore" (Ps 16:11 NRSV). Just as the Logos creates natural law to which all life necessarily subscribes, the Logos knows the one path that leads to human joy. Beauty led Lewis from *sehnsucht* to Absolute logic, to the knowledge essential to generative living.

Christianity sees all truth originating with the Logos—with God himself. This Logos directs the natural world, generating life. Across the wisdom books, Scripture exhorts man to look at this Logos as empirical proof for the rightness of God's total authority and wise ordering of willful human hearts. Nature submits and thrives. Oh man, submit and join in life's resonance!

The first garden sets the pattern for life: Submit and thrive. Adam and Eve are placed in Eden so that they can learn this pattern. Eden pulses with life. Bio-logic traces its way through climate and soil, plant and animal diversity, through rivers teeming with creatures that breathe water and skies alive with birds who perfectly orient themselves to home. There are insects and amphibians, vines and trees. How many shades of green? This is a multi-dimensional diverse place ordered by the Logos. Adam and Eve, beauty has signposts everywhere; study, for you have a test.

> The LORD God took the man and put him in the garden of Eden to till it and keep it. And the LORD God commanded the man, "You may freely eat of every tree of the garden; but of the tree of the knowledge of good and evil you shall not eat, for in the day that you eat of it you shall die." (Gen 2:15–17 NRSV)

Alexander Schmemann writes in *For the Life of the World* that "the world of nature, cut off from the source of life, is a dying world."[39] Due to their special position as culture-keepers, human beings will either lead the world to its life source or away from it. Adam and Eve have their free choice, but whichever way they choose has its ultimate end.

Here is the heart of Christian doctrine, and it is established in a garden: The visible world testifies to invisible realities that must be accepted by faith. This is not Platonic dualism where true reality exists in the forms and particulars merely reflect that reality. This is unified Christian truth. Reality is both visible and invisible and is unified by its source—the Logos. Human beings join the life-preserving and life-creating source when they submit by faith to that source. Adam and Eve's task in the garden was cultivation. This is a generative task. Increase! Spread out! Order! Diversify! By what rubric

---

39. Schmemann, *For the Life of the World*, 17.

shall they do this? What logic will govern such a magnificent task? As Paul says, "the righteousness of God is revealed through faith for faith, as it is written, 'The one who is righteous will live by faith'" (Rom 1:17 NRSV). The world achieves its "ought" when human beings submit by faith to the Logos found solely in God.

This pattern finds its ultimate expression when "the Word became flesh and lived among us" (John 1:14 NRSV). Adam and Eve did not order their dominion by faith. They attempted to select a value-rubric that was not consistent with reality. Knowledge of good and evil apart from submission to God is no knowledge at all. It is, as Schmemann says, "cut off from the source of life." As such, the world directed by the descendants of Adam is cultivated into death. This is the first stepping outside of the *Tao* and, therefore, into the void. But God's Logos will have its way. The Second Adam also finds himself in a garden. Where the garden of Eden pulsed with light and life, Gethsemane was overshadowed by suffering and death. The religious choice in front of the Second Adam was the same: Either submit to what the Logos requires and attach the world to its life-source or reject what the Logos requires and unhitch the world from its life-source. The Second Adam, the incarnate Son of God, Christ Jesus, agonized before his own crossroad: "Father, if you are willing, remove this cup from me; yet, not my will but yours be done" (Luke 22:42 NRSV). The Second Adam submitted to the Logos. In his submission, he was the grain of wheat that fell to the earth and died, and in this dying, he bore much fruit (see John 12:24). The Christian sees submission as the gateway to generative participation with all that is good and just and beautiful.

In *Culture Care: Reconnecting with Beauty for Our Common Life*, artist and author Makoto Fujimura admires beauty as "a gratuitous gift of the creator God" and states that it, therefore, "finds its source and its purpose in God's character."[40] If we wish to appraise beauty for her goodness and participate in extending her reach, we must "know the full depth of the gospel of Jesus Christ" as this is the designated means by which human beings can know God's character.[41] Fujimura rejects the all-too-common reduction of the gospel as "truncated, limited to pragmatic and tribal concerns rather than the good news of the whole of the Bible—true life, the never-ending restoration and new creation of all things in Christ."[42] Biblical faith is holistic and sees in the gospel the reattachment of the visible world to its invisible life source in the Logos. Christian discipleship, therefore, is a working

---

40. Fujimura, *Culture Care*, 51.
41. Fujimura, *Culture Care*, 91.
42. Fujimura, *Culture Care*, 91.

out of submission to this Logos such that the Christian's life generates life. Fujimura writes,

> Culture care emphasizes that God cares for the *whole* of the creation (as his own artwork) and for history (as God's own story lived through our fallen reality), and that there is not one hair of our head or one moment of our journey that God does not pay close attention to (Luke 12:7). Culture care takes Jesus himself, who cared for people, his surroundings, and his culture, as a model for us all.[43]

Christians see Christ, the incarnated Logos, as the rubric that guides all generative life on earth. Furthermore, Christians see in his gospel the ability for human beings to be re-established in their co-creative labors with the Logos. This world calls us into participation, but Christians claim participation can only and ever be directed via submission to God's norms for all that he has created via Christ.

One final time, the garden instructs us. The High Line in New York City was birthed by *sehnsucht*. The beauty of a meadow poking up through post-Industrial railroad ties spoke of something worth preserving. Beauty was a signpost saying, "Join me." Bio-logic was necessarily sought out in order to create a sustainable, thriving, and diverse garden on the west side of Manhattan. Yet, once the logic was discerned and the garden planted, was the work complete? Just ask the gardeners maintaining the High Line. They work year long to organically maintain Piet Oudolf's design for this vibrant space. Each gardener "is allocated a zone for which he or she is completely responsible" and Oudolf meets annually with the garden staff to plan how each zone should evolve.[44] Gardens, after all, are not static. As plant life matures and interacts with its environment, changes occur. Oudolf and the garden staff seek to cultivate the garden in light of these changes so that the original aesthetic is maintained. When it comes time to change plants because of pests or disease or to adjust the understory as a tree matures, Oudolf and the garden staff use the overarching aesthetic, the garden's design, to make decisions about necessary adjustments. Fujimura widens the application of this process: "In its gratuity and generosity, beauty—paradoxically—helps set boundaries on how we live."[45] Because the aesthetic of the High Line is fixed and because bio-logic prescribes what can and cannot achieve that aesthetic, Oudolf and the garden staff are not stuck at the

---

43. Fujimura, *Culture Care*, 91.
44. Kingsbury and Oudolf, *Hummelo*, 334.
45. Fujimura, *Culture Care*, 52.

crossroads deliberating about which way to go. They know their way and set to work tending the garden.

In a world where truth is bifurcated into facts and values, Christians are braced by a unified Logos. Chesterton observes that insanity "is reason used without root, reason in the void. The man who begins to think without the proper first principles goes mad; he begins to think at the wrong end."[46] When a Christian begins with the authority of God over all things, as the wise creator and sustainer of all things, all of a sudden he is freed to join the resonance of the universe. He takes one mysterious leap of faith "and everything else becomes lucid."[47] Like the great tree submitting to the logic of the forest in its life and its death, the Christian submits to the logic of the universe. This submission ultimately points, alongside beauty, to the *ultimate* end—"Your kingdom come, Your will be done, on earth as it is in heaven" (Matt 6:10 NRSV).

BIBLIOGRAPHY

Aristotle. *Metaphysica*. Vol. 8 of *The Works of Aristotle*. Translated by W. D. Ross. Oxford: Clarendon, 1963.
Bloom, Allan. *The Closing of the American Mind: How Higher Education Has Failed Democracy and Impoverished the Souls of Today's Students*. New York: Simon & Schuster, 1987.
Chesterton, G. K. *Orthodoxy*. New York: Doubleday, 2001.
Dunlap, David W. "On West Side, Rail Plan Is Up and Walking," *New York Times*, December 22, 2002. https://www.nytimes.com/2002/12/22/nyregion/on-west-side-rail-plan-is-up-and-walking.html.
Fujimura, Makoto. *Culture Care: Reconnecting Beauty for Our Common Life*. Downers Grove, IL: InterVarsity, 2017.
Friends of the High Line. "History." *High Line*. https://www.thehighline.org/history.
Kingsbury, Noel, and Piet Oudolf. *Hummelo: A Journey through a Plantsman's Life*. New York: Monacelli, 2015.
Lewis, C. S. "The Abolition of Man." In *The Essential C. S. Lewis*, edited by Lyle W. Dorsett, 428–66. New York: Simon & Schuster, 1988.
———. *Surprised by Joy*. New York: HarperCollins, 1955.
Pearcey, Nancy. *Saving Leonardo: A Call to Resist the Secular Assault on Mind, Morals & Meaning*. Nashville: Broadman & Holman, 2010.
Sacks, Oliver. *Everything in Its Place: First Loves and Lost Tales*. New York: Knopf, 2019.
Schmemann, Alexander. *For the Life of the World: Sacraments and Orthodoxy*. Crestwood, NY: St. Vladimir's Seminary, 1973.
Walsh, Brian J., and J. Richard Middleton. *The Transforming Vision: Shaping a Christian Worldview*. Downers Grove, IL: InterVarsity, 1984.

---

46. Chesterton, *Orthodoxy*, 22.
47. Chesterton, *Orthodoxy*, 23.

Afterword

Dare to Be a Davey[1]

Steven Garber

Dare to be a Daniel,
Dare to stand alone!
Dare to have a purpose firm!
Dare to make it known.

A Sunday school song it is, and not great theology—abstracted as it is from the story of salvation, the Great Story which makes sense of every story—but for a host of reasons I thought of these words as I thought of Davey Naugle because at their very best they represent what I have long prized about my dear friend and brother.

In the most simple, straightforward way, I have loved Davey's loves. His commitments and passions, his deeply held visions and dreams, are born of the very heart of God and are given away with Texas charm and generosity. For the years of his life he has kept at them with an unusual wisdom and creativity, a fabric woven of grace and truth, his life being given for our lives, which in this frail, fragile world, is just about as good as it gets.

It was our common concern to understand the purposes of God, and how we might make them known that first drew Davey and me together in Charlottesville, Virginia, thirty years ago, younger men that we were, on the

---

1. From a talk I gave in honor of David Naugle on April 17, 2018.

other side of adulthood, just beginning to find our way into the lives and loves that have been ours—and we have been walking together ever since.

We have never been neighbors, as miles and more miles have separated us, but we have been brothers, sharing together a common set of questions. For years we have taught students, inviting them into our hearts, offering them the best of our minds, longing for them to learn to see the world as God sees it.

While my questions have focused on vocation and the common good, Davey's have been similar but different. A philosopher and a theologian, he has given himself to understanding the ways that human beings make sense of who they are, and why and how they live, in and through it all teaching us to order our loves well, for God's sake and ours. Washington, DC, the great city of glory and shame, has been the setting of my teaching; for Davey it has been Dallas, this great city of commerce and culture that for the wider world defines Texas, for blessing and for curse—yes, for blessing and for curse!

For many years I served as the scholar-in-residence for the Council for Christian Colleges and Universities, traveling around the United States to scores of schools like Dallas Baptist University, meeting administrators, faculty, and students far and wide. I got to know a lot of people in a lot of places. And you should know that characteristically I am not a "best this" or a "best that" kind of person; life is simply too complex for that, with too many nuances and differences that are important to us.

Simply said, I have long believed that Davey is the best professor in America. He has mastered the world of his work, understanding the integral relationship of theology to philosophy, seeing into the deepest questions of the human heart, ones that run through every son of Adam and daughter of Eve, and then guiding his students with a remarkable wisdom, grace, and skill into honest answers to their honest questions—from beginning to end, loving his students into loving the things that matter most. He has excelled at that, and together we all say, "Thanks be to God."

To press the point: Any of us who know the rigors of the academy stand in awe of someone who runs the gauntlet of doctoral study; I know that I came to believe that there were many good reasons to stop on this side of a PhD. I almost did—several times! But for someone to do it twice is truly amazing. Davey's questions mattered so much to him that he chose to do two doctoral degrees, one in theology and one in philosophy. He is a *very* smart man! But that was never the point of his life or of his learning.

Even more important, he has seen his study as a stewardship before God in service to the world. For the best of reasons he has avoided the temptation which lurks around the corner of every heart—to get all As and still flunk life. Rather, he has offered his insights to thousands of students, showing the watching world that moral intelligence is both possible and plausible. In his own inimitable way, his own life is an apologetic for the belief that worldviews can become ways of life—and done so with winsome gracefulness.

While I have often been drawn to Dallas to work alongside Davey, by his grace invited to enter his world here at DBU, meeting his students, sometimes even meeting their parents, he and I have sometimes joined our vocations together in service to other people in other places.

For example, several years ago I was invited to lecture at the Beijing Film Academy in China. As I began to understand the nature of the invitation, I asked Davey if he was interested in coming along. So very able to do so much, I knew that the Chinese translation of his book, *Worldview: A History of the Concept*, had been published by Beijing University Press and that the philosophy department would be surprisingly graced by his presence; in fact, they would be proud to have him lecture to their best students.

And so we traveled together to China, spending days seeing the city, meeting officials from every sector of the society, but then going our own ways to lecture, Davey being received at the prestigious philosophy department at Beijing University to lecture on his book, a book that is seen as the definitive text exploring the nature and character of a worldview. Hear that again: He wrote the definitive book of his generation on the nature of worldviews, and the academic world of the most populous nation on earth honored his intellectual excellence and integrity by publishing it for China.

But Davey and I have also traveled more locally, even making the drive to Austin once, stopping by Crawford on our way in the early years of the Bush presidency, wanting to see what we could of the ranch—and of course along the highway we lingered, tasting Texas's best barbecue, lip-smacking as it was! Yes, we have loved ideas, but we have also loved brisket, as all good people should!

But "Dare to be Daniel"? In what sense does this simple song remind me of Davey? While I resist any effort to abstract the man Daniel, making him a hero of heroes, there is something about the wisdom and courage of the Old Testament prophet that ripples its way across time into the life and labor of Professor Naugle. Fundamentally, I see Daniel as a faithful servant of God in the grand metanarrative of the Bible, taking up his calling in the time and place of fifth-century Babylon, called to see the world, to make sense of history for the sake of history.

I see my dear friend Davey in the same way, differently situated of course—unless we want to wonder about the relation of Babylon to Dallas! Davey is a faithful servant of God in this time and this place, called to see and hear for the sake of all, taking up his own story within the grand story of redemptive history, offering his vocation for the sake of the common good. Therefore, while I smile at the idea of Davey's being a hero of heroes, it is also true that wherever his work has taken him, he is loved and respected, a hero of theological and philosophical imagination for students and professors alike. Very personally, Davey has been that to me for the years of my life—a hero of heroes, taking up his calling with a rare wisdom and courage. Vocation is a good word here, because it is a big word, a complex word that must account for the complexity of a life, the complexity of the loves and labors, liturgy and learning that make Davey the man that we honor.

The story of Daniel is a story of vocation, isn't it? At its heart, it is that. The first half of the book, the fascinating narrative that it is—full of exile and education, of dreams and visions, of fiery furnaces and lion's dens—is the story of a man called by God to work for the flourishing of Babylon, serving as the chief political counselor to three kings, despots as they were, tyrants each one. But Daniel served them as he served their kingdoms, weighing in on taxation and economic policy, on water resources and agricultural production, on military strength and the building of highways. Having mastered the literature and culture of Babylon as a young man, he became the wisest man in the land, called by God to seek the flourishing of his city, using his office to speak prophetically into his time and place, and known by all who knew him as a man passionately committed to his commitments.

In the second half of the book, the story becomes more complex, becoming hard to read, very difficult to understand. The dreams are no longer for someone else, but they are dreams given by God to Daniel—so that Daniel will know more fully what is going on in the world and what his own part is to be in that world.

The dreams made him unsettled. He could not sleep at night. Chapter by chapter, dream after dream, he was unable to make sense of what the dreams meant for the world and for him. We have no record of Daniel faltering in his faith even as he struggled to understand. The last word we have about Daniel in the book is that he was perplexed.

Dear friends of Davey, they are words worth pondering: *Daniel was perplexed*. Reading providence is always hard, isn't it? It was for Daniel, it is for us. Especially so in the moment, when history is happening. What on earth is going on? What does it all mean? How could this possibly be the way that it is? Those are very human questions; everyone everywhere asks them.

And every one of us here today asks those questions, too, about life at large, about our world and our nation, and we ask them too about the heartache of Davey's health. Why? What? How?

As I have long lived with Daniel's story, reading and reading it again as I try to understand more fully the meaning of human vocation in the world, I have come to the surprising conclusion that Daniel's last words are a strange grace to us. *He was perplexed.* This hero of heroes was perplexed. He could not make sense of his moment in any proximate sense. Even as he trusted God with his life, believing the God of Israel to be the Lord of history, he did not understand what God was saying to him in and through the providence of his life. Daniel was looking through a glass darkly, seeing and not seeing.

In this very now-but-not-yet life and world, we are too. And in the midst of this moment of celebration of the long labor of love that has been Davey Naugle's work at Dallas Baptist University and beyond, we are seeing this day through a glass darkly. *We are perplexed.*

In my office at Regent College, my walls are full of books, but there is one book that I have chosen to stand tall on my desk. With two bronzed Trafalgar Square lions on either side, it is a book that captures the highest hope for many professors the world over, intriguingly titled *The Love of Learning and the Desire for God,* by Jean LeClerq. For years I have seen this book as the heart of my vision for my work, teacher that I am. I want my students to learn to love learning, but to do so integrally born of their desire for God. Not learning and faith, as if somehow those are different worlds, but rather a profound twining together of faith and learning, of who I am and what I believe woven together with my deepest of all desires.

As I thought about Davey for this day and remembered the lions of Daniel's life, I thought too of the lions on my desk, differently done as they are. Not roaring with hunger, but silent sentinels; once guarding and protecting the world, now they stand as bookends, holding up this unusual book that so movingly sums up the good work of the good man that Davey is. He has loved learning, and that love has grown out of his desire for God, for most of thirty years living his life among the students of Dallas Baptist University, and many more the world over. We have all learned from his loves, over his shoulder and through his heart, and that is the truest and deepest kind of learning.

Dare to be a Daniel? For this day, let it be this instead: *Dare to be a Davey.* All of us together give thanks to God for you, David Naugle—friend and professor and colleague that you are. You have shown every one of us what it means to be both holy and human, and we are blessed to be woven into the heart of your life.

A last word. I have often smiled, knowing Davey as I do, knowing DBU as I do, knowing Texas as I do. God alone knows how often it has been that good-hearted and hopeful parents have sent their dear sons and daughters to DBU, trusting that they will become even better Baptists, when all is said and done through their four years here. Little did they know that they would meet Dr. Naugle along the way, a professor who would love them into ways of seeing and hearing the world that would change them forever. Not deconstructing their Baptist theology, never that—instead drawing them into a profoundly Christian vision of life and learning, offering his students better and deeper reasons to be good Baptists, of course, but even more, to be mere Christians, committed to commitments that are the heart of true faith through the centuries, a faith that will form them for the rest of life, and beyond.

We honor you, Davey, and we love you, longing with you for the great day when everything sad will become untrue, when every hurt and hope will be finally be made whole—the great day when there will be no more perplexity at the providence that is ours in this life and world, so very now, so very not yet that it is.

Come, Lord Jesus, come.

STEVEN GARBER
Professor of Marketplace Theology
Director of the Program in Leadership, Theology, and Society
Regent College
Vancouver, British Columbia
May 2020

Appendix

Contact Work—
A Personal Letter to Davey Naugle

The following letter is part of a collection of storytelling in the form of personal letters titled "Broken Signposts," the outworking of a larger project for Regent College, which explores the relationship between knowing, teaching, and love. The project takes up the call to learn to be storytellers for the kingdom of God and seeks not only to articulate a knowing rooted in love but also to embody that knowing in the very form of the storytelling. At this level, the knowing of love framed a series of long conversations with Davey and Deemie Naugle, whereby this letter came as the fruit of prayerful listening. Davey Naugle is a witness to the best aspirations of the project as a whole, and I pray it may be a sign and foretaste of the truth he has lived and taught for so many years in the love of Christ. In one sense, it is simply a thank-you letter to a friend and teacher who shared his life story with me. In another sense, it is a labor of love to reveal the light of the glory of God in a cracked vessel—a broken signpost—that will be found by a mystery of grace, transformed in the glorious new creation.

> *And the Word became flesh and dwelt among us, and we have seen his glory, glory as of the only Son from the Father, full of grace and truth.* —John 1:14 ESV

> *But after one glance at the Lion's face he slipped out of the saddle and fell at its feet. He couldn't say anything but then he didn't want to say anything, and he knew he needn't say anything.*
> —C. S. Lewis, *The Horse and His Boy*[1]

---

1. Lewis, *Horse and His Boy*, 282.

Dear Davey,

I never had the privilege of learning from you in the classroom, but I am a student of yours. Having no background in philosophy and in need of a guide into the unfamiliar territory of theology, I remarkably discovered your book *Philosophy: A Student's Guide* through a Google search. Not only was the book a faithful field guide, but it also led me to see that you taught nearby at Dallas Baptist University. Your gracious reception of my email led to a rich conversation over coffee, where you carefully listened to my longing for a way of learning to make sense of the whole of life. I shared how Dr. Garber's book *Visions of Vocation* had captivated my imagination, and your reply would become God's way of guiding me *further up and further in*: "Steve is a good friend of mine. Would you like to talk to him?"

Though your health has made it increasingly difficult for you to speak in recent years, your beloved wife and faithful friend Deemie has given you a voice through hers. As I have learned from you through our conversations together, it is abundantly clear that the Lord has worked through you over many years to profoundly shape your students to become lovers of life in the kingdom of God. I, too, have been remarkably transformed by the "contact work" of Christ through you, and I hope that this *remembering* might contribute to the growth of your pleasure in Him. May it be a simple foretaste of that consummate fullness when "the earth will be filled with the knowledge of the glory of the Lord as the waters cover the sea" (Hab 2:14 ESV).

You grew up in a morally conscious and communally engaged family deeply rooted in Fort Worth, Texas. Your early life formed at the intersection of your father's Presbyterian tradition and your mother's Baptist background in the middle ground that was the Methodist church. Though raised in the Christian tradition, it was not until you saw Billy Graham preach through a televised service, when you were seventeen, that you came to hear the gospel clearly. You examined the scriptures to see if these things were so, and a heart charged with the gospel ignited a faith seeking understanding (Acts 17:11). Young Life became a deeply formative community where you encountered the love of Christ through the contact work of a leader. The seeds of loving students in the way of Christ were planted, and the life-giving vine that grew continues to bear fruit to this day.

An average high school student, popular but not particularly academic, your mind came alive to the love of learning through studying the Bible. Written with your own personal study notes, a three-hundred-page commentary on Ephesians serves as an early signpost to the life you have lived loving and teaching God's Word. A desire to pursue seminary education formed early on in your undergraduate years at The University of Texas at Arlington (UTA), and a course of study in history prepared the way.

Young Life laid the groundwork for what became a way of *incarnational* teaching as a college minister and professor later on, but seminary training was the next step along the way.

Though you did not have a clear sense vocationally, you enrolled at Dallas Theological Seminary (DTS) after college. The knowledge gained through seminary formed a theological architecture on which to build a life of teaching in the years to come. After seminary, a short stint as an associate pastor confirmed that attending meetings *about* ministry was not the contact work you desired, so further study followed.

During your doctoral program in systematic theology at DTS, you encountered Jesus's message of the kingdom of God through an immersive study of The Gospels. This set you on a path of research in the "realized eschatology" of C. H. Dodd through your doctoral dissertation. At the same time, you served as a college minister at UTA in an on-campus home called The Cornerstone. Under your leadership, it became a Texas-style L'Abri, creating a point of contact for students to encounter the gospel of the kingdom of God. Over time, your growing understanding of the *already-but-not-yet* character of the kingdom came into conflict with the *not-yet* eschatology deeply ingrained in the theological imagination of Dallas. Though allowed to finish your doctorate at DTS—even that came into question!—you were fired from your post as the campus minister at UTA. Deemie shared, "He said it was the worst thing that ever happened to him—he lost his ministry. He was finally doing what he felt like God had called him to do working with college students." After this, a long visit to L'Abri in Boston created space for you to hear God's call once again, to listen and obey.

While staying at L'Abri, a call from Dallas Baptist University (DBU) presented an entry-way to a life-long love for the students of this small Baptist college perched on a hill on the outskirts of Dallas. Kindled by the study of Scripture, ignited through Young Life, and flaming out in college ministry—your fire for learning found its hearth at DBU as you welcomed students into the company of the burning heart.[2] It was here that Deemie, a colleague at the university, was recommended and agreed to review the textbook you were writing for the college. Deemie gladly affirms that she fell in love with you through your writing. In time, a literary love became literal, and you entered into the delighted knowing of marriage.

As you pursued a second doctorate "for fun"—working toward what became the definitive *Worldview: The History of a Concept*—you were given the opportunity to found a philosophy department at DBU. Your service infused and energized the school with a vision of seeing all truth as God's

---

2. See Luke 24:32.

truth and that serious learning can be to the glory of God. You developed the Paideia College Society and Friday Symposium lecture series to nourish and inspire emerging scholars and to expose students to some of the brightest Christian minds in the world. The students saw that you were interested in their complete development, not merely in assigning them grades, and your home became The Cornerstone reimagined. L'Abri parties at the Naugles', movie nights humorously named Cinematic Confabulations, and Books and Coffee evenings became living traditions for the love of learning and the desire for God to grow.

Whether attending a sporting event or grieving the death of a sibling, you were interested in the lives of your students in such a way that learning and life converged. As Deemie said, "Once a Young Life leader, always a Young Life leader. It was contact work." When teaching becomes a labor of love, learning becomes a way of life: "We were always with students . . . that was just our life." Jesus taught by being with the disciples, the beloved "little children," and you sought to follow His example. You loved your students as you did your daughter Courtney, and they became like your own children. Those who took to heart the ways of your heart came to playfully call themselves "Naugle-ites," many confessing through letters the way in which your loving presence changed the course of their lives. A student named Leigh Hickman is a witness: "Since I met Dr. Naugle, the world, for me, has never been the same. Because of his life, I see all of life shot through with divine purpose and potential for worship."[3] Likewise, through all his many visits with teachers at colleges around the country, Steve Garber concludes, "I have long believed that Davey is the best professor in America."[4]

And yet, the *already* good, true, and beautiful of Christ's kingdom is held together with the *not-yet* heartbreak of physical health. A rare neurodegenerative disorder with no known cause or cure, Progressive Supranuclear Palsy, has taken much of your physical ability over recent years. Of the many wonderful words shared in our time together, perhaps Deemie's are the most striking: "All the work for the kingdom has been taken away—the writing, the speaking, the teaching—but we trust God's purposes." I asked you what God was revealing to you when I first learned of your diagnosis, and though I do not recall your exact words, I remember their effect: "I am learning the truth of what I have taught all these years." You have long known that the suffering love of God revealed in Jesus on the cross is at the heart of reality, but this disorder has come as a painfully unexpected participation in the groaning cross before the crown. Deemie shared:

3. Leigh Hickman, personal letter to David Naugle, 2018.
4. See Steve Garber's Afterword in the present volume, "Dare to be a Davey."

> We always say we know that he is sovereign, and His ways are higher than our ways, His thoughts are higher than our thoughts. We have no idea why someone who had the influence and impact that Davey had would be stricken with this disease.... But He is showing us along the way how even with that, we are still able to glorify Him. We've always said we wanted to be in the center of God's will. We know He is sovereign. There's a reason. Just show us how we can use it to glorify Him if He is going to keep us in this situation.

Though your sickness has taken much, it has not stolen your delight in life and learning. In the early days of losing fine motor skills, you wrote your contribution to a published book by typing each word one letter at time using only your pointer finger. When you lost the ability to read, audio books became a way of continuing to learn, and Augustine's *Confessions* was one of the first you listened to.

At various times in our conversations, you managed to say through painfully strained effort, "I wish I could talk." Despite the struggle, the light in your eyes and the laughter in your bones still speak. Your presence calls to mind a hymn that I love called "How Can I Keep from Singing?"

> I hear the sweet, though far-off hymn
> That hails a new creation
> Through all the tumult and the strife,
> I hear the music ringing
> It finds an echo in my soul
> How can I keep from singing?
>
> What though my joys and comforts die?
> The Lord my Savior liveth
> What though the darkness gather round?
> Songs in the night he giveth
> No storm can shake my inmost calm
> While to that refuge clinging
> Since Christ is Lord of heaven and earth
> How can I keep from singing?
>
> I lift my eyes, the cloud grows thin
> I see the blue above it
> And day by day this pathway smooths,
> Since first I learned to love it,
> The peace of Christ makes fresh my heart
> The fountain ever springing
> All things are mine since I am his

> How can I keep from singing?
> No storm can shake my inmost calm
> While to that refuge clinging
> Since Christ is Lord of heaven and earth
> How can I keep from singing?[5]

You are a living witness to the peace that Christ's love gives amidst the tumult and strife of failing health. You have long hailed the dawning new creation and taught that all things in God's very good creation are ours to steward to God's glory and our delight. There is one slight revision, though, that I want to make—the refrain should read: "Since Christ is Lord of heaven and earth / How can I keep from *laughing*?"

Your journey reminds me, seeing through a glass darkly, of a story from The Chronicles of Narnia in *The Horse and His Boy*. Through the travails of a perilous journey, Shasta finds himself wandering on a mountain path feeling the sorrow of suffering. As he walks, Shasta hears a quiet presence walking beside him, a breath, and finally a large and deep voice. The Voice invites him to share his sorrow, and Shasta laments his life's wounds, including the ones inflicted by lions that chased him and his companion Aravis. To Shasta's terror, the Voice replies, "I was the lion." Shocked and in disbelief, he questions, "Then it was you who wounded Aravis?" The exchange that follows is penetrating:

> "It was I."
> "But what for?"
> "Child," said the Voice, "I am telling you your story, not hers. I tell no one any story but his own."[6]

As Shasta comes to see that the Voice is Aslan the lion, he falls at his feet in awed silence, and the chapter concludes:

> The High King above all kings stooped towards him. Its mane, and some strange and solemn perfume that hung about the mane, was all round him. It touched his forehead with its tongue. He lifted his face and their eyes met. Then instantly the pale brightness of the mist and the fiery brightness of the Lion rolled themselves together into a swirling glory and gathered themselves up and disappeared. He was alone with the horse on a grassy hillside under a blue sky. And there were birds singing.[7]

---

5. Lowry, "How Can I Keep from Singing?"
6. Lewis, *Horse and His Boy*, 281.
7. Lewis, *Horse and His Boy*, 282.

Davey, though your body may fail, Christ continues His contact work through you beyond writing and speaking. You are teaching us to listen with our eyes as much as our ears, to see the freedom that Christ's love gives to learn and laugh through joys and sorrows, to hope for the day when we will be transformed in the new creation. Perhaps in that day, you will not be able to say anything for a while, but then you will not want to say anything and you will know that you do not need to say anything. For you shall see the High King face to face and hear Him say, "Davey, I am making all things new"—but that is not my story to tell.

The Peace of Our Lord,

Brett Bradshaw
July 9, 2020
Dallas, Texas

BIBLIOGRAPHY

Lewis, C. S. *The Horse and His Boy*. 1954. Reprint, New York: HarperCollins, 2004.

Lowry, Robert Wadsworth. "How Can I Keep from Singing?" Hymn. 1869. Public domain.

Index

Aristotle, 15, 40, 43–44, 150, 153, 169–70, 262, 272, 306, 309
Aquinas, Saint Thomas, 3, 149, 153, 157, 159–71, 286, 293, 297
Augustine, Saint, xii, 135, 144–46, 153, 170, 172, 175, 182–84, 186, 191, 201, 204, 260–83, 284, 300, 327

Bacon, Francis, 135, 140–42
Bacon, Roger, 157
Bede (Venerable Bede/Saint Bede), 148–58
Beethoven, Ludwig van, 225, 288, 293
Boethius, 170, 204

Chesterton, G. K., 170, 305–6, 307, 308, 311, 316
Cicero, xii, 17, 43, 45, 46
Confucius, 14
Craig, William Lane, 123, 175, 177

Descartes, René, 135–41, 144, 177

Eliot, T. S., 277, 300

Freud, Sigmund, 105–6, 108–10

Guinness, Os, 1, 22–23, 30, 35

Heidegger, Martin, 263, 271

Kierkegaard, Søren, 172–73, 186–91
King, Martin Luther, Jr., 245
King, Stephen, 79, 84, 89, 94, 105, 107–8
Kuyper, Abraham, xi, 3, 223
Kuyper the dog, 3

Lewis, C. S., 7–20, 63, 83, 175, 201, 204, 226, 238, 270, 272, 287–88, 291–92, 299–300, 303, 304–6, 308, 309–13, 323, 328
Lovecraft, H. P., 103–19

Melanchthon, Philip, 38–47

Nietzsche, Friedrich, 135, 142–44, 267, 310–11

Plantinga, Alvin, 120–34, 159, 162–66, 167, 169–70, 171, 175, 177
Plato, 10, 12, 43, 150, 170, 205, 262, 266, 266–68, 276, 285

Schaeffer, Francis, 286–87, 299–300, 308
Scorsese, Martin, 74, 228–40
Shakespeare, William, 50, 274

Wilberforce, William, 21–37
Wright, N. T., 177, 255–56, 299

CPSIA information can be obtained
at www.ICGtesting.com
Printed in the USA
BVHW051752060321
601769BV00007B/19